Information Technology Ethics:
Cultural Perspectives

Soraj Hongladarom
Chulalongkorn University, Thailand

Charles Ess
Drury University, USA

IDEA GROUP REFERENCE
Hershey · London · Melbourne · Singapore

Acquisitions Editor:	Kristin Klinger
Development Editor:	Kristin Roth
Senior Managing Editor:	Jennifer Neidig
Managing Editor:	Sara Reed
Copy Editors:	Sue Vander Hook
Typesetter:	Diane Huskinson
Cover Design:	Lisa Tosheff
Printed at:	Yurchak Printing Inc.

Published in the United States of America by
Idea Group Reference (an imprint of Idea Group Inc.)
701 E. Chocolate Avenue, Suite 200
Hershey PA 17033
Tel: 717-533-8845
Fax: 717-533-8661
E-mail: cust@idea-group.com
Web site: http://www.idea-group-ref.com

and in the United Kingdom by
Idea Group Reference (an imprint of Idea Group Inc.)
3 Henrietta Street
Covent Garden
London WC2E 8LU
Tel: 44 20 7240 0856
Fax: 44 20 7379 0609
Web site: http://www.eurospanonline.com

Library of Congress Cataloging-in-Publication Data

Information technology ethics : cultural perspectives / Soraj Hongladaram and Charles Ess, editors.
    p. cm.
  Summary: "This book is the first publication that takes a genuinely global approach to the diverse ethical issues evoked by Information and Communication Technologies and their possible resolutions. Readers will gain a greater appreciation for the problems and possibilities of genuinely global information ethics, which are urgently needed as information and communication technologies continue their exponential growth"--Provided by publisher.
  Includes bibliographical references and index.
  ISBN 1-59904-310-6 (hardcover) -- ISBN 1-59904-312-2 (ebook)
  1. Information technology--Moral and ethical aspects. 2. Information technology--Cultural aspects. 3. Business ethics. I. Hongladaram, Soraj, 1962- II. Ess, Charles, 1951-
  HC79.I55I5394 2007
  174'.93034833--dc22
                                   2006032162

British Cataloguing in Publication Data
A Cataloguing in Publication record for this book is available from the British Library.

Table of Contents

Section II
Specific Viewpoints

Detailed Table of Contents

Our introduction aims at summarizing the main findings of the book and presenting its orientation. Basically, we argue that as countries and regions of the world are getting closer due to globalization, there is an increased need to deliberate carefully about the basic problems in computer ethics as well as how ethical judgments are justified. Avoiding both the extremes of relativism and ethnocentrism, the chapters present the needs both for engaged dialogs and interactions among diverse cultures and for a kind of rootedness within particular local cultural traditions. How this is done is a fascinating topic.

Section I
Theoretical Concerns

Chapter I

The purpose of this chapter is to explore whether information and information technology in certain cases ought to be valued as ends in themselves, rather than as mere means to other ends. A theory of moral status is proposed; this is a theory of who or what has moral status in the sense that we, as moral agents, have an obligation to take their well-being into consideration when making ethical judgments. The theory draws on insights from both classical Western and East Asian philosophy in order to question the exclusion of all nonliving entities in most theories of moral status. The relational properties of constitutivity and irreplaceability are singled out as ethically relevant, and suggested as one possible way to ground the moral status of information and information technologies.

Chapter II

We examine some pros and cons of online communities with respect to two main questions: (1) Do online communities promote democracy and democratic ideals? (2) What are the implications of online communities for information justice and the digital divide? In examining these questions, we also consider the effects of the Internet for community life at both the local and global levels.

We already are hybrid humans; we all are constitutively natural-born cyborgs, that is biotechnological hybrid minds. Our minds should not be considered to be located only in the head. The chapter also illustrates the interplay between cultures and distributed cognition taking advantage of the so-called disembodiment of mind and stresses the problem of the co-evolution between brains and cultures. The second part of the chapter is related to the analysis of the interplay between cultures and cognition and of some consequences concerning the problem of intercultural communication in the light of the role of moral mediators, docility, and cyberprivacy.

The chapter aims at discussing the mutual influence between culture and technology on a broad inter- and trans-cultural level. We aim for a model which incorporates cultural as well as technological factors in order to provide a basis for future ICT-research which goes beyond both technological determinism and social constructivism. At the same time we are well aware that the loose notion and imprecise definition of the concept of culture allows for the exploitation of the term in empty political and techno-economical policies. Thus, we attempt to introduce the concept of culture into the socio-responsible ICT research on equal terms with technology, economy, and society.

Stemming from philosophical analyses by Habermas and Heidegger, this chapter aims at showing how our latest hi-tech devices of communication (e.g., the mobile phone) affect our autonomy in the mobilization era. It seems that mobile phone systematization needs its own conception and understanding of what individuals are, and that conception is not similar at all to what we are familiar with through our cultural and philosophical reflections.

How do we deal with diversity and difference in information technology? In this chapter two cases are explored in which dealing with difference is a particular political and ethical concern. The designs of Indymedia, an Internet-based alternative media network, and TAMI, an Aboriginal database, are informed by the confrontations over different ways of knowing. They translate difference without sacrificing diversity, providing clues for building credible and sustainable design alternatives that will not hurt others.

Adoption of information technologies is dependent upon the availability of information to be channeled via such technologies. Although many cultural approaches to information control have been identified, two increasingly ubiquitous regimes are battling for dominance in the international arena. These may be termed the utilitarian and the deontological approaches and may be roughly identified with, respectively, the United States and the continental European tradition. Absent a drastic shift in international treaty dynamics, these dominant conceptions will likely curtail the development of alternate approaches that might otherwise emerge from local culture and tradition.

Perspectives of various Buddhist traditions are considered on the topic of analysis of the concept of privacy as well as its justification. The chapter begins by outlining the major literature in the West dealing with the issue. Then the thoughts of two Buddhist thinkers, representing two major Buddhist traditions, are presented. The two Buddhist traditions agree that the concept of privacy is a construct. However, this does not mean that there can be no analysis and justification of privacy in Buddhism. Instead, the concept is there and is justified through its usefulness in realizing goals.

Section II
Specific Viewpoints

This chapter examines information privacy as manifested and understood in Thai society. Multidisciplinary perspectives—philosophical, anthropological, historical, legal, policy-oriented, and communicative—are used to explore information privacy, which is arguably emerging as an ethic in Thailand. While the diffusion of ICTs along with the country's aspiration toward an information society may have given rise to this conceptual emergence, the long-standing surveillance that characterizes the Thai state is reckoned to be a major hindrance to a meaningful realization of this ethic in Thai society.

Information and communication technologies have both positive and negative impacts on Thai society. It is the ethics of the user that determine how the technology is used. This chapter examines the relations among Thai culture, ICT, and IT ethics, where all impacts are considered and described. There are various factors related to development of IT ethics, but the main factor is family background. Thus, in order to increase the ethics of users in an ICT world, the proposed solution is to create a strong family and instruct children in their religion. Although this method is long term, the outcome is worth the wait.

Chapter XI

As information and communication technology (ICT) is increasingly pervading more and more aspects of life, ethical issues will increasingly be computer-related. This view is underpinned by the assumption that progress is linear and inevitable. This notion ignores the cultural origin of computing. Computer technology is a product of the Western worldview and consequently the computer revolution is experienced differently by people in different parts of the world. This chapter argues that computer ethics must critically analyze the links between computing and its effects on cultural diversity and the natural environment. It also proposes that the Earth Charter can function as a framework for such holistic research.

Chapter XII

The ever-changing face of ICT can render its deployment as rather problematic in sensitive areas of applications, such as healthcare. The ethical implications are multifaceted and have diverse degrees of sensitivity from culture to culture. Our essay attempts to shed light on these interplaying factors in a cross-cultural analysis that takes into account prospective ICT development.

Chapter XIII

Turkey lies at the crossroad of civilizations; hence, it is difficult to define it through a generally accepted set of ethical principles. Western, Islamic, and Turkish cultures are in competition with each of them, and a synthesis is not achieved yet. This disagreement causes proliferation of unethical behavior such as the illegal copying of software. The majority of the highly-educated technical people in Turkey approve of the illegal copying of software if it is necessitated by the interests of the country. This shows that we have a long way to go to reach global ethical standards, and country-specific differences cannot be eliminated in the short term.

Chapter XIV

The U.S. has witnessed a massive infusion of computers and Internet access into homes, schools, libraries, and other neighborhood institutions. This has significantly increased citizens' physical access to information and communication technology (ICT) artifacts and enhanced citizens' opportunities for acquiring and strengthening technical skills. Does the increased physical access and technical skills signal closure of the digital divide? In this chapter, I address this question by describing the preconstructed ways in which the digital divide is conceptualized by academics and policymakers, and inferring what these conceptualizations suggest about the existential significance of the digital divide as experienced by historically underserved groups in the U.S.

Foreword

The rapid development and spread of information technology has led to the publication of a large number of books, both authored and edited, on the social and ethical questions that this technology has raised. This work has been dominated by the cultures in which the technology originally developed; that is, primarily in the United States of America and Western Europe. Common themes (e.g., privacy and intellectual property) have been discussed from a Western perspective. This is not a criticism, and given the number and seriousness of the issues raised, it is an important and perfectly reasonable approach. But this approach on its own is not adequate in the world of the 21ˢᵗ century.

The impact of Information Technology is now felt throughout the world, and it is important that this impact be studied from a variety of perspectives. This technology, and particularly the Internet, has bought about the collision of ideas as never before. International trade and business and international relations in general have necessitated some understanding among cultures, but prior to the Internet, relatively few people were involved. Now potentially anybody can interact with individuals from other cultures and can have an effect on a large number of them, as illustrated by the recent case of the publication of cartoons in Denmark that were offensive to many in the Islamic world.

Soraj Hongladarom and Charles Ess are to be highly commended for editing the first collection on the ethics of Information Technology that studies the issues from a variety of cultural perspectives. A wide range of backgrounds is brought to bear on the problems: Thai, Chinese, Turkish, European, and North American. This gives perspectives from religious traditions from both the East and the West and a range of topics different from that found in most other collections. There are discussions of some core problems in Information Technology ethics (e.g., privacy and intellectual property) but from different cultural points of view, and of the digital divide, the ontological problem of entities with moral status, cultural and ecological aspects of computing, human hybridization, autonomy, the design of technology, health care and the role of Information Technology, online communities and democracy, and Thai culture and Information and Communication Technology. These chapters with their various perspectives provide excellent new insights that generally have not been brought to bear on problems in Information Technology ethics.

Both editors have excellent credentials to edit a work of this kind. Each has published widely on multicultural and multidisciplinary topics in the ethics of Information Technology as well as in other areas, and has a deep knowledge of both Eastern and Western traditions. The chapters reflect this. *Information Technology Ethics: Cultural Perspectives* will be an important book that will extend the boundaries of the field of Information Technology ethics and, hopefully, will stimulate much more discussion of this kind. The world of the early 21ˢᵗ century needs it.

John Weckert *is a professorial fellow at the Centre for Applied Philosophy and Public Ethics, Charles Sturt University, The Australian National University, and the University of Melbourne, and Professor of Information Technology in the School of Information Studies, Charles Sturt University. He has published widely in the field of the ethics of information technology and is the founding editor-in-chief of the Springer journal* Nanoethics: Ethics for Technologies that Converge at the Nanoscale.

Preface

Crossing the river by feeling with our feet. —Japanese proverb

INTRODUCTION

Science and technology do not exist in a vacuum. Instead, they stand in a large variety of relations with their surroundings and contexts. Being manmade, science and technology have a clear link with human society in various ways. It may seem quite surprising to hear that science is manmade, but this refers to the enterprise of conducting science and its product: scientific knowledge. It may be true that knowledge exists "out there" and will continue to do so, but in order for that knowledge to become useful and relatable to human beings, some kind of methods are needed; this is when the enterprise of science comes in. Technology follows closely on the heels of science, and it is even more clearly related to the human world.

This relation of science and technology with the human world has given rise to a set of problems and agenda, and chief among these agenda are the normative aspects of the relation. Ethical problems have abounded with regard to the use of science and technology. This is so because science and technology are very powerful tools, and as such, they have a great impact on our values and on the question of what should or should not be done with regard to the processes or products of science and technology and for what reasons. Ethical deliberation on science and technology and their close relationship with the human world is thus essential in this day and age when advances in these fields are being made at a very rapid pace.

This book is aimed at continuing this deliberative attempt. More specifically, it deals with information technology, which arguably is the most pervasive and powerful technological tool that has been invented in recent decades. The evidence of the pervasiveness of information technology is everywhere. The book that you are reading now is a result of a joint editing effort by two college professors, one living in Thailand and the other in the United States. It is furthermore a collection of 14 chapters written by scholars who live and work in places far away from one another, such as Austria, Norway, the U.S., Turkey, and Thailand, to name but a few. All this, of course, is made possible through information technology. It may seem rather commonplace to say so in this day and age, but it points to the deep pervasiveness of the technology, so much so that it would be very difficult to imagine what it would be like to live without (i.e., checking e-mails or opening up a Web site).

Another aspect of the book, one which makes it particularly distinctive and interesting, is that it deals with ethics of information technology from cultural perspectives. In fact, it is not possible to view anything from an utterly neutral perspective with no angle from the peculiar standpoint of the observer. In Thomas Nagel's famous book, *The View from Nowhere* (1986), the author argues precisely this point: no observer-neutral perspective is possible, and all lookings have to be from somewhere and through someone's eyes.[1] Consequently, when information and communication technologies (ICTs) interact with humans and their communities within their social and cultural worlds, these ethical dimensions are interwoven deeply with the peculiar standpoints from which humans and their particular communities look at the world. Scholars who study cultures agree that the term *culture* is one of the most slippery concepts in the entire vocabulary (Eagleton, 2000). Nonetheless, culture always crops up in attempts to understand the human world because it is such a useful concept, and to do without it would make the task of understanding human society almost impossible. Broadly speaking, culture is what separates the human world from the natural world that operates solely on physical and chemical principles. But it is well-known in the social sciences that to rely on these physical vocabularies alone would miss the point by a wide margin in understanding what human beings are up to. What is broadly understood as the domain of culture differentiates the human world from the natural one, even though physically there are no differences at all. But if this so, then to look at the ethics of information technology through the perspectives of culture would be a most important undertaking.

Talking about cultures also implies another important dimension, for cultures are not the same all over the world. Of course, one can talk about the universal traits of human beings (e.g., they become hungry, they want to have sex, etc.), but that is part of the natural world, and when one focuses on culture as what distinguishes the human world, one cannot fail to find a tremendous variety of cultures, many of which are very different from one another. Hence, ethical deliberation on information technology and its role in the human world must not fail to include the notion of culture; and to so include culture further involves taking in the differences among the cultures of the world, such as those existing between the West and the East, for example. This is so because if one failed to incorporate these cultural differences, then one would risk, in his or her attempt to understand the ethical judgments pertaining to information technology, viewing the whole issue from an observer-neutral perspective all over again. That would defeat the purpose of staying on the ground in order to really understand the human world from the beginning.

OVERVIEW OF THE BOOK

This book, then, deals with information ethics, viewed from various cultural and intercultural perspectives. This branch of information and computer ethics is altogether a new field of study, as most books and research works in information ethics have dealt almost exclusively with what is happening in the West and relied mostly on the Western tradition of ethics and sociopolitical philosophy for their conceptual and theoretical underpinnings. However, both the global reach of the Internet and the forces of globalization more broadly are rapidly expanding the use of ICTs in non-Western countries—so much so, for example, that there are now as many users of the Internet in Asia and the Pacific Rim countries as in North America. Yet discussions of and scholarship devoted to information ethics in non-Western countries are comparatively recent, and discussions of and scholarship devoted to cross-cultural approaches to information ethics, especially across East-West boundaries, are only in their beginning stages. The book thus fills this important lacuna through an investigation of what the non-Western intellectual traditions have to say on the various issues in information ethics, both at the first-order level of proffering normative judgments on such difficult and controversial issues as intellectual property rights, the digital divide, privacy, and so forth, as well as at the second-order level of theoretical arguments and debates concerning, for example, definitions of culture and technology, their interrelationships, our frameworks for evaluating their impacts and resolving conflicts, and so forth. Along the way, the book further aims at identifying salient problems in information ethics that exist solely or more prominently in non-Western cultures and suggesting ways toward their solution that might preserve local cultural values and traditions, but in consonance with shared, more global approaches as well. Finally, a number of new syntheses—both in theory and in praxis—that conjoin prominent features of Western and Eastern traditions emerge here. These syntheses—especially in the work of Johnny Søraker, Theptawee Chokvasin, Maja van der Velden, Soraj Hongladarom, and Barbara Paterson—thus contribute novel and, we believe, substantial insight to a nascent but genuinely global information and computer ethics that extends beyond Western origins to more fully represent and incorporate Eastern cultural values and their correlative philosophical and religious traditions and frameworks.

The book, then, is aimed at achieving the following objectives. First, it introduces the dimensions of cultures into the deliberation on information and computer ethics. Second, it aims at contributing to the ongoing discussions on information ethics and gathering the best research on the field. It thereby aims to equip practitioners, policymakers, and various stakeholders in information and computer ethics with a heightened sensitivity to cultural concerns. Most broadly, the book introduces a new field of study—what our colleague Rafael Capurro (2005) has aptly called "intercultural information ethics"—into the discourse and discussions of not only academics but also policymakers and the various stakeholders in the area. Thereby, it intends to stimulate further discussion and research on the role of cultures on issues in information and computer ethics.

WHY INTERCULTURAL PERSPECTIVES?

One might question the rationale behind the emphasis on intercultural perspectives. Why focus on these perspectives since the spread of information and communication technologies seems to be homogenizing, if not at the level of deep awareness rooted in one's cultural tradition then at the level of sheer use of the technological products, which appear to be dictated, whether one likes it or not, by the procedures necessarily involved in getting the products to work? One might argue, for example, that the principle against software piracy should be applicable everywhere, because the interests of software producers need to be protected wherever the software is made available, and this should override any possible objection, such as one coming from particular cultures that copying software is an act of paying homage to the producer who is assumed to be acting out of altruism. The argument is that the interests of the producer trump such cultural concerns, and if these concerns are given too much weight, then the interests of the software producer will be compromised. It would be better, so the argument goes, to justify the interests of the software producer through a reliance on a single ethical system, presumably one from the West, since it is the West that is the source of much original software and other cultural production.

This argument is untenable in several ways. First, the argument ignores the fact that all kinds of technology, including information and communication technologies, do not operate in a vacuum. Again, there is no neutral standpoint on which one could stand and pronounce one's normative judgments on these matters in a way that transcends one's own peculiar or unique perspective. Hence, to assume that the ethical system of the West should be applied elsewhere in the world sounds rather odd in today's world in which there is a need for a multitude of systems, each of which originates in its own historical tradition. Nonetheless, this is not to argue that there can be no single ethical system that is normatively binding everywhere. Certainly, software piracy should be regarded as unethical and, indeed, illegal everywhere in the world. But it is our contention that there can be a plurality of ethical systems, each of which can be congruent in significant ways. If it is indeed necessary in today's world to protect the rights of software producers (after all, producers of software or other cultural products need not be in the West any longer), then there needs to be a system of intercultural information ethics (Capurro, 2005) that does justice to the wide variety of cultural traditions, while it is not reduced to mere relativism.

In the case of Thailand, for example, Buddhists usually turn to the teachings of their religion when they need guidance on ethical matters, and to assume that Buddhism should be disregarded when the act of deliberation on information technology ethics is done on Thai soil and in response to Thai concerns would be incongruous and ineffectual. When the technology is transplanted onto the life world of Thai culture, it tends to take shape on its own. On the one hand, it retains its functionality. Computers work in the same way in Thailand as in the U.S., for example. But on the other hand, computers have found themselves in a new sociocultural environment. Their relations to human beings and their communities are not necessarily the same as those in the West. In fact, numerous case studies have documented carefully that when ICTs (as originally the products of predominantly North American white middle and upper-middle class males) are exported beyond these cultural origins—whether within the Western sphere (e.g., various European countries and Scandinavia) and especially in non-Western cultures (including aboriginal cultures in Africa, Australia, and North America; South America; Middle Eastern countries, both Arabic and Islamic as well as Israel; and numerous countries in the Asia-Pacific region, including Thailand)—important traits, values, and patterns defining these local cultures still persist in significant ways.[2] If this is the case, then ethical deliberations as part of the meaning-making activities of culture should retain their particular cultural flavor, too. What this means in more concrete terms is that, taking the issue of personal privacy as an example, deliberations on the ethical concerns regarding privacy in the Thai context should be based on what Buddhism has to say or on what it can be interpreted to say. To argue and deliberate on this topic exclusively within the vocabularies of Immanuel Kant or John Stuart Mill alone simply will not work in the way as those vocabularies originally were intended.

The other reason is more immediate and practical. It is undeniable that the world is getting smaller due to the very fast spread of an unimaginably huge amount of information around the globe every second. In a way, this situation may seem to endorse the idea that ethical vocabularies from the West should be the tools of choice among those who deliberate on these matters, no matter where they are. But the situation also points in the other direction. As the world is getting smaller and more compressed, aspects of each part of the world tend to assume more highlighted significance. This is even more so in areas of the world (as is the case nowadays) in which significant portions do not belong to the cultural sphere of the West. The idea is not to swamp each corner and cultural niche with one cultural system (which includes the system of how ethical judgments are arrived at), but to find out how the differing systems can live together. The increased intensity of intercultural communication enabled by information technology indeed has resulted in a plethora of voices from all corners of the globe. As the case studies collected by Ess and Sudweeks (1999a, 1999b, 2003, 2005) make clear, one should not remain complacent and believe that the world is going to be culturally homogeneous in any way.

FROM HOMOGENEOUS UNIVERSALS TOWARD RESONANCE

Basing one's ethical deliberations on the particularities of one's cultural background, however, does not mean that ethical judgments are doomed to be bound only to those traditions with no possibility of alignments among different traditions. The lack of one overarching ethical system stemming from one particular cultural background does not imply that there is no ethical standard that can be applied across cultures. In fact, the globalizing world of today has made it the case that ethical systems belonging to many cultures have to be aligned with one another. This has become a necessity, because globalization means that the boundaries among the cultures are increasingly blurred. Elements of a culture very often are found in others in such a way that was not possible just a few decades ago. Issues in information technology ethics, such as software piracy, are the concerns not only of one cultural domain but of the world, since the software industry has become a global enterprise. But if there is to be (or should not be) an overarching ethical system, then whose system or what kind of system should there be in order to account for this need for alignment among the various ethical traditions?

The answer is that there does not have to be such a single, overarching system. Instead, the various systems that are available can be adapted and modified in such a way that they are aligned with one another as they need to be. Many chapters in this book attest to this. For example, the chapter by Soraj Hongladarom presents an analysis of the concept of privacy from a Buddhist's perspective. What emerges from Hongladarom's chapter is that the result of the analysis as well as the system of justification of privacy is not too remote from the concept of what constitutes privacy and why it is needed in today's world, based on the more familiar system of Western ethics. More simply put, Hongladarom is arguing that there is a need for more protection of privacy of individuals vis-à-vis the state, but the reasons behind the conclusion are couched in terms of Buddhist teachings. The alignment with what could be taken as a global concern on privacy protection is there, but with an obvious difference in how these conclusions are arrived at. This way of accounting for an alignment in ethical judgments is not exactly the same as Rawls' (2005) idea of overlapping consensus in a political liberalism. In Rawls' (2005) version, the problem of how, in one political state, citizens belonging to different religious or cultural backgrounds can find a way to live together in one polity through bracketing their metaphysical beliefs, leaving them at home, and engaging with their fellow citizens only on the basis of what is politically expedient. The overlapping consensus, according to Rawls, is what emerges when citizens from various cultural backgrounds have to work together; hence, in political liberalism, no metaphysical beliefs are taken into consideration. In our case, the metaphysical beliefs do not have to be as fully bracketed. The scope of our consideration is also much wider than Rawls', which focuses only on what is happening within one political state. What we would like to show, rather, is that there can be alignments among the various cultural traditions and ethical systems of the world, alignments which emerge when the world has become increasingly globalized. Indeed, these alignments also may be aptly called *resonances* or *harmonies*, precisely because these terms appear in both Eastern and Western traditions and are used to refer to an ethical pluralism that holds together the irreducible differences between diverse cultures alongside such closely parallel alignments (Ess, in press). These notions of alignment, resonance, and harmony—and the ethical pluralisms they articulate—mean that these diverse ethical systems and traditions do not have to leave their metaphysics at home; on the contrary, they bring their specific backgrounds to the table of philosophical dialogue and debate and search for ways in which their systems could or could not be aligned with the others. In the case of personal privacy, this would mean that the Buddhist tradition and the Western secular tradition compare and contrast their similarities and differences without (echoing Michael Walzer, 1994) each leaving its thick backgrounds and operating with its fellows on thin air.

Moreover, in the dialogical space created by our suspending the demand for a single, homogenous ethics, we may find that, in addition to such resonances and alignments, new and creative intercultural hybrids of ethical theories and insights emerge. In fact, in Section I, Lorenzo Magnani will call attention to this feature of intercultural dialogue (i.e., its ability to generate new syntheses as the claims and approaches of one culture are applied in new ways to the issues and approaches of an "Other" culture) as an important counter-cultural force, one that might help offset the homogenizing effect of globalized technologies in general and ICTs in particular, along with their tendencies to reduce human beings to instrumental value only. Indeed, four of our contributors in Section I—Johnny Hartz Søraker, Theptawee Chokvasin, Maja van der Velden, and Soraj Hongladarom—develop just such syntheses. Briefly, Søraker will conjoin Confucian thought with Western information ontology to develop a broader and more powerful theory of moral status—one that helps us make theoretical sense of our intuitions that at least some forms of data and ICTs should enjoy at least a limited form of moral status that entails at least a minimal level of moral respect. Chokvasin brings together Kantian and Habermasian theories of autonomy with Thai Buddhism, highlighting ways in which mobile phones create a new form of communicative space with which Habermasian theory does not fully come to grips; he warns that neither Western conceptions of autonomy nor Buddhist understandings of the individual may thereby be strong enough to overcome the tendency (as noted by Magnani) of technology use to reduce human beings to instrumental value only. For her part, van der Velden documents two ICT projects: the Indymedia global journalism project and an Australian project developing databases shaped from the ground up by local ethical traditions, approaches, and ways of knowing (in contrast to the prevailing tendency to use off-the-shelf technologies that thereby impose Western ontologies and epistemologies as embedded in the software and hardware). van der Velden thus brings to the foreground for us two real-world instantiations of the sort of intercultural syntheses developed at more theoretical levels by Søraker, Chokvasin, and Hongladarom. Hongladarom closes Section I with his extensive analysis of both the irreducible differences and the strong alignments or resonances between (Thai) Buddhist and modern Western understandings of the individual vis-à-vis the community, and correlative expectations regarding privacy. By bringing to the foreground important alignments (i.e., Western emphases on community and Buddhist emphases on individual striving and responsibility) that complement the well-known differences between these traditions, Hongladarom thus dramatically expands our theoretical understanding of how these two traditions may cooperate much more closely than initially expected in an emerging global information ethics.

Similarly, Grodzinsky and Herman Tavani introduce in Section I the central concerns of the digital divide, thereby laying the foundation for the distinctively intercultural responses and insights (again, at both theoretical and practical levels) regarding the digital divide developed in Section II by Barbara Paterson (emphasizing African cultural approaches) and Lynette Kvasny (who returns us to the U.S. but in a way that radically questions and expands upon the prevailing theoretical approaches). In the same way, Dan Burk's overview of diverse cultural approaches to the central issues of intellectual property and (data) privacy protection in Section I thereby opens up the intercultural dialogue on these topics further developed in Section II through the particular insights of Pirongrong Ramasoota Rananand's discussion of privacy from a Thai perspective and Gonca Telli Yamamoto's and Faruk Karaman's analyses of the multiple cultural backgrounds in Turkey (Western, Arabic-Islamic, and Eastern, such that Turkey thereby stands as a microcosm of the larger cultural divides confronting information and computer ethics) and their influences (or lack thereof) on attitudes toward intellectual property and copying software. Similarly, Bernd Carsten Stahl and Simon Rogerson's foundations for a new research program on how Western (specifically the UK) and Middle-Eastern/Islamic attitudes toward healthcare may complicate emerging efforts in telemedicine, as developed in Section I, introduce these cultural contrasts as more fully explored by Yamamoto and Karaman in Section II. Finally, Thomas Herdin, Wolfgang Hofkirchner, and Ursula Maier-Rabler develop a dialectical model of how culture and technology mutually shape one another—a model that foregrounds the role and importance of local cultural norms and identities in more powerful and effective ways than previous models made possible.

Taken both individually and together, then, these chapters helpfully and powerfully expand the theoretical understandings and practical approaches of a global intercultural information ethics.

PART I: THEORETICAL CONCERNS

We begin with Johnny Hartz Søraker's "The Moral Status of Information and Information Technologies: A Relational Theory of Moral Status." Prevailing (and usually atomistic) Western views tend to relegate both information and information technologies to a somewhat lower, usually material level in an ontological hierarchy that reserves meaning and value to higher levels associated especially with human agency. (Such views are at work, e.g., in the notion of technological instrumentalism as this view claims that ICTs are merely tools; that is, culturally and morally neutral artifacts whose meaning and worth only can be constituted by moral agents.) Within such an ontology, in contrast with human beings as holders of intrinsic moral status and value, information and information technologies can enjoy only an extrinsic and instrumental moral status and value. By contrast, Søraker turns to East Asian—specifically Confucian—theories that stress the relational (rather than atomistic) nature of beings. In this view, entities and beings attain existence and moral status precisely through their interrelations with other beings and entities. The upshot is an account of moral status for nonsentient beings—specifically, information and information technologies—that accords these a much more significant moral status and value than is possible solely within classical (but anthropocentric) Western frameworks.

While granting that moral status at its highest stage centers on human beings as moral agents, Søraker's theory, by utilizing relational value as an intermediate sort of moral status, is able to break out of the Western anthropocentric hierarchy in important ways. From this relational perspective, especially given the increasing importance of information technologies to our identity and functioning as persons (consider the simple examples of a PDA for organizing our important appointments, contact information, etc.), to damage at least some instances of information technology is tantamount to damaging us as persons. This allows Søraker to expand his original gradations to include nonsentient entities, including at least certain kinds of information and information technologies; these may have no moral standing per se, but they have moral status insofar as they function as irreplaceable and constitutive parts of a person's practical identity; that is, because such information and information technologies, seen in relational terms, contribute essentially to who we are as human beings and moral agents, their damage or loss immediately means damage or loss to who we are.

One of the central goals of Søraker's theory is to support what he calls a "more sustainable development of the infosphere," referring thereby in part to Luciano Floridi's (2003) efforts to develop an information ontology that begins with information as the fundamental substance out of which all beings are constituted. In its focus on ontology, Floridi's (2003) project is thus distinctively Western, while Buddhism, as Søraker notes, likewise takes up issues of ontology and epistemology (Confucian thought does not). What is thus striking about Søraker's claim is that it draws on specifically Eastern conceptions in part in order to expand and refine a more characteristically Western philosophical project. Thereby, it exemplifies at the level of theory the intercultural dialogues we see as essential to develop a genuinely global information ethics, specifically as it constructs a new sysnthesis of Eastern and Western theory.

In "Online Communities, Democratic Ideals, and the Digital Divide," Frances S. Grodzinsky and HermanT. Tavani take up one of the central most important legitimation claims for the Internet and computer-mediated communication (CMC) in Western and developing countries—that the Internet, specifically in the form of online communities, will foster democracy and democratic ideals. Grodzinsky and Tavani further examine two additional dimensions of the Internet and CMC that are equally compelling from a moral standpoint—the implications of online communities for information justice (specifically, the digital divide) and the potential effects of the Internet on community life at both the global and local levels.

Grodzinksy and Tavani begin by noting that online communities challenge more traditional understandings of community in many ways, as online communities are defined more by shared interests than by geographical proximity. In contrast to the unalloyed optimism marking much of the 1990s Western discourse on the Internet and democracy, Grodzinsky and Tavani take a more cautious stance—one that is in keeping with much of the prevailing research and theory in these areas as well (see Hubert Dreyfus's, 2001, critiques of notions of online communities, Nancy Baym's, 1995, 2000, authoritative analyses of online communities, and May Thorseth's, 2003, overviews and discussions of the literature and current theory and praxis regarding deliberative democracy).

Grozsinksy and Tavani then turn to a number of issues clustering about the digital divide, defined here in terms of access (or lack of access) to and/or knowledge (or lack of knowledge) of how to use ICTs. They seek to establish strong arguments for universal access to the Internet as a positive right, both within the U.S. and globally. They further observe that computing professionals slowly are coming to recognize the importance of resolving such digital divides.

They conclude with a modest optimism that the shared interests driving virtual communities may help such communities serve as engines in what Hans Jonas (1984) has called *neighbor ethics*—such neighbor ethics will continue efforts to overcome various forms of the digital divide on a global level. But, recalling the ways in which virtual communities may weaken traditional, real-world communities, they call us to examine whether the ethical benefits of the former are worth the costs to the latter.

This chapter should be read alongside Barbara Paterson's and Lynnete Kvasny's discussions in Section II of the digital divide, both of which expand the cultural and theoretical approaches introduced here.

Lorenzo Magnani's "The Mediating Effect of Material Cultures as Human Hybridization" begins with the recognition that the Western Cartesian mind-body split is simply false. Rather, human evolution has long been a matter of offloading cognitive tasks to external artifacts that help us to remember and think, beginning with notches on bone for counting and geometric diagrams. (As Clifford Geertz, 2001, put it earlier, "Our minds are not in our bodies, but in the world," p. 205.) For Magnani, this means that we already are cyborgs (i.e., biological-technological hybrids), and because our technologies as external artifacts that shape and are shaped by distinctive cultures, we can vary widely (a point developed more fully by Herdin, Hofkirchner, and Maier-Rabler later) and so, too, will our identities. In particular, Magnani seeks to examine how new information technologies result in new ontologies, including humans as information beings complete with external data shadows.

Magnani further includes an understanding of the brain as a semiotic machine, one that can create and manipulate signs, especially as these signs are embodied in external artifacts. In contrast with other views represented in this book (e.g., Floridi's information ontology, as expanded and reinforced by Søraker, and Hongladarom's Buddhist analysis) as well as with other contemporary understandings of mind and identity, Magnani seeks to argue that the brain as a semiotic Turing machine is thus simply reducible to meat. This again recalls 1990s postmodernism inspired in part by William Gibson's (1984) classic science-fiction novel *Neuromancer* and its account of life outside of cyberspace in terms of meat (see Barlow, 1996). (For representative criticisms and alternatives, see Borgmann, 2000, Becker, 2002, and Dreyfus, 2001).

But Magnani is also critical of the reductionism implicit in at least simple views of the mind as meat. Indeed, he raises the central moral problem that, as new technologies becoming increasingly central to our bodies and our identities, they thereby may produce cultures that treat people as instrumental means rather than as Kantian ends requiring absolute moral respect. Further echoing Kant (specifically, Kant's central notion of the human being as an absolute spontaneity), Magnani hopes that our internalized cultural representations may somehow activate a countercultural effect that will help us to resist such instrumentalization. He sees grounds for such hope, in particular, as intercultural communication and cross-cultural experiences allow members of one culture to appropriate and creatively apply to new contexts the external cultural artifacts that carry and embed the semiotic meanings of their root culture.

This leads Magnani to address one of the thematic concerns of this book: how to develop a global information ethics that will recognize and preserve local cultural values and norms. Magnani calls for a cyberdemocracy that, by exploiting the countercultural possibilities facilitated by cross-cultural and intercultural communication aided by ICTs, will generate new hybrid insights and institutions that will manage to offset the homogenizing effects of globalization.

Thomas Herdin, Wolfgang Hofkirchner, and Ursula Maier-Rabler's "Culture and Technology: A Mutual-Shaping Approach" aims to develop a sophisticated set of models not only for understanding how culture and technology interact but also for providing much-needed guidance for shaping technology design and use in ways that contribute to core values of equitable knowledge distribution, development of people's abilities to use ICTs, and social inclusion.

They first show the (now well-established) limitations of both technological determinism and social constructivism as once-prevailing views regarding technology. They point out that technology does not stand apart somehow from culture but rather is encapsulated as a part within culture as the more embracing whole. Technology thus may function as a necessary but not sufficient condition for determining the social outcomes of its own development and diffusion, a relationship further complicated by technology's ambivalence; its use and impacts in praxis are often different from the original intentions guiding its design. This leads to what Herdin et al. initially describe as a dialectical relationship.

This dialectical model is enhanced further by taking on board a continuum developed by Maier-Rabler, one defined in terms of information-friendly vis-à-vis information-restrictive societies. This work can be compared usefully with numerous discussions of ICTs in terms of Hofstede's famous—but contested and limited—cultural dimensions (see Ess & Sudweeks, 2005). This continuum involves further correlations between more democratic vis-à-vis more authoritarian regimes, respectively, thus providing a foundation for Herdin et al.'s rights-based approach in developing a normative model of ICT and culture. This model becomes still more fine-grained with regard to culture through the addition of Wolfgang Welsch's notion of transculturality—one that helpfully moves us beyond the container theory of society and culture that dominated earlier views (i.e., as stressing culture as homogenous, static, hermetically sealed from others, etc.). The resulting model then can address issues of the digital divide—for example, by stressing notions of a permeable flow of information between cultures as themselves complex structures of multiple and dynamic subcultures that often interconnect more directly in horizontal ways across national boundaries (e.g., diaspora communities) rather than in ways defined by a vertical integration with a specific national culture. This model offers the further advantage of thereby bringing the central importance of local communities, including their distinctive cultural norms, values, practices, and so forth, to the foreground.

Herdin et al. then explore three specific implications of their model: knowledge management, learning strategies, and education. They include attention here to notions of intellectual property and, thus, should be read alongside Dan Burk's chapter in this book. As well, they take up questions of potential cultural homogenization, imperialism, and fragmentation vis-à-vis various models for attempting to preserve local cultural values alongside global connectivity; their discussion of universalism vs. relativism and subsequent recommendations for pluralism are consistent with the broader philosophical discussion of pluralism as an important strategy in information and computer ethics for developing a global information ethics that preserves the irreducible differences defining distinctive cultures (Ess, in press).

In his "Mobile Phone and Autonomy," Theptawee Chokvasin takes up a careful analysis of the nature of the human being—specifically with a view toward possibilities of autonomy and self-governance as affected by hi-tech mobilization—from a distinctively Thai perspective; that is, one fully informed by both traditional Thai (Theravadan) Buddhism and a strong awareness of Western views, as manifested, on the one hand, in the philosophies of Heidegger and Habermas, and, on the other, in the Thai appropriation of modern ICTs, specifically, the mobile phone.

Drawing first on Heidegger, Chokvasin argues that our possession and use of such phones is distinctively personal, since they are used by their owners directly and exclusively as direct channels between themselves and others as distinctive individuals. Contra the prevailing view of technological instrumentalism (i.e., the notion that technologies are just tools and thereby somehow culturally and ethically neutral), Chokvasin argues that the mobile phone emerges within the larger context of a form of technological thinking that controls the individual as "a 'positioned' individual in the communicative sphere." This is done with our consent, he quickly adds, one fueled by our interests in communicative efficiency. Using Heidegger's notion of enframing, Chokvasin argues that personal mobile phones mean, presuming we have one and others know we have one, that we are always there in a constant state of connectedness. Chokvasin argues that Kantian and Habermasian notions of autonomy, especially as they entail the ability to give reasons for our beliefs and actions in a public, communicative sphere, in fact cannot take place in the distinctive communicative space constituted by the personal mobile phone. Habermasian notions of autonomy via social participation in communicative rationality thus fail to account for all forms of communication.

From here, Chokvasin develops his own account of the autonomy possible for mobile phone users—one that depends on a distinction between abstract conceptions, as found in Western philosophers and in Buddhist culture, and a concrete conception. The latter, however, lessens human nobility, in part because it values the individual solely insofar as such a being is needed as a controlled being within a technological system.

Chokvasin concludes by arguing that a concrete autonomy of the mobile phone user results in a more instrumental value for the individual, in contrast to a more intrinsic value for the individual who enjoys an abstract autonomy, whether in Kant/Habermas or in Buddhism. The mobile phone user, he observes, may appear to respect the other in ways that echo the sorts of respect commanded by either Kantian or Buddhist ethics for the (intrinsically valuable, for Kant) individual, but such a user instead does so only for the sake of sustaining his or her own position in a technological society and the distinctive communicative space constructed by mobile phones.

Chokvasin's essay is especially helpful to our larger project of fostering intercultural dialogue regarding basic concepts and specific issues in information ethics as he points out here that Kantian and Habermasian notions of autonomy, usually considered distinctively Western, insofar as they emerge out of the Western Enlightenment indeed find important counterparts in Buddhist culture, which considers autonomy in terms of someone choosing to comport himself to the right path and way of living. The concept of *Attasammapanidhi*, "the characteristic of a person who can set herself in the right course, right direction in self-guidance, perfect self-adjustment" (Phra Dhammapitaka, 1995, p. 321) in fact resonates closely with additional Western moral figures, including the *cybernetes*, the pilot or steersman who, in Plato's *Republic*, stands as the analogue for the capacity of a moral judgment to discern the right course or path and to correct oneself when error is made. As is well-known, the cybernetes becomes the basis of Norbert Wiener's foundational notion of cybernetics, information systems that can correct themselves over time. The cybernetes in Plato implicitly underlies contemporary cybernetics, and so it is perhaps not an accident that Wiener is also the primary founder of Western information and computer ethics (Ess, in press). Such self-correction, especially in an ethical context, is clearly central to Western ethics broadly and information and computer ethics in particular. Chokvasin's pointing to an analogous conception of ethical self-correction in Buddhist tradition suggests an important bridge between Western and Eastern ethics and, thereby, an important contribution to our larger project of developing a genuinely global information ethics.

Maja van der Velden's "Invisibility and the Ethics of Digitalization: Designing so as not to Hurt Others" picks up Søraker's and Chokvasins' critiques of technological instrumentalism and also returns us to the thematic concern with the digital divide, initially raised here by Grodzinsky and Tavani. van der Velden's essay brings us forward, moreover, as it highlights two real-world examples of designing information technologies that begin with the epistemological reality that peoples in diverse cultures know the world in different ways; hence, ICTs that intend to respect and preserve these diverse ways of knowing must be designed from the ground up (i.e., based on these diverse ways of knowing) in contrast to design strategies that impose a single, prevailingly Western model of knowledge and data in the name of efficiency.

To move beyond prevailing analytical frames that presume technological instrumentalism, van der Velden develops a theoretical foundation that draws on the work of Haraway, Latour, and the Portuguese sociologist Boaventura de Sousa Santos. She then builds up a conceptual toolkit (our term) of notions and examples—figu-

xx

rations, in her terms—that illustrate how contemporary technologies hide alternative meanings and histories (i.e., they make others invisible).

van der Velden then examines two projects—Indymedia, a collective of independent journalists; and TAMI, a database developed as part of the Indigenous Knowledge and Resource Management in Northern Australia (IKRMNA)—as ways to illustrate how distinctive ethical and political values *can* drive technology design in such a way to avoid making such others invisible. So, Indymedia is devoted to providing voice to the voiceless, in part by way of a principle of open publishing. However, achieving this required its founders and proponents to inscribe these values at the level of software code, first, in a code base called *Active*, developed initially in Australia and then adapted and used in Seattle during the WTP meeting in 1999. Subsequent versions of this software have been developed in light of specific local demands and conditions (e.g., the German constitutional prohibitions against publishing racist, hateful, or revisionist speech).

In philosophical terms, the result is a pluralism—a diversity of interpretations of how to effect open publishing—within a shared set of principles. Such a pluralism, we would argue, is in keeping with similar pluralisms emerging in information and computer ethics, both within Western spheres and between Western and Asian countries, for example (Ess, in press). At the same time, in the terms we have used here, this sort of pluralism highlights important alignments and resonances between otherwise irreducibly different cultural traditions and values.

van der Velden then turns to the Australian Aboriginal project for an even more powerful example of how to design with specific cultures, values, and ways of knowing in mind first. In taking an autopoetic approach to knowledge as a dynamic, social process, designers begin by looking at how people actually know and represent knowledge. The TAMI (Text, Audio, Movies, and Images) database designed for people with little or no literacy skills was developed in just this way, as van der Velden documents. In particular, the database was designed to be ontologically flat so that people with different ontologies (Westerners vis-à-vis Aborigines) would be able to refine it further by developing various user interfaces as appropriate to their specific ways of knowing.

van der Velden concludes by articulating four principles of the translation work she sees in the design approaches of Indymedia and TAMI as exemplars of designing technology so as *not* to hurt people. The principles highlight the values of democratizing technology, democratic representation, the cultivation of diversity, and the principle of autonomous self-organization—contra, she goes on to argue, the intrinsically hierarchical assumptions of prevailingly Western ways of organizing knowledge as encoded in technology design as fostered by the drive in globalization toward efficient but homogenous and homogenizing flows of information.

As van der Velden thus documents how design approaches can work to homogenize diverse cultures, so Dan L. Burk's following analysis of legal frameworks highlights the ways in which emerging global legal frameworks are likely to homogenize and thereby eliminate local differences as well.

Dan L. Burk's "Privacy and Property in the Global Datasphere" provides an invaluable, genuinely global overview of the current law regarding two of the central components of information and computer ethics; namely, intellectual property (IP) rights and privacy rights. It should be read especially alongside the contribution by Yamamoto and Karaman in Section II on cultural and economic roots of attitudes toward copying. Their account of Turkey suggests at least a partial counter-example to the larger conclusion regarding intellectual property law that Burk develops here.

Burk shares with our other contributors the view that technologies, including ICTs, bear "the value-laden imprint of its makers." Correlatively, the ethical codes and laws developed in diverse countries and cultures regarding the uses of information and ICTs likewise bear the imprint of their makers. Burk sees that two major ethical-legal frameworks currently dominate the global stage—that of the United States and that of the European Union. Burk concerns himself here with not only the sharp contrasts between these two frameworks as each vies for dominance in emerging international law and ethical codes but also with the perhaps inevitable consequence: no matter which side wins in this struggle, the further losers will be the distinctive ethical approaches and traditions of multiple but non-Western cultures now bound together by ICTs. In the face of the likely dominance of one or the other of these two frameworks, Burk glumly concludes that "prospects for any cultural diversity in approaches to informational control is relatively bleak."

Burk first takes up intellectual property (IP) in order to contrast the American and European approaches. Briefly, he shows that IP law in the U.S. is guided by a utilitarian ethic, a cost-benefit analysis that justifies IP rights in theory only insofar as they can be shown to benefit the larger public. The European approach, by contrast, takes what can be characterized as a deontological approach, one that insists on the intrinsic rights of the author as an autonomous (i.e., essentially free) person.

Similar considerations hold in the matter of informational privacy. Indeed, these sharp contrasts between U.S. utilitarianism and EU deontology have been noted by others as well (Burkhardt, Thompson, & Peterson, 2002) and in the ethical guidelines developed for Internet research by the Association of Internet Researchers (AoIR, 2002). But as Burk points out, these sharp contrasts spell trouble, as both the U.S. and the EU seek to promulgate their laws and approaches internationally. Briefly, Burk finds that the U.S. has managed to dominate emerging international law regarding copyright. By contrast, the EU approach to data privacy protection currently dominates internationally, first of all because the EU act requires that member states not release data to anyone in nations whose data privacy protections are less stringent than those defined for the EU.

From a Western perspective, these contrasts between the U.S. utilitarian and the EU deontological approaches may appear to be virtual opposites. But as Burk goes on to show, both ethical theories and approaches rest on shared and distinctively Western assumptions regarding the individual and the nature of the creative act. By contrast, for example, classical Confucian thought emphasizes emulation of revered classical works rather than innovation as creative. As Burk points out, in this view, copying (a cardinal sin in Western systems of copyright) is a cardinal virtue in Confucian thought and, therefore, in the many Asian countries deeply shaped and influenced by Confucian tradition. Similarly, communal control of what Westerners see as exclusively individual work is characteristic of a number of indigenous communities.

By the same token, it is now well-established that contemporary Western conceptions of privacy (and thus, of data privacy protection) are, indeed, distinctively Western, resting on relatively recent (i.e., Enlightenment) conceptions of the individual and, as Burk points out, relative affluence (see especially Hongladarom in this book; Floridi, in press). In addition to his use of recent publications on views of privacy in China and Japan, Burk highlights here the philosophy of *Ubuntu* in post-apartheid South Africa, one that emphasizes community welfare first.[3]

As Burk points out, emerging cultural norms, especially among young people, demonstrate that non-Western countries such as China and Japan are increasingly adopting Western-style notions of individual privacy, as emerging data privacy laws in these countries are shaped by international treaties dominated by the U.S. and/or the EU. Again, whether the U.S. or the EU manages to dominate in a particular context, it is thus clear that non-Western and/or developing nations must likely choose to take up one or the other of these Western models, if they wish to engage in global communication and trade. But this means, in light of these contrasts between Western and non-Western worldviews and ethical traditions, that these nations and peoples will do so at the cost of subordinating or abandoning their own ethical norms and traditions.

Bernd Carsten Stahl, Simon Rogerson, Amin Kashmeery's "Current and Future State of ICT Deployment and Utilization in Healthcare: An Analysis of Cross-Cultural Ethical Issues" lays the theoretical and ethical foundations for a program of culturally sensitive research on healthcare, focusing on the contrasts between Western and Middle Eastern cultures, thus complementing attention in other chapters on Asian and indigenous cultures.

Stahl and Rogerson note that the informatics of healthcare, where healthcare is deeply shaped by diverse communities and cultures, thus requires careful consideration of culture. Here, culture refers broadly to the totality of shared meanings and interpretations of a given group. This admittedly broad definition of culture further incorporates Hall's (1976) well-known distinction between high context/low content and low context/high content cultures. As well, Stahl and Rogerson make clear that this definition of culture fits with what we know to be true of culture (i.e., that it is dynamic and multiform), such that individuals are members of a variety of cultures, not simply of a single and supposedly static national culture (Herdin et al.). Finally, culture includes a normative function (i.e., it is to provide values that guide our behavior) that Stahl and Rogerson simply describe as decent conduct found in every culture.

Turning to healthcare, Stahl and Rogerson take up the distinction between value-based practice (VBP) vs. evidence-based practice (EBP). This distinction plays out in important ways in the policy vacuum originally described by James Moor (1985) to emerge alongside new developments in ICTs in general, and, for Stahl and Rogerson, in ICTs and healthcare in particular. Especially the values-based practice approach to healthcare highlights the potential conflicts between different individuals, especially as members of diverse cultures. By contrast, Evidence-Based Practice, as emphasizing accountability as verified by fact and evidence, may be less likely to lead to such conflicts.

From here, Stahl and Rogerson go on to consider possible values conflicts that can emerge in healthcare in the context of British culture, followed by six scenarios that highlight values conflicts in healthcare in the intersections between Middle Eastern and Western cultural values, especially UK-based practitioners. While these scenarios are somewhat speculative, they highlight the sorts of issues that Stahl and Rogerson expect to encounter in their further research on the actual use of ICTs in healthcare in the UK and a Middle Eastern country. We will see, moreover, that Yamamoto and Karaman powerfully supplement Stahl and Rogerson's examples here with their analyses of how the diverse cultural streams in Turkey (including Western and Islamic-Arabic) indeed lead to profound conflicts between these two cultural traditions.

Soraj Hongladarom's "Analysis and Justification of Privacy from a Buddhist Perspective" offers an invaluable philosophical analysis of privacy as centrally important to information and computer ethics, especially from a comparative perspective.

As others in this book help to document (Chokvasin, Ranananda, Bhattarakosol), the cultural, ethical, and legal dimensions of privacy in contemporary Thailand are especially complex and problematic. As Hongladarom points out, while Thailand is moving quickly in its appropriation and development of ICTs, and while Thailand, as with all other Asian countries, is profoundly influenced by Western notions of privacy and privacy protection laws (Burk), there is, as yet, no data privacy protection law in force in Thailand. Given the central importance of Buddhism to Thai culture, Hongladarom seeks to define and justify privacy from a Buddhist perspective. In addition, his analysis of privacy provides us with important new insights regarding both irreducible differences and perhaps surprising similarities between Western and Buddhist views.

Indeed, it would seem that the primary Buddhist teachings (i.e., self, as opposed to Western ontologies that insist on the primary reality of the self, especially in the modern era as shaped by Descartes and Kant, does not really exist) thereby undermine the basic ontological and ethical justifications for privacy in the modern West. By exploring the work of Nagasena and Nagarjuna, foundational figures for both Theravada and Mahayana Buddhism, Hongladarom argues, however, that Buddhism nonetheless sustains a pragmatic conception of privacy, one that will clearly work with better cultural and philosophical fit in Thailand and, perhaps, other countries and cultures deeply shaped by Buddhist tradition.

Hongladarom first provides a comprehensive overview of the extensive range of Western philosophical approaches to privacy. Despite important differences among Western theorists, Hongladarom makes clear that these approaches all rest precisely on a shared but distinctively Western assumption of the existence of the individual self or individual as an autonomy whose privacy, however defined, must be protected. (For additional discussion of Western conceptions of privacy, see Floridi, in press).

Hongladarom then takes up the phenomenon of hybridization of Western and Eastern notions of the individual and correlative expectations of privacy, as documented in a recent special issue (Ess, 2005). Here, he notes important similarities between Buddhist and Confucian notions of the self as a relational being, in contrast with modern Western views of the self as an isolate, something of a psychic atom that exists prior to and independently of all relationship with others. At the same time, however, Hongladarom helpfully warns against our conceiving these contrasts too sharply. Western traditions and philosophies further understand that individuals are interrelated (as emphasized especially in communitarian traditions), and Eastern views have ways of highlighting individuals as separate beings as well. Such parallels, as potential common grounds and/or what Ess (in press) characterizes as important resonances between Eastern and Western traditions, are critical, as Hongladarom notes, to the central task of a global information ethics that requires "a system of justification of privacy which respects these diverse cultural traditions, but at the same time is powerful enough to command the rational assent of all involved."

In his distinctive contribution to the development of such a system, Hongladarom begins by pointing out how Buddhism asserts the existence of the individual self at a conventional level in contrast to an absolute level, and thus, in Hongladarom's view, thereby insists on privacy as at least an instrumental good, one that counters abuse of power. This distinction, moreover, works to suspend the Western contrast between privacy as an intrinsic vs. instrumental good, and in this way, Hongladarom argues, Buddhism can make an important contribution in the form of a novel resolution of this particular debate in Western philosophy.

Turning to Nagasena, Hongladarom highlights a central argument for the Buddhist rejection of a self or a soul, understood as the unifying receptor of sense data. This reinforces the understanding of a unitary self as an empirical reality at a conventional level; while seen from an ultimate or absolute standpoint, this empirical self is simply conventional (i.e., not an absolute reality).

For Buddhists, however, the distinction between conventional and ultimate reality does not mean an ontological dualism that places less weight or value on the conventional vis-à-vis the ultimate. Indeed, for Buddhists (as well as for Kant), these are one and the same reality. Hence, Hongladarom argues, there is here a prima facie reason to respect privacy of such individuals. Indeed, he goes on to argue that the Buddhist injunction for which each person is responsible for his or her own liberation thereby sustains notions of equality and democracy that are at least closely similar to those developed and endorsed in Western societies. (The resonance suggested here thus compliments a similar alignment or harmony pointed out by Chokvasin between Buddhist versions of autonomy and Kantian and Habermasian notions, an alignment that, we suggest, further extends between the Buddhist notion of *Attasammapanidhi*, of ethical self-direction and self-adjustment, and Plato's model of the cybernetes, the pilot or steersman who symbolizes a similar capacity for ethical self-correction.)

Hongladarom further points out how Buddhism highlights the motive for efforts to violate one's privacy; namely, greed for the power, material gain, and so forth that would result from such violations. The antidote is not simply, as in the West, to insist on privacy rights as a protection against such violations. In addition, Buddhism endorses the cultivation of love and compassion as well as the extinction of the empirical self and its strong tendencies toward greed and so forth. In this way, Buddhism more directly addresses the basic source of potential privacy violations, not simply their effects.

Hongladarom concludes by noting that Buddhist ethics thus come closer to a Western-style virtue ethics as well as the pragmatic ethics of Richard Rorty (1975). In this way, his analysis helps to identify and reinforce a second key resonance between Eastern and Western thought, one noted by many comparative philosophers; namely, between Western virtue ethics (whether in Socratic, Aristotelian, and/or contemporary feminist forms) and the ethical systems of Confucian thought and Buddhism (Ess, in press).

SECTION I: SUMMARY REFLECTIONS

A number of important themes and larger insights thus emerge here. For example, many of these chapters share a clear rejection of the notion of technological instrumentalism, the view that our technologies are somehow cultural- and value-neutral. On the contrary, Søraker, Chokvasin, and van der Velden especially make clear how distinctive cultural values are embedded in ICTs, in particular, thus raising the threat of what Ess has called computer-mediated colonization (i.e., the covert, but thereby even more insidious, imposition of specific cultural values, norms, and preferences upon others as ICTs, including the Internet and the World Wide Web rapidly diffusing throughout the globe). Happily, as we have seen documented elsewhere (beginning, in fact, with the work of Hongladarom, 1998, and more broadly in the various publications by Ess and Sudweeks), local cultures and peoples are often more than capable of resisting such colonization. Here, van der Velden documents such resistance especially clearly as she provides both principles and examples of culturally sensitive design that seeks precisely to start from the ground up (i.e., from the cultural values and communicative preferences of a given group of people as the information design starting point) rather than imposing such values and preferences upon a specific group by using off-the-shelf but thereby predominantly Western designed and, thus, Western value-laden technologies.

At the same time, however, Burk's overview of the legal frameworks defining and seeking to protect intellectual property and privacy rights makes clear that the political and economic powers of the United States and the European Union are likely to override non-Western notions of who owns intellectual property (the community rather than the individual), its relative value (as emphasizing faithful replication of past masters rather than contemporary innovations), and notions of privacy (as generally more negative when individual, in contrast to familial or collective privacy as more positive).

Nonetheless, echoing van der Velden's arguments and examples regarding design, especially Søraker, Chokvasin, and Hongladarom demonstrate that a respectful philosophical dialogue between Western and Eastern traditions is not only possible—respectful in the sense that such dialogue is committed first of all to articulating, preserving, and enhancing the cultural values and preferences that define distinctive cultural identities in contrast to running over them roughshod in the name of a putative but, in fact, only Western universality; in addition, these contributors offer highly creative and fruitful syntheses out of such dialogue—but are also syntheses that, as alignments or resonances, help to bridge the irreducible differences between Eastern and Western cultures, while simultaneously preserving their irreducible differences. In this way, these insights may exemplify what Magnani has called the countercultural possibilities (in his example, of Islamic refinements of finance and economic development in light of traditional, Abrahamic critiques of interest) facilitated precisely by the cross-cultural and intercultural communication made possible by ICTs. As we will argue more fully in the Preliminary Conclusions, these alignments and resonances will prove critically useful in our larger project of developing a genuinely global information and computer ethics.

SECTION II: SPECIFIC VIEWPOINTS

We now turn to more specific analyses, beginning with two contributions that analyze the issue of privacy in Thailand. Subsequent chapters will turn to Africa, Turkey, and, finally, the United States, expanding upon initial discussions of cultural, theoretical, and practical analyses and concerns initially raised in Section I, especially as the correlative contributions in Section II provide more concrete details regarding specific cultural backgrounds and perspectives on specific issues such as privacy, software copying, and the digital divide.

Pirongrong Ramasoota Rananand's "Information Privacy in a Surveillance State: A Perspective from Thailand" focuses primarily on the historical, anthropological, and legal backgrounds of Thai notions of privacy, thereby helpfully supplementing the more philosophical approaches we have seen in Section I (Chokvasin, Hongladarom).

Rananand begins with a review of how far Buddhism may have played a role in the relative lack of an ethic of privacy in Thailand. Rananand makes the now-familiar point that, for Buddhists, the self is to be overcome in order to achieve enlightenment, or *nirvana*. Moreover, the Buddhist emphasis on interrelatedness, expressed first in the doctrine of co-emergent existence, contrasts with the Western dichotomy between the individual and the State, and thus between the private and the public.

These observations are problematic, however, in the sense that contemporary Thais may be understood to be exemplary hybrids (i.e., reflecting the powerful and extensive incorporation of Western cultural norms and beliefs); contemporary Thais, as secularized Buddhists, do not hold so strictly to traditional Buddhism as once might have been the case. For example, traditional Thai peasant houses included private spaces, but spaces that were for family activities and rituals, thus fostering a sense of collective privacy (Ramasoota, 2001). More recently, however, rooms for individuals are increasingly common in Thailand, which we might expect to foster a Western-like sense of individual privacy; we can note that such a pattern, in fact, is apparent among younger people in China (Lü, 2005) and Japan (Nakada & Tamura, 2005). Nonetheless, Rananand argues that the Thai tradition of a surveillance society, manifested in traditional wrist tattoos and contemporary smart ID cards (Kitiyadisai, 2005), has countered any similar emergence of a sense of individual privacy in Thailand. In particular, despite the clear and manifold potentials for abuse of individual privacy in the new system of smart ID cards, Rananand finds that their introduction, justified first as a way of curbing violence in the Muslim-majority provinces bordering Malaysia, has resulted in no criticism against it whatsoever. (For a somewhat different view, see Kitiyadisai, 2005.)

Rananand then provides an overview of current privacy legislation in Thailand. Briefly, while there has been some movement toward such legislation (pushed in part by globalization and the influence of Western notions and laws regarding privacy), currently in Thailand, reflecting longstanding traditions, government information is well-protected by statute and by practice, while individual/personal information is not. This means, in particular, that, thanks to the techniques of data mining between diverse bureaucratic databases, an extensive amount of information may be garnered about individuals without their knowledge or consent. This situation further reflects, on Rananand's showing, with a general public apathy in Thailand toward the issues of privacy. Even the relatively affluent Thais, who make frequent use of the Internet, see privacy as having a primarily instrumental value (rather than, say, standing as an intrinsic right, as is often defended in Western views), and if trading off individual privacy might result in economic benefit, especially users from lower socioeconomic groups seemed willing to make such a trade.

Rananand nonetheless sees some hope for further expansion of interests in individual privacy in Thailand. But he concludes with the observation that despite the pressures of globalization and the influence of notions of Thailand as an information society (the countervailing forces of Thailand's traditions as a surveillance society) coupled with a Buddhist underpinning that, contrary to Hongladarom's analyses, may undermine especially Western notions of privacy, seems to still hold the upper hand.

Pattarasinee Bhattarakosol's "Interactions among Thai Culture, ICT, and IT Ethics" provides an alternative perspective on the ethical dimensions of ICTs in Thailand, one that analyzes multiple ethical problems that have emerged in Thai society as a result of the introduction of ICTs. She begins with an extensive account of Thai culture, including nine value clusters, ranging from ego orientation to achievement-task orientation, that constitute a uniquely Thai set of orientations toward various dimensions of individual and community life. Reinforcing the dialectical understanding of the relationship between technology and culture developed by Herdin et al. in Section I, Bhattarakosol observes that most of the multiple factors influencing Thai culture are mutually interdependent (i.e., Thai culture may shape IT ethics, but as IT ethics change with new technologies and technological possibilities, so it may reshape Thai culture, in turn). Crucial to her later arguments, the sole exception here is religion: Bhattarakosol asserts that at least the ethical precepts of religion do not change.

In an analogy of computer programming languages, Bhattarakosol suggests that earlier Thai society could be understood in terms of a function-oriented language (e.g., Fortran); by contrast, she argues, contemporary Thai society is better understood as analogous to an object-oriented language. For example, earlier, a colleague could temporarily take over some of the functions of a sick colleague until that colleague was able to return to work. Such a behavior would seem to be an expression of Thai helpfulness toward others. But in contemporary Thai society, rather than function, life and work are organized in terms of objects in the sense that only particular persons can perform particular tasks. This is especially true under the regime of ICTs. Each individual user must login to a computer system using a unique user ID and password in order to be able to exercise certain functions and responsibilities. This electronic identity—another object—a cannot be shared or temporarily taken over by another. Even more bluntly, Bhattarakosol observes that people increasingly are oriented toward the consumption of objects, whether they be consumer items such as mobile phones or other persons as sex objects.

In particular, Bhattarakosol argues that as Thai children are brought up in homes increasingly inundated with the open information environments of the Internet (while their working parents are increasingly absent), such children increasingly call into question the ethical precepts that their parents try to teach. For Bhattarakosol, this is not only an argument for filtering of information, especially in light of the apparent fact that such children likely will grow up into less-than-ethical adults, but it is also an argument for renewed family structures, including a renewed emphasis on religion as the primary source of ethical precepts. Bhattarakosol proposes that such changes be implemented in small-scale pilot projects in hopes that, to remain with her analogies from computer science, the children who emerge from these projects will help the larger society to scale up in ethically positive directions.

Barbara Paterson's "We Cannot Eat Data: The Need for Computer Ethics to Address the Cultural and Ecological Impacts of Computing" takes up the urgent problems of the digital divide. Paterson points out that the usual solutions for solving this problem (basically, more machines and infrastructure) ignores the fact that computers, as we saw in several ways in Section I, embed a Western world view and its values of efficiency, speed, and economic growth. Paterson's analysis is distinctive, however, as she links the Western worldview, as embedded in ICTs, thereby leading to what she calls information colonialism with another feature of Western societies; namely, the environmental crises of global warming, natural resource depletion, and accelerated species extinction as consequences of Western ways of life.

Paterson begins by rightly pointing out that much of computer ethics has been framed by the assumptions of its almost exclusively Western developers, beginning with the presumption of a technological determinism that sees technological progress as inevitable and unstoppable. This technological determinism, moreover, is supported both by technological instrumentalism, a view examined by several authors in Section I (i.e., the belief that technology is cultural- and value-neutral, or just a tool), and by a presumed evolutionary (more precisely, Social Darwinist) view that assumes that societies and cultures are engaged in a ruthlessly competitive struggle. Paterson further identifies contemporary writers in computer ethics whose presumptions of competitive evolution reflect an unfortunate ethnocentrism. Their dominance in the field thus reinforces yet again the dominance of Western views over other cultural narratives, norms, and values. In this way, Paterson reiterates the point made by van der Velden in Section I with regard to Western design approaches as homogenizing, but now with regard to the literatures of information and computer ethics as themselves potentially homogenizing and, thereby, overriding local cultural values, norms, and decision-making approaches.

Paterson reinforces this point by reviewing the roots of the computer in Western culture—more specifically, in the emergence of mechanistic philosophy and the atomism/determinism of Thomas Hobbes. The subsequent Enlightenment built on these assumptions a (now strongly contested) view of natural science, a capitalist economics, a sociology that presumed that societies functioned like machines, and an industrial revolution literally built by machines. Paterson concludes, "The computer is thus a result and a symptom of western culture's high regard for abstraction and formalisation: it is a product of the mathematician's worldview, a physical device capable of operation in the realm of abstract thought."

A telling contrast then emerges between Western assumptions as embedded in computing technologies and African assumptions. Readers who recall Søraker's use of Confucian thought and Hongladarom's account of Buddhist thought will find these African assumptions familiar; here (again), persons are defined in terms of their relationships with other persons, such that "*participation* integrates individuals within the social and natural networks of the world" (emphasis added). As in Confucian ethics and, to be fair, Western virtue ethics, to be a person is a project of becoming a person. Personhood is not given at birth in the form of an isolated, atomistic self (as in Hobbes); Paterson cites Menkiti (1979), who notes that "personhood is something at which individuals could fail" (p.159).

Clearly, the digital divide is at least as much about cultural differences as it may be about disparities in income and infrastructure. Moreover, contra the frequent claim that ICTs inevitably (i.e., deterministically) will lead to economic prosperity and democratic polity, Paterson points out that ICTs facilitate or afford a phenomenon that Cass Sunstein (2002) has aptly captured under the phrase "The Daily Me" (i.e., my ability on the Internet to exclude others and to focus solely on communicating with and receiving information from only like-minded cohorts. Paterson (along with Sunstein and others) rightly worries that this fragmenting feature of computer-mediated communication may exacerbate existing ethnic divides in a number of African countries.

Moreover, Paterson argues that the computer, reflecting its Western roots, is, quoting Berman (1992), "a technology of command and control." Coupled in Africa with the authoritarian state inherited from colonialism, computer technology actually may increase the possibility of anti-democratic politics rather than inevitably lead to them. Moreover, as computerization apparently reinforces Western attitudes toward nature as a resource to be exploited (first of all, by making it quantifiable and separate from human beings; all are atomic isolates), and as computerization thereby reinforces models of consumption and commodification central to Western life styles,

Paterson argues that the introduction of ICTs indeed threatens to overrun local African values and knowledge and thereby to expand the environmentally unsustainable lifestyle of the West.

The solution—one anticipated, for example, by the syntheses we have seen in Section I between Confucian and Western thought (Søraker) and Buddhist and Western thought (Hongladarom), as well as in the examples of technological design from the ground up (van der Velden) and the dialectical relationship between technology and culture developed by Herdin et al.—is, instead, to work to ensure that African values and norms may work to reshape ICTs in their design and use. Paterson calls for a dialogue that will lead to information and computer ethics that is not simply global, while preserving local cultural norms and values; in addition, such a dialogue must focus on developing the ethics needed to guide the use of ICTs for the sake of sustainable development. The environment, in effect, becomes a central partner in such a dialogue.

Paterson thereby expands for us the broad parameters of the global dialogue on information and computer ethics that we endorse with this book, one that, we hope with Paterson, will develop "an inclusive ethical vision that recognizes the interdependencies of environmental protection, human rights, equitable human development, and peace."

Gonca Telli Yamamoto and Faruk Karaman's "Business Ethics and Technology in Turkey: An Emerging Country at the Crossroad of Civilizations" takes up information ethics as a subset of business ethics on the one hand and of IT and technology more broadly on the other. They note that what one country or culture may consider unethical is accepted as ethical in another culture or country—most notoriously, copying software is widely accepted in a number of Asian countries (in part, to recall van der Velden's observation, because Confucian traditions valorize copying great work)—as it is, according to Yamamoto and Karaman, in Turkey.

Yamamoto and Karaman first develop a broad approach to IT, one that echoes Herdin et al. and others in Section I by rejecting simple notions of technological determinism; rather, IT and information ethics will be shaped by a range of cultural factors, in turn, including religious and philosophical views, scientific developments, social and economic developments, and so forth. Information ethics thus must pay attention to a range of factors, beginning with IT first, since digital technologies especially develop rapidly and diffuse themselves extensively throughout all aspects of human existence (echoing Magnani).

Yamamoto and Karaman show that increasingly complex technologies issue in increasingly complex ethical issues, many of which we may not be immediately prepared to be resolved. Their analysis is of special interest, because Turkey represents a distinctive, perhaps exemplary, case study for anyone interested in the possibilities of a global information ethics that respects diverse cultural traditions. Turkey long has been shaped at the intersection of three world cultures: Western, Islamic, and Eastern. In this way, Turkey represents a microcosm of the global macrocosm: any resolutions and developments in information ethics that work in Turkey may be very suggestive for resolutions and developments in the larger world.

In their extensive review of these diverse cultural roots, Yamamoto and Karaman observe that notions of private property—especially property conceived in intangible forms, such as intellectual property—are alien to the originally nomadic peoples of the central Asian Turkish culture. Moreover, they suggest that the Islamic prohibition against stealing is less effective in Turkey in light of a larger sense that the wealthy West has taken advantage of the relatively poorer Islamic countries; hence, retaliation in the form of copying rather than paying for Western-produced software (and other goods) is seen to be justified. Finally, while Turkey is often touted as the most Western of Islamic countries (e.g., in the contemporary debates regarding Turkey's admission to the EU), Yamamoto and Karaman argue that the Westernization of Turkey, begun by its founder Ataturk, has not succeeded in changing prevailing beliefs that justify, or at least allow for, copying.

Finally, Yamamoto and Karaman point out a number of economic and social factors that likewise make it difficult for Western notions of intellectual property rights to be taken seriously in the Turkish context. More broadly, given the wide disparities among the diverse cultural views at work in Turkey as a microcosm of the larger world, they are not optimistic that a more universal IT ethic will emerge anytime soon.

Yamamoto and Karaman should be read in conjunction with Dan Burk's chapter in Section I, in part as at least as a partial counterexample to Burk's view that the intellectual property regimes of the United States eventually will dominate the global marketplace. He may well be right—in the long run. What Yamamoto and Karaman make clear for us is that local cultures, especially as reinforced by the problems of developing and/or struggling economies, may have the roots to resist such dominance for quite some time to come.

We close with Lynette Kvasny's "The Existential Significance of the Digital Divide for America's Historically Underserved Populations." Understandably enough, our other contributors, concerned with the digital divide (especially Grodzinsky and Tavani, van der Velden, and Paterson), have focused on its global expressions. But there are important global lessons to be drawn from the U.S. experience in this matter.

As the homeland of much of ICT invention and development as well as its preponderant consumer in the 1990s, the U.S. early on addressed the issues of the digital divide. Kvasny begins by observing that our answer to the question, "Has the digital divide become passé?" depends very much on what we mean by the "digital divide." In her view, academics and policymakers tend to conceive the digital divide as a gap in access and skills. In contrast to this technology-centric approach (i.e., one that emphasizes overcoming the digital divide in terms of increasing public access and training), Kvasny takes a broader existential perspective, which includes attention to emotional experience and how such experience influences decision making. From this perspective, much more is needed to overcome the digital divide than simply setting up more terminals in public libraries.

Indeed, frequently cited models and statistics based on the technology-centric approach suggest that the digital divide in the U.S. is gradually closing. But Kvasny observes that these statistics, along with their less encouraging global counterparts, come prepackaged in ways that help to create and justify categories of the information have-nots—ones that highlight typical problem populations (the unemployed, low income families, etc.). Kvasny further argues that doing so constructs the discourse regarding the digital divide in a racist way—one that argues for aid to those (at least implicitly) believed to be inferior. Put more broadly, Kvasny suggests that the prevailing discussion of the digital divide only reinforces, rather than radically calls into question, pre-existing inequalities.

Instead, Kvasny calls for a more contextually nuanced discussion of the digital divide in its social and technical as well as its economic dimensions. Some studies along these lines, in fact, exist and thereby highlight the limitations of the U.S. government's framing of, and thus proposed resolutions to, the problem. For her part, Kvasny portrays the digital divide in terms of a complex human evil that takes many forms—existential, institutional, social, political, and economic. Her recent research on ICT experience among low-income residents of a predominantly African American community shows, in fact, that ICT presents a double-bind oppression (Frye, 1983); whatever options are made available, there is no way to win. So a low-income black father, for example, characterizes the Internet as a white man's invasion of his home, one that programs his family to want "stuff" that he cannot provide.

Kvasny concludes with a series of critical questions that she argues are necessary for researchers to confront if they are to overcome prepackaged frameworks and discourse for dealing with such issues as the digital divide. She highlights Cornel West's observation that "there can be no democratic tradition without non-market values." But in the market-driven and market-dominated culture of the U.S., she goes on to point out, "nonmarket values are relatively scarce," including, in her view, the basic democratic interest in "the relationship of public interest and common good to the most vulnerable among us as human beings."

PRELIMINARY CONCLUSION

The contributors to this book, both individually and collectively, thus offer significant new insights and approaches at both theoretical and practical levels and from a wide range of cultural perspectives with regard to newly emerging global and intercultural information ethics. We conclude by noting how these contributors significantly expand what we might think of as the conceptual toolkit, research agenda—and, indeed, the very definition of this new field.

Contributors to Section II first help to sharpen our understanding of the irreducible differences among diverse cultural traditions and the challenges for any global information ethic that these differences entail. Gonca Telli Yamamoto and Faruk Karaman help to expand our understanding of the fundamental differences between Western,

Arabic/Islamic, and Eastern attitudes at work with regard to the issue of copying software, and Barbara Paterson highlights the contrast between traditional African understandings of the individual vis-à-vis the community, as these sharply contrast (in ways similar to Confucian and Buddhist views, we may note) with the Western understandings and values embedded in ICTs at both the software and hardware levels. Similarly, Pirongrong Ramasoota Rananand's and Pattarasinee Bhattarakosol's analyses of the problems of privacy in Thailand reiterate the contrasts highlighted by Hongladarom in Section I between the cultural and religious backgrounds that shape Thai notions and values and those underlying prevailing Western views. In particular, Western ethicists may be somewhat startled by Bhattarakosol's prescription for curing the ills of too much Westernization in Thailand; namely, a restoration of family life and adherence to traditional religion. That is, Western ethics, especially in the U.S. context, tends to strongly separate rationalist ethics and morality on the one hand and religious frameworks and beliefs on the other. But neither Hongladarom nor Bhattarakosol hesitate to offer strong ethical advice based in Buddhism first of all. As we are about to see, this sharp difference nonetheless may work to build a new and more comprehensive synthesis of Western and Eastern approaches, one that expands extant information and computer ethics in ways that may well be required if such an ethic is to enjoy a global legitimacy.

In fact, our contributors have offered a number of new syntheses—what we call here alignments or resonances—among diverse cultural traditions, beginning in Section I with Søraker's conjunction of Confucian and Western thought; ranging through Chokvasin's and van der Velden's conjunctions of Western theory with local values, ontologies, and ways of knowing; and concluding with Hongladarom's development of a close alignment between (Thai) Buddhist and Western approaches to issues of privacy.

Søraker takes up especially a classical Confucian understanding of human beings as relational entities and applies this notion to a distinctively Western information ontology in order to establish and defend the distinctive moral status of informational entities. In doing so, he adds a distinctive and important element not only to Luciano Floridi's highly influential information ontology but also thereby to a larger understanding, articulated perhaps most extensively by Terrell Ward Bynum, of information and computer ethics as oriented toward the moral value of flourishing. Especially as Bynum draws together here the work of Floridi, Norbert Wiener as the foundational figure of Western information and computer ethics, and other prominent contributors to that ethic, his account stands (currently, at least) as the most comprehensive such effort in Western philosophy (Bynum, 2006). Very much to his credit, Bynum seeks to incorporate important Eastern insights as well, precisely for the sake of developing a genuinely global information ethics that will recognize and preserve local cultural norms and values, both Western and non-Western. In our view, Søraker's theory of informational moral status makes a significant contribution toward that more comprehensive goal.

Similarly, Hongladarom's analysis of Buddhist understandings of the individual self and, thus, possible notions of individual privacy centrally contribute to resolving what otherwise appears to be an intractable contradiction between Western and Eastern views—and this in two ways. To begin with, Hongladarom points out that the apparent contradiction between a Western (more precisely, modern) insistence on the reality of an individual, atomic self as the moral autonomy whose rights, including the rights to privacy, must thereby be respected, and a Buddhist understanding of the individual self as an illusion that must be overcome in the name of genuine Enlightenment is not as black-and-white as it first appears. On the contrary, Western traditions certainly include understandings of the importance of relationships and community, and Eastern traditions include ways to understand the individual as an isolate as well. Moreover, the distinction in Buddhism between conventional and absolute standpoints allows for an understanding of an individual self as an empirical self as seen from the conventional standpoint—a self that thereby deserves privacy protections along the lines developed and justified in the modern West. Of course, from the absolute standpoint, this self ultimately will be seen (again) as an illusion that must be overcome if one is to overcome suffering (*dukha*); but until such Enlightenment is reached, we live as such selves and must take them and their rights, as justified by social and political requirements, seriously.

In this light, the contradiction between Western and Eastern ontologies remains, but it is ameliorated by the possibility of what we might think of as a Buddhist approximation of the Western view, one that is real enough to justify individual privacy rights as a serious matter. This resonance thus complements Chokvasin's account of Buddhist notions of autonomy, including the concept of *Attasammapanidhi*, the self-directed, self-correcting person, as thereby closely aligned with Kantian and Habermasian understandings of moral autonomy. Indeed, we have suggested that the concept of *Attasammapanidhi* resonates in particular with the Platonic model of the cybernetes, the pilot who symbolizes ethical self-correction—a resonance clearly critical for a global intercultural information ethics that seeks to take up cybernetics as not simply informational but, more centrally, ethical self-correction.

In these multiple ways, then, this alignment or resonance emerging from Hongladarom's analysis builds an important structure of ontological and ethical pluralism—one that holds together both incommensurable differences (i.e., precisely the differences in terms of beliefs, norms, values, etc.) that define distinctive cultural identities, thereby protecting cultural identities, alongside close similarities and/or shared beliefs and views (Ess, in press). Hongladarom's analysis of a close resonance between Buddhist and Western views, especially as complemented and reinforced by Chokvasin's account and the alignment we have seen between *Attasammapanidhi* and the cybernetes, hence provides critically important examples of such a pluralism and resonance.

Indeed, and perhaps most importantly, Hongladarom's account of how Buddhism approaches the problem of privacy protections is especially notable, as it shifts Western attention away from its characteristic focus on privacy as a right that must be protected to the source of the attacks on that right; namely, greed. In this way, the Buddhist injunctions to practice love and compassion—injunctions shared, obviously, by all world religions and most ethical frameworks—have us attack the problem of privacy not simply as a matter of insisting that others leave us alone, allow us to control our own information, and so forth, but rather as requiring us to assert positive responsibilities toward others (i.e., to approach them first of all out of a posture of love and compassion).

Such a solution will ring oddly in many Western ears, as it will sound more like a religious—specifically, Christian—than a rational/philosophical injunction. At the same time, however, such a solution is coherent not only with other Eastern philosophies (Confucian thought, first of all); it is also in keeping with Western virtue ethics especially, as Hongladarom points out. As well, its coherence with the Western, Abrahamic religious traditions should be seen as a strength, especially for countries such as the United States, whose citizens remain overwhelming defined in their ethics by their religious (predominantly Christian) beliefs. Moreover, this Buddhist emphasis on compassionate posture toward others very closely resonates with Hans Jonas' (1984) neighbor ethics, as endorsed in this book by Grodzinsky and Tavani. In any event, Hongladarom's Buddhist resolution, as is characteristic of virtue ethics generally and Buddhist thought in particular, makes clear that resolving the problems of privacy is not simply a matter of straightening out important but difficult conceptual problems and definitions at a purely rational level, as is the prevailing approach among Western philosophers. Rather, resolving the problems of privacy further requires us to reflect upon the motives for its violations and thereby resolve for our selves first of all to behave and thereby become more compassionate beings.

In Section II, at least one additional alignment emerges; namely, Barbara Paterson's insistence that traditional African understandings of the individual vis-à-vis the community be preserved in the face of the Western values embedded in ICTs. Paterson hereby complements Maja van der Velden's account in Section I of two ICT projects that accomplish just such a preservation of local values—but expands it to include traditional African understandings that, in turn, we can now see closely resemble Confucian and Buddhist accounts of the relationship between the individual and the larger community. But this expansion includes an additional element; namely, Paterson's linking our concerns with the homogenizing dominance of Western technologies and ethics in extant applications and information and computer ethics with the ecological consequences of a Western, consumer-oriented lifestyle. To be sure, more Western-rooted ICE systems (perhaps most notably the works of Terry Bynum, 2006, and Luciano Floridi, 2003) make explicit links between information ethics and ecological understandings of the world. But as reinforced by her standpoint in traditional African worldviews, Paterson radicalizes these linkages: ICE cannot focus narrowly on ICTs. But if it is to be a genuinely global ethic, ICE must take a genuinely comprehensive view, one that includes explicit attention to how we must live as human beings, not simply how we behave as users of technology.

This more comprehensive agenda for an emerging intercultural information ethics is still further fleshed out, for example, by Lynette Kvasny's call for researchers to critically evaluate their frameworks and research data in order to avoid simply reinscribing extant social and political injustices and, instead, to bring forward the evil that is at work in those injustices and inequalities. In this way, Kvasny makes clear that strongly prescriptive—indeed, ethically challenging and demanding—insights and claims are not restricted, for example, to the overtly religious appeal of Bhattarakosol. On the contrary, she makes clear that a comprehensive information ethics (i.e., one that steps beyond the comparatively narrow boundaries that have defined that ethics in much, though by no means all, of its Western development and expression) will issue in strong medicine (our term) (i.e., even more ethically demanding and challenging conclusions than follow from predominantly Western views).

In sum, our contributors thus help to extend and redefine intercultural information ethics in a number of striking ways. Our contributors, especially as they draw from diverse non-Western traditions (Confucian, Buddhist, Arabic/Middle-Eastern, and the indigenous traditions of Africa and Australia) thus broaden our understanding of both the irreducible cultural differences and resonances and alignments at play here, as these further apply to central issues in ICE such as privacy and intellectual property rights. They thereby highlight the dangers of remaining too closely within Western views, including assumptions of technological instrumentalism and technological determinism, and of uncritically accepting the Western assumptions both embedded in ICTs and even in specific research methodologies. As first steps beyond the Western views and approaches that have been predominant in both theory and praxis on both theoretical and practical levels, our contributors then offer up new syntheses, alignments, or resonances that help to constitute a more comprehensive, genuinely global approach to the issues of information and computer ethics (e.g., by way of new conjunctions between Western and Confucian thought [Søraker] and between Buddhist and Western thought [Chokvasin and Hongladarom]). Finally, our contributors make clear that Western tendencies to isolate and specialize (so as to separate, for example, ethics from religion and technology from ecology) will not do. Rather, a comprehensive intercultural information ethics will explicitly attend not only to the widest possible range of human cultural traditions, seeking to ensure their survival and flourishing in the face of otherwise homogenizing forces, but also thereby to the larger natural order and the potential consequences for that order that follow upon our design, construction, and diffusion of ICTs. By the same token, a comprehensive intercultural information ethics will seriously attend to the ethical demands of what Westerners may be tempted to dismiss as religious traditions, whether this be an overt call to return to traditional religious belief and family structure (Chokvasin) or to shift our attention from a primary focus on privacy protection to the more demanding awareness that the solution to data privacy may include prevention of such violation by bringing to the foreground the strongly positive obligation to cultivate within ourselves the postures of love and compassion that thereby overcome the motivating roots of privacy violation (Hongladarom). Such a call, we may note, constitutes still another alignment or resonance with the ethical posture suggested by Kvasny as necessary for Western researchers as well, insofar as the latter includes a heightened awareness of systemic evil in society and of the ways that prevailing research methodologies and data resources may collude with that evil.

While thus enhancing and expanding the emerging field of intercultural information ethics in these compelling and significant ways, we and our contributors would be the first to insist that these are but initial steps in the global intercultural dialogues that are needed for any further development of information and computer ethics on a global scale. We cordially and humbly invite our readers to take up these dialogues further.

REFERENCES

AoIR (Association of Internet Researchers). (2002). Ethical guidelines for Internet research. Retrieved from www.aoir.org/reports/ethics.pdf

Barlow, J. P. (1996). *A declaration of the independence of cyberspace.* Retrieved from http://homes.eff.org/~barlow/Declaration-Final.html

Becker, B. (2002). Sinn und Sinnlichkeit: Anmerkungen zur Eigendynamik und Fremdheit des eigenen Leibes. In L. Jäger (Ed.), *Mentalität und Medialität* (pp. 35-46). München: Fink Verlag.

Berman, B. J. (1992). The state, computers, and African development: The information non-revolution. In S. Grant Lewis & J. Samoff (Eds.), *Microcomputers in African development: Critical perspectives* (pp. 213-229). Boulder, CO: Westview Press.

Borgmann, A. (2000). *Holding on to reality: The nature of information at the turn of the millennium.* Chicago: University of Chicago Press.

Burkhardt, J., Thompson, P. B., & Peterson, T. R. (2002). The first European congress on agricultural and food ethics and follow-up workshop on ethics and food biotechnology: A US perspective. *Agriculture and Human Values, 17*(4), 327-332.

Bynum, T. W. (2006). A Copernican revolution in ethics? In G. Dodig-Crnkovic & S. Stuart (Eds.), *Computing, philosophy, and cognitive science.* Newcastle-upon-Tyne, UK: Cambridge Scholars Press.

Capurro, R. (2005). Privacy: An intercultural perspective. *Ethics and Information Technology, 7*(1), 37-47.

Dreyfus, H. (2001). *On the Internet.* London: Routledge.

Eagleton, T. (2000). *The idea of culture.* Oxford: Blackwell.

Ess, C. (Ed.). (2001). *Culture, technology, communication: Towards an intercultural global village.* Albany, NY: State University of New York Press.

Ess, C. (2005). Lost in translation? Intercultural dialogues on privacy and information ethics. *Ethics and Information Technology, 7*(1), 1-6.

Ess, C. (in press). Ethical pluralism and global information ethics. In L. Floridi, & J. Savulescu (Eds.). *Ethics and Information Technology.*

Ess, C., & Sudweeks, F. (Eds.). (1999a). Cultural attitudes towards technology and communication. *AI and Society, 13,* 329-340.

Ess, C., & Sudweeks, F. (Eds.). (1999b). Global cultures: Communities, communication and transformation. *Javnost—The Public,* 6.

Ess, C., & Sudweeks, F. (Eds.). (2002). Liberation in cyberspace ... or computer-mediated colonization? (Liberation en cyberspace ou colonisation assistee par ordinateur?). *Electronic Journal of Communication (La Revue Electronique de Communication), 12*(3, 4). Retrieved from http://www.cios.org/www/ejc/v12n34.htm

Ess, C., & Sudweeks, F. (Eds.). (2003). Liberatory potentials and practices of CMC in the Middle East. *Journal of Computer-Mediated Communication, 8*(2). Retrieved from http://www.ascusc.org/jcmc/vol8/issue2

Ess, C., & Sudweeks, F. (Eds.). (2005). Culture and computer-mediated communication: Toward new understandings. *Journal of Computer-Mediated Communication, 11*(1). Retrieved October, 2005, from.http://jcmc.indiana.edu

Floridi, L. (2003). On the intrinsic value of information objects and the infosphere. *Ethics and Information Technology, 4*(4), 287-304.

Floridi, L. (in press). Four challenges for a theory of informational privacy. *Ethics and Information Technology.*

Geertz, C. (2001). *Available light: Anthropological reflections on philosophical topics.* Princeton, NJ: Princeton University Press.

Gibson, W. (1984). *Neuromancer.* New York: Ace.

Hall, E. T. (1976). *Beyond culture.* Garden City, NJ: Anchor Press.

Jonas, H. (1984). *The imperative of responsibility: In search of an ethics for the technological age.* Chicago: University of Chicago Press.

Kitiyadisai, K. (2005). Privacy rights and protection: Foreign values in modern Thai context. *Ethics and Information Technology, 7*(1), 27-36.

Lawrence, L. (2004). *Free culture: How big media uses technology and the law to lock down culture and control creativity*. New York: Penguin.

Lü, Y. H. (2005). Privacy and data privacy issues in contemporary China. *Ethics and Information Technology, 7*(1), 7-15.

McErlean, J. (2000). *Philosophies of science: From foundations to contemporary issues*. Belmont, CA: Wadsworth.

Menkiti, I. A. (1979). Person and community in African traditional thought. In R. A. Wright (Ed.), *African philosophy* (pp. 157-168). New York: New York University Press.

Moor, J. (1985). What is computer ethics? In T. W. Bynum (Ed.), *Computers and ethics*, (pp. 266-274). Oxford: Blackwell.

Nagel, T. (1986). *The view from nowhere*. New York: Oxford University Press.

Nakada, M., & Tamura, T. (2005). Japanese conceptions of privacy: An intercultural perspective. *Ethics and Information Technology, 7*(1),17-26.

Phra Dhammapitaka (Payutto, P. A.). (1995). *Dictionary of Buddhism* (8th ed.). Bangkok: Mahachulalongkorn University Press.

Ramasoota, P. (2001). Privacy: A philosophical sketch and a search for a Thai perception. *MANUSYA: Journal of Humanities, 4*(2), 89-107.

Rawls, J. (2005). *Political liberalism*. New York: Columbia University Press.

Rorty, R. (1975). *Philosophy and the mirror of nature*. Princeton, NJ: Princeton University Press.

Sudweeks, F., Zhu, J., & Ess, C. (Eds.). (2002). Internet adoption in the Asia-Pacific region. *Journal of Computer-Mediated Communication, 7*(2). Retrieved from http://www.ascusc.org/jcmc/vol7/issue2

Sunstein, C. (2002). *Republic.com*. Princeton, NJ: Princeton University Press.

Tavani, H. T. (2004). *Ethics and technology: Ethical issues in an age of information and communication technology*. Hobcken, NJ: John Wiley and Sons.

Thorseth, M. (2003). *Applied ethics in Internet research*. Trondheim: Norwegian University of Science and Technology.

Walzer, M. (1994). *Thick and thin: Moral arguments at home and abroad*. Notre Dame, IN: University of Notre Dame Press.

Acknowledgments

We are living in an interconnected world, and this interconnectivity can hardly be more evident than in this particular book. To begin with, this interconnectivity makes our volume possible; while most of us have never met one another in person, everyone involved with the production of this book—the authors who live in faraway places, the publisher, the two editors who live in separate continents—all communicate with one another almost seamlessly through the wonders of information and communication technologies. Second, this interconnectivity is the impetus of the book itself; we share the deep conviction that such interconnectivity entails new demands in and from the fields of information and computing ethics. First of all, we must address the cultural perspectives of these ethics, as they now implicate technologies that virtually interconnect all peoples and cultures around the globe. This book is a result of our shared effort.

Intercultural information ethics, to use the term introduced by Rafael Capurro, has become much more significant in today's world due to a variety of reasons. Information and communication technologies, while originating in and conveying the values of Western cultures, now have spread throughout the world; the non-Western traditions need to reflect on what is available in the intellectual and spiritual resources of their traditions to find out how best to respond to the challenges posed by these technologies. In particular, many issues, as is well-known, do not know of any national or cultural boundaries; yet, these issues very often carry an impact locally. It is the local people and local communities that feel these impacts most acutely. Most systems underlying current computer and information ethics, however, have not, to our minds and those of the authors, adequately addressed how culture plays a role in reflecting, pronouncing judgments, interpreting, and reinterpreting their resources and environments in such a way that well-informed and carefully thought through ethical deliberations within local dimensions could take place. This book is a result of this common effort.

We certainly owe a great deal to a large number of people and institutions who have unfailingly helped with this project. First of all, we would like to thank Chulalongkorn University, which established the Center for Ethics of Science and Technology in March 2006 as a research unit serving as a virtual center in which faculty members from various academic disciplines can find common ground on which to discuss and delve into the intricacies of today's ethical and social aspects of science and technology. The atmosphere provided by the Center has been very conducive to sustained reflection and thinking, and we would like to thank all of Soraj Hongladarom's students who have dedicated their time and effort to editing and related tasks. Jantima Eamanond has meticulously looked over all the chapters to check their compliance with the style sheet and compiled the index list. Vajradhara Amitabhaporn also helped with the editing and compiling tasks. Don Sandage has contributed his expertise in carefully checking the grammar, style, and spelling in some of the chapters. Many thanks.

Second, we would like to thank Kristin Roth from Idea Group Inc., who has worked closely with the editors since the inception on the idea that led to this book. Her care and gentle guidance, and most of all her patience and understanding during the process of editing and reediting the chapters are appreciated with gratitude. We also would like to thank the reviewers who have generously given their invaluable time to comment and save the authors from many possible errors. We are especially grateful to Luciano Floridi, John Weckert, Terry Bynum, Rafael Capurro, and many others, who generously shared their time and expertise in support of this project—not only as reviewers but also as central figures in information and computing ethics who have shaped these fields in important ways and provided us with insight and encouragement.

This book is partially supported by a grant from the Thailand Research Fund, grant number BRD4680020. Its generous support is hereby gratefully acknowledged.

Soraj Hongladarom and Charles Ess
May 2006

Section I
Theoretical Concerns

Chapter I
The Moral Status of Information and Information Technologies:
A Relational Theory of Moral Status

Johnny Hartz Søraker
Norwegian University of Science and Technology, Norway

ABSTRACT

The purpose of this chapter is to explore whether information and information technology in certain cases ought to be valued as ends in themselves rather than as mere means to other ends. I will address this problem by proposing a theory of moral status: a theory of who or what has moral status in the sense that we, as moral agents, have an obligation to take their well-being into consideration when making ethical judgments. The proposed relational theory of moral status draws on insights from both classical Western and East Asian philosophy in order to question the exclusion of all nonliving entities in most theories of moral status. The relational properties constitutivity and irreplaceability are singled out as ethically relevant and are suggested as one possible way to ground the moral status of information and information technologies.

INTRODUCTION

In its *Charter on the Preservation of the Digital Heritage*, the United Nations Educational, Scientific and Cultural Organization (UNESCO) states that a vast amount of information "is at risk of being lost. Many of these resources have *lasting value* and significance, and *therefore ... should be protected and preserved* for current and future generations" (UNESCO, 2003, pp. 67-68, emphasis added). UNESCO further states that the seriousness of this threat has not been grasped fully and stresses the important role of information technologies (IT) in preserving this information.

The purpose of this chapter is to explore one possible theoretical grounding for the claims made by UNESCO. In what sense does information have lasting value, what kind of value can it be, why should we protect and preserve it, and what is the role of IT? I will address these problems by proposing a theory of moral status: a theory of who or what has moral status in the sense that we, as moral agents, have an obligation to take their well-being into consideration when making ethical judgments. I have termed this general, stand-alone theory *the relational theory of moral status*. It consists of an intrinsic and relational component, ascribing moral status in virtue of intrinsic and relational properties, respectively. The intrinsic component is based on traditional Western accounts of moral status, whereas the relational component is based on insights borrowed from classical East Asian philosophy. By proposing this theory, I wish to question the exclusion of all nonliving entities in most theories of moral status and explore whether it is at all possible to extend the notion so as to include information and information technologies.

The argument proceeds in several steps, gradually extending the range of entities whose well-being we have an obligation to take into consideration. Due to constraints on space, I will limit myself to opening up the possibility of ascribing moral status to nonliving entities in very special circumstances. I also will outline in what sense this can be a step toward identifying in what sense information has lasting value. In line with UNESCO's claim, it is important to emphasize the importance of preventing irreversible loss of our informational heritage, which often follows when information is ascribed value only in virtue of its perceived utility. The goal is a more sustainable development of the infosphere.[1]

THE MORAL STATUS DEBATE

The debate on who or what has moral status has been prominent in animal and environmental ethics in the last couple of decades, and the notion is central to the controversies surrounding abortion and stem cell research. The notion *moral status* signifies whether or not we have an obligation to take an entity's well-being into consideration when making ethical judgments. In order not to

beg the question, well-being initially should be defined in a broad sense. The broad definition of well-being is analogous to *soundness*, which can describe the condition of both living and nonliving-entities. A sound entity is free from disease, damage, and decay; it is unimpaired, uninjured, and in good condition.[2] We should at least start out with this broad definition and then make it more restrictive once we know what entities to include among the class of entities whose well-being should be taken into consideration.

Some entities have moral status in virtue of certain properties that are deemed ethically relevant. This is based upon the Principle of Formal Equality, which is a guideline for consistent thinking when it comes to practical matters. The principle can be formulated as follows: entities that are relevantly similar should be treated in a similar manner; a differential treatment requires an ethically relevant difference (Wetlesen, 1999). Thus, the crucial questions in the moral status debate become as follows:

1. What properties are ethically relevant in the sense that a differential treatment of x and y can be justified on the basis that x has property F, whereas y does not (or at least not to a sufficient degree)?
2. What entities are in possession of these properties?

Mary Anne Warren (1997) has introduced a helpful distinction between uni-criterial and multi-criterial theories of moral status. Unicriterial theories single out one property; for instance, rationality (Kant, 1996), sentience (Singer, 1990), or self-consciousness (Regan, 1983), and claim that all entities that satisfy that criterion should be treated equally. Multi-criterial theories (Warren, 1997; Wetlesen, 1999) utilize a number of criteria, resulting in theories in which some entities have higher moral status than others.

Among the most prominent theories in Western accounts of moral status, we find the theories of

Immanuel Kant, Tom Regan, and Peter Singer. Kant famously held that only moral persons have moral status; moral persons are the only entities toward whom we have direct moral duties. For Kant, the capabilities of free will, reason, and linguistic competence are necessary and sufficient criteria for being a moral person (Wetlesen, 1999). It is important to emphasize that a moral person in this context does not signify a person who is morally good but rather a person who is worthy of moral respect due to the fact that he or she is capable of moral agenthood. In practice, only humans are regarded as moral persons, but other entities are not excluded by definition. Tom Regan, although a deontologist of a Kantian bent, criticizes what he sees as Kant's anthropocentrism and singles out the ability to see oneself as a subject-of-a-life as sufficient for having moral status. *Subject-of-a-life* can be described roughly as being self-conscious and having the ability to see oneself as a temporal agent with future plans and goals. Being a subject-of-a-life also includes having experiences and beliefs from which future plans and goals are derived. Peter Singer, a utilitarian, mirrors Bentham's original utilitarian concept of measuring morality in terms of pain and pleasure, and singles out the ability to be sentient (capable of feeling pain and pleasure) as sufficient for having moral status.

Based in part on these efforts, Jon Wetlesen proposes a theory that combines the ethically relevant properties of Kant, Regan, and Singer. His biocentric, gradual theory of moral status also extends moral status even further, and *conation* (i.e., a striving to maintain one's existence or will to live) is seen by Wetlesen as sufficient for having moral status. In Wetlesen's theory, however, this is only the minimal criterion for having moral status, and moral status comes in degrees. With decreasing levels of moral status:

1. Moral persons (for convenience, I will sometimes refer to these as persons; in practice, they include humans only)

2. Merely self-conscious beings (e.g., dogs)
3. Merely sentient beings (e.g., fish)
4. Merely striving entities (e.g., microorganisms)[3]

THE INTRINSIC COMPONENT

The intrinsic component of the relational theory of moral status is based on Wetlesen's gradual theory of moral status. The underlying premise of Wetlesen's theory is that persons have moral status and that moral status is ascribed on the basis of an entity's relevant similarities with persons.[4] This seems to follow from the principle of formal equality already mentioned, but requires an analysis of what it means to be a person and what it means for something to be relevantly similar. Wetlesen answers these questions in terms of Christine Korsgaard's notion of practical identity, and I follow his lead.

In *The Sources of Normativity*, Korsgaard gives an insightful analysis of what she terms *practical identity*. According to Korsgaard (1996), one's practical identity is best understood as "a description under which you value yourself, a description under which you find your life to be worth living and your actions to be worth undertaking" (p. 101). The ethically relevant properties that constitute my practical identity are properties that I endorse and recognize as valuable in myself and, if I am to act consistently, properties that I ought to value in others. It seems evident that the properties that make me a person in a Kantian sense constitute an important part of my practical identity. Hence, free will, reason, and linguistic competence are ethically relevant properties. But, as Wetlesen (1999) points out, these properties alone leave us with a "fragmented and inadequate conception of ourselves" (p. 311). Having a practical identity without the ability to make plans on the basis of one's experiences makes little sense. Consequently, Regan's subject-of-a-life is an integral part of our practical identities and an additional ethically relevant property. Furthermore, it seems arbitrary to exclude our sensations of pleasure and pain, since the experience of pleasure is an important part of what makes life worth living. Wetlesen also adds the criterion *conation* (i.e., an entity's striving to maintain its own existence) as an integral part of our practical identity and ethically relevant property. Conceiving one's life as worth living almost by definition includes our having a conscious experience of striving or will to live. Thus, at the very least, the properties singled out so far are arguably integral parts of my practical identity. They are all fundamental properties that I value in myself by an act of reflective endorsement.[5] Violating these properties is a violation of my core identity and my very reasons for living and, consequently, places an obligation on both myself and others to not impede upon these properties. Furthermore, if I am to act consistently I ought to value these properties in you, and recognize that it would be morally wrong for me to impede upon them. According to this line of reasoning, it is morally wrong to hinder someone from actualizing their reason and linguistic competence—and to obstruct their free will.[6] It is morally wrong to hinder their ability to make plans for their lives (being a subject-of-a-life), and it is morally wrong to willingly inflict pain upon them. Evidently, it is also morally wrong to impede upon their will to live. If we are to act consistently, we should respect those properties in others—not only those that satisfy all of them but also any entities that satisfy one or more of these criteria. Therefore, according to Wetlesen, we should not impede upon a dog's self-consciousness, a fish's sentience, or a microorganism's will to live.

A couple of further points must be addressed in order to establish the intrinsic component: (1) Is there an ethically relevant difference between humans and highly evolved nonhuman animals? and (2) Is there an ethically relevant difference between biological life and other highly complex entities?

First, the ascription of higher moral status to persons (in practice, human beings) than certain highly evolved nonhumans is vulnerable to what is often called the *argument from marginal cases.* This argument is utilized by both Regan and Singer in order to criticize what they see as Kant's anthropocentrism. Many so-called marginal cases of humans lack free will, reason, or linguistic competence. At the same time, it is plausible that many nonhuman animals—at least to a higher degree than marginal humans—possess some degree of free will, reason, and possibly even linguistic competence. According to the principle of formal equality, differential treatment requires an ethically relevant difference.

Thus, if we are to act consistently, we should either (1) exclude marginal humans—among them the severely retarded and newborn—from having the same moral status as "normal," adult humans or (2) include animals that are relevantly similar to marginal humans among the ones with moral status. Since most would find the former absurd, the conclusion becomes that we cannot make a sharp distinction between humans and animals that are equivalent to marginal humans.

In reply to this objection, Wetlesen defends his differentiation between persons and other animals by differentiating between abilities and capabilities (Wetlesen, 1999). Most humans, including the marginal cases, have the capability for free will, reason, and linguistic competence. Although some never actualize these capabilities into operative abilities, the mere capability is what sets humans apart from other animals. The capability is sufficient for being a moral person, whereas having the operative ability makes you a moral agent. I agree with Wetlesen that when it comes to moral status, we should not differentiate between moral persons and moral agents. The latter have additional moral duties and responsibilities, but not a higher moral status. At the same time, there is an ethically relevant difference between those who have the capabilities in question (e.g., an infant or a comatose person) and those who do not (e.g., a chimpanzee). The latter will never become moral agents, whereas the former might actualize their capabilities into operative abilities, and it is therefore morally wrong to harm them in ways that will hinder this actualization. The human exceptions are those who are so severely retarded or injured that they have no chance of regaining their free will, reason, or linguistic competence; not only the abilities but also the capabilities are lost. Consequently, they have no moral status whatsoever. This poses a problem for Wetlesen and many other accounts of moral status, which is one of my reasons for adding the following relational component.

Second, the ascription of moral status to all living entities and none whatsoever to nonliving entities runs into a similar problem with marginal cases. Wetlesen argues that the conation found in all life is an ethically relevant property due to its similarity with the conscious experience of a will to live, which is central to our practical identities. This seems to be an unnecessary and inconsistent favoring of biological life. In order to encompass all living entities, conation must be defined very broadly, and a broad concept of conation does not seem to follow from a Korsgaardian notion of practical identity.[7] My conscious experience of being a striving individual with a will to live, which rightly belongs to my practical identity, is qualitatively different from that of a microorganism. I agree with Wetlesen that any integral part of my practical identity should be respected in others, but this requires that the property is relevantly similar. It is possible to describe an amoeba or a light switch, for that matter, as having a painlike reaction, but there is, of course, nothing "to be like" that amoeba or light switch. Consequently, that "pain" is not relevantly similar to the experience of pain felt by a sentient being. I believe the same holds for Wetlesen's comparison of the conation found in nonsentient beings with the conscious will to live found in the practical identity of a person. They can be described in a similar manner, but the unconscious reflexes of an

amoeba or the growth of a plant is not relevantly similar to our conscious experience of a will to live. If we define conation in a broad way, as non-conscious striving, then this property also can be satisfied by a number of nonliving entities (e.g., advanced robots). In short, conation considered as an unconscious striving is not relevantly similar to our conscious experience of a will to live, nor is it a property unique to living entities.

Based on these considerations, the intrinsic component of the relational theory of moral status follows Wetlesen's theory of moral status with the exception of conation. To summarize, moral status (or what I later will refer to as the subclass moral standing) comes in three degrees:

1. **Moral Persons:** (Satisfying the capability for free will, reason, and linguistic competence) enjoy full and equal moral status; no moral person has a higher moral status than other moral persons do.
2. **Merely Self-Conscious Beings:** (With future plans and goals based on beliefs and experiences and with the ability to see themselves as temporal agents) have moral status but less than moral persons.
3. **Merely Sentient Beings:** (With the ability to experience pain and pleasure) have moral status as well, although less than self-conscious beings and considerably less than moral persons. [8]

Although Wetlesen and the intrinsic component of my theory abandon the traditional uni-criterial approaches to moral status, they rest upon what is known as intrinsic properties only. There are multiple definitions of what an intrinsic property is, but often it is defined as a property that it is possible for an entity to possess, even if it were in isolation. Being sentient is an intrinsic property because it is logically conceivable that an entity can be sentient even if it were the only thing in existence. Being married, on the other hand, is an extrinsic, or relational, property, since it is logically inconceivable that an entity can be married if it were the only thing in existence. The reason that intrinsic properties, explicitly or not, often form the basis of moral status is that intrinsic properties are the only properties that can give rise to intrinsic value; that is, value in itself. In order for moral status to be objective and independent from outside valuers, the properties upon which this is based must persist, even if there were no valuers around. G. E. Moore (1971), to whom I will return next, stated, "This is, in fact, the only method that can be safely used, when we wish to discover what degree of value a thing has *in itself*" (p. 91, emphasis added). This commitment to objectivity and noncontingency, which is apparent in most theories of moral status, seems to be a reflection of the two-world metaphysical order inherited out of classical Greece, which has given Western philosophy its tradition for seeking objectivity and universality (Ames, 2000).

MORAL STATUS IN LIGHT OF WESTERN AND CLASSICAL EAST ASIAN PHILOSOPHY

Most ethical theories come with metaphysical commitments, and theories of moral status are no exception. In Western philosophy, since the ancient Greek philosophers, the distinction between reality and appearance has been a central topic of discussion. This is reflected in the fundamental questions in Western philosophy, such as "What is the Being behind beings?" and "How do we attain knowledge about the world itself, not merely its appearance?" This two-world metaphysics is the very basis for separating objectivity and subjectivity, and has had a profound impact on Western philosophy ever since. Wittgenstein (1958) characterized Western philosophy as having "a contempt for the particular case" (p. 18). The same focus on objectivity is also dominant in Western accounts of moral status. The exclusive focus on intrinsic, objective, and noncontingent

properties became even more evident after the notorious early 20th-century dispute between G. E. Moore and F. H. Bradley over internal and external relations.[9] In short, Bradley argued that all relations are internal in the sense that the essence of an object is contingent and influenced by all the relations in which it stands. Moore's (1993) reply is complex, but in short, he argues that Bradley's dogma of internal relations implies that any entity "which does in fact have a particular relational property, could not have existed without having that property. And in saying this it obviously flies in the face of common sense" (p. 88). Moore, who is generally regarded as one of the founders of analytic philosophy and who has made a major impact on Western ethics, reinforced the objective/subjective distinction, now in terms of intrinsic/extrinsic. In addition to the preference for the objective and universal, a related notion of our consciousness as distinct from the physical world also has been dominant in classical Western philosophy. This is especially evident in Plato's notion of kinship between the soul and the world of ideas, and the Cartesian separation between *Res Extensa* and *Res Cogitans*.

In classical East Asian philosophy, however, the starting point is not the search for Being behind beings or the ultimate objective reality of the world, nor is the mind typically construed as distinct from the physical world. Instead, the point of departure is the assumption that there is only this one continuous concrete world. Rather than asking what lies behind the world as it appears, classical East Asian philosophy asks how the different objects in this continuous world are related, seen from our own specific place in the world (Ames, 2000).[10] Entities do not have essences in an Aristotelian sense, but differing relations at different times define their very nature—much in line with Bradley's notion of internal relations. The difference between classical East Asian and Western philosophy also is reflected in their respective languages. "Essentialism is virtually built into … all Indo-European languages" (Ames &

Rosemont, 1998, pp. 21-22). In Western languages and philosophy, the world typically consists of discrete substances and essences, and objects are only extrinsically related, "so that when the relationship between them is dissolved, the [previously related entities] are remaindered intact" (Ames & Rosemont, 1998, p. 24). In classical Chinese language and philosophy, however, a "dissolution of relationships is surgical, diminishing both parties in the degree that this particular relationship is important to them" (Ames & Rosemont, 1998), p. 24). From this perspective, certain relations between myself and other living or nonliving entities are constitutive of my identity, and consequently, this relation places restrictions on how one ought to treat the related object.

Most Western accounts of moral status inherit the metaphysical preference for objective and noncontingent criteria. Likewise, the intrinsic component ascribes moral status based on intrinsic properties alone. Are there good reasons for grounding moral status solely on intrinsic properties? The main reason is that intrinsic properties supposedly give an entity objective, independent, and noncontingent value in itself. We thereby avoid the relativist threat. If we insist that moral status must be objective and observer-independent, then intrinsic properties are clearly the only viable criteria for ascribing moral status. My claim in outlining the following relational component is that moral status does not have to be objective and observer-independent. On the contrary, a number of undesirable consequences follow from relying on intrinsic properties alone and the conflation of nonintrinsic and instrumental value. The same holds for the way in which Western accounts of moral status usually treat our conscious faculties as separate from the body and the rest of the world. The relational component is inspired by the Chinese way of viewing entities in the world as centers of mutually constitutive relationships and our identities as extended into the world. Although this approach faces some serious problems of its own, the purpose is to challenge the Western

preferences mentioned previously and explore in what way it can make sense to ascribe moral status to certain nonliving entities.

THE RELATIONAL COMPONENT

Recall Wetlesen's inclusion of the severely retarded and newborn among moral persons based on their possession of the capability of moral agency. This is all fine, but consider the following example. Imagine a comatose father with no possibility of regaining free will, reason, or linguistic competence—nor self-consciousness, sentience, or a conscious will to live. According to Wetlesen, the intrinsic component, and most other accounts of moral status, this comatose father has no moral status; if the capability is gone, then the moral status is gone. Wetlesen (1999) would reply that we should give the comatose father the benefit of the doubt but admits that this is a somewhat ad hoc assumption (p. 302). In any case, if there were no doubt, there would be no moral status. The comatose father would have, at best, instrumental value. The same holds for stillborn children or children born without a functioning brain. Does it make sense to speak of these entities as having no moral status whatsoever? Can I do whatever I please with the stillborn child? One might be tempted to answer these questions instrumentally by saying "yes, as long as nobody knows," but at the same time, I believe our moral intuition tells us something more fundamental. If Achilles had dragged the corpse of Hector around without anyone knowing, would that have made it permissible? If I am not mistaken, our moral intuition tells us something more fundamental. There is something morally wrong with treating certain dead entities in this manner, despite the fact that there were no ethically relevant intrinsic properties in the corpse of Hector. As long as we are limited to intrinsic or instrumental value, then a comatose father, a stillborn child, and the corpse of Hector has, at best, instrumental value; they deserve no value as an end and only have value insofar as they serve some other end.[11]

Intrinsic, Relational, and Instrumental Value

One common feature of most theories of moral status, explicitly or not, is that having intrinsic value—value in itself—is necessary for having moral status. The two terms often are equated, since they both are contrasted with mere instrumental value. Furthermore, value in itself is often conflated with value as an end, which both are contrasted with instrumental value. In "Two Distinctions in Goodness" Korsgaard (1983) attempts to clarify these concepts and distinguishes between the following:

1. **Final and Instrumental Value:** Entities with final value are valued as an end for their own sake, whereas entities with instrumental value are valued as means to something else.
2. **Intrinsic and Extrinsic Value:** Entities with intrinsic value have value in themselves; the source of their value is their own existence. Entities with extrinsic value, on the other hand, have their value derived from some other source.

Intrinsic value entails final value, but not the other way around. More importantly, instrumental value entails extrinsic value, but not the other way around. If the value of an entity is derived from some other source (extrinsic value), this entails that it cannot have value in itself (intrinsic value), but not necessarily that it has no value as an end (final value). The conflation between extrinsic and instrumental value is dangerous, because entities that do not meet the criteria of intrinsic goodness then become mere instruments. This includes, for instance, the original *Mona Lisa* and the corpse of a loved one. By stressing the third category—extrinsic final value—we can avoid

the counterintuitive implications of operating with only two categories. The *Mona Lisa* and the corpse of a loved one do not have intrinsic value, but do they have final value—do they have value as ends? Let us refer to this nonintrinsic, final value as *relational value*. If an entity has relational value, this means that it has value as an end but that this value is derived from some other source; hence, it is contingent, nonobjective, and dependent upon an external valuer.

Interestingly, Wetlesen seems to be open to the idea of a third category between intrinsic and instrumental value.[12] According to Wetlesen (1999), an object can have final value "in so far as someone has an interest in it for its own sake. [This is] a relational term, relative to the interests ... of some subject" (p. 291). Nevertheless, Wetlesen states that having final value in virtue of mere relational properties does not add up to moral status. Wetlesen agrees that certain objects can have final value by virtue of their relational properties but still reserves moral status for intrinsic final value. Presumably, the reason is that final value based on mere relational properties is derived from some other source; hence, the value is not objective and noncontingent, and our duties are not direct. Thereby, they are excluded from having moral status according to his definition. This is a clear indication of the Western preoccupation with objective and intrinsic properties. If we are operating only with intrinsic and instrumental value in which only the former has moral status, a comparison between the respective ranges of valued objects within those categories becomes somewhat counterintuitive. For instance, Wetlesen (and Singer) extend moral status in order to include all sentient beings, which yields that a fish (given that fish are capable of experiencing pain) has moral status, whereas the original *Mona Lisa* has none. Add to this the fact that the original *Mona Lisa* in reality is valued far beyond most animals (i.e., we have a stronger obligation to preserve the well-being of the *Mona Lisa* than a merely sentient being). Consequently, it seems strange to preserve moral status for intrinsically valued entities only.

Granted, the original *Mona Lisa* does not have intrinsic value, but at the same time, its value seems to be vastly higher than the intrinsic value of a fish, let alone, in Wetlesen's case, a microorganism. Since many entities are, and ought to be, valued far beyond merely sentient beings and not only in terms of utility, the notion of moral status loses its significance if, despite this fact, it includes only intrinsically valued entities. This raises the need for operating with relational value in addition to intrinsic and instrumental value and to extend moral status so as to include this category. The well being of a human being, a dog, and the *Mona Lisa* should be taken into consideration when making ethical judgments, because they have value as ends, regardless of whether the source of this value is intrinsic or relational. We do not need to investigate any further consequences of destroying a human being, a dog, or the original *Mona Lisa* in order to say that it is morally wrong; their well being matters in itself.

The Anthropocentric Objection

A common objection to the previous line of reasoning is that intrinsic value is radically different from what I have called relational value. Only the former entities have value independently of someone actually valuing them. In order to have genuine value as an end, an entity must have value as an end, even if it were the only thing in existence. By caring for the well being of anything but persons, we are caring, in fact, for the well being of the person(s) to whom this entity is related. If I take the well being of a corpse into consideration, this is just an indirect way of taking the well being of the ones who care for the corpse into consideration. Thus, the corpse serves merely as a means to an end; namely, taking the well being of a person into consideration. Consequently, its value is only instrumental—or so the objection goes.

This objection is forceful, but only if we consider it possible at all to have moral status if there were no conscious valuers around. In an anthropogenic approach, however, "the moral language game has its origin in human culture, not in nonhuman nature. It only makes sense to humans" (Wetlesen, 1999, pp. 296-297). Consequently, nothing has moral status if there are no conscious beings around to ascribe this moral status. Moral status, defined as the class of entities whose well being we have an obligation to take into consideration, only makes sense to someone who actually is able to take the well being of someone into consideration—and capable of letting that consideration guide one's actions. As seen from an anthropogenic standpoint, the very notion of something having moral status independently of human beings makes little sense. Entities with intrinsic value by definition retain their intrinsic value in isolation, but not their moral status. In this view, we should be concerned with value as an end, not value in itself. As long as the starting point is that nothing has moral status independently from human judgment, then the question of moral status is not "What has value in itself, independently from humans?" but rather "What ought we, as humans, to treat as an end in itself?" In terms of well being and moral status, "What has moral status in the sense that we, as moral agents, have an obligation to regard their well being as an end in itself, not merely as a means to another end?"

Based on these considerations, we can distinguish between three kinds of values: intrinsic, relational, and instrumental. The task remains, however, to provide reasonably precise criteria for entities that do not have the necessary intrinsic properties yet have a value independent of their utility. If something has value as an end, this means that it is not a mere means to an end and that it has value independent of its utility. For instance, the *Mona Lisa* and the corpse of a loved one are valuable, regardless of their use. These entities seem like clear candidates for having moral status without having intrinsic value, but what makes them so? What are the criteria for being an ethically significant relation?

Organic Unities and the Irreplaceability Criterion

Perhaps the most important difference between instrumental and relational value is that instrumentally valued entities are replaceable, whereas relationally valued entities are not. Money has mere instrumental value, since the individual tokens are replaceable. Whether I have this or that $100 bill does not make much of a difference. This is also a clear indication that it has no value as an end, since a similar entity, by appearance, function, or convention, can take its place and receive the same value. This is not the case with the original *Mona Lisa*. It is not possible to replace the original *Mona Lisa* for any other entity and retain its value, not by appearance, function, nor convention. If it is destroyed, it is irreversibly destroyed. The irreplaceability of an entity is important because this in itself requires us to treat it differently from replaceable entities; this in itself can provide sufficient reason for taking its well being into consideration precisely because its destruction never can be rectified.

As we can see, relational value is linked closely to the uniqueness and irreplaceability of an entity, but this is not a sufficient criterion. A grocery list scribbled on the back of an envelope is also unique and irreplaceable in a very weak sense, but that does not mean that it has moral status. If an entity has no value for anyone, its irreplaceability does not make a difference. We need additional criteria for defining when an irreplaceable entity has value as an end. I have previously mentioned Moore's critique of Bradley's notion of internal relations, and at first glance, the Moorean view appears to be the antithesis of the relational theory of moral status put forward in this chapter. Nonetheless, his concept of organic unity comes very close to the relational component presented here.

According to Moore, an entity has intrinsic value if and only if a universe containing only that entity would be good; it would be a better universe than no universe at all. Although this definition requires a further clarification of what a good universe would be, it is at least a good test to find out what does not have intrinsic value. Regardless of whether or not we think the *Mona Lisa* has any value in our actual universe, it is hard to see how the *Mona Lisa* could have any value if it were the only thing in existence. This also signifies the difference between the intrinsic component discussed previously and the relational component. Entities that satisfy the intrinsic criteria singled out in the intrinsic component—rationality, self-consciousness, and sentience—have value in isolation because their well being matters to themselves. The well being of the *Mona Lisa*, on the other hand, does not matter to anyone in isolation. However, Moore's definition of intrinsic value takes on an entirely new meaning when he introduces his notion of organic unity. According to Moore, the intrinsic value of an organic unity (a whole) can be different from the intrinsic value of its parts. For instance, "a whole formed by a good thing and an indifferent thing may have immensely greater value than that good thing itself possesses" (Moore, 1971, p. 28). In other words, an entity with no value in isolation can, by being part of an organic unity, make that unity more valuable. Thus, the existence of that entity brings more goodness into the world, not in isolation, but if considered as part of an organic unity, if it stands in a certain relation to an intrinsically valuable entity. To illustrate this point, Moore uses a beautiful object as an example:

A beautiful object ... is commonly held to have [no intrinsic value] at all. But the consciousness of a beautiful object is certainly a whole of some sort in which we can distinguish as parts the object on one hand and the being conscious on the other. ... We cannot attribute the great superiority of the consciousness of a beautiful thing over the beautiful thing in itself to the mere addition of the value of consciousness to that of the beautiful thing. (Moore, 1971, p. 28)

The *Mona Lisa* in isolation has no intrinsic value, whereas a conscious being in isolation has intrinsic value. A whole consisting of the *Mona Lisa* and a conscious being in isolation have even higher intrinsic value. In terms of isolation, a universe in which only a conscious being capable of aesthetic appreciation existed would be worse off than a universe in which the organic unity of this being and the *Mona Lisa* existed. Thus, the *Mona Lisa* cannot bring value into the world as long as it exists in isolation, but together with such an intrinsically valuable entity, it can and does.

If we combine the intrinsic component, the anthropogenic presupposition and Moore's notion of organic unity, this yields that an entity with relational value is an entity that is capable of increasing the intrinsic value of an organic unity consisting of itself and a person (i.e., an entity with rationality, self-consciousness, and sentience). The related entity does not thereby attain intrinsic value, but by being a necessary part of a unity that has intrinsic value, it attains value as an end. In contrast with being a mere instrumental part of a unity, the criteria for being part of an organic unity is that "the good in question cannot conceivably exist, unless the part exist also … [it] is a necessary condition for the existence of that good which is constituted by the whole" (Moore, 1971, p. 29). If an entity is a mere instrumental part of a unity, this means that the good constituted by the unity in question can continue to exist, even if the instrument is annihilated; the instrument can be replaced. In other words, one criterion for having relational value is that the annihilation of such an entity means that the good constituted by the whole also is annihilated; it is an irreplaceable part of an organic unity. Furthermore, in order to have intrinsic value as a whole, the organic unity

must be a unity between the related entity and something that has intrinsic value.

Practical Identities and the Constitutivity Criterion

The intrinsic criteria singled out as integral parts of our practical identities are sufficient for having intrinsic value. But, as Moore pointed out, certain entities can form part of a whole with a higher intrinsic value than the parts. This means that the intrinsic value of a whole consisting of our practical identities and a related entity can have a higher intrinsic value than our practical identities alone. Paraphrasing Korsgaard, if a related entity is constitutive for seeing one's life as worth living and one's actions as worth undertaking, then the organic unity of the person and the related entity have a higher intrinsic value than the person alone—it is an organic unity in the Moorean sense. Furthermore, it is not the consequences of destroying such an entity that makes it morally wrong, but the very fact that it is a part of an organic unity with a person. If no one were aware of Achilles' mistreatment of Hector's corpse, this does not make that action morally good or indifferent. It is even conceivable that Achilles' mistreatment of Hector's corpse overall had positive consequences (e.g., if the pleasure felt by Achilles was the only relevant utilitarian consequence); still, it is morally wrong due to the fact that it formed an organic unity with those who loved him. Whether or not they were, in fact, harmed by Achilles' deeds does not make a difference as to the moral wrongness. In this sense, the relational theory of moral status, in contrast with utilitarianism, does not measure the harming of an entity in terms of mere consequences. It is monotonic in the sense that intentional damage to the well being of entities with moral status may be inevitable due to conflicting obligations but never can be morally good or indifferent due to lack of negative consequences.

The way in which we are related to other entities also can be seen as an extension of our practical identities beyond the inside of our skulls. As Ames and Rosemont (1998) puts it when describing Chinese philosophy, "As the quality and quantity of our relationships proliferate, so, too, are we extended in the world" (p. 24). Moore's notion of organic unity escapes his somewhat abstract notion that only things in isolation have intrinsic value. Furthermore, the mere logical conceivability of something having value in isolation is too far removed from our actual world of ethical dilemmas, considerations, and complex interdependencies. It also stands in contrast to the knowledge we have about the very source of our practical identities: Although Descartes might have been right in assuming that it is logically conceivable for our minds to exist distinct from our bodies, cognitive science has long since abandoned the Cartesian, self-contained mind. It is empirically inconceivable. Nevertheless, many accounts of moral status hardly consider the relation between mind and body. The brain and our practical identity, if anything, constitute an organic unity. Beyond reasonable doubt, the brain is constitutive of the mind, in a strong sense. All theories of moral status considered in this chapter stress our conscious faculties and not those parts of our bodies that actually give rise to these sensations. For instance, persons have moral status in virtue of their rationality, but there is little mention of the role of the brain in all of this. Does my brain have moral status or mere instrumental value? The brain is not replaceable, and, save religion and superstition, there is little reason to deny that it is constitutive of having a practical identity. Consequently, the brain is not a mere instrument for bringing about our rationality, self-consciousness, and sentience—it is the physical aspect of our practical identities. Thus, harming the well being of a brain is morally wrong as long as it is forming an organic unity with our practical identities. It is irreplaceable and constitutive of our practical identities. Evi-

dently, few entities are constitutive of someone's identity in the same degree as a brain. I will return to the question whether there are degrees of replaceability and constitutivity and whether or not these are necessary or sufficient criteria. First, however, I will focus on my primary task in this chapter, which is to argue that information and information technology in certain very special circumstances should be ascribed moral status. In certain circumstances, information and information technology can be both constitutive of my practical identity and irreplaceable—far beyond a metaphorical sense.

INFORMATION TECHNOLOGY AS STRONGLY CONSTITUTIVE

In the intrinsic component, I argued, in line with Korsgaard (1996) and Wetlesen (1988), that our practical identity is the source of why we have moral status. If we, for the sake of argument, at least, agree that the brain is a necessary condition for (and a physical aspect of) our practical identities and, consequently, deserves moral status, then the crucial question becomes, as Clark and Chalmers (1988) put it, "Where does the mind stop and the rest of the world begin?" (p. 7). Do we draw the line at the brain?

Consider the following example (Clark & Chalmers, 1988): Otto suffers from Alzheimer's disease, and he has become dependent upon a notebook in which he writes down everything that he needs to remember. He carries the notebook wherever he goes, and whenever he needs some old information, he looks it up. For Otto, the notebook plays the same role as our biological memories. The information technology (notebook) plays the same role as our brain's storage of information, and the information (entries in the notebook) plays the same role as information stored in the brain.

At first glance, there might appear to be a number of radical differences between the notebook and the brain, but on closer inspection, none of them is really that radical. Our biological memories also can be unavailable in some circumstances, can be permanently lost, and others can insert false information. Furthermore, to say that Otto's memory disappears when he is not consulting his notebook would be equivalent to saying that our biological memories disappear when we are not conscious of them. There is nothing sacred about information that happens to be stored on the inside of our skin. The causal role played by Otto's notebook mirrors the causal role of our biological memories in every important respect. Clark and Chalmers put the point in terms that come very close to Korsgaard's and the argument from practical identity:

The information in Otto's notebook ... is a central part of his identity as a cognitive agent. [Otto] is best regarded as an extended system. ... To consistently resist this conclusion, we would have to shrink the self into a mere bundle of occurrent states. ... In some cases interfering with someone's environment will have the same moral significance as interfering with their person. (Clark & Chalmers, 1988, p. 18; emphases added)

In this example, Otto's notebook is clearly something different from ordinary notebooks, and destroying the notebook (i.e., information technology) would be ethically equivalent to tampering with the mind/brain. The notebook is irreplaceable in the same sense that our brains are irreplaceable; if the notebook were destroyed, most of Otto's memories and beliefs would be irreversibly lost. In Moore's terminology, Otto's notebook is a necessary part of an organic unity, together with Otto's practical identity—its destruction would be irreversible. Indeed, Clark and Chalmers (1988) echo Moore's (1971) notion of organic unity and the constitutivity criterion in describing what is so special about the notebook: "[T]he relevant parts of the world are *in the loop,* not dangling at the other end of a long causal chain. [They] play

an ineliminable role" (p. 9). Entities at the other end of a long causal chain would be so distant that they have, at best, instrumental value. But, as in classical Chinese philosophy and language, the very interconnectedness and co-relation of our minds and certain entities makes the dissolution of this relation surgical. The brain is not dangling at the other end of a long causal chain, and neither is Otto's notebook; they are in the loop; that is, constitutive and irreplaceable—their destruction cannot be rectified. Furthermore, it satisfies Korsgaard's description of our practical identity in the sense that it is something that makes Otto's life worth living and his actions worth undertaking. To paraphrase Wetlesen, without the notebook, Otto's identity would be fragmented and inadequate. Thus, in the same sense that we should respect and value someone else's practical identity and its physical aspects, we should respect and value Otto's practical identity, including the notebook.

The case of Otto's notebook suggests that IT can become inextricably linked to our practical identities. Although the strong relation between Otto and his notebook is not a common one, the expected convergence between biotechnology and increasingly powerful information technologies suggests that the gap between our practical identities and IT will become increasingly narrow. As the case with Otto shows, we by no means need to conjure up future scenarios in order to realize that IT can be an inextricable part of one's practical identity. For most of us, IT is still a mere tool, hence deserving of nothing but instrumental value, but there are cases in which technologies take on a completely different role—and, therefore, deserve a completely different status.

STRONG IRREPLACEABILITY AND STRONG CONSTITUTIVITY

The case with Otto's notebook suggests that information and information technology can have moral status, but only if they are constitutive and irreplaceable in a strong sense. My primary conclusion in this chapter is that in these special cases, there are good reasons to extend moral status so as to include nonliving entities. But this claim is still rather exclusive and fails to include entities that many intuitively regard as having value as an end.

Throughout this chapter, I have used the original *Mona Lisa* and the corpse of a loved one as prime examples of something that does not have value in itself but, at the same time, is valued far beyond whatever uses to which it can be put. Although the *Mona Lisa* seems like an intuitive case of value as an end, it is hard to give a precise account of why it has value as an end. The *Mona Lisa* does occupy a special place in the practical identity of many, and it is certainly irreplaceable. As Matthew Humphrey (2002) wrote:

There are at least a group of people who insist that their lives go significantly better knowing that they live in a world in which the Mona Lisa exists ... [it] serves to give their lives meaning. ... [K]nowing this to be true, those who see little, or even no value in the Mona Lisa, and think it would be better used as fuel, should be prepared to share in the burden of keeping the Mona Lisa in existence. It is strongly irreplaceable. Although it can be reproduced and copied, none of the copies would embody Leonardo's genius, none would be authentic. ... These give us all good reasons (although not always trumping reasons), to engage in Mona Lisa preservation. (p. 193)

At the same time, it is too strong to claim that the *Mona Lisa* actually constitutes someone's practical identity. Is it enough to be important for someone's practical identity, to merely contribute to making someone's life worth living? By itself, this seems like a vague criterion, since it is possible to include a vast number of entities in this category. But, as mentioned, the strong irreplaceability of certain entities ought to make us more sensitive

to their well being, based on the simple fact that damage to such entities would be impossible to rectify. This suggests that the question of relational value is a question about the correlation between irreplaceability and constitutivity: The more irreplaceable an entity is, the less constitutive it has to be, and vice versa. For instance, the original *Mona Lisa* can be said to have relational value due to being important (constitutive in a weak sense) for someone's practical identity and irreplaceable in a strong sense, while various technical aids can have relational value if they really are constitutive of someone's practical identity but irreplaceable in a somewhat weaker sense. The problem is that these criteria become too vague and inconclusive as soon as we start operating with degrees of irreplaceability and constitutivity. For instance, Musschenga (1998) tries to make a claim about the importance (weak constitutivity) of certain cultural artefacts and, consequently, that we have moral duties toward them, but fails to provide precise criteria for when cultural artefacts are constitutive enough. He states:

[They] are the components or constituents *of the good life. A life enjoying [these] entities is richer than a life in which these values are absent. ... Although cultures do not have moral standing comparable to that of humans, we do have moral duties to cultures insofar as they* contribute to the richness of life. (Musschenga, 1998, p. 214; emphasis added)

Intuitively, I agree with Musschenga, but "contribute to the richness of life" is too vague and ultimately may lead to supererogatory obligations. This is not an argument against extension of moral status to cultural artefacts, but it shows that more work must be done in terms of precision in order to make such a claim. This is the reason why I have focused on the case with Otto in which the related entity (the notebook with its entries) really is constitutive of his practical identity and irreplaceable in the sense that its annihilation would be irreversible. I limit myself to suggesting that the correlation between irreplaceability and constitutivity might be the way to go if we are to extend moral status even further—if we are to provide a theoretical grounding for how an even wider range of information can have lasting value and ought to be protected. [13]

THE RELATIONAL THEORY OF MORAL STATUS

I have made the point somewhat dramatically so far, and I willingly admit that there is, of course, a difference between moral status grounded in intrinsic properties and moral status grounded in relational properties. Nevertheless, they should not be considered completely different phenomena followed by completely different obligations. In order to underline that relational properties can give rise to moral status *and* acknowledge the difference between moral status based on relational and intrinsic properties, I propose to refer to value as an end in general as moral *status,* and refer to value as an end based on intrinsic properties as moral *standing.* If an entity has value as an end in virtue of its relational properties alone, it has moral status but not moral standing. In other words, moral standing is a subclass of moral status. The moral status of an entity comes in degrees in the following order (again, these claims are *ceteris paribus*):

1. **Moral Persons:** (Satisfying the capability for free will, reason, and linguistic competence) enjoy full and equal moral standing; thus, the moral status of a person cannot be augmented by relational properties.
2. **Merely Self-Conscious Beings:** (With future plans and goals based on beliefs and experiences and with the ability to see themselves as temporal agents) have moral standing but less than moral persons. Their moral status can be augmented by relational properties, but only minimally (e.g., an

owned and loved dog has a higher moral status than a stray dog). [14]

3. **Merely Sentient Beings:** (With the ability to experience pain and pleasure) have moral standing as well, although less than self-conscious beings and considerably less than moral persons. Their moral status can be increased significantly by their relational properties (an owned and loved fish has significantly higher moral status than a fish in the wild).
4. **Non-Sentient Entities:** Have no moral standing but can have moral status by being an irreplaceable and constitutive part of someone's practical identity (e.g., Otto's notebook).

As stated in the previous section, the inclusiveness of the fourth category depends on how strictly we define irreplaceability and constitutivity, which I have left as an open question.

Problems with the Relational Theory of Moral Status

Although I have tried to argue that the relational theory of moral status deals with living and non-living entities in a manner consistent with our moral intuitions (at least as long as we interpret these criteria in a strong sense), the theory faces quite a few problems of its own.

First, the theory itself rests upon a couple of presuppositions that have not been discussed sufficiently due to constraints on space. In addition to the anthropogenic presupposition discussed previously, some of the arguments appeal to our moral intuitions. These presuppositions are not uncontroversial, but a full discussion and defence is beyond the bounds of this article.

Another problem is that moral status often is defined in terms of direct duties, which, in practice, entails that entities must be able to recognize their own well being in order for us to have direct duties toward them; they must have preferences that can be satisfied or frustrated. I agree that this is necessary for having intrinsic value; hence, the intrinsic component of the theory. However, the rejection of ascribing moral status to everything else stems from the conflation between moral status and intrinsic value. They both are seen as having to be objective, non-contingent, and still exist in isolation. If the notion of who or what has moral status is meant to be an anthropogenic guideline for moral actions, as opposed to a metaphysical claim, I have tried to make the case that value as an end rather than value in itself should be conflated with moral status. Value as an end, as opposed to value in itself, can be derived from another entity and does not presuppose that an entity is conscious.

Finally, ascribing moral status to information and IT, even in very special circumstances, might be considered too strong, and it can be objected that it will lead to supererogatory obligations. This is especially problematic if we weaken the irreplaceability or constitutivity criteria. The case with Otto, however, rests on seeing our practical identities as the ultimate source of normativity. Consequently, if anything at all can form the basis of moral status, it is our practical identities. If this is agreed upon, the objection would have to reject (1) that being a constitutive and irreplaceable part of our practical identities, even in a strong sense (e.g., our brain) is sufficient for having moral status, or (2) that information and IT cannot possibly satisfy these criteria. With regard to (1), I cannot see how any physical entities at all should be taken into consideration if not the human brain, and I hope the case with Otto's notebook (which is an information technology) provides sufficient reason to reject (2) in some very special circumstances.

CONCLUDING REMARKS

In this chapter, I have tried to make the case that information and information technology, at least in very special circumstances, ought to be ascribed moral status. Inspired by the East Asian way of viewing the world as consisting of mutually constitutive relationships, I have argued that relations, in some cases, can give us sufficient reason to take the well being of an entity into consideration. More specifically, an entity that is an irreplaceable and constitutive part of an organic unity together with a person thereby attains value as an end and moral status. I have limited myself to arguing that this is reasonable, at least in certain very special circumstances. Although the potential value of nonliving entities must be contingent, dependent upon human subjects, and might have originated for purely instrumental reasons, their value ought not to be regarded as such once they have become an irreplaceable and constitutive part of someone's practical identity. How far we are to extend the criteria of constitutivity and irreplaceability and thereby widen the range of nonliving entities with moral status is an issue that has been left open.

There are certainly other ways to reach a similar conclusion, and this theory struggles with problems of its own, but the reason I have chosen an approach in terms of moral status is to underline the threat of always treating information and information technologies as mere means to other ends. Instrumental value derived from human interest easily can be sacrificed for other, more immediate human interests and thereby lead to shortsighted irreversible decisions and an unsustainable development of the infosphere.

ACKNOWLEDGMENTS

I would like to express my gratitude to Jon Wetlesen, Kristian Ekeli, and Charles Ess for carefully reading earlier drafts and for their valuable remarks and suggestions. I also would like to thank two anonymous referees, Luciano Floridi, Charles Ess, and Soraj Hongladarom, for their insightful comments and encouragement.

REFERENCES

Ames, R. T. (2000). East Asian philosophy. In E. Graig (Ed.), *Concise Routledge encyclopedia of philosophy* (pp. 225-229). London: Routledge.

Ames, R. T., & Rosemont Jr., H. (1998). *The analects of Confucius—A philosophical translation*. New York: Ballantine Publishing Group.

Bradley, F. H. (1959). *Appearance and reality: A metaphysical essay* (2nd ed.). Oxford: Clarendon Press.

Clark, A., & Chalmers, D. (1988). The extended mind. *Analysis, 58,* 7-19.

Floridi, L. (1999). Information ethics: On the theoretical foundations of computer ethics. *Ethics and Information Technology, 1*(1), 37-56.

Floridi, L. (2002). On the intrinsic value of information objects and the infosphere. *Ethics and Information Technology, 4*(4), 287-304.

Humphrey, M. (2002). *Preservation versus the people? Nature, humanity and political philosophy.* Oxford: Oxford University Press.

Kagan, S. (1998). Rethinking intrinsic value. *The Journal of Ethics, 2,* 277-297.

Kant, I. (1996). *Groundwork of the metaphysics of morals* (M. Gregor, trans.). Cambridge: Cambridge University Press.

Korsgaard, C. M. (1983). Two distinctions in goodness. *The Philosophical Review, 92,* 169-195.

Korsgaard, C. M. (1996). *The sources of normativity.* New York: Cambridge University Press.

Moore, G. E. (1971). *Principia ethica.* Cambridge: Cambridge University Press.

Moore, G. E. (1993). External and internal relations. In T. Baldwin (Ed.), *G.E. Moore: Selected writings* (pp. 79-105). London: Routledge.

Musschenga, A. W. (1998). Intrinsic value as a reason for the preservation of minority cultures. *Ethical Theory and Moral Practice, 1,* 201-225.

Pearce, T. R. (2004). *Spinoza's naturalism: Conatus as a universal principle.* Retrieved November 3, 2005, from http://www.littlesputnik.net/trpearce/Spinoza-Conatus.htm

Regan, T. (1983). *The case for animal rights.* Berkeley, CA: University of California Press.

Singer, P. (1990). *Animal liberation* (2nd ed.). New York: New York Review of Books.

UNESCO. (2003). *Cultural and linguistic diversity in the information society.* Paris: UNESCO.

Vlahos, M. (1998). Entering the infosphere. *Journal of International Affairs, 51,* 497-525.

Warren, M. A. (1997). *Moral status: Duties to persons and other living things.* Oxford: Oxford University Press.

Wetlesen, J. (1999). The moral status of beings who are not persons: A casuistic argument. *Environmental Values, 8,* 287-323.

Wittgenstein, L. (1958). *The blue and brown books.* Oxford: Blackwell.

Wong, D. B. (2004). Relational and autonomous selves. *Journal of Chinese Philosophy, 31,* 419-432.

ENDNOTES

[1] The infosphere is "shorthand for the fusion of all the world's communications networks, databases, and sources of information into a vast intertwined and heterogeneous tapestry of electronic interchange … which creates a network ecology" (Vlahos, 1998, p. 498).

[2] See the *Oxford English Dictionary* (http://dictionary.oed.com) for more uses of the term *soundness.* For a more detailed analysis of

what it means for nonliving entities to have well being, I refer the interested reader to Floridi (2002). Floridi (2002) presents a comprehensive list of features (p. 47) that are "related to the well-being of (regions of) the infosphere not in a contingent, external and means-end relation, but internally and in a constitutive sense" (p. 45).

3   Let me hasten to add that the examples used to illustrate subjects-of-a-life and sentient beings throughout this chapter are meant as illustrative and for the sake of the argument only. I am concerned mainly with which properties are ethically relevant, not which entities satisfy these criteria. In other words, I am not insisting that dogs are (merely) subjects-of-a-life or that fish are (merely) sentient.

4   This is known as casuistic argumentation, which aims to analyze a moral problem by drawing parallels between paradigmatic cases upon which we agree and the case at hand.

5   See especially pp. 49-89 in Korsgaard (1996).

6   The Kantian caveat is, of course, as long as your free will does not impede upon the free will of others. As Kant (1996) puts it, "[I]f a certain use of freedom is itself a hindrance to freedom in accordance with universal laws (i.e., wrong), coercion that is opposed to this (as a *hindering of a hindrance to freedom*) is consistent with freedom in accordance with universal laws, that is, it is right" (p. 25 [6:231]).

7   This broad concept of conatus seems to be what Spinoza had in mind, but, as an ethically relevant property, Wetlesen attributes it to living entities. In Spinoza, all entities in the universe, including nonliving entities, have conatus as they strive to preserve their being. See Pearce (2004) for an analysis of Spinoza's wide-reaching notion of conatus.

8   These are *ceteris paribus* claims in the sense that we cannot justify the killing of an animal based on a minor violation of the moral status of a person. If I had to inflict a small wound on a moral person in order to save the life of a merely self-conscious being, I should, of course, save the merely self-conscious being's life. If I had the choice between saving the life of a merely self-conscious being and that of a moral person, I should save the life of the moral person.

9   For the views of Moore, see especially chapter 1 of Moore's *Principia Ethica* (1971, pp. 1-36) and "External and Internal Relations" (1993). Bradley's view on the intrinsicality of relations appears first and foremost in chapter XXIV and Note B in the appendix of the 2nd edition of his *Appearance and Reality* (1959).

10 This short presentation of East Asian and Western metaphysics is inevitably a very generalized picture. My intention is by no means to deny or to gloss over the tremendous diversity these labels cover, but they are used here in order to analyze some of the broader, more common issues generally shared by the respective traditions. I especially rely on Ames (2000), Ames and Rosemont (1998), and Wong (2004) when it comes to the general features of classical East Asian philosophies, primarily Confucian philosophy. As Wetlesen has pointed out to me, Buddhism constitutes one important exception from the generalized picture of East Asian philosophy, since all schools of Buddhism stress the Western distinction between highest/objective truth (*paramarthasatya*) and apparent/conventional truth (*samvrtisatya*).

11 See Floridi (1999, p. 55) for an alternative way to defend the value of Hector's corpse and how death poses a problem for many traditional ethical theories.

[12]   Wetlesen's (1999) terminology is somewhat confusing, since he refers to value in itself based on relational properties as *intrinsic value* (p. 291). Kagan (1998), however, cites value as an end based on intrinsic properties as the common meaning given to intrinsic value (and goes on to criticize that definition).

[13]   Strictly speaking, an entity also can attain value as an end by being a constitutive and irreplaceable part of an organic unity with merely self-conscious or sentient beings since they also have intrinsic value. I have left out this issue, but this can provide the basis for ascribing moral status to ecosystems.

[14]   Some might find that ascribing a higher moral status to owned and loved dogs than to stray dogs sounds counterintuitive. Let me reiterate that, as subjects-of-a-life, the difference is only minimal and normally would come into play only if somehow we were forced into sacrificing one for the other.

Chapter II
Online Communities, Democratic Ideals, and the Digital Divide

Frances S. Grodzinsky
Sacred Heart University, USA

Herman T. Tavani
Rivier College, USA

ABSTRACT

We examine some pros and cons of online communities with respect to two main questions: (1) Do online communities promote democracy and democratic ideals? and (2) What are the implications of online communities for information justice and the digital divide? The first part of the chapter will examine online communities in general and will attempt to define what we mean by "community" and more precisely, "online communities." It will then examine ways of building online communities, that is, what brings people together online. The second part of the chapter will look at the positive and negative contributions of online communities in light of democratic ideals and will address the issue of information justice and the digital divide. In examining these questions, we also consider the effects of the Internet for community life at both the local and global levels.

ONLINE COMMUNITIES

Before examining some of the pros and cons of online community life, we begin by elucidating the notion of a virtual or online community. First, however, we consider what *community* means in general.

What is a Community?

According to *Webster's New World Dictionary of the American Language*, *community* is defined as "people living in the same district, city, etc., under the same laws" (1996, p. 269). The first part of this definition stresses the geographical aspects of community via an association with concepts such as *district* and *city*. In the past, community life typically was constrained by geographical limitations. In the 20th century, various forms of transportation, including the automobile, made it possible to extend, even if only slightly, the geographical boundaries of a community. However, traditional communities for the most part have continued to remain limited by physical constraints such as geography.

The advent of the Internet and the forms of social interaction it makes possible causes us to reexamine our thinking about the concept of a community. Individuals who are separated physically by continents and oceans can participate daily in electronic communities. As a result, more recent definitions of community tend to focus on the second part of the definition—"under the same law"—which can include common rules and common interests that one or more groups of people share, rather than on criteria involving geographical districts and physical constraints. In order for a community to exist, there must be some degree of shared beliefs, values, and goals among members who share a common vision and who desire to perpetuate it through the socialization of new members. Two values that traditionally have been associated with strong communities are trust and commitment.

We should point out that communities do not need to be homogenous in population, even though many are. Consider that, in many cases, individuals with diverse backgrounds participate and belong to communities because of their commitment to the shared values of the community, which often manifest themselves in a set of rules that embodies these beliefs.

What is an Online Community?

Howard Rheingold (2001) suggests that online communities can be understood as "computer-mediated social groups." He describes his initial experience in joining the WELL (the Whole Earth

'Lectronic Link), one of the earlier electronic communities, in which norms were "established, challenged, changed, reestablished, rechallenged, in a kind of speeded-up social evolution." The WELL was a community, Rheingold maintains, because of the kinds of social contracts and collaborative negotiations that happened in that setting. The WELL and other early electronic communities, including listservs, were instrumental in the initial formation of women's groups online. For example, WOW (Women on the Well) was a forum for women who belonged to the WELL, creating a community within a community. And SYSTERS-l, formed in 1990, was an early online community that supported women working in science and technology (Shade, 2002).

Michelle White (2002) notes that in cyberspace, the term *community* is a popular way of describing synchronous online settings because it suggests that they offer "social exchange, emotional support, and learning environments." Synchronicity, in this definition, can apply to location in cyberspace as well as to time, because, while chat rooms and instant messaging services—two forms of technology that facilitate online communities—are synchronous in terms of time and space, listservs and newsgroups are only synchronous in space and not time. (This point supports our emphasis on the latter part of the definition of community in the preceding section.) White also points out that describing online settings as communities acknowledges the "complex and important activities that people engage in through those sites." In effect, it also legitimizes these structures by making them seem as if they are physical and real.

Building Online Communities

In the preceding section, we noted that common interests can bring people together to form an online community. But what exactly are some of the common interests that define these individuals as members of a given community? Traditionally, people have been inclined to think of themselves in terms of factors related to national heritage, religious and political affiliations, gender, and so forth. Many of our traditional notions of identity, including the concept of nationality, are becoming antiquated in the age of the Internet. For example, young people who have grown up using the Internet may prefer to define themselves in terms of their consumer interests rather than in terms of some particular country or state that they happen to inhabit in the off-line world. Geographic and national boundaries may mean far less to this group of persons than they have to those who came of age in the era preceding the Internet, when distance and geographical remoteness precluded the formation of natural communities that included international participants.

Yet, for other groups, the Internet has facilitated connections that would have been impossible in physical space. A young gay teenager, for example, who may feel isolated in his or her local community, can find support and encouragement from other gay teens online. Women can connect to other women on the Web and can access information not always readily available in physical space. There are online communities that support cyberfeminism, women's health issues, anti-cyberstalking, and anti-harassment actions. There also are parenting chat rooms as well as groups dealing with the glass ceiling and work-related issues, date rape, incest, divorce, and so forth. As more and more women embrace cybertechnology and as women begin to trust those in their particular online communities, they are more likely to self-represent and identify as part of the group in a way that they already do in physical space.

Another form of online community has been the weblog or blog. Blogs typically are initiated by an author as a form of online journal, yet they fall under White's definition of online community (see previous section) because they attract people of like-minded interests who read, learn, and communicate in the blog through postings. A recent Google search for women's blogs offered up among others: Christian women, technology, finance, clothes, body image, relationships, health, and feminism. In the past few years, blogging has become more popular, and people often have blogs to which they contribute regularly. Blogging has become what "meetings" were in the age prior to the Internet: a place to discuss and share ideas and opinions on certain issues.

DO ONLINE COMMUNITIES PROMOTE DEMOCRATIC IDEALS?

In the first section, we suggested that many of the new possibilities for social interaction made possible by online communities could be viewed as positive contributions. Also consider that on the Internet, people can meet new friends and future romantic partners; can form medical support groups; can join chat rooms, list-servers, and discussion forums to disseminate material to like-minded colleagues; and can communicate by e-mail with individuals with whom they otherwise would not likely bother to correspond by physical mail or telephone. However, we also need to examine some negative effects of these new forms of interaction, especially in terms of their implications for democracy and social justice. For example, hate speech has proliferated; harassment and stalking incidents have occurred (see Grodzinsky & Tavani, 2004); and there has been at least one incident involving a virtual rape in cyberspace (see Dibbell, 1993). Also, the Internet has minimized the need for face-to-face communications and has made it much easier to deceive people about who actually is communicating with them. These concerns lead us to ask whether the Internet also threatens some of the important values underlying community life.

Overall, have online communities had a positive effect on communication and interaction? Gordon Graham (1999) points out that the Internet enables a "reconfiguration of human communities" based on individual choices provided users. So, one advantage of online communities is that they empower the individual to choose a community in which to interact instead of simply having to accept the default community or society in which he or she is already situated. Graham believes that online communities also further promote freedom in the sense that members, if they choose, can disregard more easily certain kinds of personal properties or attributes, such as gender and ethnicity, which are more obvious in traditional communities.

If Graham is correct, then the Internet has provided individuals with greater choice and freedom with respect to joining communities. Values involving freedom, choice, openness, and so forth, certainly would seem to favor democratic ideals. However, others see the relationship between the Internet and democracy quite differently. Richard Sclove (1995), for instance, believes that technologies—and, by implication, Internet technologies—tend to undermine rather than facilitate democracy and community life. Cass Sunstein (2002) argues that the Internet has both democracy-enhancing and democracy-threatening aspects. He believes that the Internet enhances democracy in the sense that it provides greater access to information by lowering the costs involved in finding and getting information. Because that information also can be filtered so easily, however, he suggests that the Internet threatens what he calls "deliberative democracy" (see Thorseth, 2005, for a detailed discussion of deliberative democracy and the Internet). Graham (1999) has also suggested that the Internet, perhaps unwittingly, might strengthen the worst aspects of democracy, because Internet technology facilitates political and social fragmentation by isolating individuals and insulating groups. These factors tend to increase polarization.

To appreciate the level of polarization and fragmentation made possible by technology, consider a hypothetical scenario envisioned by

Richard Epstein (2000) set in the year 2028, in which our personal (electronic) agents prepare a personalized electronic newspaper for us each morning. The newspaper contains information about only those topics that we individually have selected; and the information is presented to us from an ideological perspective that we choose. In other words, our electronic agents have been carefully instructed to filter information to meet all of our specifications and tastes. Contrast this kind of personalized newspaper of the future, which Nicholas Negroponte (1995) refers to as *The Daily Me*, with conventional newspapers of today. Imagine what it would be like to have your daily newspaper tailored to your own individual interests and tastes.

Epstein describes a (hypothetical) dinner party in which the guests, all of whom subscribe to personalized newspapers, assemble around the dinner table. The guests soon discover that they have no common vocabulary, no common shared memories, and no common conceptual framework in which to share their conversations. For example, one guest reads only news about sporting events, while another reads only about the virtual economy. And even if two or more guests happen to read news reports about the same general topic, the perspectives from which the information is disseminated to them via their electronic agents is so radically different that they still would likely be unable to find any common ground for conversation. Not surprisingly, there is complete silence at the dinner party.

Epstein asks how we could maintain a democracy in a world in which there is no shared vocabulary of civic concepts and principles. The character in Epstein's story who describes the conversation at the dinner party laments, "We have the frightening proliferation of extremists groups who have their own private vocabularies and ideologies." Epstein also asks how the "public square," which has been fragmented into "tens of thousands of highly specialized communities that do not communicate with one another," can be recreated. So, we have seen that while the Internet may promote democratic ideals such as choice and freedom, it also seems to undermine those ideals by fragmenting society and polarizing individuals.

INFORMATION JUSTICE AND THE DIGITAL DIVIDE

We have examined the growing emergence of online communities and their implications for democracy and democratic ideals. Will the notion of physical community become obsolete in the future? In order to investigate this question, we need to examine local and global communities through the perspective of information justice, an aspect of social justice. Information justice is tied to questions about whether the digital network can help people to better manage their lives through an access to technology, while avoiding the dangers of exploitation and discrimination that often exist in physical space. In an article entitled "Reconceptualizing the Digital Divide," and in his book, *Technology and Social Inclusion*, Mark Warschauer (2002, 2003, respectively) observes that technology projects around the world too often focus on providing hardware and software and pay insufficient attention to the human and social systems that also must change in order for technology to make a difference. According to Warschauer (2002):

[Access to ICT] is embedded in a complex array of factors encompassing physical, digital, human, and social resources and relationships. Content and language, literacy and education, and community and institutional structures must all be taken into account if meaningful access to new technologies is to be provided.

To understand the impact of the Internet for questions involving information justice at both the local and global levels, it is important to understand issues surrounding the digital divide. According to Benjamin Compaine (2001), the phrase *digital divide* is essentially a new label for an earlier concept: information haves and have-nots. It describes the disparity that exists between those who have access to information and communication technology (ICT) and those who do not. Compaine (2001) defines the digital divide as the perceived gap between those who have and do not have access to information tools *and* the ability to use those tools. Hence, the digital divide can be understood as the gap, perceived or real, between those who have and do not have either (a) access to ICT or (b) the knowledge and ability to use that technology, or both.

To speak of *the* digital divide might suggest that there is one overall divide—that is, a single divide as opposed to many divides or divisions. Although multiple divisions exist, we limit our discussion to two broad categories: a divide *within nations* and a divide *between nations*. Within nations, divisions exist between rich and poor persons, racial majority and minority groups, men and women, young and old, disabled and nondisabled persons, and so forth. On the other hand, there is a division that sometimes is referred to as the global digital divide that exists between information-rich and information-poor nations. We examine some of the effects of the digital divide at the local and global levels, respectively in the next two sections.

Some Effects of the Digital Divide at the Local Level

In response to concerns about a growing digital divide at the local level, we briefly consider some issues in the U.S. In 1993, the Clinton administration announced its plans for a National Information Infrastructure (NII). One objective of the NII was to ensure that all Americans would have access to ICT. To accomplish this goal, the National Telecommunications and Information

Administration (NTIA) was charged with investigating the status of computer and Internet access among Americans. In 1995, the NTIA issued its first report, *Falling through the Net*, which confirmed the commonly held belief that Internet access was related to socio-economic factors. This report also noted that a disproportionate number of information have-nots lived in rural areas and inner cities. The NTIA's 1999 report, *Falling through the Net: Defining the Digital Divide*, noted that while more Americans were accessing the Internet, significant discrepancies in access still existed with respect to socio-demographic factors involving race, education, income, and marital status. According to the NTIA's 2000 report, *Falling through the Net: Toward Digital Inclusion*, the rate of digital inclusion is increasing in the U.S. across all socio-demographic sectors. Some have interpreted this report to imply that the divide between ICT haves and have-nots in the U.S. is narrowing; others, however, dispute this interpretation.

A key issue in the debate about the digital divide in the U.S. is the question whether some kind of universal service policy is needed to ensure that all Americans will have the appropriate level of access to computer and Internet technologies. Prior to the Internet era, the issue of universal service in America had been debated in the context of telephony (or telephone technology). When telephones became available in the early part of the 20th century, there was some concern that people living in less-populated rural areas in the U.S. would not be able to afford this new technology. Because having a telephone was considered essential for one's well being, the Communications Act of 1934 was enacted into law, and telephone usage rates were subsidized in order to ensure that all Americans would have affordable telephone service. A question currently debated is whether having Internet access also is or soon will be at the point of becoming essential for one's well being.

Recent proposals have recommended special e-rates in the form of federal technology discounts to subsidize the cost of Internet access for public schools and libraries. Whereas prior universal service policies involving telephony aimed to provide telephone access at the residential level, e-rates are targeted for public schools, libraries, and other community points of access. In effect, e-rates aim to provide universal Internet access for Americans, but critics point out that those rates do not ensure universal service. Why is a policy that ensures universal service, as opposed to universal access, to ICT necessary? Gary Chapman and Marc Rotenberg (1995), representing Computer Professionals for Social Responsibility (CPSR), have argued not only that everyone must have access to the Internet but also that pricing should be structured so that full Internet service is affordable to everyone. In their view, merely providing community points of access to the Internet, such as at public schools and libraries, would not be sufficient. Chapman and Rotenberg argue that just as placing telephones in public locations would not meet the requirements for a universal telephone service policy, simply providing Internet access in public places cannot satisfy the conditions needed for universal Internet service.

Whereas advocacy groups such as CPSR have lobbied the U.S. Congress for a universal Internet service policy, others have opposed such legislation. Opponents generally have used three kinds of arguments (Tavani, 2004). One type of objection is based on the notion that a universal Internet service policy would create an entitlement that could grow out of control and possibly set a precedent for entitlements for other kinds of government-subsidized services in the future. Another kind of objection is based on the concern that the revenue needed to implement a universal Internet service policy would have to be generated by tax subsidies. Here, it is argued that a tax of this type would be unfair to taxpayers in moderate-income brackets who would shoulder the greatest burden, as well as to the telephone and utility companies who also would be taxed. A third type of objection is based on the view that issues concerning Internet access for poorer citizens are, at bottom, issues involving personal priorities and values for those citizens. Critics who appeal to this line of reasoning point out that nearly everyone in the U.S. who wishes to own a television and subscribe to TV cable service can find a way to purchase those items and pay for those services. Hence, they conclude that no universal service policy for ICT is needed. Supporters of universal service, however, argue that their opponents have either overly simplified or greatly underestimated the problems faced by those who are unable to afford Internet access in their homes. This brings up the underlying philosophical issue of whether Internet access should be viewed as a positive right.

What are positive rights, and how are they different from negative rights? Negative rights are like liberties in the sense that we have a (legal) right not to be interfered with in exercising them. So if I have a (negative) right to own a computer and purchase Internet access, then no one is permitted to interfere with my purchasing these items and services. Can one's legal rights involving Internet access also possibly be understood as a positive right in which full Internet service must be provided to everyone? There are very few positive rights. In the U.S., for example, one's right to have access to healthcare is considered a negative rather than a positive right because the government is not required to provide citizens with healthcare. In the European Union countries, on the other hand, access to healthcare generally is considered a positive right. One of the few positive rights enjoyed by U.S. citizens is the right to receive a free public education through high school (grades 1-12). This is a positive right in the sense that the U.S. government legally is required to provide each citizen with access to such an education.

Perhaps the rationale used for determining why one has a right to receive a free public education in the U.S. can help us to frame an argument for why universal Internet access also should be required by law. We can begin by asking why public education is a positive and not merely a negative right. One answer is that without adequate access to an education, a child will not have equal access to opportunities involving jobs, careers, and so forth. If it also could be shown that having Internet access at home is essential in order for students to participate adequately in the educational process, then it would seem that students should have a positive right to Internet access. But why would not having access to ICT necessarily deprive someone of access to goods that are important or vital to one's well being? Jeremy Moss (2002) has argued that not having access to a form of technology that is "instrumentally vital for access to other goods (employment, knowledge about one's health outcomes or access to democratic institutions)" is essentially a "threat to one's well being." It is for this reason that Moss believes that persons who do not have access to ICT are "constrained through not having the resources to do *something important*" (2002, p. 162; emphasis added).

What does Moss mean when he suggests that having access to ICT is important because it provides a means for certain resources that are "vital for one's well-being"? He argues that without access to ICT, people are unfairly disadvantaged for three reasons: (1) their access to knowledge is significantly limited; (2) their ability to participate fully in the political process and to receive important information is greatly diminished; and (3) their economic prospects are severely hindered. We elaborate briefly on each point. First, Moss claims that because access to knowledge is lessened or prevented by the digital divide, people who are deprived of access to ICT are not able to benefit from the increasing range of information on the Internet and, thus, are falling further behind. Second, because of barriers to participation in the decision-making process in developing countries, people in remote areas may have no other means to participate in national debates or to receive information about important developmental matters and policies that can affect them significantly. Third, not having access to digital resources can severely hinder the prospects that developing countries have for economic growth. Moss believes that because so much of world growth is driven by the information and communication sector, people living in countries that are not part of this sector will be disadvantaged. If Moss is correct, then it would seem that a strong case could be made for declaring that universal Internet access should be construed as a positive right (Tavani, 2003). Doing so also would help to bridge the global digital divide between developed and developing nations.

Some Effects of the Digital Divide at the Global Level

Most people in the non-Western world do not have Internet access. Those in many developing countries who are fortunate to have Internet access often are required to deal with technical problems involving poor connectivity and low bandwidth. Consider, for example, some of the challenges faced by Internet users in Malawi, given the current state of telecommunications in that African nation. Levison, Thies, and Armarasinghe (2002) point out that people living in this developing country must contend with a very expensive form of telephone service (and corresponding Internet access) that is metered in terms of minutes used. Not only is Internet access prohibitively expensive in Malawi, but also those who can afford access must cope with many practical difficulties and limitations. For example, telephone connections there are so slow and telecom failures so frequent that using the Internet for conventional purposes (e.g., for interactive searches that most Internet users residing in North

America and Western Europe take for granted as part of a Web interface) is generally impractical. The kinds of problems experienced by Internet users in Malawi should not be viewed as isolated or as peculiar to countries in sub-Saharan Africa. Rather, they are typical of those encountered by users in many developing nations.

Efforts to address problems involving the ICT divide between industrialized and developing countries can be traced back to the early 1990s, when the idea of a Global Information Infrastructure (GII) emerged. Al Gore described the initial plan for a GII in an address to the International Telecommunication Union in Brazil on March 21, 1994. A principle objective of Gore's plan was to develop a global infrastructure that would support universal access to ICT. Critics argue that very little has resulted from this and other earlier proposals aimed at addressing global concerns about unequal access to ICT. Recently, however, there have been signs suggesting that concerns about a global digital divide are being taken seriously. In the summer of 2000, for example, the Okinawa Charter on Global Information was announced at an annual Group of Eight (G8) summit in Japan. At that summit, the G8 leaders formed the Digital Opportunities Task Force (DOT), which some see as a first step in a serious effort to narrow the global digital divide or what some now refer to as the international information and knowledge divide. Leslie Regan Shade (2002) refers to "globalizing from below" in describing the way women in the Philippines, Latin America, Africa, and Asia have developed grass roots initiatives for democracy and social justice. At the second global knowledge conference in Malaysia in 2000, there were two initiatives introduced: a gender and ICT replication and learning fund that promotes an exchange of initiatives on gender equity and women's empowerment using ICT; and support to women entrepreneurs, which provides incentives either through ICT businesses, online mentoring, or financing (Shade, 2002).

In an article titled "Equity of Access: Adaptive Technology," (Grodzinsky, 2000), the author addressed the problems faced by users with disabilities. She argued that in the age of information technology, the computer equipped with adaptive devices can be the equalizer that allows people with disabilities to participate in and compete for jobs that require computer access, because it supports autonomous learning and empowers the user. Since the publication of that article, there have been several advances in assistive devices and interface design that address disability issues. There is now a disability setting, for example, in the Windows Control Panel. Sun Systems (a computer company) has developed an accessibility program and in March 2001, "the American Foundation for the Blind cited the achievements of Sun's Accessibility Team, recognizing Sun with the 2001 Access Award. The Java Accessibility API provides a complete and consistent interface that makes it easy for mainstream developers and for assistive technology vendors to make fully accessible applications available to users with disabilities" (Sun, 2001). For those with vision impairments, Sun's products are compatible with a number of specialized assistive technologies, including freeware and open source solutions. Gnome 2.0 provides software to make the desktop user-accessible and customizable.

While these technologies have moved in the right direction, accessibility on the Web has remained a problem. Since the mid-1990s, the world of Internet computing has expanded significantly. With the advent of e-commerce, shopping has moved online, and library access and research are now available through large online databases and accessed through search engines. Web sites invite us into their domains with applications that include movie clips, animations, hyperlinks, and shopping carts. But are these applications accessible to all? How useful is the movie clip to the hearing impaired user? Can the blind user find the hyperlink to get to the next page of a Web site?

Given that the infrastructure of the information age is the Internet, why aren't all Web sites accessible to everyone? The World Wide Web Consortium (W3C) has a Web Accessibility Initiative (WAI) whose technical activity section is dedicated to ensuring that the core technologies of the Web are accessible to those with disabilities (World Wide Web Consortium). Then why haven't Web designers taken advantage of the free expertise and built their sites to be accessible to those with disabilities? There are several issues: a lack of mandate for the private sector, cost, speed, and sensitivity to the problem of accessibility for the disabled. Because Section 508 of the Americans with Disabilities Act only applies to organizations receiving government funds, those in the private sector can ignore the mandate on accessibility. But even universities that receive federal monies have been slow to make their sites accessible to disabled persons. In terms of cost, it is more expensive to create a Web site with a multimodal interface. Developers have to become familiar with accessibility issues and how to overcome them. It takes longer to develop these Web sites, because it is often difficult to translate into accessible code all the bells and whistles that make a Web site interesting. Sometimes, these must be limited as a developer builds in text redundancy so that accessibility can be realized. Also, some companies perceive that these Web sites generally are larger and take longer to load, which translates into a speed issue. In general, this is not the case. Given the current processor speeds, network capabilities, and memory capacity of personal computers, we must ask if these are real issues or simply excuses. Slowly but surely, computer developers are recognizing that users with disabilities form a viable international community that has joined the professional ranks of not only computer programmers, engineers, and scientists, but also computer users with purchasing power.

CONCLUSION

Assuming that the digital divide can be bridged at both the local and global levels, important questions still remain. One question has to do with whether increased online communities at the global level threaten our traditional community life, especially as it exists in the off-line world. Philosopher Hans Jonas (1984) speaks of "neighbor ethics." Traditionally, we have had a presumptive responsibility to consider our neighbors as people deserving special moral consideration. Historically, we have banded together with our neighbors in the face of external threats, and we have enjoyed and benefited from the mutual support and reciprocal relationships with our neighbors in physical communities. But who are our neighbors in the global community? If we band together in online communities comprised of people living on several different continents, we can offer our "electronic neighbors" support in some sense and to some degree. But, in so doing, do we also risk the possibility that we will lessen our commitment to our neighbors in physical space? If so, we can ask whether this tradeoff is one worth accepting or is one that needs to be reevaluated.

ACKNOWLEDGMENTS

This chapter draws from and expands upon material in two previously published works:

Grodzinsky, F. S., & Tavani, H. T. (2006). The Internet and community building at the local and gloabl levels: Some implications and challenges. In J. Frühbauer, R. Capurro, & T. Hausmanninger (Eds.), *Localizing the Internet: Ethical issues in intercultural perspective.* Munich: Fink Verlag.

Tavani, H. T. (2004). *Ethics and technology: Ethical issues in an age of information and communication technology.* John Wiley & Sons.

REFERENCES

Chapman, G., & Rotenberg, M. (1995). The National information infrastructure: A public interest opportunity. In D. G. Johnson & H. Nissenbaum (Eds.), *Computers, ethics & social values* (pp. 628-644). Englewood Cliffs, NJ: Prentice Hall.

Compaine, B. (2001). *The digital divide: Facing a crisis or creating a myth.* Cambridge, MA: MIT Press.

Dibbell, J. (1993, December 21). A rape in cyberspace. *Village Voice*, pp. 36-42.

Epstein, R. G. (2000). The fragmented public square. *Computers and society.* Retrieved from http://www.cs.wcupa.edu/~epstein.fragmented.htm

Graham, G. (1999). *The Internet: A philosophical inquiry.* New York: Rutledge.

Grodzinsky, F. S. (2000). Equity of access: Adaptive technology. *Science and Engineering Ethics, 6*(2).

Grodiznsky, F. S., & Tavani, H. (2004). Ethical reflections on cyberstalking. In R. A. Spinello & H. T. Tavani (Eds.), *Readings in CyberEthics* (2nd ed.) (pp. 561-570). Jones and Bartlett.

Jonas, H. (1984). *The imperative of responsibility: In search of an ethics for the technological age.* Chicago: University of Chicago Press.

Levison, L., Thies, W., & Amarasinghe, S. (2002). Providing Web search capability for low-connectivity communities. In J. R. Herkert (Ed.), *Proceedings of the 2002 International Symposium on Technology and Society (ISTAS'02)* (pp. 87-92). Los Alamitos, CA: IEEE Computer Society Press.

Moss, J. (2002). Power and the digital divide. *Ethics and Information Technology, 4*(2), 159-165.

National Telecommunications and Information Administration (NTIA). (1995). *Falling through the net: A survey of the have-nots in rural and urban America.* Washington, DC: US Department of Commerce. Retrieved November 15, 2005, from http://www.ntia.doc.gov/ntiahome/fallingthru.html

National Telecommunications and Information Administration (NTIA). (1999). *Falling through the net: Defining the digital divide.* Washington, DC: US Department of Commerce. Retrieved November 15, 2005, from http://www.ntia.doc.gov/ntiahome/fttn99.html

National Telecommunications and Information Administration (NTIA). (2000). *Falling through the net: Toward digital inclusion.* Washington, DC: US Department of Commerce. Retrieved November 15, 2005, from http://www.ntia.doc.gov/ntiahome/fttn00/contents00.html

Negroponte, N. (1995). *Being digital.* New York: Alred Knopf Books.

Rheingold, H. (2001). *The virtual community: Homesteading on the electronic frontier* (rev. ed.). Cambridge, MA: MIT Press.

Scolve, R. E. (1995). *Democracy and technology.* New York: Guilford Press.

Shade, L. R. (2002). *Gender and community in the social construction of the Internet.* New York: Peter Lang.

Sun Microsystems. (2001). *Java's support for accessibility.* Retrieved November 16, 2005, from http://www.sun.com/access/java.access.support.html

Sunstein, C. R. (2002). *Republic.com.* Princeton, NJ: Princeton University Press.

Tavani, H. T. (2003). Ethical reflections on the digital divide. *Journal of Information, Communication and Ethics in Society, 1*(2), 99-108.

Tavani, H. T. (2004). *Ethics and technology: Ethical issues in an age of information and communication technology.* Hoboken, NJ: John Wiley and Sons.

Thorseth, M. (2005, March 18). *IT, multiculturalism and global democracy—ethical challenges.* Paper presented at the Workshop on Positive Discrimination. Institute for Philosophy, Pedagogy, and Rhetoric, Copenhagen University. Retrieved November 16, 2005, from http://trappe13.dynamicweb.dk

Warschauer, M. (2002). Reconceptualizing the digital divide. *First Monday, 7*(7). Retrieved December 21, 2002, from http://www.firstmonday.dk/issues/issue7_7/warschauer

Warschauer, M. (2003). *Technology and social inclusion: Rethinking the digital divide.* Cambridge, MA: MIT Press.

Webster's New World Dictionary of the American Language. (1996). World Publishing Company.

White, M. (2002). Regulating research: The problem of theorizing research in LambdaMOO. *Ethics and Information Technology, 4*(1), 55-70.

World Wide Web Consortium. Retrieved from http://www.w3.org/WAI/Technical/Activity.html

Chapter III
The Mediating Effect of Material Cultures as Human Hybridization

Lorenzo Magnani
University of Pavia, Italy
Sun Yat-sen University, China

ABSTRACT

We already are hybrid humans, fruit of a kind of co-evolution of both our brains and the common, scientific, social, and moral knowledge we have produced by ourselves, starting from the birth of material culture with our ancestors until the recent effects generated by the whole field of information and communication technologies (ICTs). We all are constitutively natural-born cyborgs; that is, biotechnological hybrid minds. Our minds should not be considered to be located only in the head; human beings have solved their problems of survival and reproduction, distributing cognitive and ethical functions to external nonbiological sources, props, and aids, which originate cultures. This chapter also illustrates the interplay between cultures and distributed cognition, taking advantage of the so-called disembodiment of mind, and stresses the problem of the co-evolution between brains and cultures. The second part of the chapter is related to the analysis of the interplay between cultures and cognition and of some consequences concerning the problem of intercultural communication in light of the role of moral mediators, docility, and cyberprivacy. Finally, I discuss some suggestions concerning the problem of what I call the principle of isolation of cultures, with respect to the effects of ICTs.

CYBORGS AND DISTRIBUTED COGNITION

Following Clark's (2003) conclusions on the relationships between humans and technology, especially information-and communications technologies (ICTs), we all are constitutively natural-born cyborgs; that is, biotechnologically hybrid minds[1]. Less and less are our minds considered to be in our heads; human beings have solved their problems of survival and reproduction by distributing cultures and cognitive functions to external nonbiological sources, props, and aids. Our biological brains have delegated to external tools many activities that involve complex planning and elaborate assessments of consequences (Clark, 2003, p. 5). A simple example might be how the brain, when faced with multiplying large numbers, learns to act in concert with pen and paper, storing part of the process and the results outside of itself. The same occurred when Greek geometers discovered new properties and theorems of geometry; they manipulated external diagrams to establish a kind of continuous cognitive negotiation with a suitable external support (e.g., sand or a blackboard) in order to gain new important information and heuristic suggestions.[2] The use of external tools and artifacts is very common; cognitive skills and performances are so widespread that they become invisible, thus giving birth to something I have called *tacit templates* of behavior that blend internal and external cognitive aspects (Magnani, 2001a).

New technologies will facilitate this process in a new way: on a daily basis, people are linked to non-biological, more-or-less intelligent machines and tools like cell phones, laptops, and medical prosthetics. Consequently, it becomes harder and harder to say where the world stops and the person begins. Clark contends that this line between biological self and technological world has always been flexible and that this fact has to be acknowledged both from the epistemological and the ontological points of view. Thus the study of the new anthropology of hybrid humans becomes important, and I would add that it is also critical for us to delineate and articulate the related ethical issues.

I certainly share Clark's (2003) enthusiasm in philosophically acknowledging our status as cyborgs, but I would like to go further in order to do more than just peer through the window of his book at the many cyberartifacts that render human creatures the consumer cyborgs we are.

Our bodies and our selves are materially and cognitively extended; that is, meshed with external artifacts and objects. This fact sets the stage for a variety of new philosophical and moral questions related to the role of cultures in our technological world. For example, because so many aspects of human beings are now simulated in or replaced by things in an external environment, new ontologies can be constituted, and Clark would agree with me. Pieces of information that can be carried in any physical medium are called *memes* by Dawkins (1989). They can stay in human brains or jump from brain to brain to objects, becoming configurations of artificial things that express meaning, like words written on a blackboard or data stored on a CD, icons and diagrams on a newspaper, configurations of external things that express meanings and cultural units like an obligatory route. They can also exist in natural objects endowed with informative significance (e.g., stars), which offer navigational guidance. In my perspective, the externalization of these chunks of information is described in light of the cognitive delegation on which human beings concentrate in material objects and structures. Like memes, cultural units are distributed everywhere, thanks not only to their dissemination in brains but also to their embodiment in various kinds of external materiality, objects, and artifacts of various types (see section on Artifacts and Intercultural Communication and section on Cultures, Counter Cultures, and Docile Humans).

Beyond the supports of paper, telephone, and media, many human interactions are strongly mediated (and potentially recorded) through ICTs (e.g., the Internet). What about the concept of identity, so connected to the concept of freedom? At present, identity has to be considered in a broad sense; the externally stored amount of data, information, images, and texts that concern us as individuals is enormous. This storage of information creates for each person a kind of external data shadow that, together with the biological body, forms a cyborg of both flesh and electronic data that identifies us or potentially identifies us (see the subsection Mediating Individual Privacy and Identity and the Principle of Cultural Isolation: The Role of ICTs). I contend that this complex new information being depicts new ontologies that, in turn, involve new moral problems. In turn, these new ways of building intercultural relations tend to depict uniform behaviors and habits because of the effect of their globalization. We no longer can apply old moral rules and old-fashioned arguments to beings that are at the same time biological (concrete) and virtual, situated in a three-dimensional local space but potentially globally omnipresent as information packets. For instance, where we are located cybernetically is no longer simple to define, and the increase in telepresence technologies will affect this point further. It becomes clear that external, nonbiological resources contribute to our variable senses of who and what we are and what we can do.[3]

MATERIAL CULTURE AND THE DISEMBODIMENT OF MIND

If, as Clark (2003) holds, the line between the biological self and the technological world is flexible and continually shifting, then biological self and the technological world are intertwined in cyborgs that present a variety of cases and degrees. This story, related to the birth of hybrid humans, is completely intertwined with the birth of culture, which intrinsically is immediately material and informational.

Let us first consider the case of what I call *tool-using humans* (i.e., related to clothing, shelters, etc.) (Magnani, 2007), appearing at least from the birth of the so-called material culture when hand axes were constructed and so offering new cognitive chances to the co-evolution of the mind of some early humans such as the Neanderthals. These hominids already possessed isolated cognitive domains, which Mithen (1996) calls *different intelligences*, probably endowed with different degrees of fleeting consciousnesses about the thoughts and knowledge within each domain (natural history intelligence, technical intelligence, social intelligence) (see the next sec-

tion). Unfortunately, when examined in light of its evolutionary history, the human mind is quite evidently limited as to the types of ideas it can hold and transmit between generations without material support.

It is extremely important to stress that material culture is not just the product of this massive cognitive chance but also the cause of it. In this perspective, we acknowledge that material artifacts are tools for thoughts as is language; that is, tools for exploring, expanding, and manipulating our own minds. In this regard, the evolution of culture is linked inextricably to the evolution of consciousness and thought.

The early human brain became a kind of universal and creative intelligent machine, extremely flexible so that we no longer needed different separated intelligent machines doing different jobs. A single one should have sufficed. As the engineering problem of producing various machines for various jobs was replaced by the office work of programming the Turing's universal machine to do these jobs, so the different intelligences very soon became integrated with a new universal device endowed with a high-level type of consciousness. This achievement was accomplished thanks to the birth of (material) culture. From this perspective, the expansion of the mind is, in the meantime, a continuous process of disembodiment of the mind itself into the cultural material world around it; the evolution of the mind is inextricably linked with the evolution of large, integrated, material cognitive/cultural systems.

Other more recent types of cyborgs appeared, and others will appear—the ones we call *enhanced humans* (related to the exploitation of prosthetics, pacemakers, artificial organs, etc.) and so-called *medical cyborgs* (fruit of IVF, cloning, genetic enhancement, etc.). We also have the *cognitively enhanced cyborgs* (using abacus, laptops, external cognitive representations in general, cell phones) and the *super-cyborgs* (endowed with stimulator implants, silicon chip transponders, etc.).

It is now clear that the biological brain's image of the body is protean and negotiable, an outgoing construct that changes as new technologies are added to our lives (Clark, 2003). Take the human visual system, for example, where much of the database is left outside of the head and is accessed by an outward-looking sensory apparatus (principally, the eyes). As opportunistic cyborgs, we do not care whether information is held within the biological organism or stored in the external world in, for instance, a laptop or cell phone. Not only do new technologies expand our sense of self, they also can induce changes in the actual physical body; increased finger mobility has been observed among people under 25 as the result of their use of electronic game controllers and text messaging on cell phones (Clark, 2003, p. 86).

THE CO-EVOLUTION OF BRAINS AND CULTURES

What I call *semiotic brains* (Magnani, in press, 2006c) are brains that make up a series of signs and that are engaged in making, manifesting, or reacting to a series of signs; through this semiotic activity, they are engaged at the same time in being minds and, so, in thinking intelligently. An important effect of this semiotic activity of brains is a continuous process of disembodiment of mind that exhibits a new cognitive perspective on the mechanisms underlying the semiotic emergence of cultures.

Following Turing's (1969) point of view, a big cortex can provide an evolutionary advantage only in the presence of a massive storage of meaningful information and knowledge on external supports that only an already developed small community of human beings can possess. Evidence from paleoanthropology seems to support this perspective. Some research in cognitive paleoanthropology teaches us that high-level and reflective consciousness in terms of thoughts about our own thoughts and about our feelings (i.e., consciousness not considered merely as raw sensation) is intertwined with the development of modern language (speech) and material culture. More than 250,000 years ago, several hominid species had brains as large as ours today, but their behavior lacked any sign of art or symbolic behavior. If we consider high-level consciousness related to high-level organization (in Turing's sense) of human cortex, then its origins can be related to the active role of environmental, social, linguistic, and cultural aspects.

Hand axes were made by Early Humans and first appeared 1.4 million years ago, and still were made by some of the Neanderthals in Europe just 50,000 years ago. The making of hand axes is intertwined strictly with the development of consciousness. Many needed capabilities constitute part of an evolved psychology that appeared long before the first hand axes were manufactured. It seems that humans were pre-adapted for some components required to make hand axes (Mithen, 1996, 1999):

1. **Imposition of Symmetry:** (Already evolved through predator escape and social interaction). It has been an unintentional byproduct of the bifacial knapping technique but also deliberately imposed in other cases. It is also well-known that the attention to symmetry may have developed through social interaction and predator escape, as it may allow one to recognize that one is being directly stared at (Dennett, 1991). It also seems that "Hominid handaxe makers may have been keying into this attraction to symmetry when producing tools to attract the attention of other hominids, especially those of the opposite sex" (Mithen, 1999, p. 287).
2. **Understanding Fracture Dynamics:** (Evident from Oldowan tools and from nut cracking by chimpanzees today).
3. **Ability to Plan Ahead:** (Modifying plans and reacting to contingencies, such unex-

pected flaws in the material and miss-hits), still evident in the minds of Oldowan tool-makers and in chimpanzees.

4. **High Degree of Sensory-Motor Control:** "Nodules, pre-forms, and near finished artefacts must be struck at precisely the right angle with precisely the right degree of force if the desired flake is to be detached" (Mithen, 1999, p. 285). The origin of this capability usually is tracked back to encephalization (the increased number of nerve tracts and the integration between them that allows for the firing of smaller muscle groups) and bipedalism (requires a more complex integrated highly fractionated nervous system, which, in turn, presupposes a larger brain).

The combination of these four resources produced an important semiotic revolution: the birth of what Mithen calls technical intelligence of early human mind, which consequently is related to the construction of hand axes and their new semiotic values. Indeed, they indicate high intelligence and good health. They cannot be compared to the artifacts made by animals, like honeycombs or spider webs, deriving from the iteration of fixed actions that do not require consciousness and intelligence.

Private Speech and Fleeting Consciousness

Two central factors play a fundamental role in the combination of the aforementioned four resources:

• The exploitation of *private speech* (speaking to oneself) to trail between planning, fracture dynamic, motor control, and symmetry (also, in children, there is a kind of private muttering that makes explicit what is implicit in the various abilities).

• A good degree of *fleeting consciousness* (thoughts about thoughts).

In the meantime, these two aspects played a fundamental role in the development of consciousness and thought:

So my argument is that when our ancestors made handaxes there were private mutterings accompanying the crack of stone against stone. Those private mutterings were instrumental in pulling the knowledge required for handaxes manufacture into an emergent consciousness. But what type of consciousness? I think probably one that was fleeting one: one that existed during the act of manufacture and that did not endure. One quite unlike the consciousness about one's emotions, feelings, and desires that were associated with the social world and that probably were part of a completely separated cognitive domain, that of social intelligence, in the early human mind. (Mithen, 1999, p. 288)

This use of private speech certainly can be considered a semiotic internal tool for organizing brains and, thus, for manipulating, expanding, and exploring minds—a tool that probably evolved with another: talking to each other. Both private and public language act as cultural tools for thought and play a fundamental role in its evolution, opening up our minds to ourselves and, thus, in the emergence of new meaning processes.

Material Culture and Semiosis

Another semiotic tool appeared in the latter stages of human evolution; it played a great role in the evolution of primitive minds; that is, in the organization of human brains. Hand axes also are at the birth of material culture so new cognitive chances can co-evolve:

• The mind of some early humans, like the Neanderthals, were constituted by relatively isolated semiotic cognitive domains that Mithen calls *different intelligences*, probably endowed with different degrees of consciousness about the thoughts and knowledge within each domain (natural history intelligence, technical intelligence, social intelligence). These isolated cognitive domains became integrated, also taking advantage of the role of public language.

• Degrees of high-level consciousness appear; human beings need thoughts about thoughts.

• Social intelligence and public language arise.

As I already have anticipated, it is very important to stress that material culture is not just the product of this massive cognitive chance but is also the cause of it. "The clever trick that humans learnt was to *disembody* their minds into the material world around them: a linguistic utterance might be considered as a disembodied thought. But such utterances last just for a few seconds. Material culture endures" (Mithen, 1999, p. 291).

In this perspective, we acknowledge that material artifacts are cultural tools for thoughts as is language: tools—as new signs—for exploring, expanding, and manipulating our own minds. In this regard, the evolution of culture is inextricably linked with the evolution of consciousness and thought.

As I already have illustrated, the early human brain became a kind of universal intelligent machine, extremely flexible so that we no longer need separated intelligent machines doing different jobs. A single one suffices. There is a clear analogy to the engineering problem of producing various machines for various jobs, which is replaced by the office work of programming the universal machine to do these jobs; so the different intelligences become integrated in a new universal device.[4]

From this perspective, the semiotic expansion of the mind is, in the meantime, a continuous pro-

cess of disembodiment of the minds themselves into the material world around them. In this regard, the evolution of the mind is inextricably linked with the evolution of large, integrated, material cultural semiotic systems.

Finally, given the fact that the problem of bringing connection between the world within the skull and the world outside of it always has been a central interest of anthropology; it is not a surprise that this perspective also is shared by anthropologists like Geertz (2000) who (also citing Clark's [2003] emphasis on the question, "Where does mind stop and the rest of world begin?") concludes that the question is analogous to the anthropological one, "Where does culture stop and the rest of self begin?" Geertz clearly explains the relevance of distributed cognition theories for cultural anthropology:

At least since the circumstantial description of the incipient, prelinguistic stages of hominization (small skulls, erect stature, purposed implements) began about a half a century ago with the discovery of prepithecanthropine fossils and early Pleistocene sites, the fact that brain and culture coevolved, mutually dependent the one upon the other for their very realization, has made the conception of human mental functioning as an intrinsically determined intracerebral process, ornamented and extended, but hardly engendered by cultural devices—language, rite, technology, teaching, and the incest tabu—unsustainable. Our brains are not in a vat, but in our bodies. Our minds are not in our bodies, but in the world. And as for the world, it is not in our brains, our brains, or our minds: they are, along with gods, verbs, rocks, and politics, in it. (Geertz, 2000, p. 205)[5]

Building Cultures through the Disembodiment of Mind

A wonderful example of meaning creation through disembodiment of mind is the carving of what most likely is the mythical being from the last

Figure 1. In Mithen (1999)

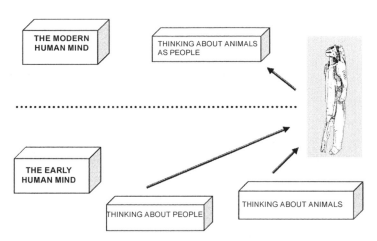

ice age (30,000 years ago), a half-human/half-lion figure carved from mammoth ivory found at Hohlenstein Stadel, Germany.

An evolved mind is unlikely to have a natural home for this being, as such entities do not exist in the natural world: so whereas evolved minds could think about humans by exploiting modules shaped by natural selection, and about lions by deploying content rich mental modules moulded by natural selection and about other lions by using other content rich modules from the natural history cognitive domain, how could one think about entities that were part human and part animal? Such entities had no home in the mind. (Mithen, 1999, p. 291)

A mind consisting of different separated intelligences cannot come up with such entity (Figure 1). The only way is to extend the mind into the material word, exploiting in a semiotic way rocks, blackboards, paper, ivory, and writing, painting, and carving: "artefacts such as this figure play the role of anchors for ideas and have no natural home within the mind; for ideas that take us beyond those that natural selection could enable us to possess" (Mithen, 1999, p. 291).

In the case of our figure, we face an anthropomorphic thinking created by the material representation serving to semiotically anchor the cognitive representation of supernatural being. It is a kind of ancestor of our current ICTs in which informational and knowledge are stored and manipulated externally. In this case, the material culture disembodies thoughts that otherwise will soon disappear without being transmitted to other human beings, and realizes a systematic semiotic delegation to the external environment. The early human mind possessed two separated intelligences for thinking about animals and people. Through the mediation of the material culture, the modern human mind can arrive to think internally about the new concept of animal and people at the same time. But the new meaning occurred over there in the external material world where the mind picked it up.

Artifacts as external semiotic objects allowed humans to loosen and cut those chains on their unorganized brains imposed by their evolutionary past, chains that always limited the brains of other human beings, such as the Neanderthals. Loosing chains and securing ideas to external objects was also a way to creatively reorganize brains as universal machines for thinking.

In the remaining part of this chapter, I will describe the centrality to semiotic cognitive information processes of the disembodiment of mind from the point of view of the cognitive interplay between internal and external representations in cultural settings. I consider this interplay critical in analyzing the relation between meaningful semiotic internal resources and devices and their dynamic interactions with the externalized semiotic materiality already stocked in cultural environments. Hence, minds are extended in material cultures and, at the same time, artificial in themselves.

Material and Immaterial Cultures

The tradition of studies on intercultural relations (Roth, 2001) distinguishes between material and immaterial cultures. Immaterial interactions would focus "on language, non-verbal expressions, and behaviors of the actors as well as on their perceptions, attitudes, and values" (Roth, 2001, p. 564). On the contrary, material culture refers to people's material environments consisting of food, dwellings, and furniture, and deals with social or territorial behaviors mainly related to intracultural aspects of national, regional, and cultural identities but not to personal intercultural communications.

In the previous sections, I have depicted a different perspective on material culture, taking advantage of some results coming from the area of embodied and distributed cognition. In this perspective, every culture is material. There is not something immaterial (mental?) in terms of words, perceptions, or values that we can distinguish from objects like hammers or laptops. Beyond Cartesian dualism, I have illustrated that our (material) brains delegate meaningful cognitive (and ethical) roles to externalities and then tend to adopt what they have checked occurring outside, over there, in the external invented structure. Consequently, a large part of culture

formation takes advantage of the exploitation of external representations and mediators.

My view about the disembodiment of mind certainly involves the Mind/Body dualist perspective as less credible as well as Cartesian computationalism. Also the view that Mind is Computational independently of the physical (functionalism) is jeopardized. In my perspective, on human cognition we no longer need Descartes dualism; we only have brains that make up large, integrated, material cognitive, and cultural systems. The only problem seems how meat knows that we can reverse the Cartesian motto and say *sum ergo cogito*—it is meat that makes up external material cultures. In this perspective, what we usually call *mind* simply consists in the union of both the changing neural configurations of brains together with those large, integrated, material cultural, and cognitive systems that the brains themselves are building continuously.

Cultures and Cognition

Peirce's philosophical and semiotic motto, "man is an external sign," is very clear about the materiality of mind and about the fact that the conscious self is a cluster actively embodied of flowing intelligible signs.[6] This semiotic perspective provides a good framework in which we can depict a more satisfying and modern concept of culture that can better account for many aspects related to the impact of recent information and communication technologies (ICTs). Peirce says:

It is sufficient to say that there is no element whatever of man's consciousness which has not something corresponding to it in the word; and the reason is obvious. It is that the word or sign which man uses is the man himself. For, as the fact that every thought is a sign, taken in conjunction with the fact that life is a train of thoughts, proves that man is a sign; so, that every thought is an external sign, proves that man is an external sign.

That is to say, the man and the external sign are identical, in the same sense in which the words homo and man are identical. Thus my language is the sum total of myself; for the man is the thought. (Peirce, 1931-1958, vol. 5, p. 314)

We can exploit this fundamental philosophical argumentation to modernize the concept of culture with respect to the tradition of historical, sociological, and anthropological studies. It is by way of signs that we ourselves are semiotic processes; for example, a more or less coherent cluster of narratives. If all thinking is in signs, it is not true that thoughts are in us because we are in thoughts (Magnani, in press). This centrality of thoughts is the centrality of signs, and everywhere there are signs, there are cultural units. External materialities, like laptops or brains, can acquire cultural meanings and roles insofar as they are endowed with cognitive/semiotic delegations. One of the central properties of signs is their reintepretability. This occurs in a social process in which signs are referred to as *material cultural objects*. In this sense, natural and artificial objects become what I propose to call *cultural mediators*.[7]

Both trained neural networks in a human brain able to express cognitive skills, concepts, or emotions, and natural objects like stars endowed with cognitive delegations (e.g., to help the navigation) become cultural units because they are inserted in a process of human cognitive signification, epistemic, moral, emotional, aesthetic, economical, and so forth. The same happens in the case of material external artifacts, such as, for example, a cell phone, a laptop, or another ICT. They are the effect of cognitive delegations that make them cultural units over there in the same time intertwined with human beings; we do not have to forget that we already are semiotic and, thus, cultural processes, and in this sense, we also are defined partially by those external cultural units that continually affect us, transforming humans in those cyborgs that I have depicted in the previous section.

It is clear in this perspective that the Peircian person-sign, which is culturally determined, is future-conditional; that is, not fully formed in the present but depending on the future destiny of the concrete semiotic/cultural activity (future thoughts and experience of the community) in which he or she will be involved. If Peirce maintains that when we think we appear as a sign (Peirce, 1931-1958, vol. 5, p. 283) and, moreover, that everything presented to us is a phenomenal manifestation of ourselves, feelings, images, diagrams, concepts, schemata, and other cultural representations, are phenomenal manifestations that become available for interpretations and, thus, are guiding our actions in a positive or negative way. They become signs when we think and interpret them. It is well known that, for Peirce, all semiotic experience also is providing a guide for action. Indeed, the whole function of thought is to produce habits of action.

ARTIFACTS AND INTERCULTURAL COMMUNICATION

In light of the considerations illustrated in the previous sections, we can see every technology (and, obviously, information and communication technologies [ICTs], which are built expressly to carry information) as strictly intertwined with human beings through a continuous interplay of semiotic activities. In our era of increasing globalization, ICT artifacts, such as the Internet, databases, wireless networks, and so forth, become crucial mediators of cross-cultural relationships between human beings and communities. I will treat this problem in this and in the following sections dealing with some effects of ICT technologies on the concept of human docility, identity, and privacy, and with respect to the properties of what I call *moral mediators*.

Clark (2003) correctly depicts a Nokia mobile phone as something that is "part of us," taken for granted, an object regarded as a kind of "prosthetic limb over which you wield full and flexible control, and on which you eventually come to automatically rely in formulating and carrying out your daily goals and projects" (Clark, 2003, p. 9). It is well known that Heidegger distinguished between a tool's or artifact's being ready-to-hand, like the hammer and the cell phone, and its being present-at-hand. A ready-to-hand tool does not demand conscious reflection. "We can, in effect, 'see right through it,' concentrating only on the task (nailing the picture to the wall) [or, we add, writing an SMS message on a cell phone]. But, if things start to go wrong, we are still able to focus on the hammer [or on the cell phone], encountering it now as present-at-hand that requires our attention, that is, an object in its own right. We may inspect it, try using it in a new way, swap it for one with a smaller head, and so on" (Clark, 2003, p. 48). Using a tool becomes a continuous process of engagement, separation, and re-engagement. Just because they are ready-to-hand, these tools are called transparent or invisible technologies.[8] Tools of this type express cultures that we call *implicit.*

This brings me to the following point: Okay, I also possess a Nec mobile phone and have, consequently, gained a new degree of cyborgness. I am no longer only intertwined with classic tools like hammers, books, and watches, but I am also wired to a cell phone through which I work, live, and think. The problem is that our enthusiasm for information and communication technological advances may blind us to the intercultural and ethical aspects of the processes of engagement, separation, and reengagement that they make possible.

To heighten my awareness of such processes, I hope to acquire, as I use my cell phone and other tools yet to come, the moral knowledge necessary to maintain and even reinforce my identity, freedom, responsibility, and the ownership of my future; I would hope for the same for all other hybrid humans. I respect the new object or artifact that integrates its cognitive abilities with its users,

but we must be mindful of the responsibilities that technology brings so that it enhances rather than diminishes us. Moreover, does the cognitive value of the artifact count more than some basic biological cognitive abilities of the human body? What is the dignity of human beings as special brain/body cultural materials with respect to the remaining externalized cultural objects and structures?

Everyone has experienced the difficulty and complexity of unsubscribing from some cyber-service suppliers like cell phone companies or Internet providers. Such obstacles testify to the fact that even if they are effective tool-based cognitive extensions of our bodies, then they also are tool-based economic institutions aiming to cast themselves as cognitively necessary and irreplaceable things. Because they satisfy market needs, which can be highly aggressive, they in some sense acquire more importance than the biological life itself.

As I have already illustrated, new artifacts become ready-to-hand, but at what ethical and cultural cost? We still must be able to extricate, if we so choose, the technology that has appeared in our lives. Terminating a cell phone service contract, for example, should be an easy process without extended hassles or unexpected costs.[9] What way of ethical thinking fully explicates that right and will lead to new policies and laws that will protect human dignity in the future technological world? What countercultural strategies and cognitions do I need if a sophisticated new neurophone (Clark, 2003) is wired into my cochlear nerve as a direct electronic channel? Or how will one get rid of an affective wearable that monitors your stress levels and provides daily profiles and other data to you but, in the meantime, is generating an intolerable information overload? (Picard, 1997). You start to think you have another self, and it feels as if you no longer own some of the information about yourself—that damn affective wearable also monitors all your frustrations and shows you an interpretive narrative on how things went. It is not simple to have the maturity necessary to deal with a kind of another self, fruit of technology, that monitors and tells us another story about ourselves. Certainly, scientific advances like the neurophone that Clark describes and the affective wearable will come first and only later on the moral and legal rules. As I will illustrate better in the following section, the production of an appropriate counterculture is central in order to avoid the blindness to the dangerous ethical consequences of ICTs and other technologies.

Beyond simple cochlea implants and heart pacemakers, other intrusions into the human body currently are tested or imagined. Warwick (2003) lists new super-cyborgs formed by human (or animal) machine brain/nervous system coupling. Their diffusion will be able to produce new cultures endowed with unexpected consequences. There are stimulator implants that counteract electronically the tremor effects associated with Parkinson's disease; implants that permit the transmission signals from brain of stroke victims to the computer to cause the cursor on the computer screen to move left, right, up, and down (so spelling out words and making requests); silicon chips transponders surgically implanted in the upper left arm able to transmit unique identifying radio signals. In this last case, it is also possible to install direct links with the nervous fibers in the arm, able to transmit and receive signals, that have permitted experiments on movement signals. Experiments also were made on transmitting signals across the Internet directly from a human brain implant to a robot in order to move its hand. Furthermore, extrasensory inputs sent to robots suitably sensing the world using ultrasonic sensors were sent to human brains that were able amazingly to make sense of the signal.

Of course, as Warwick and Clark claim, these super-cyborgs can size and control the process of evolution so that evolution is based entirely on technology rather than biology. Evolution will become even more than today (i.e., co-evolu-

tion from the viewpoint of human beings) as the organism and the environment (disseminated by super-cyborgs) find a continuous mutual variation. The organism modifies its character in order to reach better fitness; however, the environment, and, thus, cultures that develop in it, equally are continuously changing and very sensitive to every modification. Within this complex system of changes, many organisms might fit the same environment (niche), which becomes highly sensible—and active—with regard to the organisms that live in it.

There is a profound tension between the biological and the cultures engendered by technological spheres of human hybrids, who are composed of a body plus cell phone, laptop, the Internet, and so forth. Sometimes, the two aspects can be reconciled by adjusting and redistributing various new cultural and ethical values, but the struggle is ongoing, and the final results are unknowable; the outcome simply depends on the moral targets that hybrid people identify and advocate. Do the cultural functions spontaneously engendered by a cell phone count more than some pre-existent cultural values related to the biological body without artifacts or with other old-fashioned artifacts? Are the new delegation of tasks to the cell phone and the consequent cultural modifications really compensated by new positive capabilities and chances, or does a biological body's lack of cognitive autonomy become intolerable at some point?

In the book *Morality in a Technological World*,[10] I describe in detail how the economic value of technological objects that are grafted on to human beings makes it dangerously easy to produce cultures in which people are treated people as means, and it is well-known that the market economy is inherently inclined to regard human beings this way. In a market economy, qualities and worth of human beings—their intelligence, energies, work, emotions, and so forth—can be arbitrarily exploited and/or disregarded in favor of solely promoting the sales of artifacts, items that may or may not be that useful. Situations like these, of course, inevitably generate frustration. Central to this issue is the fact that many people are used to being considered things; they are, in Kantian terms, treated as means (and only as means). In the book, I offer a way to recalibrate the cultural and ethical value of things so that respecting people as things becomes a positive way to regard them.

To give an example, imagine people who have used certain devices so much that some of their biological cognitive abilities have atrophied. Such people may yearn to be as respected as a cell phone—perhaps the expensive one of the future that I mentioned before, the direct electronic channel wired into my cochlear nerve that features a sophisticated processor, spectacular AI tools, and a direct Internet connection. In that cultural framework, the hybrid person at hand will feel himself or herself dispossessed of the moral cognitive worth already attributed to nonbiological artifacts. It is very simple to imagine how this situation will be much more complicated by the appearance of future super-cyborgs endowed with huge amounts of extra memory, enhanced mathematical skills, extrasensory devices, and (why not) able to communicate various signals by thought. They will be more powerful than humans, with brains that are directly part human and part machine, so the "epicentre of moral and ethical decision making will no longer be of purely human form, but rather it is a mixed human, machine base" (Warwick, 2003, p. 136).

Being cared for and valued is not always considered a human right; for instance, collectives do not have moral (and legal) rules that mandate the protection and preservation of human beings' cognitive skills. As a result, we face a paradoxical situation that inverts Kant's thinking, one involving people who are not sufficiently or appropriately treated as means, as things. Yet people's biological cognitive skills deserve to be valued at least as

much as a cell phone; human cognitive capacities warrant moral credit, because it is thanks to them that things like cell phones were invented and built to begin with. In this way, human hybrids can reclaim moral recognition for being biological carriers of information, knowledge, know-how, autonomy, cultural traditions, and so forth, and gain the respect given to cognitive artifacts for being external cultural repositories (e.g., books, PCs, works of art). That human hybrid, who exhibits knowledge and capacity to reason and work, will expect to play a clear, autonomous, and morally recognized role at the level of his or her biological intellectual capacities.

What I have just illustrated will hold also in the case of the future super-cyborgs that I depicted previously, fruit of the most advanced ICTs revolution, just with slight modifications. Two moral problems will still be at stake: (1) the problem of the equal distribution among human beings/brains of those sophisticated artificial endowments like extrasensory devices; and[11] (2) the fact that super-cyborgs possess biotechnological cognitive skills deserves to be valued in a very balanced way; super-cyborgs' biological cognitive capacities will have to be valued very much, not to consent the priority and the dominance of the artificial aspects, so determining cyborgs with intelligent prostheses but dull brains.

CULTURES, COUNTER CULTURES, AND DOCILE HUMANS

We have seen in the previous sections that material culture disembodies thoughts that otherwise will soon disappear, without being transmitted to other human beings, and realizes a systematic semiotic delegation to the external environment. I contend that cultures are formed through semiotic anchorage of informational content to external material objects and structures. I have described this process as a kind of disembodiment of mind.

We also have seen that unorganized brains organize themselves through a semiotic activity that is reified in the external cultural environment and then reprojected and reinterpreted through new configurations of neural networks and chemical processes. I also think the disembodiment of mind can account nicely for semiotic processes of creation of countercultures.

Material Cultures and Moral Mediators

We have said that through the mediation of the material culture the modern human mind can, for example, arrive to internally think the new meaning of animals and people at the same time, so generating a conceptual and cultural change. We can account for this process of disembodiment of our ancestors from a theoretical cognitive point of view. I maintain that cultural representations are external and internal. We can say that:

- **External Cultural Representations:** Formed by external cultural materials that express (through reification) concepts and problems that are not necessarily present in the brain of some human beings.
- **Internalized Cultural Representations:** Internal reprojections, a kind of recapitulation (learning) of external representations in terms of neural patterns of activation in the brain. It is in this way that human beings take part in a culture or in a new culture. The representations sometimes can be manipulated internally like external objects and can originate new internal reconstructed representations through the neural activity of transformation and integration. It is at this level that a countercultural effect can be activated. When the fixation of external (new) cultural units, derived from the interplay between the two levels, is reached, they, in turn, can be externalized to the aim

of constituting new cultural devices open to a further possible diffusion.

In our technological world, there is a huge expansion of private and public objects and artifacts that have gained great importance in everyday life and for the self-definition of people, especially in industrialized societies. The global trade and continuous exchange of commodities is one of the central aspects of our lives in the cyberage. Regional and national products have become available worldwide, and some of them have become international commodities, marketed and consumed globally.

I have illustrated how these artifacts play the role of cultural mediators. Let us now describe some details of this effect of mediation, paying special attention to some ethical consequences. All artifacts embed a fragment of cultural knowledge and experience and are the fruit of complicated cognitive delegations. These delegations explain, in the case of the cell phone (explicitly related to ICTs) but also in the case of furniture or food why artifacts can influence many communicative processes. Roth (2001) illustrates some important cultural roles played by artifacts. Artifacts can be (1) topics or themes of (intercultural) communication that carry internationally the know-how about products; (2) material contexts that wrap each act of communication; (3) media for intercultural communication; (4) transferred and communicated across cultural boundaries as merchandise; (5) entertainers of various relationships with humans, related to the available culture specificity; (6) used symbolically; and (7) ways to overcome the difficulties in interpreting foreign cultures.

Furthermore, artifacts play a spatial role in separating public and private spaces, workplaces, and so forth, as in the case of buildings and streets, chairs, and tables in houses and offices; they also have a personal dimension at the communication level, as in the case of clothes, utensils, ritual objects, fences, and so forth; and an actional dimension in eating, working, celebrating, and so forth. These dimensions usually are related to standard roles that the artifacts play, and only special interactions with humans can change these default characters. In the case of globalized artifacts, it is through the cyclic process of internalization/externalization previously described that they culturally can acquire new ethnic, regional, or national ethical values and new identifications and meanings (Teuteberg, Neumann, & Wierlacher, 1997) in a process that sometimes is characterized clearly by a countercultural disposition that can arise at both the cognitive and emotional levels (Lindner, 1997). In the EU, controversies about Italian pasta, Dutch clogs, French champagne, and German beer have demonstrated "the extent to which regional and national identities are tied to material cultures and local cultures are used as countercultures to globalization" (Roth, 2002, p. 573).

The insistence on the home country artifacts in the case of the emigrants demonstrates how values of objects can acquire new meanings and change their disposition once removed from their standard places; in other cases, foreign objects and artifacts are often responsible for a kind of culture shock. The so-called countercultural effects of creolization (Howes, 1996) and localization (Lindner, 1997; Roth, 2001) have affected the international cultural identity of goods like Coca-Cola, which certainly represents the symbol of the globalization of products.

Similarly, in the case of new media and technical instruments that work at the level of worldwide transmission of information and/or at the level of global communicative networks, there is evidence (Bredin, 1996) that in their use (but also in the use of technological equipment like cell phones and laptops), there are significant cultural differences. In some cases, the transfer of technology might not appreciate local values and also might undermine those values later on (Moss, 2005) so that a great part of the globe as

well as the majority of the world population do not enjoy the fruits and benefits that information technologies are supposed to bring (Hongladarom, 2005). In other cases, some positive impacts have been experienced.

In this domain of the complex interaction between culture, technology, and intercultural communication, the literature of the so-called Social Construction of Technology (SCOT) is also relevant (Sismondo, 1993; Winner, 1993). It is in this area of studies that Latour's notions of the dehumanizing effect of technologies emerge and are based on the so-called actor network theory.[12] The actor network theory basically maintains that we should think of science, technology, and society as a field of human and nonhuman (material) agency. Human and nonhuman agents are associated with one another in networks, and they evolve together within these networks. Because the two aspects are equally important, neither can be reduced to the other; "An actor network is simultaneously an actor whose activity is networking heterogeneous elements and a network that is able to redefine and transform what it is made of. ... The actor network is reducible neither to an actor alone nor to a network" (Callon, 1997, p. 93).

A different but related perspective (one that, like Latour's, avoids anthropomorphic prioritization of human agency and addresses the dissolution of boundaries between things and people) is offered by Andrew Pickering in his writing on science studies of post-humanism. He describes externalities (representations, artifacts, tools, etc.) as kinds of nonhuman agencies[13] that interact with a decentered human agency in a dialectic of resistance and accommodation called the *mangle of practice*.[14] The resistance is a failure to capture material agency in an intended form, while accommodation amounts to reconfiguration of the apparatus that might find a way through its resistance. When human and nonhuman agencies are brought together, as often has occurred throughout history in mathematics, natural sciences, and technology, it is impossible to predict the results.

An example of a positive impact and of re-invention of roles of Western technology in a developing country is given by the substantial role played by cell phones in ensuring in the Republic of the Philippines the success of the EDSA II people power revolution in 2001, which forced President Joseph Estrada to resign (Valdez, 2005). In this case, technology was used effectively by civil society to raise new cultural consciousness of the Filipino people. During the height of the impeachment trial against President Estrada, the total volume of the SMS text messages exchanged by Filipinos in a single day exceeded the total volume of text messages in all of Europe. A similar event, of course, is inconceivable in Western countries.

In my book *Morality in a Technological World* (Magnani, 2007), I have introduced the concept of moral mediator. A moral mediator is a cultural mediator in which ethical aspects are crucial and the importance in potential intercultural relationships is central. What exactly is a moral mediator? Morality often is performed in a tacit way, per se, through doing. Moreover, part of this doing can be seen as an activity of cultural manipulation of the external word for just building moral mediators. They can be built in the aim of getting ethical effects, but they also consist in beings, entities, objects, and structures that objectively, beyond human beings' intentionalities, carry ethical or unethical consequences. Hence, a significant portion of manipulations also is devoted to building that vast new source of distributed information and knowledge that originates external moral mediators.

Moral mediators represent a kind of redistribution of the moral effort through managing objects and information in such a way that we can overcome the poverty and the unsatisfactory character of the moral options immediately represented or found internally (e.g., principles, prototypes, etc.). I also think that the analysis

of moral mediators can help to account for the mechanisms of the macroscopic and growing phenomenon of global moral actions and collective responsibilities resulting from the invisible hand of systemic interactions among several cultural agents at the local level (Floridi & Sanders, 2003). A cultural object, such as an Internet Web page on which some commodities are sold online, not only realizes an economical transaction but also carries ethical effects insofar as it implies certain customers' behaviors related to some policies and constraints.

Natural phenomena also can serve as external artifactual moral mediators; many external natural objects (e.g., animals) create opportunities for new ethical knowledge, as in the case of endangered species. Thanks to utilitarianism and environmentalism, some animals have acquired the moral definition of endangered; in turn, people learned something new by discovering (through those animals as moral mediators) how human beings also can be redefined as endangered. Many external things that traditionally have been considered morally inert can be transformed into moral mediators. In general, we can use animals to identify previously unrecognized moral features of human beings or other living creatures, as we can do with the Earth or (non-natural) cultural entities; we also can use cultural external tools such as writing, narrative, ritual, and various kinds of pertinent institutions to reconfigure unsatisfactory social orders. Hence, not all moral tools are inside the head—many are shared and distributed in external objects and structures that function as ethical devices.

External moral mediators function as components of a memory system that crosses the boundary between person and environment. For example, they are able to transform the tasks involved in simple manipulations that promote in an agent further moral inferences. When an abused child is moved to a house to reconfigure his or her social relationships, this new moral mediator can help him or her to experience new inferences (e.g., new emotions concerning adults and new imageries about his or her past abuse).

Moreover, I can alter my bodily experience of pain through action by following the template control of sense data, as we previously outlined, that is through shifting (unconsciously) the position of my body and changing its relationships with other humans and nonhumans experiencing distress. Mother Theresa's personal moral rich feeling and consideration of pain certainly had been shaped by her closeness to starving and miserable people and by her manipulation of their bodies. In many people, moral training often is related to these kinds of spontaneous (and lucky) manipulations of their own bodies and sense data so that they build morality immediately and nonreflectively through doing. It is obvious that these processes involve a cultural (often countercultural) redefinition of the role of bodies with respect to the received perspectives.

What is the suggestion we can get from the concept of moral mediator with respect to the problem of intercultural communication? I think that the main teaching regards the need to understand the language of objects of other cultures. Given the huge cognitive and emotional role played by things and external representations, it is through them that we can increase the effects of commensurability even in the hardest cases of conflicting cultures. Let us illustrate the example of Islamic fundamentalists and Western capitalist culture in which a counterculture is activated to the aim of reinterpreting capitalistic rules, transactions, and loans.

Islamic fundamentalists have resumed medieval objections to the charging of financial interest as part of a more extended attack on Western influences and look for different ways of financing commerce and industry that, in their eyes, do less violence to Islamic society and countries. They consider international loans from Western governments and banks as basically exploitive but expect to find and retain elements of capitalism within their domestic economies as tools for promoting development within the family. "So the medieval debate about the clever new forms of contract, aimed at circumventing the moral objection to interest, is being repeated in contemporary Islam, in the hope of squaring the needs of commerce with the traditional injunctions of the *Sharīya*"(Jonsen & Toulmin, 1988, p. 310).

Here, we see that using an old financial practice in a new context (modern Islam) generates problems; difficulties arise when international loans are made between countries with different cultures. The medieval conflict between moral investing and immoral money lending acquires new relevance. Simply applying a general principle against usury is not particularly productive, for it limits opportunities for commerce between Muslim nations and the rest of the world; instead, new ways of conducting business must be considered able to act as moral mediators of the puzzling situation. The underlying lesson here is that the concrete case—the seemingly irreconcilable conflict between cultures—takes agents beyond the reach of rules and compels them to take into account a particular set of circumstances, the fact that there are other commercial practices that are acceptable in Islamic business communities. In other cultural cases, similar situations can be found when some abstract principles are not always universally good principles to use when deciding how (and whether) to treat particular cases, because their application can be techniques that often can be very useful but can have unacceptable negative side effects for both the children and their families. In the usury problem, abstract rules must be modified suitably and mediated to fit particular circumstances.

Docile Humans Externalize Cultures

Following Simon's perspective, human beings first of all always and constitutively operate in a situation of bounded rationality; human beings and other creatures do not behave optimally for their fitness, because they are not able to get knowledge and make inferences that would support optimization. Moreover, in order to survive, humans are docile in the sense that our fitness is enhanced by "the tendency to depend on suggestions, recommendations, persuasion, and information obtained through social channels as a major basis for choice" (Simon 1993, p. 156). In other words, we support our limited decision-making capabilities, counting on external data obtained through the senses, from the social environment. The social context gives us the main data filter, available to increase individual fitness (Secchi, 2006).

The concept of docility is related to that of altruism in the sense that one cannot be altruistic if he or she is not docile. In this perspective, the intelligent altruist is the fittest. However, the most important element seems to be docility more than altruism, because docility is the condition of the possibility of the emergence of altruism. In Simon's work, docility also is related to the idea of socializability, and certainly it is an aspect of both the human beings' continuous cognitive delegations to the external environment and to other social members.

The problem here is twofold. First, people delegate data acquisition to their experience and to the external cultural resources and individuals, as I have illustrated in the first three sections of this chapter. Second, people do trust others to learn. I have already illustrated how a big cortex, speech, rudimentary social settings, and primitive material culture furnished the conditions for the birth of the mind as a universal machine. I contended that a big cortex can provide an evolutionary advantage only in the presence of a massive storage of meaningful information and knowledge on external supports that only an already developed small community of human beings can possess. If we consider high-level consciousness as related to a high-level organization of human cortex, its

origins can be related to the active role of environmental, social, linguistic, and cultural aspects. It is in this sense that docile interaction lays on the very basis of our social (and neurological) development.

It is obvious that docility is related to the development of cultures, their availability, and to the quality of cross-cultural relationships. Of course, the type of dissemination of cultures and their possible enhancements affect the chances that human collectives have to exploit docility and so to increase their fitness. I guess the conflicts and lack of dialogue between cultures and the excessive normalization generated by globalization can diminish the positive effects of docility. I strongly think research on these and similar aspects must be established and encouraged.

Mediating Individual Privacy and Identity and the Principle of Cultural Isolation: The Role of ICTs

In chapter four of the already cited book by Magnani (2007), I have contended that knowledge has to be considered a duty. Of course, the problem of its dissemination and distribution in cultures immediately arises. I also showed that from my examination of knowledge as duty considered to be a consequence of the current technological complexity of external things, a warning can be made naturally in the case of the problem of identity and cyberprivacy. I am now realizing that this warning has to be made not only at the micro level of the individuals but also at the macro level of cultures. I contend that if a lot of knowledge is incorporated in external artificial things through current ICTs (and we need knowledge to deal with external things, both natural and artificial), human beings are so intertwined with those external things that their visibility can be excessive and dangerous.

At present, identity has to be considered in a broad sense; the amount of data, information, images, and texts that concern us as individuals are enormous and are stored in external things/means. This storage of information about human beings creates a kind of external data shadow for every human individual who, together with the biological body, generates a kind of cyborg, also consisting of electronic data that identify us or potentially identify us. New moral ontologies are created; for example, a new human being is individuated, biologically local, and cybernetically global. In the cited book I have illustrated and discussed some ideas about the Panopticon effect as a metaphor of the mechanisms of large-scale social control that characterizes the modern world. As we have said, a detailed computational shadow of the person's private life can be built by storing collected pieces of information about people. I think we no longer can apply old moral rules and old-fashioned arguments to beings that are at the same time biological (concrete) and virtual, situated in a three-dimensional local space, but potentially globally omnipresent as information packets. People have to be protected not only from being seen but also from feeling visible in order to avoid ostracism and stigmatization about minorities, to be protected from insult, to avoid becoming more conformist and conventional, and so to avoid the possibility of being oppressed.

I think something similar can be discussed and examined at the macro level of cultures. The process of globalization jeopardizes local cultures from the point of view of their identities but also from the point of view, per se, of their privacy. I think cultures also need appropriate thresholds of isolation and self-protection. If the identity and isolation of cultures are harmed beyond a certain degree, we have consequences for the specific freedom of the related affected collectives.

For example, surely at the micro level of individuals, the role of identity cards and other tools for identifications have positive effects, for instance, in terms of the enhancement of equality; we all have the identity card, then we are all

citizens. Unfortunately, we can reach negative outcomes in terms of repressive acts just made possible by the kind of imprisonment of subjectivity caused by the excessive identification policies, as Foucault (1979) magisterially described (Kaboré, 2005). Similarly, globalization effects of ICTs can enhance local cultures, magnifying their identities, but they also can contaminate them in a way that generates the loss of isolation and so the loss of their role in the identification of the related collectives.

I contend that what I call the *principle of isolation* of cultures resorts to the protection against interference with the collectives' ways of realizing and developing their interests, both in the sense of interests related to their practical objectives or merely intertwined with strands of their identity over time.[15] I also contend that this protection has to be equilibrated with the need to promote cyberdemocracy, which will be a real kind of counter-culture counterposed to the negative effects of globalization (Bardone & Magnani, 2006; Cavalier, 2004).

CONCLUSION

The main thesis of this chapter is that the disembodiment of mind is a significant cognitive perspective that is able to unveil some basic features of the creation of cultures. Its fertility in explaining the interplay between internal and external levels of cognition is evident. I maintain that various aspects of culture formation could take advantage of the research on this interplay; for instance, study on cultural mediators can provide a better understanding of the processes of intercultural communication.

From the paleoanthropological perspective, we have learned that an evolved mind is unlikely to have a natural home for new concepts and meanings, as such concepts and meanings do not exist in the already known artificial and natural world;

the cognitive referral to the central role of the relation between meaningful behavior and dynamic interactions with the environment becomes critical to the problem of the origins of cultures.

I think the role of what I call *cultural mediators* can be further studied, also taking advantage of the research on the interplay between cultures and distributed cognition and appropriately stressing the problem of the co-evolution between brains and cultures. The final part of the chapter aims at offering new suggestions related to the analysis of the interplay between cultures and cognition and of some consequences concerning the problem of intercultural communication in light of the role of moral mediators, docility, cyberprivacy, and the problem of isolation of cultures with respect to the effects of ICTs. I think that because of the relationship between docility and culture, further research has to be promoted on the chances that human collectives have to exploit docility and, thus, increase their fitness with respect to the role of intercultural communication. Furthermore, taking advantage of an analogy with research on cyberprivacy and identity, I contend that what I call the principle of isolation of cultures resorts to the protection against interference with the collectives' way of realizing and developing their interests, both in the sense of interests related to their practical objectives or merely intertwined with strands of their identity over time.

REFERENCES

Bardone, E., & Magnani, L. (2006). The Internet as a moral mediator: The quest for democracy. In L. Magnani & R. Dossena (Eds.), *Computing, philosophy, and cognition* (pp. 131-145). London: College Publications.

Barlow, J. P. (1996). *A declaration of the independence of cyberspace.* Retrieved from http://www.eff.org/~barlow/Declaration-Final.html

Bateson, G. (1972). *Steps toward and ecology of mind.* Novato, CA: Chandler.

Bredin, D. (1996). Transforming images: Communication technologies and cultural identity in Nishnawbe-Aski. In D. Howes (Ed.), (pp. 161-177).

Bynum, T. W., & Rogerson, S. (Eds.). (2004). *Computer ethics and professional responsibility.* Malden, MA: Blackwell.

Callon, M. (1994). Four models for the dynamics of science. In S. Jasanoff, G. E. Markle, J. C. Petersen, & T. J. Pinch (Eds.), *Handbook of science and technology studies* (pp. 29-63). Los Angeles: Sage.

Callon, M. (1997). Society in the making: The study of technology as a tool for sociological analysis. In W. E. Bjiker, T. P. Hughes, & T. Pinch (Eds.), *The social construction of technological systems* (pp. 83-106). Cambridge, MA: MIT Press.

Callon, M., & Latour, B. (1992). Don't throw the baby out with the bath school! A reply to Collins and Yearley. In A. Pickering (Ed.), *Science as practice and culture* (pp. 343-368). Chicago: The University of Chicago Press.

Cavalier, R., (2004). Instantiating deliberative democracy. Project PICOLA. In *Proceedings of the European Conference Computing and Philosophy (E-CAP2004_ITALY),* Pavia, Italy.

Clark, A. (2003). *Natural-born cyborgs: Minds, technologies, and the future of human intelligence.* Oxford: Oxford University Press.

Dawkins, R. (1989). *The selfish gene.* Oxford, UK: Oxford University Press.

Dennett, D. (1991). *Consciousness explained.* Boston: Little, Brown, and Company.

Dennett, D. (2003). *Freedom evolves.* New York: Viking.

Donald, M. (1998). Hominid enculturation and cognitive evolution. In C. Renfrew, P. Mellars, & C. Scarre (Eds.), *Cognition and material culture: The archaeology of external symbolic storage* (pp. 7-17). Cambridge, MA: The McDonald Institute for Archaeological Research.

Donald, M. (2001). *A mind so rare: The evolution of human consciousness*. New York: W.W. Norton & Company.

Floridi, L., & Sanders, J. W. (2003). The method of abstraction. In M. Negrotti (Ed.), *Yearbook of the artificial. Nature, culture, and technology: Models in contemporary sciences*. Bern: Peter Lang.

Foucault, M. (1979). *Discipline and punish: The birth of the prison* (A. Sheridan, trans.). New York: Vintage Books.

Geertz, C. (2000). *Available light: Anthropological reflections on philosophical topics*. Princeton, NJ: Princeton University Press.

Hameroff, A. R., Kaszniak, A. W., & Chalmers, D. J. (Eds.). (1999). *Toward a science of consciousness III. The third Tucson discussions and debates*. Cambridge, MA: MIT Press.

Haraway, D. (1991). A cyborg manifesto: Science, technology, and socialist-feminism in the late twentieth century. In D. Haraway (Ed.), *Simians, cyborgs and women: The reinvention of nature* (pp. 149-181). New York: Routledge.

Hongladarom, S. (2005, January 7-9). *The digital divide, epistemology and global justice*. Papers presented at the 2nd Asia-Pacific Computing and Philosophy Conference, Chulalongkorn University, Bangkok, Thailand.

Howes, D. (Ed.). (1996). *Cross-cultural consumption: Global markets, local realities*. London: Routledge.

Hutchins, E. (1995). *Cognition in the wild*. Cambridge, MA: MIT Press.

Johnson, D.G. (1994). *Computer ethics* (2nd ed.). Englewood Cliffs, NJ: Prentice Hall.

Jonsen, A. R., & Toulmin, S. (1988). *The abuse of casuistry: A history of moral reasoning*. Berkeley: University of California Press.

Kaboré, B. (2005). Vie privée, identité et vol d'identité. In *Proceedings of the Technology and Changing Face of Humanity Conference*, Ontario, Canada.

Latour, B. (1987). *Science in action: How to follow scientists and engineers through society*. Cambridge, MA: Harvard University Press.

Latour, B. (1988). *The pasteurization of France*. Cambridge, MA: Harvard University Press.

Law, J. (1993). *Modernity, myth, and materialism*. Oxford: Blackwell.

Lindner, R. (1997). Global logo, local meaning. *Focaal, 30*(31), 193-200.

Magnani, L. (2001a). *Abduction, reason, and science: Processes of discovery and explanation*. New York: Kluwer Academic/Plenum Publishers.

Magnani, L. (2001b). *Philosophy and geometry: Theoretical and historical issues*. Dordrecht: Kluwer Academic.

Magnani, L. (2002). Epistemic mediators and model-based discovery in science. In L. Magnani, & N. J. Nersessian (Eds.), *Model-based reasoning: Scientific discovery, technology, values* (pp. 305-329). New York: Kluwer Academic/Plenum Publishers.

Magnani, L. (2007). *Knowledge as a duty: Morality in a technological world*. Cambridge, UK: Cambridge University Press.

Magnani, L. (2006). Mimetic minds, meaning formation through epistemic mediators and external representations. In A. Loula, R. Gudwin,

& J. Queiroz (Eds.), *Artificial cognition systems.* Hershey, PA: Idea Group Publishing.

Magnani, L. (in press). Semiotic brains and artificial minds: How brains make up material cognitive systems. In R. Gudwin & J. Queiroz (Eds.), *Semiotics and intelligent systems development.* Hershey, PA: Idea Group Publishing.

Magnani, L., & Nersessian, N. J. (Eds.). (2002). *Model-based reasoning: Scientific discovery, technology, values.* New York: Kluwer Academic/ Plenum Publishers.

Mithen, S. (1996). *The prehistory of the mind: A search for the origins of art, religion, and science.* London: Thames and Hudson.

Mithen, S. (1999). Handaxes and ice age carvings: Hard evidence for the evolution of consciousness. In A. R. Hameroff, A. W. Kaszniak, & D. J. Chalmers (Eds.). *Toward a science of consciousness III. The third Tucson discussions and debates* (pp. 281-296). Cambridge, MA: MIT Press.

Moor, J. H. (1985). What is computer ethics? *Metaphilosophy, 16*(4), 266-275.

Moor, J. H. (1997). Towards a theory of privacy in the information age. *Computers and Society, 27,* 27-32.

Moor, J. H., & Bynum, T. W. (Eds.). (2002). *Cyberphilosophy.* Malden, MA: Blackwell.

Moss, J. (2005, January 7-9). *Fixing the digital divide; sustaining or undermining local values?* Papers presented at the the 2nd Asia-Pacific Computing and Philosophy Conference, Chulalongkorn University, Bangkok, Thailand.

Norman, D. A. (1999). *The invisible computer.* Cambridge, MA: The MIT Press.

Peirce, C. S. (1931-1958) (*CP*). *Collected papers* (8 vols.). In C. Hartshorne & P. Weiss (Eds.), (vols. I-VI) and A. W. Burks (Ed.), (vols. VII-VIII). Cambridge, MA: Harvard University Press.

Perkins, D. (2003). *King Arthur's round table: How collaborative conversations create smart organizations.* Chichester: Wiley.

Picard, R. W. (1997). *Affective computing.* Cambridge, MA: MIT Press.

Pickering, A. (1995). *The mangle of practice: Tome, agency, and science.* Chicago: The University of Chicago Press.

Roth, K. (2001). Material culture and intercultural communication. *International Journal of Intercultural Relations, 25,* 563-580.

Secchi, D. (2006). A theory of docile society. Submitted to *Mind and Society.*

Shore, B. (1996). *Culture in mind, cognition and the problem of meaning.* Oxford: Oxford University Press.

Shweder, R. A. (1991). *Thinking through cultures: Expeditions in cultural psychology.* Cambridge, UK: Cambridge University Press.

Simon, H. (1993). Altruism and economics. *The American Economic Review, 83*(2), 156-161.

Sismondo, S. (1993). Some social constructions. *Social Studies of Science, 23,* 515-553.

Sundari, K. (2005, January 7-9). *Internet booths in villages of India.* Papers presented at the 2nd Asia-Pacific Computing and Philosophy Conference (pp.1-28), Chulalongkorn University, Bangkok, Thailand.

Tamura, T. (2005, January 7-9). *Japanese feeling for privacy.* Papers presented at the 2nd Asia-Pacific Computing and Philosophy Conference (pp. 88-93), Chulalongkorn University, Bangkok, Thailand.

Teuteberg, H. J., Neumann, G., & Wierlacher, A. (Eds.). (1997). *Essen und kulturelle identität: Europäische perspektiven.* Berlin: Akademie.

Toulmin, S. (1985). *The inner life: The outer mind.* Worcester, MA: Clark University Press.

Turing, A. M. (1969). Intelligent machinery. In B. Meltzer & D. Michie (Eds.), *Machine intelligence* (Vol. 5, pp. 3-23).

Turing, A. M. (1992). *Collected works of Alan Turing: Mechanical intelligence.* (D. C. Ince, Ed.). Amsterdam: Elsevier.

Valdez, V. J. (2005, January 7-9). *Technology and civil society.* Papers presented at the 2nd Asia-Pacific Computing and Philosophy Conference, Chulalongkorn University.

Warwick, K. (2003). Cyborg morals, cyborg values, cyborg ethics. *Ethics and Information Technology, 5*, 131-137.

Weiser, M. (1991, September). The computer for the 21st century. *Scientific American, 9*, 99-110.

Winner, L. (1993). Upon opening the black box and finding it empty: Social constructivism and the philosophy of technology. *Science Technology and Human Values, 18*(3), 362-378.

ENDNOTES

[1] My enthusiasm echoes well-known 1996s discussions, including Barlow's "A Declaration of the Independence of Cyberspace" (1990), which states, "We will create a civilization of the Mind in Cyberspace," as well as the foundational work of Haraway (1991), even if the concept of disembodiment I will introduce in the following chapter in the perspective of current cognitive research was not present.

[2] I have devoted part of my research to analyzing the role of diagrams in mathematical thinking and geometrical discovery (Magnani, 2001b, 2002).

[3] A survey on new moral problems and ontologies caused by ICTs is given in Bynum and Rogerson (2004), Johnson (1994), Moor (1985, 1997), and Moor and Bynum (2002).

[4] On the relationship between material culture and the evolution of consciousness, see Donald (1998, 2001) and Dennett (2003).

[5] Many related works in the field of so-called cultural psychology address the problem, per se, in a precognitive way—of the role of culture in the development of the mind (Bateson, 1972; Toulmin, 1985; Shore, 1996; Shweder, 1991).

[6] Consciousness arises as "a sort of public spirit among the nerve cells" (Peirce, 1931-1958, vol. 1, p. 354).

[7] I draw the concept of cultural mediator from that of epistemic mediator and of moral mediator that I have respectively introduced in Magnani (2001a, 2007). The cognitive anthropologist Hutchins (1995) already coined the expression *mediating structure* to refer to various external tools that can be built to cognitively help the activity of navigating in modern as well as primitive settings. Any written procedure is a simple example of a cultural mediator with possible various cognitive aims. Language, mental models, mathematical procedures, furniture, buildings, rules of logic, and so forth are all mediating cultural mediators. Some of them, like traffic lights or supermarket layouts, also are endowed with various specific mediating roles, economic, moral, legal, and so forth, and the contexts we arrange for one another's behavior. Of course, cultural mediators are artifacts, institutions, ideas, and various systems of social interaction, usually made existent and effective with the help of hybrid components: laws, habits, buildings, learned emotions, and so forth.

[8] Weiser (1991). On the so-called invisible technologies, see Norman (1999).

[9] A human being may feel that while all people are mortal, one's subscription to the

Internet provider will never die. The life of these small external artificial things tends to overcome our own.

[10] Magnani (2007).

[11] It is evident that already current human brains are provided in various degrees with external natural (e.g., teachers, parents, other human beings, etc.) and artificial cognitive mediators (e.g., books, schools, laptops, Internet access, etc.) because of biological differences and social inequalities. For more information about cognitive delegations to organizations, institutions, and so forth, see Perkins (2003).

[12] This theory has been proposed by Callon, Latour himself, and Law (Callon, 1994, 1997; Callon & Latour, 1992; Latour, 1987, 1988; Law, 1993).

[13] As a form of what Pickering calls disciplinary agency, nonhuman agency also includes conceptual tools and representations—such as scientific theories and models or mathematical formalism. "Scientific culture, then, appears as itself a wild kind of machine built from radical heterogeneous parts, a supercyborg, harnessing material and disciplinary agency in material and human performances, some of which lead out into the world of representation, of fact and theories" (Pickering, 1995, p. 145).

[14] p. 17 and pp. 22-23.

[15] The modification of the concept and feeling of privacy induced by the Internet in young Japanese people is illustrated in Tamura (2005), who depicted the new role in privacy of the Web diaries.

Chapter IV
Culture and Technology:
A Mutual-Shaping Approach

Thomas Herdin
University of Salzburg, Austria

Wolfgang Hofkirchner
University of Salzburg, Austria

Ursula Maier-Rabler
University of Salzburg, Austria

ABSTRACT

The aim of this chapter is to discuss the mutual influence between culture and technology on a broad inter- and transcultural level. Especially, how does information culture shape the meaning of information, communication, and knowledge, and consequently, the design, spread, and usage of ICTs in certain societies? Vice versa, we are interested in the ways in which the spread and usage of ICTs affect the predominating culture. We aim for a model that incorporates cultural as well as technological factors in order to provide a basis for future ICT research that goes beyond both technological determinism and social constructivism. We believe that new technologies indeed can contribute to more justice in the world in terms of access to knowledge and wealth, if sociocultural factors are taken into account more seriously. Current developments in the context of the UN World Summit on the Information Society raise awareness in this direction. At the same time, we are well aware that the loose notion and imprecise definition of the concept of culture allows for the exploitation of the term in empty political and techno-economical policies. Culture degenerates to an indispensable buzzword in the current ICT debate. This chapter is an attempt to introduce the concept of culture into the socioresponsible ICT research on equal terms with technology, economy, and society.

THE RELATIONSHIP BETWEEN CULTURE AND TECHNOLOGY

How can technology be defined? Technology often is considered a means to a particular end, the means being artificially created, not natural, and something that is not directly necessary for the individual or the end user; it serves, rather, to fulfill the need to produce something that is later to be consumed. However, we use the term in a broader sense. We regard technology as being more than just the sum of such artefacts, which are merely the crystallized, concrete manifestations of human behavioral patterns. A method is the *how*, the way in which a goal is reached and which involves the use of means. A means is a medium in that it mediates between the starting point and the desired result, regardless of what sort of action is involved. Thus, one could speak of social technology (e.g., psychotherapy) as a technology and not merely of technology as something used for (material) production in a society. So, technology also includes the know-how involved in the use and application of the artefacts. In short, technology embraces the ways and means of acting in pursuit of a goal (Hofkirchner, 1999).

How can culture be defined? Using the same analogy for technology, it could be understood to be an equally artefact-based concept, which is not a means to an end but rather an end in itself. That is to say, it is not in itself an essential of life, but rather something that represents a human desire (i.e., what makes humans distinct from other living beings). Here, too, there is a notion that culture is not only the result of a process but also this very process as it moves toward the goal; that is to say, culture is a characteristic of goal-oriented actions (i.e., the striving toward goals as well as the goals themselves) (Hofkirchner, 1999). It is this notion of culture that we refer to in this chapter.

Are there imaginable connections between culture and technology? The two ideal-typical extreme positions are well-known, each making a single direction of determination (Hofkirchner, 1999).

The first position can be referred to as technological determinism, which postulates the total, or at least dominating, influence of technology on culture. Technology is supposed to develop more or less on its own, pushing social development along as it goes. This may be interpreted positively or negatively. An uncritical opinion of Marxist origin saw social advancement as an inevitable result of technical achievements, just as the ideology of the bourgeoisie justified the progress of the technically possible as socially desirable. This view is opposed entirely by fundamentalists who hold technological development responsible for the loss of important values in society. Neither philosophy accepts the possibility of technological development being influenced in any way. Both ignore the fact that there would be no such development if multinational corporations and national governments were to stop investing in research and development; if there were no economic, military, or political interests to divert their resources into these areas; and if there were no values, morals, or norms that underlay these economic, military, or political interests. The fact that on a micro-level there are countless thousands of engineers constantly involved in technology design, and that on a macro-level managers and politicians decide which technological options are realized, supports the second theory—social constructivism—that technology is constructed deliberately to be a part of society. According to this view, the interests of those groups that dominate the genesis of technology finally are embodied in the technology, which in itself cannot be neutral. Here again, both a critical and an approving variant may be distinguished. While the one bemoans the inability of existing technology to pursue ethically justified, socially acceptable, and peaceful and environmentally sound objectives, the other sees the existing economic, democratic, and human rights structures as the best guarantee of developing optimal technological options. Both versions neglect the inherent dynamism within technological development.

Do the two theories—technological determinism and social constructivism—together give a realistic view of the relationship between technology and culture? This would mean that two equally matched factors—the technical and the cultural—would not be complete without the other. Furthermore, one also might break away from strict determinism and grant each side a measure of independence, thus denying that one side totally dominates the other. But would we then have a workable proposition to discuss, or would we be reduced to the assumption that one factor partly influences the other but is itself partly influenced by its counterpart? This is a superficial answer. Is it not rather the case that the actions we are talking about, whose dependence on mediating factors we want to stress if we are talking about technology and whose immersion in value judgments we wish to highlight when we are discussing culture, not only have an individual character, but rather, through the availability of technological methods and cultural values on the part of society, acquire a deeply societal nature? The use of technology makes every action no longer unique to any individual person. Technology is based on cooperation, be it in the application of special methods, the implementation of these in specific social areas, their invention and development, or in any situation in which the skills and knowledge of other members of society are required. The same holds true for convictions, value judgments, instructions, standards, behavioral patterns, and the like. These are just as much a part of the context of life of the individual, and they promote certain technological methods but discourage others. Technology makes every technologically mediated action into a socially determined one, and its use is a human characteristic. Technological development is part of cultural development; this means that technology is part of culture, and so their relationship to each other is one of part

and whole. Culture is the all-embracing factor in this context.

In each part-whole relationship, the parts are the necessary preconditions for the emergence of the whole but are not the sufficient condition for the complete determination of the result. The whole arises from the parts but then exerts control over them in the form of downward causation; the parts are no longer independent of each other as separate entities but are dominated by the whole. The relation of part and whole in regard to technology and culture is, therefore, as follows: technology has the meaning, the purpose, and the task of functioning as means and method for solving social problems. Social interests, cultural values, norms, and morals are thus in the origin and manifestation of technology in its invention, diffusion, and application in the entire process of its development, as its reason for existence. This, however, is insufficient to enslave technology completely. Technology is ambivalent; sometimes it appears to resist our intentions by wholly or partly failing to do what is wanted of it, and other times it not only fulfills our expectations but goes on to do other useful tasks that originally had not been anticipated. Technology represents potential for the realization of social goals. These technologically realizable goals may correspond to pre-existing goals within society; the practical attainment of these by technological means, however, may cause them to change, at least slightly. It is, of course, also possible that the intended goals may differ from those that can be reached with technological support. In this case, new technology may be developed in order to meet the requirements, or the requirements may, as it were, be adapted to fit the reality of what is technically possible. Realizable goals, therefore, do not always exist at the start of the process but may be discovered as options made available by technology. Whether society decides to pursue these goals on the grounds that they are possible is no longer a question of technology but rather of social decision making (Hofkirchner, 1994).

To conclude, we consider the relationship of technology and culture to be dialectic. A relationship is usually called *dialectic* if, first, the sides of the relation are opposed to each other; second, both sides depend on each other; and third, they form a relation that is asymmetrical (Hofkirchner, 2004). A part-whole relationship is dialectic since part and whole represents opposites, the whole depends on the parts as well as the parts on the whole, and parts and whole build up a hierarchy in which the different levels cannot be replaced by each other.

Considering this notion of the relationship between technology and culture on a broad and general level, the following section attempts to add further thought in the context of information and communication technologies (ICTs) and culture. The specific meaning of information and communication for different societies, which is predominantly the result of a special culture, determines the meaning and, therefore, the spread and usage of ICTs. Vice versa, ICTs have been developed and will be developed in the future in certain (information and communication) cultures, which leads to the functions and practices of use we are facing when we implement ICTs.

INFORMATION AND COMMUNICATION CULTURES

When referring to information and communication cultures, we address the basic significance of having access to information and knowledge and the practices of communication and cooperation in a specific society. The most important consideration involves the relationship between those who have access to information that has a profound effect on the distribution of power of control over flows of information within society. It is assumed that within societies with a strong hierarchical structure, the flow and dissemination of public information is restricted to just a

few people, while in more liberal societies, there is a far broader basis for direct access to public information. Furthermore, more hierarchically structured societies are less likely to be expected to adapt to the Internet than liberal societies with a flatter hierarchy (Maier-Rabler, 1995, 2002).

The general attitude toward access to information, toward transparency of structures and processes, and toward empowerment and freedom of expression pertaining to a specific society or state is deeply rooted in traditions and practices of social and cultural conditions. The cultural-social framework of a society is formed mainly by the political-social system, by the legislative system, and particularly by the predominating ethic and religious values. As a result of these diverse dimensions, a continuum between the poles of information-friendly vs. information-restrictive cultures emerges (Maier-Rabler & Sutterlütti, 1992; Maier-Rabler, 1995).

Information-friendly societies foster the development of knowledge throughout all groups of a society by providing equal and universal access to all available public information. In information-friendly societies, people have access to public information, freedom of speech is guaranteed to individuals and institutions, and the concept of universal access is understood as the equitable and affordable access to information infrastructure and to information and knowledge essential to collective and individual human development for all citizens. In information-friendly societies, curiosity is encouraged by education systems, and skills for information retrieval are taught rather than just being fed information. Questions count more than answers, and students are encouraged to research instead of memorize given information (Maier-Rabler, 2002).

The political system in information-friendly cultures is likely to be in a form of communicative democracy within a developed system of civil society. Direct democratic participation is a living practice enjoyed by all social groups. The legal system is likely to be an information-rich, case-based system in which access to information is vital for legal practice.

The economic system in an information-friendly environment strongly depends on access to information and its dissemination to shareholders and customers. Wealth and success are highly valued, and information on turnovers, revenues, and profits are publicly available. Information-friendly societies experience a great expansion in their limitations, especially through the new information and communication technologies. At the same time, it has become clear that without a capable citizenship and without capable institutions, unintended and even unwanted consequences take place. What is more, the current crises of the stock markets have been due to access to information that neither has been audited nor controlled. On a political level, we face a threat to well-established forms of representative democratic systems through populist political trends. New ways of direct democratic participation turn into the opposite, if utilized by people who have not had the chance to acquire the needed skills. However, in information-friendly societies, the chances to implement successful programs to provide equal chances for all members of society to acquire capabilities (in the context of ICT) are higher than in information-restrictive societies.

If we turn to information-restrictive societies, however, we see that they are characterized by a strong hierarchical order throughout society, leading to fewer chances for social, economic, and cultural movement. In such environments, people obtain access to relevant public information when needed, whereby the information is predominantly defined by the authorities or other higher-ranking institutions or persons within the respective hierarchical system. In such societies, people are accustomed to information simply being provided and not having to actively retrieve it. This attitude characterizes the relationship between citizens and authorities, customers and businesses, the public and the media, and students

and teacher. The education system in information-restrictive cultures does not encourage curiosity or question-based learning. The "right" answer is the measure of success. What is right and what is wrong again are defined by authorities in the education system. People are not trained to address their environments and to pose questions critically. These answer-oriented societies are an obstacle for the optimal utilization of new information and communication technologies. Digital communication networks such as the Internet work best with a question-oriented approach that leads to a variety of plausible answers in different contexts. Expecting the right and only answer (as people in information-restrictive societies are trained) leads to predictable disappointments and, therefore, less motivation to get involved in new media.

In information-restrictive cultures, the flow of information between authorities and citizens as well as between businesses and customers follows the push principle, whereby authorities and businesses decide which information is being passed on. In such cultures, the Internet is perceived merely as a new and additional (mass) medium to transfer information to a mass audience. Consequently, a huge amount of information and communication capacities of the Internet simply are left unused. As there are not any geographical, national, or cultural borders within digital communication networks, information and applications from information-friendly cultural environments compete with those from information-restrictive cultures on a global stage.

We assume that information-friendly cultures provide a competitive advantage for their members in the global information society.

THE HUMAN-CENTERED AND CULTURALLY SENSITIVE ICT ADOPTION PROCESS

This chapter aims toward a better understanding of ICT adoption processes being dependent

Figure 1. Model of a human-centric and culturally sensitive ICT adoption process

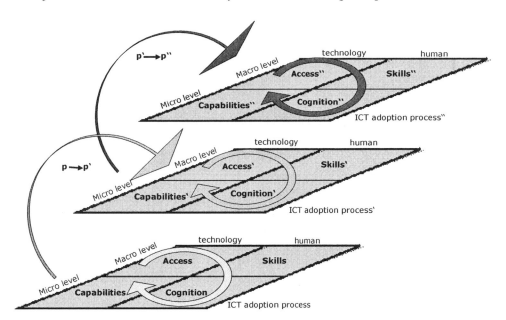

from different information and communication cultures. This process, in most societies, is driven by predominantly techno-economic e-policies that are still striving to overcome the Digital Divide and to foster economic growth by means of ICTs on the macro-level of state policy. This approach has been criticized by various authors in recent years (Preston, 2004; van Dijk, 2005; Warschauer, 2002).

Most critics have in common the need to turn away from techno-deterministic viewpoints to human-centered and culturally sensitive approaches. This also can be characterized as a shift from building infrastructures to creating identities, or from bridging the digital divide to closing the knowledge gap. This means putting the individual in the center of the adoption process of technology; therefore, cognitive, cultural, and social factors must be considered in order to achieve a comprehensive understanding.

Following Mansell (2001) and Garnham (1997), we suggest adopting a rights-based capabilities approach in the ICT adoption process to ensure that people have the possibilities to make informed

decisions about the specific ways in which they want to make use of ICTs. Acquiring those capabilities first demands awareness processes on an individual cognitive level. Only when people understand the individual and social implications of ICTs will they be able to make informed choices about their specific usage patterns. The stage when people shift from technology-driven skills to culturally embedded understanding is the stage that brings the ICT adoption process from the macro-level of state e-policy to the micro-level of the individual—an indispensable precondition to bring about the skilled user.

This process requires socially or culturally motivated individuals on the one hand and governments who want to offer a set of alternative choices for their citizens to allow them to achieve whatever new-media-lifestyle they want on the other.

As we have already mentioned, the development of these adoption processes depends strongly on the predominating information and communication culture in a given society. In information-friendly environments, people have a greater chance of developing capabilities in the context of ICT and, therefore, making informed decisions based on the degree of their involvement with new information and communication technologies.

The following model aims to visualize two dimensions of the ICT adoption process: (1) the stages from access to capabilities and (2) the helical transformation of adoption processes (p) as a result of the mutual relation between technology and culture. Every culturally embedded adoption process leaves the new capable user on an advanced stage that itself is the ground for the access step to technology.

Model of a Human-Centered and Culturally Sensitive ICT Adoption Process

The adoption process, which also can be considered the major stage for targeted ePolicy measures, starts with the problems of technology-determined access. We need access to technology in order to make experiences and to trigger the following steps. Unfortunately, many processes get stuck in the access stage; "If they build it, they will come" could be the motive for access-only strategies. Most countries favor this access-dominated strategy, which is predominantly in the interest of the technology industry and, therefore, an industry policy measurement.

The critique of the access-only strategy led to a human-oriented enhancement of the same strategy. People need to have adequate skills in order to use the accessed technology. At first glance, this could solve the problem—not only provide people with technology but also train them to use it. Similar to the access stage, the skills stage also is geared predominantly to the interest of the technology industry; in this case, the big international or global software monopolists. Acquiring skills means dealing with a given technology. The creative potential of people in the context of technology is not addressed (National Research Council, 2004).

A further step has to be taken in order to involve the individual in the process of adopting new information and communication technologies. People must know why they should make use of ICTs and not only how to use them. On the cognitive level, the awareness of technology in the specific cultural sphere has to be raised. Here, there is a cultural translation of technology. Only when people understand the diverse patterns of different practices of ICT usage will they be able to make the informed choices as preconditions for gaining capabilities. And only the capable user will provide the basis for economic growth and competitiveness for which most countries, regions, and cultures are striving.

The capable user is the point of departure for the next iteration of the ICT adoption process (p'). Capable users have different demands for access to new technology and also represent a different level for skills training. Such qualified users, who differ in terms of cultural and social backgrounds, represent the input into p'', and so forth.

DIGITAL CULTURES

Cultural Shifts: Transculturality

In recent decades, the concept of interculturality has been very popular and influential in regard to the fairly young discipline of intercultural communication (Leeds-Hurwitz, 1998). In this context, communication was understood to be an action taking place between countries that were perceived as self-contained units. In this traditional definition, cultures are seen as types of autonomous islands that are virtually completely closed-off, which Beck (1997) called metaphorically the "container theory of society" (p. 49). But modern societies are very diverse entities. They contain and incorporate many elements of different origins, and the boundaries between foreign and indigenous cultures get blurred and finally become untraceable. Tsagarousianou (2004) suggests that diasporas should not be seen as "given communities, a logical, albeit deterritorialized, extension of an ethnic or national group, but as imagined communities, continuously reconstructed and reinvented" (p. 52). Welsch (1999) developed a new approach of connected cultures, which he called *transculturality*. This approach emerged due to cultures being interconnected and similar lifestyles merging and being assimilated. Cultures cannot be perceived as homogenous units anymore, because they are complex and diverse in themselves. "Cultures today are extremely interconnected and entangled with each other. Lifestyles no longer end at the borders of national cultures, but go beyond these, are found in the same way in other cultures. The way of life for an economist, an academic or a journalist is no longer German or French, but rather European or global in tone" (Welsch, 1999, 197f.).

This also can be observed in the Internet community. People from different countries use a sort of transcultural ideological language in chat rooms and are united by common interests. Even though they come from very different parts of the world, they have more in common with each other than they have with some members of their respective national communities. The mutuality derived from their similar interests prevails over the mutuality derived from nationality.

Enhancing Welsch's (1999) concept of transculturality, we consider that this concept needs a more focused perspective on the permeability between global and local cultures, which means that transculturality allows the individual to switch between different identities according to current needs, feelings, interests, and demands. People want to belong to a certain group and want to be identified as a member of such a group; they do not want to constantly act, think, and live on a global level. The identity of the self cannot exist only on a global level, and therefore, "the search for identity, collective or individual, ascribed or constructed, becomes the fundamental source of social meaning. ... Yet identity is becoming

the main, and sometimes the only, source of meaning in an historical period characterized by widespread destructuring of organizations, delegitimation of institutions, fading away of major social movements, and ephemeral cultural expressions" (Castells, 2001, p. 3).

LINKING CULTURE, KNOWLEDGE, AND ICTS

At this point, we introduce the extended concept of culture, which is intertwined with the concept of knowledge with the aim to discuss the correlation between culture, knowledge, and the role of ICTs. This endeavor eventually should lead to an approach that allows us to connect the complex concept of cultures with its impact on various spheres of our respective lives and, therefore, on our identity. Therefore, the term *digital culture* will be used to describe the model of mutual influence between culture and technology, which we use as a fundamental framework to develop a new understanding of the use of ICTs. This model aims at an understanding of cultural differences in handling information to guarantee a beneficial development of society.

If the concept of transculturality is introduced into the notion of knowledge, there is a rapid increase of global knowledge. ICTs allow direct communication between vast numbers of people with different cultural backgrounds but do not automatically distribute access to knowledge equally. In fact, many citizens cannot gain access to global knowledge or even local knowledge other than to their own knowledge because of their low economic status (digital divide) and their low educational levels (cultural divide). These divides create groups of haves or have-nots, communication-rich or communication-poor, winners or losers in the globalization process. Concerning identities, these divides determine the different opportunities of switching identity levels. However, the more people are capable of

Figure 2.

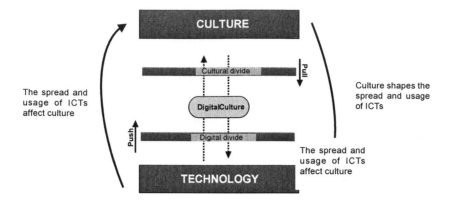

assuming different identities, both on a local and global level, the more they are capable of gaining advantages in the digital culture.

To avoid getting caught in this gap-trap and to guarantee a sort of mutual benefit, we have to find a way to reconcile some aspects of knowledge production and acquirement, which means that global knowledge has to be incorporated locally (pull factor) in order to allow people to benefit from global knowledge on a local level. Also, local knowledge has to be introduced into the cycle of global knowledge production (push factor) in order to make sure that there is an awareness of the existence of this local identity in a global society. Thus, developments in this global society can be influenced with regard to local positions. We face the challenging task of creating a permeable flow of communication that allows for global and local knowledge bases to interact.

COMBINING ICTS AND CULTURE TO A NEW APPROACH

As already mentioned, technology and culture influence each other and are mutually dependent on each other. It is, however, important to discuss the terms *culture* and *technology* and the respective points of view. It is equally important to demon-

strate that culture and technology influence each other by using the term *digital culture*.

Drawing upon these basic insights, we will discuss the dialectic of shaping, diffusion, and usage of ICTs in societies and different cultural knowledge bases along the following dimensions: content, distribution, and context.

DIGITAL CONTENT CULTURE

This indicator refers to the concept of knowledge production or, in other words, how data are converted into knowledge. According to Willke (2004), one has to distinguish between data and knowledge, even though knowledge management often is mistaken for data preparation and data exchange.

In fact, data are nothing but raw material for knowledge, and in the age of ICT, getting ahold of useful data is not difficult. What is difficult, however, is reducing and filtering huge amounts of potentially useful data and converting them into information first by putting them into a broad context that adds relevance to them; knowledge is gained by putting information into a practical context and modifying or creating a practical due to it in order to make the information practically useful (Willke, 2004).

ICTs, like the Internet, can transport and make available huge amounts of data and information. The content to be distributed is taken from this basic range of knowledge. In a metaphorical sense, the Internet can be linked to a sea of information, all of which is useful in principle. Yet, to get ahold of the invaluable essence of relevant information, we have to siphon off all irrelevant information. The focus is on translating data and information into helpful insights that can be used to improve real-life situations by adding practical relevance to the data.

To guarantee the success of knowledge transfer and the adaptation of new knowledge, a transdisciplinary approach, in addition to an interdisciplinary approach, has to be adapted. This means that different scientific approaches are used, but an effort also is made to involve the local community in the process. In that way, one can ensure that the goals are adapted to the local culture, which increases the likelihood of locals accepting them.

There are three main topics that have to be discussed: knowledge management, learning strategies, and educational approaches.

DIGITAL DISTRIBUTION CULTURE

The second dimension illustrates the relationship between the channel that is used for information transport and the dissemination of knowledge—the pull/push strategy.

The first aspect is the communication code: if a message is to be transported, it has to be converted into numbers, text/words, and/or pictures (Willke, 2004). There are limits to the amounts and kinds of information that can be transported in a certain channel. This depends on the type of channel as well as the respective circumstances (e.g., legal, technical, environmental, infrastructural) that, in fact, might influence the usage of the channel.

If we distinguish between explicit and tacit (i.e., structured and unstructured) knowledge, we can see how difficult it is to distribute knowledge. While explicit knowledge (represented in documents, databases, products, and processes) is easy to transfer, tacit knowledge "is more dependent on action, context and personal experience, which makes it difficult to formalize and communicate" (Martin, 2003, p. 44).

The next aspect can be observed in culturally influenced communication rituals. Each and every one of our actions is influenced by culture (i.e., norms, values, beliefs), and by performing these actions repeatedly, we permanently reinforce our cultural understanding. A similar cycle of conditioning can be found in technology. We develop technology by drawing upon our cultural understanding. We then use this technology on a daily basis and, thereby, cause it to impact our identity (reinforcement).

This development can be observed with the personal computer. The term *personal* already indicates that this technology was invented in a very individualistic culture. The more time we spend interacting with computers/technology in this way, the more our patterns of thought and conveying knowledge are assimilated to those used by computers/technology. Our way of thinking becomes more abstract, and knowledge is reduced to mere words and graphics, which lead to future inventions being more abstract as a logical result. The term *digital culture* means that we shape our ICTs and are shaped by them in reverse.

The same applies to the Internet, whose basic technology was developed in the academic-military information culture in California in the late 1950s and early 1960s. This implies a certain practice of converting data into knowledge using the Internet as a practical source for information. In similar information cultures, it is clearer how one can use this kind of data. But people from a different cultural setting who have a different concept of knowledge acquisition might not be

Table 1.

Dimensions	Digital Divide	Cultural Divide	Digital Culture
Content	Data, Information "knowing that ..."	Knowledge "knowing how ..."	Data, Information, Knowledge "knowing why ..."
Distribution	Channels limited to technical possibilities	Inadequacy between text and channel	Sharing and dissemination of knowledge
Context	Limited to technical Connectivity	Skills Realization Application	Inclusion Awareness Capabilities

able to make adequate use of the Internet. They might not be familiar with the work processes dominating the information culture within which the Internet was developed. Therefore, it could lead to difficulties to connect to and make use of the Internet. Besides, the way the Internet is used might not cohere with their cultural behavior.

DIGITAL CONTEXT CULTURE

There are factors that influence culture and technology on a meta-level. The central questions are: What culture do we live in? What culture do we work in? What culture do we act in?

An important indicator is knowledge as a commodity or as a free public good. First, costs are linked to the question of whether knowledge can be circulated freely or whether it should be treated as property (IPR—intellectual property rights; DRM—digital rights management). Second, costs refer to the investment and maintenance of infrastructure (hardware, software, bandwidth), and finally, we have to calculate the costs for educating people to use ICTs successfully and to develop the ability to convert data into knowledge.

Another important indicator deals with power, which can be explained by using the game theory. It seems that most political and economic decisions are based on the zero-sum game theory, which

means that any gain for one player represents an equal loss for the other. We have to face the fact that empowering people also means a loss of power for the powerful to some extent. The powerful create new competitors by empowering other people, societies and/or subcultures. This is not so much about unlimited development as it is about creating a situation of equal opportunities.

Content, distribution, and context are influenced by technology as well as culture. It is not enough to focus only on the digital divide but also on the cultural divide, and by using the concept of digital culture, we can develop a kind of empathy with the goal that we have to create inclusion and development as a central value, if we really want to change from a segregated to an inclusive society.

THE ONE AND THE MANY

In this respect, it is worth discussing the relationship of the one and the many. Due to global challenges that endanger the species as a whole and that must be met by a single set of intelligently coordinated actions, the partitions of humankind are on the brink of forming a unit on a planetary scale, and many cultures are on the brink of forming one culture. The awareness of this required delicate relationship between the one and the many may serve as a normative idea that guides the measures to be taken to advance world society.

The question is how one of the many relates to another one and how the many relate to the oneness that is made up of the manifold. Is the world society to become the common denominator of the various identities? Or is one of the many the only one? Or are the many merely summands of the individual? Or do the many participate in a one that goes beyond them?

The reductionist way of thinking in intercultural discourse is called *universalism*. Cultural universalism reduces the variety of different cultural identities to what they have in common. Identities are homogenized by a sort of melting pot that was named McWorld (Barber, 2001). Modernism (i.e., the pursuit of human rights, democracy, and capitalism based on the same mode of metabolism carried out by the same technology everywhere) is universalistic—shimmering between a claim to liberalism and pompous imperialistic behavior as it is witnessed by its adversaries. In either case, it gets rid of the richness of cultural identities, the many are reduced to a shallow one, and there is no diversity in the unity.

A second strand in intercultural discourse revolves around the way of thinking that overuses projection. It may be called *particularism* or *totalitarianism*. Cultural particularism or totalitarianism extrapolates what separates one cultural identity from the rest and construes an imaginary common. It also leads to homogenization. The melting pot in this case, however, was named Jihad (Barber, 2001), because it is the anti-modern fundamentalism that may be a good example for imposing a certain one out of the many on the rest of them. Here, a culture that is accredited with very specific social relations is raised to the level of the ideal, which is to serve as a model for all other cultures to copy. Thus, a specific form is built up to be the general norm. Inasmuch as it is something particular that is raised in this manner, it concerns particularism.

Inasmuch as it reaches the status of the general norm, it concerns totalitarianism. This results also in unity without diversity.

A third way to conceive intercultural discourse is *relativism*. Cultural relativism rests on the figure of dissociation. By denying any commonality of different cultural identities, it yields fragmentation. The many fall apart. These concepts of multiculturalism and separatism suit postmodern thoughts. Here, each of the many cultures is seen as something with the right to exist and remain free from external interference. Each special case is made into a norm in its own right. Inasmuch as it is one of many that is made into a norm, we may speak of pluralism. Inasmuch as every special case is treated thus, we must, however, speak of indifferentism. Relativism does not claim general validity and does not wish to unify anything or anyone. The postmodernist form leaves differences as they are. World society would simply be diversity without unity.

None of these three options can satisfy. Either the one is regarded as the necessary and sufficient condition for the many, the many are considered necessary and sufficient for the one, or one and many are deemed independent.

Cultural thinking that reconciles the one and the many is achievable only on the basis of an integration and differentiation way of thinking. It integrates the differences of the manifold cultural identities and differentiates the common as well. Welsch (1999) coined the term *transculturalism* and notions of *glocalization* (Robertson, 1992) or *new mestizaje* (a term coined by John Francis Burke in "Reconciling Cultural Diversity With a Democratic Community: Mestizaje as Opposer to the Usual Suspects" in Wieviorka (2003), which are useful in this context.

The process of emergence of a new sustainable world society may be sketched in terms of dialectics. Diversity is not abolished but rather sublated and leads in an evolutionary leap to a unity through diversity, which, in turn, enables and constrains diversity in order to make it diversity in unity, which then builds the new base for unity through diversity. World culture is located on the macro-level; the partitions of world culture that are located on the micro-level take care of the world culture in order to preserve humanity.

CONCLUSION

Starting with a critique of both techno-deterministic and social-constructive approaches toward the relationship between technology and culture, we argue for a dialectical, mutual-shaping approach. Especially in the context of information and communication technologies (ICTs) and society, this dialectical relationship between culture and technology is important. To strive for the capable user, cultural dimensions have to be incorporated into a model that transfers the spread and usage of technology on the one hand and the social shaping of technology on the other. The concept of digital culture represents a framework that embraces the techno-cultural dimensions of content, distribution, and context. This framework provides an applicable instrument that allows addressing the important questions in the context of technology and society, such as equal knowledge distribution, provision of capabilities, and social inclusion.

REFERENCES

Barber, B. (2001). *Jihad vs. McWorld*. New York: Ballantine.

Beck, U. (1997). *Was ist Globalisierung?* Frankfurt am Main: Suhrkamp.

Castells, M. (2001). *The information age: Economy, society and culture: The rise of the network society* (vol. 1). Oxford: Blackwell.

Garnham, N. (1997). Amartya sen's "capabilities" approach to the evaluation of welfare: Its application to communications. *The Public, 4*(4), 25-34.

Hofkirchner, W. (1994). On the philosophy of design and assessment of technology. In S. Katsikides (Ed.), *Informatics, organization and society* (pp. 38-46). Vienna-Munich: Oldenbourg.

Hofkirchner, W. (1999). Does electronic networking entail a new stage of cultural evolution? In P. Fleissner & J. C. Nyiri (Eds.), *Cyberspace: A new battlefield for human interests? Philosophy of culture and the politics of electronic networking* (vol. II) (pp. 3-22). Innsbruck, Áron, Budapest: Studienverlag.

Hofkirchner, W. (2004). Unity through diversity: Dialectics—Systems thinking—Semiotics. In H. Arlt (Ed.), *The unifying aspects of cultures* (CD-ROM). Wien: INST.

Leeds-Hurwitz, W. (1998). Notes in the history of intercultural communication: The foreign service institute and the mandate for intercultural training. In J. N. Martin, T. K. Nakayama, & L. A. Flores (Eds.), *Readings in cultural contexts* (pp. 15-29). Mountain View, CA: Mayfield.

Maier-Rabler, U. (1995). Die neuen Informations—und Kommunikationstechnologien als gesellschaftspolitische Herausforderung. *Informatik Forum, 9*(4), 157-168.

Maier-Rabler, U. (2002). Cultural aspects and digital divide in Europe. *Medien Journal, 3*, 14-32.

Maier-Rabler, U., & Sutterlütti, E. (1992). *Pressestatistik im internationalen Vergleich. Endbericht des Teilprojekts Pressestatistik und Datenkoordination im Rahmen des Forschungsprogramms "Ökonomie und Zukunft der Printmedien"*. Salzburg: Research Report.

Mansell, R. (2001). *New media and the power of networks* [Inaugural Professorial Lecture, Dixon's Chair in New Media and the Internet]. London School of Economics and Political Science. Retrieved February 25, 2006, from www.lse.ac.uk/collections/media@lse/pdf/rmlecture.pdf

Martin, B. (2003). Knowledge management and local government: Some emerging trends. *Asia Pacific Management Review, 8*(1), 43-57.

National Research Council. (2004). *Beyond productivity. Information technology, innovation, and creativity.* Washington, DC: National Academy Press.

Preston, P. (2004). European Union ICT policies: Neglected social and cultural dimensions. In J. Servaes (Ed.), *The European information society* (pp. 33-58). Bristol: Intellect Books.

Robertson, R. (1992). *Globalization.* London: Sage.

Tsagarousianou, R. (2004). Rethinking the concept of diaspora: Mobility, connectivity and communication in a globalised world. *Westminster Papers in Communication and Culture, 1*(1), 52-66.

van Dijk, J. (2005). *The deepening divide. Inequality in the information society.* Thousand Oaks, CA: Sage.

Warschauer, M. (2002, July 1). Reconceptualizing the digital divide. *First Monday, Peer Reviewed Journal on the Internet, 7*(7). Retrieved from http://www.firstmonday.org/issues/issue7_7/warschauer/index.html

Welsch, W. (1999). Transculturality—The puzzling form of cultures today. In M. Featherstone, & S. Lash (Eds.), *Spaces of culture: City, nation, world* (pp.194-213). London: Sage. Retrieved February 2, 2006, from http://www2.uni-jena.de/welsch/Papers/transcultSociety.html

Wieviorka, M. (2003). *Kulturelle differenzen und kollektive identitäten.* Hamburg: Hamburger Edition.

Willke, H. (2004). *Einführung in das systemische wissensmanagement.* Heidelberg: Carl-Auer-Systeme.

Chapter V
Mobile Phone and Autonomy

Theptawee Chokvasin
Suranaree University of Technology, Thailand

ABSTRACT

This chapter is to offer a critical study of what the human living condition would be like in a new era of hi-tech mobilization, especially the condition of self-government or autonomy, and how, in the Thai perspective, the condition affects culture. Habermas' analysis of individuation through socialization and Heidegger's question concerning technology and being are used in the study, and it is revealed that we are now confronted with a new technological condition of positioned individuals in the universe of communication through mobile phones. This situation surely will be realized in a world highly mobilized by the phenomenon of connectedness. This means that we are concerning ourselves with our concrete individuality for our self-expression in that universe. I offer an interpretation that we would hold this kind of individuality to be valuable because of an effect from technological thinking. In addition, comparing this view on individuality with Buddhism, I found that the view offered here is not similar to the Buddhist concept of self as a construction. I offer an argument to show that these concepts are basically different for ethical reasons; while the Buddhist concept still preserves the nobility of the moral agent (Buddhism, after all, is a religion and needs to concern itself with morality), the concrete individuality discussed here is considered only as an instrumental value in a world of hi-tech mobilization.

PROBLEM AND SIGNIFICANCE

Does the formulation of autonomy come from inside or outside an individual? From the investigation in the theory of subjectivity comes Habermas' individuation through socialization; one can achieve greater autonomy when he or she is engaged in a process of social integration to become socialized individuals (Habermas, 1992). His approach is sketched out in an intersubjective understanding that emerges from communicative action when individuals enter a public sphere to share their volition or opinion in order to make a reasoned agreement that later becomes a so-called universal law (Habermas, 1990). It is interpreted that, while Kantian pure reason inside us is the source of autonomy (as interpreted in Guyer, 2003), Habermas' theory of communication sheds light on the question by suggesting that an outer source, the process of socialization by communication, is the case.

If we accept for the sake of argument that Habermas' theory of communication is suitable to explain autonomy, one question still remains, particularly in our time of modernity: Can the same explanation be applied simultaneously to communication on mobile phones, especially the hi-tech ones? Habermas' theory primarily aims at our communication when we are face-to-face with those with whom we are communicating, but we did not see how a situation will be realized when the communication occurs between a distance, not a face-to-face one. The term *hi-tech mobile phones* that I used here means a kind of cellular phone that can be a credit card, Internet connection, e-mail port, voicemail junction, and so forth, according to the usage of Myerson (2001). We may imagine that it will be like a pocket personal computer. This concept of a hi-tech mobile phone somehow would be realized in the future. It sticks with its owner everywhere he or she goes, even in water (if waterproof and not easily broken). However, its dominant characteristic is that it is an important item of personal belongings. Its owner is the only one to hold and use it. If we were to routinely share the mobile phone with another person, there would be no difference at all between it and a public telephone or a house telephone. Therefore, a real mobile phone has a characteristic of being able to identify its owner in order for it to become the most efficient way to communicate with the one with whom we are trying to connect in such a way that is not possible when one receives (or sends) a call from (to) an unexpected person. Certainly, the communication on mobile phones is not a face-to-face one; we are not in a position of being body-to-body with him or her with whom we are talking. Sometime in the future, there might be a great development in mobile phone technology so we can see faces on the screens of mobile phones, but still, we normally do not consider this a face-to-face communication.

My topic, "Mobile Phone and Autonomy," may lead someone to think that the mobile phone itself becomes a thing that keeps us always in control. It sticks with us all the time; we have to use it in our daily lives, and we find it so indispensable that we will never reject it. Therefore, it is a channel through which another person can reach us directly and control us so that we behave according to the rules of social conduct. We may be afraid of being monitored by an online e-policeman through the channel of our mobile phone, and that feeling would prevent us from doing something illegal. In that kind of social management, everywhere we went surely would be known by the police, so if we did something against the rules, we could be abruptly caught, or we could be tracked down by the system in our mobile phone. Or we would be shocked by a dangerous flow of electricity caused by a police officer through the battery of the mobile phone to prevent us from escaping the scene. However, even though it seems that those situations might be possible in the near future or that someone might want to say that a side effect of using a personal mobile phone is a utopian society in which people dare not commit a crime, I do not have any intention in this chapter to talk about these surveillance roles of the mobile phone. As the highest status of moral development, autonomy or self rule of a moral agent is not explained as fear of being punished by the law. Autonomy is understood as a concept of self-expression as an agent who has his or her own freedom and intention to do according to his or her volition for his or her end for himself or herself. Moreover, the concept of autonomy always goes along with the concept of rationality rather than with emotion or any stimulus that does not stem from pure reason. I consider the concept of autonomy only in a dimension that involves rationality. It is possible that in the mobilization era, people will be aware of being monitored and controlled, and they will have to conduct themselves strictly according to the law and social rules, but I think that this consequence is only the tip of the iceberg. There seems to be a hidden and more important phenomenon.

OBJECTIVES

In this chapter, I would like to accomplish two things. First, I would like to study how hi-tech mobile phones affect our self-governance (autonomy), depending largely on Habermas' and Heidegger's theories of communication. Second, I analyze whether the mentioned theories lead one to a conclusion that the mobile phone is strengthening one of the crucial aspects of autonomy: our self-responsibility or self-positioning in the universe (of communication).

WHAT WILL YOU BECOME WHEN YOU ARE IN COMMUNICATION? BECOME CONNECTED

Mobile phones make us closer. How should we understand the meaning of this sentence, especially its deep meaning lying at the heart of communicative acts on mobile phone? One may say that we are connected with one another, and we ourselves want to make that connection. Mobile phones are only tools that obliterate any distance between us and those with whom we want to communicate. Anyway, if we look at this phenomenon carefully and in a very different way, we may encounter something striking. Is it the case that the phenomenon of communication itself is using mobile phones as tools to tie our interlocutor and us in the line of communication? The communication cannot exist without us and the one with whom we are talking, and certainly without the tool functioning as a medium; therefore, it needs all of these factors in order to exist. This kind of technology really brings us closer.

Receiving a call from someone or, in other words, being connected can be considered a phenomenon that occurs. A question then arises: What is a characteristic of this phenomenon? Following Heidegger's (1977) phenomenological assumption that we should begin to answer from the first thing on our minds after a question is

asked, perhaps the question could be answered that the most distinct characteristic of communication is connection. Only when at least two units of communication (the speaker and the receiver) are connected (i.e., related in some context of discourse) is the communication accomplished. If the communication analysis of Habermas is correct, it may be said that the relationship is the source of our own self-understanding as a unit in the accomplished communication. But Heidegger may have something more to say; that is, self-understanding is a phenomenon that already presumes some ontological status of the one who understands his or her own being in that sphere. This entity who understands his or her own being and can take being as an issue is what Heidegger calls Dasein ("being there"). To take being as an issue is a Heideggerian term that refers to Dasein's unique ability to conceive the *being of beings*; in other words, to have a preontological understanding of beings. Because this self-understanding has its source from communication, it means that the self becomes known as being there in that connection through communication. The self is not lying somewhere outside or beyond that connection in order for it to enter inside that sphere of connection with the other self. He or she learns of the being of himself or herself only when he or she is connected in the sphere of communication with his or her interlocutor (even when his or her interlocutor is himself or herself). I would call this phenomenon that occurs in communication *connectedness*. Connectedness means that that a person understands his or her own self or his or her own existence through the connection with the other person in the sphere of accomplished communication. Accomplished communication means any talks about any thing that the speaker and his or her interlocutor have a consensus in understanding. Therefore, it may be considered that this meaning of communication is rather close to what Habermas called *meaning* and *communicative rationality* that constitute a mutual understanding between the speaker and the interlocutor (Habermas, 1979). Consequently, from a successful communication through which we are connected to the other person in conversation, the sphere of communication is where we infer our own existence from that person's response in a communicative action (we listen to him or her, or he or she hears us). Communication on telephone brings people near, even though there is a long distance between their physical bodies, and especially on mobile phones, we could say that there is always nearness between them.

What is this nearness, anyway? I would like to offer an investigation of the meaning by comparing communication on mobile phones with other forms of communication. Imagine a case in which we want to talk to a prime minister; it is possible that we have at least some chance of having a conversation with him or her directly. Nevertheless, the possibility is not so high, because we might be obstructed by the prime minister's staff. The next day, we write a letter of inquiry and send it by e-mail; however, it is possible that the answer we receive back is not directly from the prime minister but from an assistant. Even when we try to connect to the prime minister on a workplace telephone line and ask to talk to him or her directly, we could be obstructed again by an assistant, or an assistant might persuade us that we should leave our message with him or her or use him or her as a medium to talk to the prime minister (which means that the prime minister actually was sitting nearby but did not want to accept the line directly, so we actually receive the prime minister's answer but not directly). However, the situation will be totally different if we have a communication with the prime minister on a mobile phone. If our call is accepted, we certainly will be sure that the one who accepts the call is the prime minister (in the case that a personal mobile phone is allowed to be used only by its owner). If that call is outgoing from our own mobile phone, then the prime minister also will know who wants to talk to him or her. In any case, whatever answer the prime minister

is telling us via the connection on a mobile phone is not an interesting characteristic to investigate here, because I find two more interesting characteristics to consider; namely, that the mobile phone is a source of constructing a sphere in which a real individual meets a real individual, and it is a hi-tech device to guarantee the connectedness between those individuals. In what follows, I will explain why these two characteristics are the two aspects that answer what nearness is.

Based on Habermas' critique of communicative rationality that can be found in a successful communication, I infer that there also may be some kind of rationality in a communication on a mobile phone. If this is the case, communication on a mobile phone will be a source of the smallest sphere in which rationality can be found. That is because this type of communication typically requires only one speaker and one hearer on the line. They are being connected; in other words, getting near each other. Being near, which occurs in that type of communication, can be understood clearly from our experience using a mobile phone. We experience more convenience reaching the one with whom we are trying to connect when using a mobile phone rather than when using nonmobile devices. This phenomenon of being near could be called the phenomenon in which two real individuals can talk to each other without being intruded by a third party and without a medium messenger. The situation in which we can talk directly to a prime minister, as mentioned previously, is of this type—a real individual encounters a real individual. So I am inclined to say that this situation always occurs when people are connected by their mobile phones, but the possibility would be lessened if the communication were not via a mobile device. Mobile phones make human beings get closer as two real individuals in connection with each other. From here, I have some further questions: Why is this communication technology aimed at allowing this phenomenon to reveal itself? What is the value of this phenomenon? In other words, why is a real individual so necessary to develop from the hi-tech tool of communication? I will elaborate my argument further in the next section to show that, in the mobilization era, an instrumental value of the individuality is indispensable. Communication technology needs it for its own best efficiency.

Imagine two people—Mr. Black and Mr. Jones. Black has owed Jones a sum of money for a long period of time, and today, Jones needs his money back. Jones tries to find Black by visiting him at his company to have a face-to-face communication about the debt. It is possible that Black can see from afar that Jones is coming. Black goes straight to a doorway of a fire exit and hides himself behind the door, peeping through a little space between the door and the wall to see what Jones is going to do. Jones cannot see that his cunning debtor has run away, but could he be sure that Black did not want to see him and already escaped? It does not seem so. Could he be sure to believe in Black as before and console himself that this is because Black is not at work today? Not either. From this event, I conclude that between Black and Jones there is no connection. Moreover, there is no connectedness either, because Jones cannot be certain to infer any meaning or message from that disconnection.

Two hours later, Jones wonders whether Black is at his house, so he dials Black's house phone. His call is not received at all. Again, Jones cannot be certain to infer that this is because Black is not there. Black might guess correctly that the call was from Jones and did not want to receive it. Jones cannot be certain that Black tries to evade talking with him about the debt, because it could be the case that Black was then actually not at his house. From this event, I again conclude that there is no connection and connectedness, because Jones cannot be sure to infer any meaning from that disconnection.

However, would all these problems still happen in the case of communication on a mobile phone? If Jones uses his mobile phone to connect with Black's and finds that his call is not accepted at all, there is almost a zero probability that Jones would infer another meaning except that Black is trying to avoid meeting him or does not pay attention to Jones' needs. If a great development of mobile phone technology makes it so convenient that we could accept every call at any time and any place, except when we are dead, this would mean that when we live in this world, we are always in connectedness with other people in the sphere of communication. In the latter case between Black and Jones, even though there is no connection because of Black's not receiving the call, there already is connectedness. Jones can infer that Black pays no heed to him from the very act of Black's not receiving the call. There is connectedness without successful connection, but not without meaning, so we may conclude that this time there is an accomplished communication. From this investigation, I conclude that a mobile phone brings us near, because it always guarantees connectedness, and it is the most suitable channel for two individuals to have an immediately direct conversation. Even through the act of not receiving our calls, we can at least infer that our expected recipient is loath to do so. In a face-to-face communication or on a nonmobile phone, there is noticeably no guarantee of connectedness, but in mobile phone communication, there is a guarantee that none of the real individuals can ever escape from connectedness.

INDIVIDUATION, AUTONOMY, AND RATIONALITY

The next questions are: Why does this modern technology of communication need to control an individual to be present in the sphere of communicative world? Why is there such a strong need for such exact identification of individuals? Communication on the mobile phone is aimed so much at the individual being that it seems to be itself a cause of that individuation. But could we then conclude that the mobile phone is a tool of individuation? Some might not say so, because the mobile phone is considered only as a tool of convenient communication that was invented by human beings. We have already individuated a person as an individual being long before the tool was invented, so it does not seem to make any sense to argue that individuals are individuated through mobile phones. Or could we say that the mobile phone is a tool of identification? Some might not agree either, because it would be more reasonable to explain that the mobile phone is only a tool that stores personal information, and to do so, we must identify in the first place which mobile phone is our own in order to keep our information in it. In sum, the process of individuation is not causally relevant to the invention of mobile phones, whether as cause or effect. It is only for the sake of our convenience that direct communication is done best via a mobile phone, and the process of individuation is only a necessary condition for that.

I find, however, that the previous summary is too big a leap to conclusion. The claim underlying that summary is that a communication device is only a tool for a more convenient orientation. There are some questions that those who argue along this line did not ask; for example, if a mobile phone is only a tool, then why is this technology aimed so much at the individuality of its owner, and why does it have a role of controlling its owner to be always within the sphere of connectedness, as shown in the previous analysis?

I would like to offer an argument to show that the role of technological thinking is to control the individual person as a positioned individual in the communicative sphere. This is all because of our need for efficiency in communication. I do not say that the communication technology is about to have an influence on us without our consent to it. This is not a matter of willing to be or not willing to be in that influence. It is a matter of necessity of the best communicative efficiency that we have to be individuated from each other in order to be in an exact position of receiving or sending a call.

If we consider its efficiency as a desired end of communication, then mobile phone technology is here to help us reach that end. Everything that is involved in bringing about that efficiency is provided by a systematized technology of the mobile phone, and all of them are considered only in terms of resource preserving for the technology, or, in the Heideggerian term, a standing-reserve. A human being in the mobilization era would rather be revealed as a unit provided for technological efficiency. The best technology of communication reveals its own essence--Enframing, as Heidegger (1977) called it. If this is true, I am inclined to say that human beings are the resource of it; not the concept of a human being as a living person or an agent capable of intentional action, but a human being as revealed in its essence, which is its being there as a positioned individual. In other words, in the best communication technology, the position in a communicative sphere of human beings is resource-preserving for its own efficiency. To consider the mobile phone technology only as tool is not a way to see its underlying essence, because there is another aspect of it that is not merely a tool. Ironically, we ourselves are considered vital tools playing our exact individual roles in that world of the most efficient communication.

Again, the mobile phone always guarantees that the connectedness of meaning occurred in communication or, at least, some meaning that could be inferred from it. No, we are not influenced to receive any calls, especially those to which we are loath to do so. We are not influenced to receive any connection via our hi-tech mobile phone with a reason of efficiency in our communication with each other. But are we always in connectedness? In other words, are we always "there" to be inferred some meaning from this communicative sphere? The answer is yes. Surely, in our common sense, we feel that we are not compelled to do the connection, but it is necessary for us to be in the connectedness.

From here, I am in a position to offer a critique of mobile phone technology and its impact on our autonomy or our self-directing. I have presented an argument purporting to show that the technology is really there to make our load much lighter, even in our nearest task of self-directing. Then what is the significance of this situation that has an impact on autonomy at all? As I have said, if, in the new age of modern technology, human beings are necessarily tied to the connectedness, then a question arises: Can we consider that human beings have freedom to choose their own lives as they prefer? If we are unavoidably tied to the sphere of communication in which everyone is in connectedness, how are we to speak of our freedom? Here, I will use a concept of autonomy from Habermas to clarify this problem. An interpretation of the Habermasian concept of autonomy by Warren (1995) is that Habermas considers autonomy a normative ideal with six implications, shown in Habermas' works. These are as follows:

- Self-identity (one can locate oneself in terms of biographical projections)
- Capacities of agencies and origination
- Capacity of having freedom (one can distance oneself from social context)
- Capacity for critical judgment (in Habermas, it means an individual's capacity to participate in communication with reason)
- Capacity of reciprocal recognitions of the identities of speaking subjects
- Some measure of responsibility (by giving reasons for behaviors to others)

For the sake of argument, I consider here that all of these implications are interwined with the concept of freedom of choosing the best lifestyle for the individual who lives that life of his or her own. Nevertheless, the freedom is developed from a communicative rationality when one participates in the social sphere to share his or her own judgment of the lifestyle, defend its validity claims in the argumentation, and, of course, be morally responsible for his or her own self conduct. But

wait. Can this kind of freedom be realized in a sphere of hi-tech mobilization age? If human beings are about to comport themselves in a mobilization way of life that involves one-dimensional thinking of the efficiency of technology, then how can we have that freedom?

This question is explained in a book by Myerson (2001), *Heidegger, Habermas and the Mobile Phone*. Myerson suggests that Habermas' theory will not be so smooth when applied to the communication in the mobilization world. In that world, the idea of communication is changed dramatically. What is being communicated—message or meaning? asked Myerson. He says that communication on a mobile phone is transformed into a one-dimensional version of meaning, which is the message. Anyway, what Habermas needs for his theory to work well is that people should be in a suitable circumstance to provide reasons for their expressions; therefore the message version of communication is not a good one in Habermas' view (Myerson, 2001). The result is that a mobilization world is not a sphere in which the source of rationality can reside. However, rationality is one of the crucial aspects of autonomy. Then how can autonomy be developed, if a mobilization world is not a place for rationality at all? Unfortunately, Myerson has no answer for this, but it is one that I am trying to figure out. Is autonomy possible in that world? If it is, then what would it be like? Would autonomy in this case be in a similar formulation, as in Habermas or Kant? I am inclined to say no.

How can Habermas compromise the thesis that autonomy is developed from social participation with communicative rationality in a public sphere with my thesis that something, which can be called self-positioning, is developed from connectedness in mobile phone communication? If the compromise does not work, Habermas may have to accept that his theory cannot explain some aspects of communication. In a public sphere, face-to-face communication can be represented fully in processes of engaging in reasoning or in a critical examination of self and others, and one can be recognized as an individual from the processes. But one can be recognized as an individual via mobile phone communication, for I showed that communication on the mobile phone is where a real individual meets a real individual and where there is no other but only those individuals connecting on the line. When the processes come to terms with the development of autonomy, must we limit the autonomy development only to the extent of face-to-face communications in a public sphere? Or do we have to say that we are seeing a new consequence from this hi-tech communication that has an impact on autonomy development? What we are seeing is that the mobile phone is bringing about a new phenomenon of sphere revealing, the smallest sphere in which communicative rationality can be developed. This sphere is where a real individual meets another real individual to make an intelligible communication on the line. However, what kind of rationality is there on that sphere? The individuals are able to have intelligible communication with each other on their mobile phones, as they do when they participate in a face-to-face communication. So must there be some kind of rationality in that sphere? I would venture to say yes.

We know that the mobile phone is the best way to communicate efficiently. This new technology gradually is necessitating itself within our modern age. People can have a conversation about politics, for example, face-to-face with one another with communicative rationality. They also can talk about the same political story via mobile phones with communicative rationality. But there surely is something more in this mobile phone talking. This is because we only can make the communication best via mobile phones to feel like being together when we really are some distance from each other. The mobile phone proves itself to be the only way to guarantee efficiency in communication; therefore, it has its own process of rationalization of itself. The process is that it guarantees that the one with whom we are to connect is exactly the

one with whom we want to connect, and that connection always transmits some significance, even when the connection is rejected or that it always guarantees the connectedness. What this means is that, despite the fact that we are in conversation with our partners and epitomize communicative rationality when we reach understanding with each other, we also are guaranteed by the mobile phone that our interlocutor is the individual exactly and always positioned in a communicative sphere in order for us to infer some meaning from our connection, and vice versa from the other person to us. In this system, we cannot escape from connectedness, because we already are positioned in the sphere. The technological system always sees us as an individual unit that is always available as a mechanic of the most efficient communication. As Habermas has said about communication in a social sphere, that we could infer our individuality as well as others' from the sphere, our being individual means very much to the technological systematizing that reveals itself very clearly in communication technology.

SELF-EXTENSION AND SELF-EXPRESSION: CONCRETE VERSION OF AUTONOMY THROUGH THE MOBILE PHONE

In the other aspect of the mobile phone, we know that it is a tool for communication. It is a technological tool that enhances our capacity to talk and hear; in other words, communication. This nature of the mobile phone is one of the technological characteristics—self-extension. This characteristic of selfhood is a crucial aspect of autonomy; it is our self-governance or self-rules in accord with our social being with others (Berofsky, 2003). From this, I have a question: What is it about our autonomy when our selves are not restricted to our bodies, minds, or living conditions? Imagine a mobilization world in which there is a need for the best efficiency in communication; every single person must have a personal mobile phone. Inevitably, our mobile phone will be with us everywhere and every time when we are not in a face-to-face communication in order for us to remain in this social universe of communication. This is a universe in which the mobile phone is indispensable. Each of us is connected to our own mobile phone; it is like one of our organs. Surely, the concept of autonomy is involved with self-identity; therefore, questions arise. What will become of autonomy when self-identity is enhanced that way? Will the duty of our self-governance be left to the mobile phone because we begin to feel being monitored by anyone in this universe of communication who also knows where we are by tracking the position of the phone? If the mobile phone is highlighting this way of our self-governance, what will be the kind of autonomy from the influence of communication in this modernity? Is that still a so-called freedom? These are the other questions I try to answer.

I believe that a critique of technology by Heidegger (1977), his superb writing of *Being and Time* (1962), and a reinterpretation from Habermas' theory could provide an interesting answer. I do not agree with Myerson that Habermas' theory does not provide at all a plausible account for communication on mobile phones. If this relation of our being and the mobile phone is an inconvertible one, this means that the phone contains a technological essence in the Heideggerian sense—Enframing. I already have shown why I am inclined to think that the essence will rationalize the necessity of itself. If this is the case, some aspect of autonomy surely will be revealed, though not one that Habermas expects as a normative ideal or as freedom. From here, I offer the last argument developed from my own terminology: the abstract and the concrete version of autonomy and their difference in an ethical aspect of human nobility. I will show that the old concept of autonomy found in philosophers or in

Buddhist culture is an abstract one and preserves human nobility. In contrast, the new concept of autonomy derived from a reflection of mobile phone technology is a concrete one that lessens human nobility and values the positioned individuality as indispensable in a control for technological systematization.

We may imagine people in the mobilization era having their own mobile phones. When they are in communication with each other, they become connected. Are they only connected to their interlocutor? No. It is also that sphere of communication with which they are connected. Besides communication with a friend, the speaker also communicates with the world. There is also an activity of reporting to the world that he or she is there in the sphere in which he or she and the friend intersubjectively guarantee each other as being in the world. This means that, at least, there is knowledge of their existence as unique and irreplaceable individuals in that sphere. Anyway, are our friends initiating themselves to have this knowledge as individual being by themselves? No. Human beings cannot conceive themselves as individuals solely standing without the world. But the answer is the communication technology—the mobile phone. It constitutes a way of being individuals as valuable for the most efficient characteristic in communication technology. It is valuable because anyone in the mobilization era must preserve it for himself or herself in order to continue one's own way of being in the sphere. From here, I have an interpretation developed from Heidegger's concept of the two interdependent ontological statuses of entities: presence-at-hand and readiness-to-hand (Heidegger, 1962). The characteristic I would like to interpret from Heidegger is not about the theoretical and practical aspects of entities like those that other philosophers have done (Ihde, 1979) but is about the ontological characteristic of readiness-to-hand as unobtrusiveness (Dreyfus, 1991). Heidegger says that a hammer is always at work as the most efficient tool, if and only if it is an entity as or working as a hammer without our awareness that it is in the hand. But if it is broken, we have to look carefully at what was wrong with it. Nevertheless, when we hold it in our hand and conceive it as a hammer, we do not call it a hammer merely because we want to. Heidegger points out that because it is in a context of being an equipment for a carpenter that we conceive it as one of necessary tools in that context. A hammer has it own status as an individual entity, if and only if it is in a broader context than itself with the other tools. Moreover, the context itself never reveals itself to us; it is always unobtrusive, but it is where the hammer is conceived as an entity. In Harman (2002), the readiness-to-hand is called *tool-being*, because it is interpreted in his work that every aspect in Heidegger's work is about theory of objects, which are tool-beings. I use that interpretation for my purpose here to offer an argument that the individuality of an individual person is considered valuable in the context of the best communication when two persons do not have a face-to-face communication. Consequently, the two persons can claim that they are individuals connecting on the line, because the hi-tech communication creates a context for that communication to be possible. The exact positions of the two persons are only tools for the efficiency of communication, and the individuality is a valuable characteristic derived from the context. The value I mention here is a kind of instrumental value, the value that human beings would have for the era of hi-tech mobilization as tool-beings.

If this speculation turns out to be true, then in the new era of hi-tech mobilization, each of us is always seen as an individual unit in the context of efficient communication. The individuality is valued for every unit; therefore, we must be responsible to preserve our own individuality. (Always keep your mobile phone with you and never let anyone use yours). This positioned individual is considered concrete, because he or she always reports himself or herself to the sphere of communication. Furthermore, in terms of responsibility, individuals have to preserve the very individuality of themselves, I have to conclude that there also is a crucial aspect of autonomy in that activity. This is concrete autonomy. It means that when everyone has their own mobile phone and are positioned individuals in the sphere of communication, then at least one obligation they have is to promise to preserve their own positions in the sphere. This kind of promise is not merely some kind of thinking supported by pure reason in a person's mind without being seen by anyone else outside. The very act of position preserving when people are connected on mobile phones is the right act to show that this obligation is kept and not violated.

Therefore, this concrete version of autonomy can be defined as a self-responsibility in the mobilization era. Your position must be revealed in the sphere, and you must keep it for your own sake of living. The old version of autonomy is aimed at self-government and self-expression in a moral understanding of agency. We can find this concept in Kant; autonomy is a self-government according to the universal laws derived from pure reason. We accept those universal laws and comport ourselves to them, because they are from our own pure reason. This concept also can be found in Habermas. Nevertheless, universal laws are not derived from pure reason but from communicative rationality, according to Habermas. We have to comport ourselves to them, because they are from the consensus we had with the other people who are involved in a public sphere making a reasonable agreement. However, this version of autonomy cannot be seen by anyone outside. We just believe in each other that we have a promise to keep according to what agreement we have. This is not a version of autonomy that we can see from outside a self-responsibility of a moral agent except when his or her behavior is expressed. I call this old version of autonomy *abstract* because of the reason I mention. Everybody who came out of the public sphere is credited as a citizen in a political system and knows well how to behave according to the agreement he or she made. To violate the agreement means that he or she is no longer credited as a citizen; therefore, in this version of autonomy, what it means is that the moral agent is preserving, in my word, his or her own status of nobility. He or she can choose his or her own style of living, as long as that choice of living is not against the agreement. His or her freedom also is derived from the public sphere.

Surprisingly, besides the notion of self-government, the concept of autonomy in many philosophies is involved with the notion of human nobility. Even in Thai culture, which derives the concept of autonomy mainly from Buddhism, to talk about autonomy consists of considering how someone comports himself or herself to the right course of living. In Phra Dhammapitaka (1995), there is a concept of *Attasammapanidhi*, which means the characteristic of a person who can set himself or herself on the right course, in the right direction of self-guidance or perfect self-adjustment. This moral characteristic is among the 38 highest blessings (Mangala, 38). Also, in a set of seven qualities of a good man (Sappurisa-dhamma, 7), there is a characteristic, *Atthaññuta,* which means to know the meaning and to know the purpose and the consequence of *dhamma* (Phra Dhammapitaka, 1995). From those characteristics, we have to understand more of a crucial aspect of the Buddhist concept of the self. The doctrine of *anatta* is the crucial doctrine, which encourages the Buddhist practitioner to detach himself or herself from clinging to his or her own individual self. In reality, the self has no existence of its own, because it is a construction from many causes and conditions. When those causes and conditions cannot engage with one another, the self can persist no more. So, to understand what the Buddhist teachings are telling us about self-adjustment or self-government is not to understand in such a way that those characteristics belong to a self or that there is a persistent person who acts as their bearer; it is to understand the matter in such a

way that those characteristics are occurrences in a moment of conceiving by a person's mind (or *citta*). Autonomy, in Buddhist concept, is some noble characteristic that occurs with a mind that conceives *dhamma*. It is reflected in those noble persons who can adjust themselves to the right course of living. In order for other people to know that someone has autonomy, they also must be in that right course of living. Therefore, from my previous definition, I have to conclude that the version of autonomy in Buddhist concept is an abstract version involved with nobility of the mind. It can be conceived only in the minds of those who know the *dhamma*, or the Buddhist teachings, not a characteristic that we can see from outside of them.

Moreover, there also is a kind of freedom in the Buddhist concept of autonomy. In Phra Dammapitaka (1999), there is a notion of *Attanovatti*, which means the freedom of the mind that conceives the *dhamma* of three characteristics of existence: impermanence (*Anitya*), suffering (*Duhkha*) and not-self (*Anatta*). The mind of those who thoroughly understand the teaching will never cling to the impermanence of existence. This freedom (*Attanovatti*) of mind will guarantee that the person autonomously will never commit any immoral act. But if anyone who is still clinging to the existence of, say, wealth or social reputation, which actually are impermanent, he or she will never have that freedom, because his or her mind is still tied to those illusions, and he or she still has a chance of doing something immoral.

In sum, the Buddhist concept of autonomy has something involved with a nobility status of a person. We may have to conclude that the old concept of autonomy is an abstract version and that we can find it in Kantian or Habermasian philosophies; namely, that nobility of person is still preserved in a political status as well as in Buddhist philosophy—that nobility of person can be found in the *dhamma*, or the teachings. Nevertheless, all of these philosophies conceive autonomy with a notion of freedom. Finally, what is left to say about these versions of abstract autonomy when one compares them with the concrete version that we have obtained from our reflective investigation of the mobile phone and connectedness? I will offer only a description of a near future that is predicted to occur as an answer to the question.

CONCLUSION

Based on the arguments I have offered so far, I am inclined to conclude that the mobile phone has its own way of developing autonomy in people, because it has its own rationalization in a technological system. The version of autonomy derived from it is a new way of self-expression in the sphere of communication. This is the case, because the self-identity of the mobile phone's owner is extended to the tool of communication; therefore, the position of any individual owner always is expressed by the guarantee of connectedness. Moreover, as the very being of a positioned individual is so valuable in the sphere in which people are responsible to preserve it, any individual person is considered only an instrument in the most efficient mobilization system. Coyne (1995) points out that this is a matter of our being controlled by hi-tech communication, which reveals the clearest essence of technology that Heidegger calls Enframing. However, here, I have more to say about it, for it is a new concept of autonomy that still involves freedom; this technology does not exclude all aspects of freedom. We still feel free to receive or not to receive connections from other people. But in the aspect of our status in the mobilization era, are we really free to escape from being a positioned individual? No. Are we free to leave the obligation of preserving our own individuality that guarantees the efficiency of hi-tech communication? No. It is just that in this time of modernity, we have a new way of thinking how it is to be an individual person. In the old concepts, we have political or ethical ways of

thinking about it, and we have preserved human nobility in those ways of thinking. We find our freedom from ethical characteristics of life. In contrast, the new concept from the mobile phone replaces the old value with a new one: the instrumental value of individuality. In the mobilization era, people with their own mobile phones are the best mechanics that guarantee the best efficiency in the communication system.

People in that time of modernity may have very good behavior. It seems that all the time they respect the nobility of the other and of himself or herself. But in reality, they have it because they have to preserve their own positions and not to misbehave, for it could lessen the best technological efficiency in their societies. They do not do good deeds because they feel that it is morally good, but rather because they feel that it is technologically good instead.

REFERENCES

Berofsky, B. (2003). Identification, the self and autonomy. *Social Philosophy & Policy, 20*(2), 199-220.

Coyne, R. (1995). *Designing information technology in the postmodern age: From method to metaphor.* Cambridge, MA: The MIT Press.

Dreyfus, H. L. (1991). *Being-in-the-world: A commentary on Heidegger's Being and Time, division I.* Cambridge, MA: The MIT Press.

Guyer, P. (2003). Kant on the theory and practice of autonomy. *Social Philosophy & Policy, 20*(2), 70-98.

Habermas, J. (1979). *Communication and the evolution of society* (T. McCarthy, trans.). Boston: Beacon Press.

Habermas, J. (1990). *Moral consciousness and communicative action* (C. Lenhardt & S. W. Nicholsen, trans.). Cambridge, MA: Polity Press.

Habermas, J. (1992). *Postmetaphysical thinking: Philosophical essays* (W. M. Hohengarten, trans.). Cambridge, MA: The MIT Press.

Harman, G. (2002). *Tool-being: Heidegger and the metaphysics of objects.* Chicago: Open Court.

Heidegger, M. (1962). *Being and time* (J. Macquarrie, & E. Robinson, trans.). New York: Harper & Row.

Heidegger, M. (1977). *The question concerning technology and other essays* (W. Lovitt, trans.). New York: Harper & Row.

Ihde, D. (1979). *Technics and praxis.* Dordrecht: D. Reidel.

Myerson, G. (2001). *Heidegger, Habermas and the mobile phone.* Cambridge, MA: Icon Books.

Phra Dhammapitaka (Payutto, P. A.). (1995). *Dictionary of Buddhism* (8th ed.). Bangkok: Mahachulalongkorn University Press.

Phra Dhammapitaka (Payutto, P. A.). (1999). *Buddhadhamma* (8th ed.). Bangkok: Mahachulalongkorn University Press.

Warren, M.E. (1995). The self in discursive democracy. In S. K. White (Ed.), *The Cambridge companion to Habermas* (pp. 167-200). Cambridge, MA: Cambridge University Press.

Chapter VI

Invisibility and the Ethics of Digitalization:
Designing so as not to Hurt Others

Maja van der Velden
University of Bergen, Norway

ABSTRACT

The diversity of knowledge is crucial for finding credible and sustainable alternatives for living together. Yet, a preoccupation with content and connectivity obscures the role of information technology by making invisible different ways of knowing and other logics and experiences. How do we deal with diversity and difference in information technology? In this chapter, two cases are explored in which dealing with difference is a particular political and ethical concern. The designs of Indymedia, an Internet-based alternative media network, and TAMI, an Aboriginal database, are informed by the confrontations over different ways of knowing. They translate difference without sacrificing diversity, providing clues for building credible and sustainable design alternatives that will not hurt others.

ETHICS OF DIGITALIZATION: DESIGNING SO AS NOT TO HURT OTHERS

Now we are faced with a global conflict that is so nebulous, so ill-defined and ill-conceived, that it may never end. All we are told is that there is our side, and there is the other side. ... But the horror of never ending war brings with it the chance for a truly global resistance. And so we will create a new side—the side that wants to understand, the side that seeks out the root causes of our struggle, the side that will triumph over conflict itself. (Adbusters, 2005)

Information technology is one of the pillars of the global war. It is also a technology of development, as information and communication technology for development (ICT4D). Behind both lurks the metaphor of the digital divide. For the Pentagon, the digital divide is manifested in technological superiority over enemies on the battlefield. In development, the digital divide is a metaphor for the barriers to the digital flow of information and knowledge and the social and economic consequences thereof. In both, the digital divide metaphor suggests that information and communication technologies are solutions, bridges across the divide that enable the flows of knowledge and information to reach new territories and new targets.

The digital divide metaphor implies a conceptualization of knowledge as commodity, something that can be extracted and transported from one place to another. Accordingly, efforts to overcome the digital divide are connected closely with ideas about a global knowledge society in which everyone has the right of access to information and knowledge.[1] But the perception that technology has no intrinsic value, that it gets its meaning through use (UNDP, 2001), has obscured the social and political processes that led to the design or selection of a particular technology through which that information and knowledge is transmitted.

If we understand knowledge not as a commodity but as a process of knowing, something produced socially, we must ask about the nature of digitalization itself. As the Aboriginal elders say, "Things are not real without their story" (Indigenous Knowledge and Resource Management in Northern Australia, 2005a). The technology that produces digital connectivity also produces the nonexistence of people and their stories, the fabric of the social nature of knowledge. When confronted with the social embeddedness of knowledge, the digital divide becomes a divide, not between the information and knowledge haves and have-nots but between what can be digitalized (commodities) and what cannot be digitalized (social processes).

Whose knowledge and experiences, or what forms of knowledge and logic, have become invisible in the categories (Bowker & Star, 1999) and technological designs chosen to organize information and knowledge? How can we promote differences in a world in which credible alternatives are rendered invisible by the very solutions that claim to bridge the divide?

The Portuguese sociologist Boaventura de Sousa Santos (2004) argues that the richness of human knowledge and experience is actively rendered invisible. In a sociology of absences, Sousas Santos (2004) presents five modes in which this richness is produced as nonexistence, as noncredible alternatives to what exists:

- **The Monoculture of Knowledge and the Rigor of Knowledge:** The way in which modern science and high culture are the sole producers of truth and aesthetic quality. This monoculture produces nonexistence in the form of ignorance and lack of culture.
- **The Monoculture of Linear Time:** The way in which history has a unique and known direction and meaning (e.g., in the forms of progress, development, globalization). This monoculture produces nonexistence in the form of describing as backward whatever is not declared forward.
- **The Monoculture of the Naturalization of Differences:** The way in which the distribution of people according to categories, such as race and sex, naturalize hierarchies. This monoculture produces nonexistence in the form of insurmountable inferiority.
- **The Logic of the Dominant Scale:** The way in which the dominant scales of the West, the universal and the global, prevail and ignore contexts. This logic produces nonexistence in the form of noncredible alternatives such as the local and the particular.
- **The Logic of the Productivity:** The way in which productive nature and productive labor maximize fertility and profitability in a given production cycle. This logic produces nonexistence as nonproductiveness in nature in the form of sterility and nonexistence and in labor in the form of laziness.

How we deal with different ways of knowing is reflected in our moral choices about technology (Hamelink, 2000). In *The Companion Species Manifesto,* Haraway (2003) describes "caring about and for other concatenated, emergent worlds" (p. 61). Haraway's new manifesto is her "political act of hope in a world on the edge of global war" (p. 3). In a similar vein, Latour (2002) echoes Santos by warning against a "false peace," a peace in which the right to construct remains in the hands of "culture-free scientists, engineers, economists, and democrats" (p. 16).

In short, we must confront the threat of invisibility by technological design. The social embeddedness of knowledge and the problem of invisibility imply the need to go beyond a rights-based approach in search of an ethics of digitalization itself. Elsewhere, I have proposed an ethical framework for how to deal with social differences in designing information technology (van der Velden, 2004, 2005). This framework deals with issues of democratization, representation, cultivation of diversity, and self-organization. Next, I examine the problem of the invisibility of other forms of knowledge, logic, and experience as a particular ethical challenge for people designing and selecting information and communication technology. I will examine information technology as a site in which invisibility is produced by looking at Indymedia and TAMI, two information systems in which different ways of knowing are interpreted and negotiated. Indymedia, a collective of independent media centers and hundreds of journalists, has a global reach (Indymedia, 2005). TAMI is part of the Indigenous Knowledge and Resource Management in Northern Australia (IKRMNA) project. TAMI is a database constructed for and by Aboriginal people (Indigenous Knowledge and Resource Management in Northern Australia, 2005b).

FIGURATIONS

Places where choices about technology are made are design processes. Design processes can be understood as translation processes; stories, concepts, values, and facts are translated into material representations (Mörtberg, 2003). When information technologies become available to us as users, we have no clue about the experiences and concepts that played a role in the design process. Seldom do we realize what our technologies make invisible and that those technologies could have been designed differently.

In this section, I discuss figurations as a lens to look at how information systems deal with difference. A figuration is a metaphoric framing (Braidotti, 1994). It is both a mode of differentiation to provide different ways of looking at one account as well as a mode of production of alternative accounts. Rosi Braidotti (1994) considers a figuration as political fiction; it allows one to move across established categories, to think them through, and to establish alternative ones. For example, she uses the nomad as a figuration of a post-colonial feminist subject, a conceptual form of self-reflexivity to think through and to move across established categories and connections. The nomadic subject is inspired by nomadic people but refers more to a nomadic state than nomadic traveling (Braidotti, 1994). A nomadic state presents a particular politics of location: "A location is an embedded and embodied memory. It is a set of countermemories that are activated by the resistant thinker against the grain of the dominant representations of subjectivity" (Braidotti, 2002, p. 3). The nomadic subject results in a call for a new kind of ethics, which Braidotti (1994) presents as the ethics of sustainable nomadic shifts. Nomadic shifts are creative ways of becoming through otherwise unlikely encounters of experience and knowledge.

The figurations discussed below have in common that they establish alternative categories and accounts by bringing in a more ecological perspective and by making already existing but invisible connections and agencies visible and different outcomes possible. Figurations imply a discursive ethics: "that one cannot know properly, or even begin to understand, that towards which one has no affinity" (Braidotti, 2002, p. 241). Figurations provide us with a language to describe and map difference.

Palimpsest: Reworking the Linear

Artists Lyn Moore and Tracey Andrews (2001)[2] use the figuration of the palimpsest to make the history of the Lake Mundo region in Australia visible. Moore and Andrews researched the many ways in which the Lake Mundo region has been mapped. Andrews, a member of the Barkindji people, painted her ancestor tracks across satellite images of the region. In an art installation, these images were juxtaposed with a colonial map of 1835, showing the colonial discovery of the land (Moore & Andrews, 2001).

Moore and Andrews call their artworks *palimpsests*. In its original meaning, a palimpsest is a manuscript, usually papyrus or parchment, on which an earlier text has been removed (literally, scraped away) in order to make place for a new text. The original text often is not completely erased and still is or can be made legible. The palimpsests of Moore and Andrews rearrange the seemingly linear order of the different texts by scraping the ancestor history in the image, revealing the deceptiveness of satellite technology as a reflection of a reality. They show that what is not visible on the satellite image, a nonexistence, is produced actively as such by the technology.

In this meaning of palimpsest, the dominant text is not scraped away, but the still legible older texts are made visible. This scraping makes visible what is produced as nonexistence by the satellite technology. With the figuration of the palimpsest, the artists are able to create an alternative account of the history of the region. Through writing ancestor history back into the satellite image, connections are created between past and present.

Friction: Creative Power of Diversity

Another figurative approach is friction. In *The Global Situation*, Anna Tsing (2000) describes globalization as preoccupied with "the *ur* object of flow—instead of the social conditions that allow or encourage the flow" (p. 337). Tsing suggests that if we imagine the flow as a creek, we would notice not only what flows but also the channel that makes the flow possible. She points to the importance of looking at the process of channel making.

Tsing (2005) reminds us that we need to look at the political and social processes that build the channels that enable or restrict flows. By prompting us to think of the friction in channels, Tsing focuses attention on the false dichotomies of flow and nonflow, such as immobile and mobile, local and global, particular and universal, connected and unconnected. The figuration of friction enables us to see the diversity in speeds, change, place, scale, and connectedness, and to see how people and places become disconnected and reconnected and how flows slow down or take a different course.

Tsing (2005) describes how "knowledge of the globe" and "globally traveling knowledge" depends on friction: "[F]riction reminds us that heterogeneous and unequal encounters can lead to new arrangements of culture and power" (p. 5). Friction is a figuration of emergent accounts, of fragments of global connections. Sometimes, one account gathers enough power to seem global, argues Tsing (2005), but investigating the friction surrounding it will reveal its connectedness with other accounts. Friction is a figuration for the creative power of diversity.

Diffractions: Making a Difference

Donna Haraway's (2000) figuration of diffraction refers to the broken-up light rays on a screen. It is not a reflection, the displacement of the same somewhere else. "Diffraction patterns record the history of the passage of light rays through slits, the history of interaction, interference, reinforcement, difference" (Haraway, 1997, p. 273).

With the figuration of diffraction, history, not representation, is used as a tool to foreground something, to make a difference. Haraway's

Companion Species Manifesto can be read as the record of history of the companionship of people and dogs. Diffracting is showing something in all its contexts and meanings, mapping the effects of difference. Diffraction is, above all, a figuration for the commitment of making a difference in the world.

Figurations are materialist mappings, drawing a network of connections in which otherwise disconnected experiences and knowledges meet. Moore and Andrews' artwork shows how the vision of a satellite produces a nonexistence of other ways of seeing and knowing. They use the palimpsest to make the layers of the past visible in the present. In the same way, diffractions draw a record of history in order to make difference visible and to make a difference in the world. Frictions draw an image of the flow of information and knowledge in information systems and networks as a creek (Tsing, 2005) with obstacles, diversions, transformations, branches, and dead ends. Braidotti's nomadic subject incorporates a nonunitary vision, a freedom of thinking in the flow of connections, imagining new becomings.

Christina Mörtberg (2003) discusses the use of figurations as interventions in system design. Using the examples of diffractions and the nomadic subject, she compares them with techniques used in the design of information systems, such as prototyping and development of scenarios. Mörtberg proposes to use figurations as a way to foreground the significance of materiality, the techniques, technologies and methods we use to produce a technical solution. Figurations thus contribute to making the materiality in system design visible in order to open up the design processes toward using different models, techniques, and technologies, as well as to make interconnections between use and design and to create new techniques and methodologies and new solutions.

In the next section, I will present two information system designs. Both designs are the result of a struggle over knowledge and over whose knowledge counts in the technological design. I will use figurations to describe the confrontations and negotiations over difference in the design process.

TRANSLATING DIVERSITY INTO TECHNOLOGY

The technological design of an information system controls, to a large extent, how information is produced, categorized, archived, and shared in the system. This design reflects the politics, culture, and even race, gender, class, and ethnicity of the people involved. The technological design often is perceived as the result of a set of neutral technical choices. For example, decisions about the information architecture of a database supposedly are based on neutral considerations of efficiency and effectiveness, as the structuring of data and metadata is deemed crucial for the location and retrieval of the data as well as the interoperability with other systems.

One of the effects of such neutral design processes is what O'Hara (Bowker, 2000) calls the grooving effect. Grooving is a process of convergence (Bowker, 2000): "A set of data structures and retrieval models are set up so that a particular, skewed view of the world can be easily represented. ... Thus the world that is explored scientifically becomes more and more closely tied to the world that can be represented by one's theories and in one's databases" (p. 17).

After the process of grooving, a subsequent process of reverse bootstrapping can take place in which the structures of data in the database become the lens through which we make assumptions about the world (Bowker, 2000; Christie, 2004).

As we will see in the following examples of the Indymedia network and the TAMI database, it is possible to work the other way around. The technology underlying these two projects was designed to accommodate the way people produce and share information and knowledge, the way they *do knowledge* (Bowker & Star, 1999; Christie, 2004; Verran, 2005).

Doing knowledge refers to an understanding of human knowing as a continuous, dynamic social process rather than a commodity. In an autopoetic perspective (Graham & Rooney, 2001; Maturana & Varela, 1987), knowing is understood as effective action. In the context of designing information technology, it is crucial to look at how people know and how people represent that knowing. Can the design process be located where the users do knowledge, where they live and produce knowledge?

The examples of Indymedia and TAMI are selected because their explicit mission is to provide voice to the voiceless, to design a technology that does not exclude other ways of knowing and experience. In this chapter, I analyze the documents produced in and around the design processes of these two systems. I was able to access Indymedia, as it is freely accessible on the Internet.

Doing Information and Knowledge

Indymedia (www.indymedia.org) is a collective of independent media organizations and hundreds of journalists, forming a diverse network of Independent Media Centers. They can be found in more than 100 countries and cities and in more than 20 languages.

The mission statement of Indymedia states (Indymedia Document Project, 2005a):

The specific purpose of the Confederated Network of Independent Media Centers (CNIMC) is to facilitate the use of media production and distribution as a tool for promoting social, environmental and economic justice, and to develop a global decentralized communications network to provide a voice for the voiceless. It is also the purpose of this network to give expression to a wide diversity of social movements in order to assist the distribution of intellectual, scientific, literary, social, artistic, creative, human rights, and cultural expressions not covered by the commercial press.

Each Indymedia Media Center is asked to subscribe to the membership criteria (Indymedia Document Project, 2005b) and the Principles of Unity (Indymedia Document Project, 2005c). The Principles of Unity is a work in progress. It contains 10 principles, including the principle of Open Publishing, which is still in its proposal phase: "All IMC's, based upon the trust of their contributors and readers, shall utilize open web based publishing, allowing individuals, groups and organizations to express their views, anonymously if desired" (Indymedia Document Project, 2005c).

Providing voice to the voiceless and the principle of open publishing form the basis of the Indymedia network. The principle of open publishing is, at the same time, the most problematic, as it is in conflict with the legislation on restricting freedom of speech as well as with the values and local politics in some of the countries in which Indymedia centers are established. Indymedia centers in these countries have implemented their own editorial policies to deal with these local realities. Aspects of these policies are inscribed in the source code.

At the moment, there are about 14 code bases in use in the Indymedia network (Indymedia Document Project, 2005d). The first source code, *Active*, was developed by activists in Australia to run a small activist media center. In the same year, software was adapted and used for the independent media center in Seattle, Washington, during the activities surrounding the World Trade Organization (WTO) meeting in 1999. The success of the media center in Seattle led to the establishment of many more Independent Media Centers. Coleman (2004) and Hill (2003) describe how soon after discussions started on how to improve Active.

What was initially dubbed *Active2*, resulted in many more source codes with names such as *SF-Active*, *Mir*, *FreeForm*, and *DadaIMC*.

As Hill (2003) discusses, each of the Active spinoffs reflects the different evaluations and approaches to the problems of the first Active software. For example, Mir was developed for the German IMC site, reflecting "a legal environment which prohibits racist, hateful, and revisionist speech in ways that necessitates prior restraint story moderation in a way that many IMCs are uncomfortable with" (Hill, 2003, p. 5). Other spinoffs dealt with the authentication process. Active had no authentication process, allowing anonymous postings. This is still possible with IMC software such as *DadaIMC*. Other IMC softwares now require a name, while some also allow you to post under a nickname.

Other points of contention were the way feature articles were implemented, the system's user friendliness, and the internationalization and localization of the systems (Hill, 2003). Each of the Active spinoffs dealt with these issues in a particular way. The result was that the Indymedia Technical Collective never developed Active2. The politicization of each design choice made it impossible to rewrite the original source code into one that would satisfy every Indymedia center in the world (Hill, 2003).

What the variety of IMC source codes shows is that there are different interpretations of open publishing possible within the Principles of Unity. These interpretations are politically motivated and "grant us a meaningful form of freedom, the independence to choose the socio-technical terms on which we communicate" (Hill, 2003, p. 8).

The ongoing negotiations in the Indymedia network in order to balance unity, difference, and autonomy show that part of these negotiations need to be expressed on the level of the source code, the software programs on which the individual IMCs run. New participants in the Indymedia network can choose which source code serves their values best or develop a new one.

Another example of doing knowledge is the Indigenous Knowledge and Resource Management in Northern Australia (IKRMNA). IKRMNA is a project to support and develop Indigenous databases that maintain and enhance the strength of local languages, cultures, and environments in Northern Australia. Verran (2005) and Christie (2004) present a design process in which users are designing their technology by using it. Christie (2004) proposes to rid the database "as far as possible of its ontological presumptions" (p. 9) and to start with a minimal metadata structure and a limited dataset. A focus on the use of this database then will inform the design of the interface, search engine, and data structures.

One of the projects is TAMI, which stands for Text, Audio, Movies, and Images,[3] and is designed to be useful for people with little or no literacy skills. The users become designers when they group and order resources by simple drag and drop, and they can print or save their collection on DVDs. An important feature of the database is that it is designed to be ontologically flat so that indigenous knowledge traditions are not preempted by Western assumptions. The user encodes the structure in the database; for example:

- Objects can be uploaded and searched without metadata
- There are no preexisting categories
- Users can give metadata to their own collections
- One way of searching objects in the database is by browsing through the full set of thumbnail resources

An ontologically flat database offers the possibility of adding different interfaces to it. Besides the interface configuration used by TAMI, it is possible to imagine another configuration, one that embeds the way of knowing of Western science (Verran, 2005). Such a database even may help to negotiate what Verran (2005) has called *ontic differences*, the different ways in which people give meaning to things.

Programming for Diversity

The Indymedia network and the TAMI database were selected because dealing with difference and giving voice to the voiceless were clear objectives in both projects. I was interested particularly in how their dealing with difference worked out on the level of computer code of the software programs underlying the two projects. This computer code functions as law (Lessig, 1999). Code regulates, to an important extent, how we can use a database, a content management system, or an Internet service. As code regulates the production and communication of our expressions, it can interfere with our own values.

I used the figurations presented in the previous section as guides and lenses while exploring Indymedia and TAMI. Using these figurations helped me to focus on the history of the systems. In these histories, moments and places of friction became visible where confrontation, negotiation, and translation take place. In the case of the Indymedia, using figurations helps to understand that the network is very different from other distributed content management systems on the Internet. The diversity in the source codes of the Indymedia network enables the expression of the diversity found within the participating communities, countries, and peoples. The disagreements over the values inscribed in Active, the first Indymedia source code, can be read as creative friction (Tsing, 2005), resulting in the development of several new source codes.

At the same time, the Indymedia network shows that confrontations and negotiations are ongoing. Someone who doesn't agree with the policies of the local center (e.g., the option to post anonymously is disabled) can still use other centers with different policies. The laws of Indymedia, the network's source codes as well as its membership criteria and Principles of Unity, are sites of translations of the differences found in the network. These differences are not negotiated and translated into one source code or into a set of principles accepted by all. Translations take place only where the Indymedia centers connect in order to share information.

Translations are one common way to deal with difference in information technology. Translation in this context normally refers to the localization and internationalization in software design. Localization refers to the customization of software and documentation for a particular country or people, including the translation of menus and messages into the native spoken language as well as changes in the user interface to accommodate different alphabets and cultures. Internationalization refers to the process of designing an application so it can be adapted to various languages, time zones, and monetary values without the need for changes in the design.

The examples of Indymedia and TAMI suggest a new dimension in processes of translation in information technology. In different ways, their designs reflect a commitment to diversity in the source code. In the case of Indymedia, diversity is expressed in the variety of local source codes in one global network. In the case of TAMI, diversity is expressed through one local source code, which is able to negotiate its visibility globally.

Translation as a way of dealing with difference was a more conscious process in the example of the TAMI database. Helen Verran (2005), one of the scholars involved in the IKRMNA project, proposed to negotiate ontic differences by looking for the inside connection, a third translating domain at the overlap of the two ontologies. This overlap can be understood as what Tsing (2005) would call the site of creative friction or what Mary Louise Pratt (1999) has called contact zones: "social spaces where cultures meet, clash, and grapple with each other, often in contexts of highly asymmetrical relations of power, such as colonialism, slavery or their aftermaths as they are lived out in many parts of the world today." Pratt describes an almost 400-year-old heterogeneous text deploying European and Andean systems of meaning making as a contact zone. She argues that the position of a person in the contact zone will decide how the text is read.

The development of the TAMI database shows that an information system is a contact zone, a sociotechnical space in which different ontologies, knowledges, and experiences meet, clash, and grapple with each other." The TAMI project shows how a database becomes the contact zone in which Aboriginal and Western scientists create dialogues on resource management. As was the case with Pratt's text, people from different ontologies will read the Aboriginal database differently. Its ontological flatness will allow for different user interfaces and different readings.

For non-Aboriginal database designers, an ontologically flat database with its lack of schemas[4] and other structures that make connections between the data in a database possible may seem illogical. Understanding the TAMI database as a palimpsest makes clear that the database doesn't lack anything; it inscribes a different way of making connections in the database. The database was built according to the Aboriginal way of knowing, making Aboriginal ways of doing knowledge visible.

CONCLUSION

Beyond what there is now, there is what you know. (Construction site graffiti in East-Oslo, Norway, September 28, 2005)

In this chapter, I have explored an analytical approach to the problem of difference in a world in which credible alternatives are made invisible by technology. In his sociology of emergences, de Sousa Santos (2004) shows how diversity becomes visible through "the symbolic amplification of clues" (p. 176). Clues are signals and traces of the future in the present. As the examples of

Indymedia and TAMI show, figurations help us to find clues for an ethics of digitalization.

In the case of Indymedia, difference was negotiated not into one but into several different source codes. The wide variety of media organizations is able to work together in one global networked collective because of this diversity. Each of the versions contains confrontation and negotiation. The negotiations were about the way to work together and share information. The confrontations over issues of privacy and control resulted in different ways of organizing access and information management. The different software versions each have a common component for the collective networking and a different component for networking at the level of the individual center. In the case of TAMI, negotiations resulted in a database that does knowledge the Aboriginal way. The databases of the researchers and their institutions need to adapt to the Aboriginal way of doing knowledge by constructing open and flexible databases. The adaptation is from the bottom up, from the smaller or weaker to the bigger or more powerful. This design makes it possible to imagine institutional databases that do not hurt Aboriginal people and their knowledge.

António Sousa Ribeiro (2004) describes translation as a metaphor of our times, providing "mutual intelligibility without sacrificing difference in the interest of blind assimilation." The design processes of Indymedia and TAMI can be understood as translation work. The work in Indymedia and TAMI is very different from what is called localization or internationalization in software design. Nor is this form of translation based on a dialogue between different ways of knowing, in which assimilation or consensus is being sought between two or more clearly defined cultures. This understanding of translation is based on the idea that no culture or knowledge system is complete. Thus, the designs of Indymedia and TAMI are the result of people negotiating as equals with equal rights to construct (Latour, 2002), building together as companions, sharing bread (Haraway, 2003). This kind of translation work is based on an epistemological imagination that makes it possible to create credible and sustainable alternatives and "to live so as not to hurt others" (Gandhi, 1925).

If we approach information systems as sites of translation, we can investigate how difference is negotiated into material representations. Santos proposes a sociology of translation based on a negative universalism; namely, that there is no grand theory, no universal theory of progress and development. Santos builds his sociology of translation on Raimon Panikkar's (Hall, n.d.) thesis of the incompleteness of all religions and cultures: "[N]o culture, tradition, ideology or religion can today speak for the whole of human kind." Panikkar (1979) argues for *diatopical hermeneutics*, a hermeneutics across radically different places (dia-topoi = across places). Diatopical hermeneutics is a proposal for dealing with the distance between a knower and the object to be known when they belong to different cultures or ideologies. In a similar way, the Indian scholar Shiv Visvanathan (Kraak, 1999) proposed dialogue as a positive heuristic for dealing with competing knowledges. This dialogue is based on cognitive justice; all forms of knowledge are valid and should coexist in a dialogic relationship to each other. The examples of Indymedia and TAMI show that difference also is negotiated at the level of the source code. The designers of these systems are involved in creating meaningful technology—technology that enables giving voice to the voiceless and technology that helps to make credible alternatives visible.

In this, the translation work of Indymedia and TAMI confirm the importance of the four principles of this framework of the democratization of knowledge and technology (van der Velden, 2005):

- The Principle of the Democratization of Technology can be found in Indymedia's

multiple source codes and TAMI's ontologically flat design.

- The Principle of Democratic Representation can be found, for example, in Indymedia's choice for free software and the family ownership of the TAMI database.
- The Principle of the Cultivation of Diversity can be found in Indymedia's multiple source codes and the large number of languages supported in the Indymedia network. In the case of TAMI, diversity is cultivated by the particular design of the database, which supports an Aboriginal way of knowing without excluding access by databases designed to support other ways of knowing.
- The Principle of Autonomous Self-Organization can be found in the flexible design of the Indymedia network and organization, which allows for ongoing expansion, even with the addition of new source codes and again in the particular design of the TAMI database. The database is designed at the same time when it is used, allowing users to determine the rules by which the database organizes information.

The examples of Indymedia and TAMI add to this framework that in order to give voice to the voiceless and to make silence visible, local and global information systems need to be built from the ground up, starting with the small or weak, and to be inclusive of local source codes.

Indymedia and TAMI both are examples of information technologies that challenge the idea of overpowering global flows and global media. The global flow of information in the Indymedia network is negotiated in each local Indymedia center. The TAMI database is not yet connected with other databases, but other Aboriginal databases built on the same design principles in the future will negotiate the global flow of Aboriginal knowledge through their local source code. Non-Aboriginal databases can connect if they are built flexible enough to adapt to Aboriginal databases. The conflicts and negotiations in the design processes of Indymedia and TAMI reveal the power of local code. The global flows of information are channeled through local source codes.

The people involved in these projects recognized that they were all builders—founders, designers, users, beneficiaries—and equal participants in the construction of the systems. Crucially, there was no blueprint; there is no universal way to build. The standards by which we measure if they are good or bad builders emerge through the negotiations over the right ways to build (Latour, 2002). Indymedia and TAMI became spaces for negotiations and dialogues because they performed cognitive justice. In a description of the principles of cognitive justice, Visvanathan (Kraak, 1999) mentions, among others, that "[c]ognitive justice should strengthen the voice of the defeated and marginalized" and "[e]very citizen is a scientist. Every layperson is an expert."

REFERENCES

Adbusters. (2005). Two minutes of silence. *Adbusters, 62*(13), 6.

Bowker, G. C. (2000). *Biodiversity: Datadiversity.* Retrieved September 30, 2005, from http://epl.scu.edu:16080/~gbowker/biodivdatadiv.pdf

Bowker, G. C., & Star, S. L. (1999). *Sorting things out: Classification and its consequences.* Cambridge, MA: The MIT Press.

Braidotti, R. (1994). *Nomadic subjects: Embodiment and sexual difference in contemporary feminist theory.* New York: Columbia University Press.

Braidotti, R. (2002). *Metamorphoses: Towards a materialist theory of becoming.* Cambridge, UK: Polity Press.

Castells, M. (2001). *The Internet galaxy: Reflections on the Internet, business, and society.* Oxford: Oxford University Press.

Christie, M. (2004). *Words, ontologies and aboriginal databases.* Retrieved September 30, 2005, from http://www.cdu.edu.au/centres/ik/pdf/WordsOntologiesAbDB.pdf

Coleman, B. (2004). *Indymedia's independence: From activist media to free software.* Retrieved September 30, 2005, from http://journal.planetwork.net/article.php?lab=coleman0704

de Sousa Santos, B. (2004). A critique of lazy reason: Against the waste of experience. In I. Wallerstein (Ed.), *The modern world-system in the longue durée.* New York: Ferdinand Braudel Centre.

Gandhi, M.K. (1925). On economics and bread labour. *Young India, 17*(9). Retrieved September 30, 2005, from http://home.earthlink.net/~coalition4peace/oneconomicsandbreadlabour.htm

Graham, P., & Rooney, D. (2001). A sociolinguistic approach to applied epistemology: Examining technocratic values in global "knowledge" policy. *Social Epistemology, 15,* 155-169.

Hall, G. (n.d.). *Intercultural & interreligious hermeneutic: Raimon Panikkar.* Retrieved September 30, 2005, from http://www.dialoguecentre.org/PDF/Hall.pdf

Hamelink, C. J. (2000). *The ethics of cyberspace.* London: Sage.

Haraway, D. (1997). *Modest_witness@second_millenium: Femaleman_meets_oncomouse.* New York: Routledge.

Haraway, D. (2000). *How like a leaf: An interview with Thyrza Nichols Goodeve.* New York: Routledge.

Haraway, D. (2003). *The companion species manifesto: Dogs, people, and significant otherness.* Chicago: Prockly Paradigm Press.

Hill, B. M. (2003). *Software(,) politics and indymedia.* Retrieved September 30, 2005. from http://mako.cc/writing/mute-indymedia_software.html

Indigenous Knowledge and Resource Management in Northern Australia (IKRMNAa). (2005a). *What we do.* Retrieved September 30, 2005, from http://www.cdu.edu.au/centres/ik/whatwedo4.html

Indigenous Knowledge and Resource Management in Northern Australia (IKRMNA). (2005b). *TAMI.* Retrieved September 30, 2005, from http://www.cdu.edu.au/centres/ik/db_TAMI.html

Indymedia. (2005). Independent Media Center. Retrieved September 30, 2005, from http://www.indymedia.org

Indymedia Documentation Project. (2005a). *Mission statement.* Retrieved September 30, 2005, from http://docs.indymedia.org/view/Global/MissionStatement

Indymedia Documentation Project. (2005b). *Membership criteria.* Retrieved September 30, 2005, from http://docs.indymedia.org/view/Global/MembershipCriteria

Indymedia Documentation Project. (2005c). *Principles of unity.* Retrieved September 30, 2005, from http://docs.indymedia.org/view/Global/PrinciplesOfUnity

Indymedia Documentation Project. (2005d). *Code bases.* Retrieved September 30, 2005, from http://docs.indymedia.org/view/Devel/WebHome#Codebases

Kraak, A. (1999). *Western science, power and the marginalization of indigenous modes of knowledge production* [Interpretative minutes of the discussion held on "Debates about Knowledge: Developing Country Perspectives" co-hosted by CHET and CSD]. Retrieved September 30, 2005, from http://www.chet.org.za/oldsite/debates/19990407report.html

Latour, B. (2002). *War of the worlds: What about peace?* Chicago: Prickly Paradigm Press.

Lessig, L. (1999). *Code and other laws of cyberspace.* New York: Basic Books.

Maturana, H. R., & Varela, F. J. (1987). *The tree of knowledge.* Boston: Shambala.

Moore, L., & Andrews, T. (2001). *Ancestor tracks through art.* Retrieved September 30, 2005, from http://www.icomos.org/australia/Tracks/30a%20Moore%20&%20%20Andrews,%20Ancestor%20tracks.pdf

Mörtberg, C. (2003). In dreams begins responsibility—Feminist alternatives to technoscience. In C. Mörtberg, P. Elovaara, & A. Lundgren (Eds.), *How do we make a difference; Information technology, transnational democracy, and gender* (pp. 57-69). Luleå, Sweden: Luleå University of Technology.

Panikkar, R. (1979). *Myth, faith, and hermeneutics: Cross-cultural studies.* New York: Paulist Press.

Pratt, M. J. (1999). *Arts of the contact zone.* Retrieved September 30, 2005, from http://web.nwe.ufl.edu/~stripp/2504/pratt.html

Ribeiro, A. S. (2004). The reason of borders or a border reason? *Eurozine.* Retrieved September 30, 2005, from http://www.eurozine.com/article/2004-01-08-ribeiro-en.html

Tsing, A. L. (2000). The global situation. *Cultural Anthropology, 15*(3), 327-360.

Tsing, A. L. (2005). *Friction: An ethnography of global connection.* Princeton, NJ: Princeton University Press.

UNDP. (2001). Making new technologies work for human development. Human Development Report 2001. New York: Oxford University Press.

van der Velden, M. (2004). Cultivating knowledge diversity: Reflections on cognitive justice, ICT, and development. *Proceedings of the Fourth International Conference on Cultural Attitudes towards Technology and Communication 2004* (pp. 3-13). Perth, Western Australia: Murdoch University.

van der Velden, M. (2005). Programming for cognitive justice: Towards an ethical framework for democratic code. *Interacting with Computers, 17*, 105-120.

Verran, H. (2005). *Knowledge traditions of Aboriginal Australians: Questions and answers arising in a databasing project.* Retrieved September 30, 2005, from http://www.cdu.edu.au/centres/ik/pdf/knowledgeanddatabasing.pdf

ENDNOTES

[1] For example, the Heinrich Böll Foundation initiated in preparation for the World Summit on the Information Society a charter of civil rights for a sustainable knowledge society, calling for the "unhampered and non-discriminatory use of knowledge and keeping access to information resources open" (http://reddot.xima-redaktion.de/download_en/Charta3-0-en.pdf)

[2] I was introduced to the art of Moore and Andrews in an article by Bowker (n.d.).

[3] See http://www.cdu.edu.au/centres/ik/db_TAMI.html#

[4] A schema describes the objects that are represented in the database and the relationships that exist between these objects.

Chapter VII
Privacy and Property in the Global Datasphere

Dan L. Burk
University of Minnesota Law School, USA

ABSTRACT

Adoption of information technologies is dependent upon the availability of information to be channeled via such technologies. Although many cultural approaches to information control have been identified, two increasingly ubiquitous regimes are battling for dominance in the international arena. These may be termed the utilitarian and deontological approaches and may be identified roughly with the United States and the continental European tradition. Each approach has been aggressively promulgated by its respective proponent via international treaty regimes in the areas of privacy and intellectual property, to the virtual exclusion of other alternatives. Absent a drastic shift in international treaty dynamics, these dominant conceptions likely will curtail the development of alternate approaches that might otherwise emerge from local culture and tradition.

INTRODUCTION

Technology, like all human artifacts, bears the value-laden imprint of its makers, including embedded cultural assumptions as to how technology should or should not be used. These embedded values may differ from the values of cultures outside that of the originators of the technology and may lead to cultural disruption when the technology is put to uses outside its original cultural milieu. For example, many of the controversies surrounding the proliferation of Internet technology—controversies over pornography,

intellectual property, privacy, bulk e-mail, or hate speech—may be viewed as cultural clashes between the values embedded in the technology and the values of those now using the technology (Burk, 1999b).

Law, considered a formalized expression of values, similarly embodies cultural norms and also may clash with the values embedded in alien technologies. But as Lessig (1999) and Reidenberg (1998) have shown, embedded technological rule sets in information technologies are contiguous with the explicit legal and normative rule sets of their originating culture; that is, both law and technology constrain behavior according to the value system that they express. This relationship has important implications for the proliferation and adoption of information and communication technologies (ICTs) around the globe. Development of these technologies presupposes the existence of informational content to be stored, communicated, or processed. Adoption of such technologies is, therefore, necessarily dependent upon the legal and normative regime that determines the availability and control of the information to be stored, manipulated, and disseminated via that technology. The ability to specify the legal and technical parameters for use of information is necessarily the ability to control the adoption and use of ICTs that process such information.

Consequently, as ICTs become more widely available, the provision of informational content increasingly has become a matter of intense interest, both among nations that are net information producers and among nations that are net information consumers—although perhaps for different reasons. As nations that develop information technologies export those technologies, they have consciously exported along with it particular legal and normative models for informational control, effectively spreading their value systems alongside their technologies. Issues of informational control have tended to arise in two separate sectors, contemplating, respectively, development of creative informational content and gathering of personal information. Legal regimes regulating control of these informational genres typically are labeled under the rubrics of "intellectual property" and "data privacy." In each area, the late 20th and early 21st centuries have seen a clear trend toward off-the-shelf regimes derived from the economic and political dominance of the United States and the European Union. Each of these economic powers has aggressively promoted its own approach to information control, and in doing so, have largely displaced and overwhelmed the development of local or indigenous from-the-ground-up informational regimes.

In this chapter, I examine the nature and proliferation of these off-the-shelf models that now dominate international provision of information. I shall first sketch the general outlines of the dominant approaches toward information ownership and toward control of personal information, showing how the philosophies from each side of the Atlantic parallel one another for each of these respective information denominations. Specifically, I show how both information ownership and data privacy are dominated by parallel regimes of Western utilitarian and deontological ethics. I then turn to a description of the political and legal strategies by which the dominant information regimes have been internationally promulgated and indicate the effect that these ethical juggernauts have had in an era of globalization. I then survey the type of localized or indigenous approaches that are being extinguished by the dominant Western approaches and conclude that, absent some unexpected and drastic change in the near term, prospects for any cultural diversity in approaches to informational control is relatively bleak.

INTELLECTUAL PROPERTY

The economic character of digital communication and data processing technologies hold profound implications for any regime of informational control. Once the infrastructure of these technologies is in place, they allow the reproduction and dissemination of digitized content at essentially zero marginal cost. Additionally, the equipment used to engage in such activity is increasingly available at a relatively modest cost, which continues to decline with technological advances in the fabrication of semiconductor devices for processing and storage capacity. These economic trends diminish or largely remove the economic impediments that in the past have naturally constrained the creation and dissemination of creative informational works. Consequently, any control that is to be exercised over such works must increasingly come from legal constraints. Nations that are net information exporters have a vested interest in such legal constraints, typically in the form of intellectual property regimes, in order to capture the value of the content they produce.

The American Approach

The legal constraint of intellectual property law necessarily imposes costs upon consumers of creative content; by imposing such constraints, access to creative works that digital technology might make freely available is diminished when legal controls are imposed. In the United States, these constraints are justified under a rationale that is unabashedly utilitarian, which presumes that the long-term benefits of legal constraints will justify the short-term cost. Most frequently, this calculus of cost and benefit is couched in the language of economics. Creative works are characterized as economic public goods, which may be underproduced because they can be appropriated at a cost below the cost of production. Intellectual property rights constitute an incentive to creation that allows the creator to charge for certain uses of the work and so recoup the investment required to develop such work (Landes & Posner, 1989).

Under this approach, intellectual property rights are justified only to the extent that they benefit the public in general. The constraints imposed by intellectual property rights, deterring certain uses by the public, are permissible only if outweighed by the benefit of new works that they prompt. The individual rights of authors are secondary. In copyright, the specific legal regime covering creative informational works, authors certainly may benefit from the incentives offered, but this is merely a corollary benefit. The rights of the author should at least in theory extend no further than necessary to benefit the public and conceivably could be eliminated entirely if a convincing case against public benefit could be shown.

As a practical matter, of course, those industries with a pecuniary interest in strong copyright protection essentially always can make a case for public benefit from such incentives. In contrast, much as predicted by public choice theory, the needs of the general populace remain inchoate, unrepresented by any well-organized or well-financed constituency that might argue the potential harms or downside of increasing incentives. As a consequence, little actual balancing occurs, resulting in a one-way jurisprudential ratcheting of intellectual property rights toward continual expansion. However, the rights are not absolute, as the grant of rights to one group may adversely affect the costs of another politically cogent group, which may exercise political leverage to obtain an exemption. Hence, while the overall approach of the American system may be utilitarian, the rights system is complex and riddled with special exceptions not necessarily justified by efficiency or welfare considerations.

The European Approach

While the American approach to copyright is based almost exclusively on a utilitarian rationale, the European model is based largely upon a tradition that has been characterized as author-centered or personality-based (Drahos, 1996; Ginsburg, 1990). Under this approach, copyright is justified as an intrinsic right of the author, a necessary recognition of the author's identity or personhood. Although there are variations on this rationale, with slight difference of philosophical nuance between different European nations (Dietz, 1995), the general rationale for copyright in this tradition regards creative work as an artifact that has been invested with some measure of the author's personality or that reflects the author's individuality. Out of respect for the autonomy and humanity of the author, that artifact deserves legal recognition.

Central to this jurisprudence of authorial autonomy is the provision of so-called moral rights, which specify certain uses and characteristics of creative works as a recognition of the inherent dignity and personality of the author (Stromholm, 1983). Typical moral rights accorded to authors include the right of attribution (formerly known in a more gendered form as the *right of paternity*) under which the author has the right to have the work associated or not associated with his or her name; the right of integrity, by which the author has the right not to have his or her creation altered by another; and an economic right or *droit de suite*, under which the author has the right to benefit from future resale of the work. Such rights tend toward inalienability; often, the author cannot waive, sell, or disclaim them (Netanel, 1993).

This approach might be generally termed *deontological*, based in a strong notion of absolute rights accorded to the individual. In contrast to the American cost-benefit approach, the deontological approach declines consideration of instrumental incentives as a means to an end, focusing instead on what may be necessary to honor the personhood of the individual (Hughes, 1988). Under this approach, authors should be accorded moral rights, no matter what the resulting calculus of general utility or harm. This is not to say that rights under the European system are any less complex or rife with political exceptions than under the American system. But certain features relating to authorial prerogative, which could not be justified under the U.S. system, remain under the European approach.

INFORMATION PRIVACY

The ease with which automated digital media allow collection, reproduction, and distribution of information has affected not only the law and practical governance of creative works but also other types of informational control regimes. Data related to individual transactions, movements, and activities are also easily captured, stored, and manipulated, raising issues of information

privacy and data protection. Much as in the case of intellectual property, two primary models for privacy regulation have emerged on the international scene, paralleling the models previously discussed for intellectual property: an American and a European approach, grounded respectively in utilitarian and deontological considerations.

The American Approach

The United States has adopted a so-called *sectoral* approach to informational privacy, eschewing comprehensive data protection laws in favor of piecemeal treatment of the issue (Cohen, 2000; Reidenberg, 2000). Thus, personal information records in certain industries, such as credit reporting or healthcare, may be covered nationally by specific federal regulation. States or local governments may regulate particular aspects of retention, storage, and transfer of personal data within their geographic jurisdiction. Some industries may self-regulate through trade organizations or associations, or may adopt aspirational models of good practice. This fragmented approach results in a patchwork of regulations that can only be described as maddeningly haphazard, sometimes contradictory, and frequently confusing.

This approach has been largely adopted to keep the data collection environment as business-friendly as possible, limiting the imposition of privacy regulation to specific situations in order to minimize the potential financial and administrative burden on firms. This effectively produces a regime in which individual data belongs to the firms that capture or generate it in the course of consumer transactions. The default for usage of individual data is typically set as an implied blanket permission whereby individuals must take some affirmative action to opt out of data collection or usage. Actual regulation is indirect, such as governmental imposition of sanctions for fraudulent misrepresentation upon firms that promise consumers particular data protection and then fail to deliver.

While not as explicitly utilitarian as the U.S. approach to intellectual property, this American approach to privacy has clear instrumentalist roots, arising from particular economic considerations. Much of the business-friendly sectoral approach arises out of a historical American distrust of governmental solutions and a preference for market-based behavioral incentives. Perhaps paradoxically, this preference arises from a conviction that decentralized ordering via market forces will result in greater individual autonomy than would state intervention. This entails an assumption that the coercive power of the state is to be feared, whereas the coercive power of a given business naturally will be disciplined by market forces.

Consequently, the sectoral approach avoids comprehensive regulation and relegates governmental intervention to a bare minimum. Rather, the market is expected to supply privacy protection: if consumers desire privacy protection, then it is anticipated that businesses will voluntarily supply it in order to capture their patronage. Indeed, to the extent that recognition of individual rights in private data has been discussed, market-based approaches such as propertizing individual information have been proposed. Of course, the market for privacy is notoriously prone to market failure, as no individual datum is likely to be of sufficient worth to bargain over; it is only in the aggregate the data has value. Thus, no individual consumer will have sufficient bargaining power to exploit property rights in his or her individual data, and no market is likely to emerge that would allow decentralized control over personal information.

The European Approach

In contrast to the American sectoral approach to data collection, the European Union has adopted an approach based on comprehensive legislation, and grounded in strong, even inalienable individual rights (Reidenberg, 2000). This approach is spelled out under a data privacy directive requiring EU member states to adopt conforming legislation. The directive subjects individually identifiable or sensitive data to certain legal safeguards regarding the handling of such data. Notice of data collection must be given to the affected individual as well as the opportunity to review and correct individualized records. Certain types of personal data considered especially sensitive, such as data relating to health or religion or sexuality, receive special protection. Release or dissemination of the data for purposes other than that for which it was initially collected is restricted. Perhaps most importantly, the system hinges upon consent of the individual; people must opt in before individualized data can be collected. Notwithstanding the opt-in rule for collection, many of the rights accorded to individuals with regard to notice and data handling are inalienable; individuals cannot waive them, even if they wish to do so.

Such mandatory and inalienable rights, residing with the individual, are the hallmarks of a deontological approach. Paralleling the European tradition in intellectual property, EU privacy law elevates considerations of regard for personal autonomy over considerations of cost and benefit. Indeed, compliance with EU data protection requirements imposes a substantial financial and administrative burden on a broad array of businesses that may handle personalized data. Nonetheless, the EU data directive accords strong privacy rights not only despite the cost and inconvenience to EU businesses but, indeed, despite the cost and inconvenience to businesses outside the EU, including businesses operating within the U.S. This sets the stage for direct international conflict of the deontological EU approach and the U.S. utilitarian approach.

INTERNATIONAL PROMULGATION

The deliberate international propagation of the U.S. and EU models may be largely explained by the economic characteristics of information technologies already mentioned. As such technologies are adopted, both creative content and personal data can be quickly and cheaply distributed from jurisdictions with lax regulation or oversight into jurisdictions with more stringent regulation and oversight. This creates an incentive for more stringent jurisdictions to encourage greater stringency outside their borders, effectively expanding the territory covered by their regulatory regimes to other nations.

In general, stringent informational control jurisdictions will tend to be developed nations that are net exporters of information; less stringent jurisdictions will tend to be less-developed nations that are net importers of information (Burk, 1999a). The result is a gradient of informational stringency that to some extent reflects tension between developed nations and underdeveloped or developing nations. The economic and political position conferred by information export entails the economic and political leverage to impose information control policies that are advantageous to the developers.

Copyright Treaties

International promulgation of information control models has occurred in part through standard international coercive mechanisms—unilateral treaty negotiations, diplomatic pressure, direct imposition or threat of economic sanctions, and even occasional veiled threats of military force. For the most part, however, the dominant information ownership models have been internationally promulgated via multilateral treaty negotiations. These formal agreements under international law predate the age of digital technologies, but have gained increased importance since the advent of such technology.

The Berne Convention

The oldest international treaty regarding copyright is the Berne Convention, now well over a century in existence (Ricketson, 1987). Neither this treaty nor, indeed, any other creates an international system of copyright; thus, copyright protection exists country-by-country according to the provisions of national law. But although it does not create a worldwide right for authors, the Berne Convention instead harmonizes copyright law by requiring signatory nations to provide at least a specified minimum standard of protection for creative works. The provisions of this treaty are situated firmly within the European authorial model, requiring signatory nations to accord authors with moral rights, including rights of integrity and attribution.

Because of this, the United States remained for many years a holdout to Berne membership, acceding to the treaty only in 1989 after American businesses determined that they might benefit from harmonized international copyright protection. Prior to 1989, the United States attempted to promulgate and rely on a Berne alternative, the Universal Copyright Convention (UCC), which lacked Berne's moral rights provisions. But the UCC also lacked Berne's international appeal, and U.S. businesses clamored for accession to Berne as globalization awakened them to the value of widespread international copyright uniformity. This ultimately resulted in U.S. accession to Berne, but with significant reservations. Even after joining Berne, the United States declined to enact conforming moral rights legislation, relying instead upon a patchwork of specific visual artists' rights, trademark law, and state unfair competition law to constitute the nominal equivalent of its obligations under the treaty.

WTO TRIPs

Despite the success of the Berne Convention in attracting nations to implement a harmonized minimum standard of copyright protection, the treaty falls well short of the results desired by information exporting nations. A major impediment to implementation of the Berne Convention has been the lack of any credible enforcement mechanism. Berne is, at best, aspirational; although nations acceding to the treaty promise to abide by certain standards, the treaty lacks any functional provision to punish or discipline noncompliance.

Consequently, in an era of globalization, copyright proponents sought more robust international mechanisms for advocating strong control over creative informational works. They turned to the most rapidly developing instruments and institutions of international law, integrating intellectual property into multilateral trade negotiations under the General Agreement on Tariffs and Trade (GATT) (Reichman, 1995). Ongoing rounds of treaty negotiations, intended to lower international trade barriers, culminated in the creation of the World Trade Organization (WTO), an institution intended to ensure and advance the principles of the GATT agreements. To this end, the WTO houses a dispute resolution procedure that allows signatory governments to submit treaty noncompliance disputes to the decision of adjudicatory panels (Komuro, 1995). By moving intellectual property under the umbrella of international trade, this adjudicatory mechanism could be used to enforce compliance with copyright treaty standards.

Consequently, a new agreement on Trade-Related Aspects of Intellectual Property Rights (TRIPs) was attached to the GATT treaty framework. Agreement to the provisions of the TRIPs agreement is required for admission to the WTO. TRIPs sets minimum standards for intellectual property protection in WTO signatory nations, including compliance with the major provisions of the Berne Convention (Helfer, 1998; Reichman, 1995). As a consequence, the majority of the world's nations is rapidly falling under the regime of the Berne Convention, either by explicitly becoming Berne signatories or by acceding to Berne via TRIPs. The number of nations in the latter category continues to grow as nations seek admittance to the WTO trade treaty to which

TRIPs is tied. Although at the time of this writing a few jurisdictions remain outside the WTO membership, most have either joined the WTO or are working toward membership.

This nearly universal application of Berne might appear to herald the international victory of the European model, but the appearance is deceptive. There is one important caveat to the incorporation of Berne into TRIPs: at the insistence of the United States, TRIPs does not require signatories to comply with the moral rights provisions of Berne. This effectively strips the implementation of deontological copyright from the treaty and accomplishes the goal that the United States long had sought both domestically and internationally: strong global copyright protection without strong authorial rights. Consequently, under the TRIPs regime, the utilitarian model of information control dominates the international regime of information ownership.

Privacy Law

The international profile for privacy law has developed in a strikingly different fashion than that for intellectual property. Unlike the field of intellectual property, where the United States has been highly aggressive in asserting an affirmative utilitarian position, the field of privacy and data protection has seen the United States remaining relatively passive. As a result, the utilitarian position in this area has been manifest primarily because the United States as a major international player has maintained its own domestic sectoral stance. The more assertive role has been left to the European Union, but even so, the EU has not directly advanced its position under the kind of international treaty instruments or institutions that have been so conspicuous in the contest to shape international intellectual property law.

Instead, the EU model for data privacy has proliferated by virtue of a self-replicating feature in the EU data privacy directive. This directive might be considered *viral* in the sense that this term has been applied to certain forms of legal license provisions; that is, it infects follow-on users with some aspect of its own purpose and restrictions. In this particular case, the contagion is accomplished by means of a reciprocity provision that forbids member states from releasing personalized data to users in nations whose law lacks data privacy provisions equivalent to those in the European Directive (Swire & Litan, 1998). This places other nations in an awkward position as their native businesses attempt to engage in transactions with EU-based firms; if those nations lack EU-type data protection, doing business with the EU becomes nearly impossible. In other words, the reward for adopting the European privacy model is the privilege of conducting business with EU firms.[1]

Consequently, the economic importance of the EU bloc has driven the adoption of the rights-based approach in much of the world and has, in fact, left the United States in the position it once occupied with regard to the Berne Convention: a prominent holdout against a widespread international model. Indeed, lacking privacy laws substantially equivalent to those of the EU, the U.S. has had to negotiate safe harbor provisions that allow U.S. firms to conduct business with the EU on the basis of individual data protection compliance. This in some sense co-opts the sectoral approach as individual businesses individually adopt the tenets of EU data protection, since the benefits of adopting the deontological approach outweigh the costs.

ALTERNATIVES LOST

The international dynamic described here reveals competing utilitarian and deontological models, the utilitarian model holding a dominant edge in intellectual property law, the deontological model holding an edge in data privacy. But as both models ultimately arise out of the Western European intellectual tradition, imposition of either the American or European model on the rest of the world may smack somewhat of colonialism (Hamilton, 1996). Indeed, it should; the promulgation of these models is to some degree an extension of the promulgation of intellectual property and related laws by the great powers throughout their colonial empires during the 19th and 20th centuries (Geller, 1994). Local, non-Western cultures have developed their own norms and expectations for the control of information; these cultural approaches may share some features with the dominant international models, or they may differ substantially. When off-the-shelf information control models are imposed from outside, local customs and expectations regarding the treatment of information may be neglected or even eradicated.

Ownership Alternatives

Indigenous approaches to ownership and control of creative activity may differ radically from that formulated under either the American or European approaches, which, despite their philosophical differences, share fundamental assumptions regarding individuality and the nature of the creative act that law might recognize. Thus, Alford (1995) suggests that the problem long seen by Western powers as copyright piracy in China stems, in fact, from the Confucian cultural heritage in that region. The Confucian tradition largely denied the value or desirability of novel creative contribution, instead promoting respect for the classical work of revered sages and cultural icons. Under this approach, the most desirable contribution to present culture would arise by emulating the venerable work of the past, rather than by fostering original creations in the present or future. Thus, original expression—the entire purpose of Western systems of literary ownership—is viewed as undesirable under Chinese tradition, while copying—the cardinal sin in Western systems of literary ownership—becomes the cardinal virtue under a Confucian mindset.

Chinese antipathy toward intellectual property was additionally long reinforced by a communist ideological suspicion of the U.S. market-based approach of propertization, in some cases transforming the local appropriation of Western content into a sort of geopolitical statement. Communal approaches to creative works are by no means limited to Chinese or other politically communist systems. Numerous other ethnic groups have displayed a preference for communal rather than individual control of such works, although typically on cultural grounds rather than on political ideologies. Thus, to indigenous peoples such as the New Zealand Maori, the copyright concept of "author" seems outlandish or peculiar, as creative works are deemed to belong to the tribe or group (Geller, 1994). In other cases, such as that of the North American Hopi, individuals cannot claim ownership of creative works because creativity is deemed to stem from the inspiration of a divine spirit or higher power, not from the human artisan (Gana, 1995).

Individual ownership of cultural objects or folklore is also foreign to many other indigenous communities. Among the indigenous cultures of sub-Saharan Africa, control of cultural properties may be restricted to certain families that are designated the guardians for preservation or transmission (Kuruk, 1999). In addition to situating informational control with a particular lineage rather than with an individual, the concept of ownership or control itself may differ substantially from Western concepts of property. In many African communities, guardianship or custody of cultural properties entails responsibility for the preservation and transmission of a song, chant, icon, or artifact, but not the right to exclude others in the relevant community from access to the property. In a similar vein, aboriginal Australians likewise designate certain persons as custodians or stewards of culturally significant designs, as do many Native American tribes (Gana, 1995). In such societies, the goal of ownership is largely to maintain the meaning of cultural objects within their society, rather than to generate new works.

Indeed, to the extent that dominant Western proprietary approaches affirm individual contribution and ownership, rather than collective control of cultural properties, it has been suggested that nonappropriable works are cast into the public domain for free appropriation by individual follow-on creators (Chander & Sunder, 2004). This raises the concern that the dominant models transform indigenous knowledge into a virtual resource of raw material to be mined by artists in the developed world, whose recast creative product will be fully protected against appropriation or use by those who supplied the basis for the new work (Boyle, 1996; Coombe, 1998). This outcome fuels developing world suspicion that the dominant Western models are purposefully designed to systematically disenfranchise developing world creators. But even setting aside concerns over intentional exploitation, the ownership models drawn from the Western philosophical tradition may fit poorly with indigenous cultural expectations.

Privacy Alternatives

Unlike intellectual property, where alternative local conceptions of ownership have been increasingly documented and examined, studies of indigenous privacy or data protection preferences are almost nonexistent. While scattered studies of non-Western cultural privacy considerations exist, only recently have any of them been related to the subject of data protection. The sparse literature that exists indicates that privacy practices outside the developed world may differ markedly from the individualist practices of the developed West. Privacy researchers long have recognized that Western concepts of privacy are relatively recent and highly culture-specific, arising in large measure from the social and sexual mores of Western lifestyles (Posner, 1978). To the extent that a taste for privacy stems from actual or metaphorical physical seclusion, it presupposes an industrialized asset base that would allow different groups of people to be segregated by class, gender, or age, and perhaps segregated yet again by types of activity or bodily function. Such segregation requires not only a relatively affluent lifestyle but also certain cultural assumptions as to the proper criteria for sequestering or publicizing any particular activity.

Neither of these conditions is necessarily present in the history or development of personal information treatment by other cultures. Concrete examples of alternative data protection preferences in non-Western settings remain to be documented, but extrapolating from the scattered studies of diverse cultural approaches to privacy and sensitive information, it seems plausible to expect that attitudes toward data protection also would diverge from the dominant models. In some cultures, it is likely that the basis for privacy is radically shifted away from the deontological assumption of individual autonomy and personal dignity. In many cultures, family identity may take precedence over that of the individual. In yet other cultures, the relational boundary is yet wider, and communal or group identity may take precedence. Such cultural norms may sit uncomfortably within the Western deontological model of data protection.

For example, Lü (2005) notes that while China has at present no comprehensive data protection law, some internal discussion of such laws has begun. The literature comprising these preliminary discussions appears to reflect a different balance of values than those surrounding Western data protection laws; in particular, Chinese commentators appear to give greater weight to social responsibilities than to individual rights or desires for privacy. Other sociological studies suggest that while traditional Chinese culture fosters an interest in solitude and personal reserve that parallel Western notions of privacy, concern over anonymity and government collection of data is minimal (Chan, 2000). The emphasis on social obligation and de-emphasis on state action may reflect both recent Chinese political history and more general Chinese cultural norms emphasizing social values at the expense of individual autonomy. Moreover, empirical studies of Chinese familial relations suggest that traditional Chinese interests in the control of information may lie at the boundary of the family rather than that of the individual (Chan, 2000).

Recent commentary on the indigenous norms of South Africa suggests a similar cultural pattern at odds with the Western concept of privacy. One of the guiding precepts of post-apartheid South African political, public, and private initiatives has been the philosophy of *ubuntu*, a cultural worldview that emphasizes communal values of connectedness and that places community welfare over individual welfare (Broodryk, 2002; Kwamwangamalu & Nkonko, 1999; Louw, 2001). Olinger, Britz, and Olivier (2005) observe that the communal and interpersonal philosophy of *ubuntu* leaves little purchase for concepts of individual privacy as defined in the developed world. Under *ubuntu*, personal identity is dependent upon and defined by the community. Within the group or community, personal information is common to the group, and attempts to withhold or sequester personal information is viewed as abnormal or deviant. While the boundary between groups may be less permeable to information transfer, *ubuntu* lacks any emphasis on individual privacy.

Recent analysis of Japanese cultural norms shows an analogous pattern in the disposition of personal information. Mizutani, Dorsey, and Moor (2004) argue that Japanese cultural norms of information access rely on the context of the individual within certain groups. In Japanese culture, loyalty to the group is emphasized over individuality; proper conduct is defined by situated community—the workplace, the neighborhood, age category, and so forth. Privacy within a particular group is maintained by the norm of *enryo*, or appropriate restraint in handing personal information in that context. A given individual may rely on others in the context of the group to exercise appropriate discretion, or *amae* toward handling of personal information in the context of the group. Here again, the boundary for information access lies in the context of particular groups rather than with the individual, as the dominant data protection model assumes.

A data protection model adapted to such cultural attitudes might recognize familial or community interests in reviewing and controlling data pertinent to the family group or the community, rather than being oriented toward individual data protection rights. Rather than excluding all but the individual and those authorized by the individual to access personal data, restrictions on access might exclude those outside the relevant group, or might condition access to certain information upon group affiliation. Access requirements might anticipate and rely upon cultural norms, such as *enryo*, or they might even formalize these norms, requiring handlers of personal data to act with appropriate restraint toward the information. Or, in a normative environment such as that created by the South African *ubuntu* worldview, data protection may be seen as irrelevant for many situations considered pressing in the developed nations.

At the same time, such cultural differences may reflect traditional norms that may be changing under the influence of globalized media. Mizutani et al. (2004) note that younger Japanese people are more likely to demand individual privacy over the demands of the group. Lü (2005) similarly notes that Chinese attitudes toward personal and familial privacy are changing rapidly under increasing Westernization, and legal instantiation of data protection norms similarly is being shaped by international treaty obligations. Thus, it appears that the promulgation of Western information ethics paradigms via formal treaty obligation is only a component, if nonetheless a key compo-nent, of a broader cultural shift toward Western individualism in the wake of globalization.

CONCLUSION

The developed world's paradigms of utilitarian and deontological informational control are rapidly overgrowing other indigenous models around the globe in much the same way that exotic species introduced into local ecosystems may crowd out indigenous species. To some extent, this trend comes as a general result of globalization, as the normative and ethical assumptions carried by Western media consciously or unconsciously are adopted in other sectors of the world. But to the extent that these models are promulgated by legal instruments, the imposition of the developed world's models is deliberate and calculated.

Much as in the case of lost biological species, we have only poor records of the indigenous cultural models that are being overwhelmed and forgotten by the rapid proliferation of the dominant information models. In the case of intellectual property, scholars critical of copyright and patent maximalism have documented several examples of non-Western or indigenous cultural approaches that reject or differ from the deontological or utilitarian assumptions of the developed world. But in the case of privacy and data protection, the scholarly record is sparse. Scattered accounts of non-Western privacy norms can be found in the literature on anthropology and cultural studies, but little has been done to relate these accounts to the question of data protection. This marked disparity between cultural analyses of privacy and of intellectual property may reflect the economic disparity between the two fields. The value of personal data is primarily personal, while the business value of indigenous knowledge and cultural objects raises the profile of issues related to their ownership and makes the need for analysis of those issues seem more immediately compelling.

Thus, intellectual property scholars have already analyzed the potential for application of non-Western ownership systems to intellectual property. Similar analysis is needed in the area of data protection. Studies of non-Western and indigenous cultures similarly may suggest additional misalignments with the dominant data protection models. In some cases, the cultural line between public and private may shift away from that assumed by the dominant models; it is likely that in some cultural settings, information considered highly personal by Western standards, such as wealth or spending habits, may be deemed open and public, whereas information considered relatively innocuous in Western settings, such as a nickname, might be considered extremely private. As in the examples of China, Japan, and South Africa, privacy as a matter of individual autonomy may be relatively unimportant in cultural settings in which communal or group obligations take precedence; instead, protection of communal information might be deemed more appropriate. In such cultures, access to personal information or assent to the collection of personal information might more appropriately be sited with the family, the local community, or the reference group than with the individual.

But such approaches to personal or communal information control are unlikely to be accommodated within the data protection juggernaut now sweeping across the globe. Ironically, the imposition of either dominant model is troublesome from the internal perspective of each model. From a deontological standpoint, it is unclear that the autonomy of individuals is accorded respect by imposing upon them rights to which they object or with which they disagree. From a utilitarian standpoint, there may be substantial benefits to standardization of legal regimes, including legal regimes for information control, but this comes at the high and perhaps unacceptable cost of suppressing or deterring competitive alternatives. Nonetheless, absent a radical change in current trends, it is unclear whether the benefits of indigenous information alternatives, or the respect due their originators, will be realized in the foreseeable future.

REFERENCES

Alford, W. P. (1995). *To steal a book is an elegant offense: Intellectual property law in Chinese civilization*. Palo Alto, CA: Stanford University Press.

Boyle, J. (1996). *Shamans, software and spleens*. Cambridge, MA: Harvard University Press.

Broodryk, J. (2002). *Ubuntu: Life lessons from Africa* (2nd ed.). Pretoria: National Library of South Africa.

Burk, D. (1999a). Virtual exit in the global information economy. *Chicago-Kent Law Review, 73*, 943-995.

Burk, D. (1999b). *Cyberlaw and the norms of science*. Boston College Intellectual Property and Technology Forum 1999. Retrieved October 15, 2006, from http://infoeagle.bc.edu/bc_org/avp/law/st_org/iptf/commentary /content/burk.html

Chan, Y. (2000). Privacy in the family: Its hierarchical and asymmetric nature. *Journal of Comparative Family Studies, 31,* 1-17.

Chander, A., & Sunder, M. (2004). The romance of the public domain. *California Law Review, 92*, 1331-1374.

Cohen, J. E. (2000). Examined lives: Informational privacy and the subject as object. *Stanford Law Review, 52*, 1373-1438.

Coombe, R. J. (1998). *The cultural life of intellectual properties: Authorship, appropriation, and the law*. Durham, NC: Duke University Press.

Dietz, A. (1995). The moral right of the author: Moral rights and the civil law countries. *Columbia-VLA Journal of Law & the Arts, 19*, 206-212.

Drahos, P. (1996). *A philosophy of intellectual property.* Brookfield, UK: Dartmouth.

Gana, R. L. (1995). Has creativity died in the third world? Some implications of the internationalization of intellectual property. *Denver Journal of International Law & Policy, 24,* 109-144.

Geller, P. E. (1994). Legal transplants in international copyright: Some problems of method. *UCLA Pacific Basin Law Journal, 13,* 199-230.

Ginsburg, J. C. (1990). A tale of two copyrights: Literary property in revolutionary France and America. *Tulane Law Review, 64,* 991-1031.

Hamilton, M. A. (1996). The TRIPs agreement: Imperialistic, outdated, and overprotective. *Vanderbilt Journal of Transnational Law, 29,* 613-634.

Helfer, L. (1998). Adjudicating copyright claims under the TRIPs agreement: The case for a European human rights analogy. *Harvard Journal of International Law, 49,* 357-437.

Hughes, J. (1988). The philosophy of intellectual property. *Georgetown Law Review, 77,* 287-291.

Komuro, N. (1995). The WTO dispute settlement mechanism: Coverage and procedures of the WTO understanding. *Journal of International Arbitration, 12,* 81-171.

Kuruk, P. (1999). Protecting folklore under modern intellectual property regimes: A reappraisal of the tensions between individual and communal rights in Africa and the United States. *American University Law Review, 48,* 769-849.

Kwamwangamalu, N. M., & Nkonko, M. (1999). Ubuntu in South Africa: A sociolinguistic perspective to a Pan-African concept. *Critical Arts Journal, 13,* 24-42.

Landes, W. M., & Posner, R. A. (1989). An economic analysis of copyright law. *Journal of Legal Studies, 18,* 325-363.

Lessig, L. (1999). *Code and other laws of cyberspace.* New York: Basic Books.

Louw, D. J. (2001). Ubuntu and the challenges of multiculturalism in post-apartheid South Africa. *Quest: African Journal of Philosophy, XV*(1-2), 15-36.

Lü, Y. (2005). Privacy and data privacy issues in contemporary China. *Ethics and Information Technology, 7*(1), 7-15.

Mizutani, M., Dorsey, J., & Moor, J. (2004). The Internet and Japanese conception of privacy. *Ethics and Information Technology, 6*(2), 121-28.

Netanel, N. (1993). Copyright alienability restrictions and the enhancement of author autonomy: A normative evaluation. *Rutgers Law Journal, 24,* 347-442.

Olinger, H.N., Britz, J.J., & Olivier, M.S. (2005). Western privacy and ubuntu: Influences in the forthcoming data privacy bill. Ethics of new information technology. *Proceedings of the 6th International Conference on Information Ethics: Philosophical Inquiries,* Twente, The Netherlands (pp. 292-306).

Posner, R. (1978). The right of privacy. *Georgia Law Review, 12,* 393-422.

Reichman, J. H. (1995). Beyond the historical lines of demarcation: Competition law, intellectual property rights, and international trade after the GATT's Uruguay round. *The International Lawyer, 29,* 388-483.

Reidenberg, J. R. (1998). Lex informatica: The formulation of information policy rules through technology. *Texas Law Review, 76,* 553-593.

Reidenberg, J. R. (2000). Resolving conflicting international data privacy rules in cyberspace. *Stanford Law Review, 52,* 1315-1371.

Ricketson, S. (1987). *The Berne Convention for the protection of literary and artistic works: 1886-1986.* London: Kluwer.

Stromholm, S. (1983). Droit moral—The international and comparative scene from a Scandinavian viewpoint. *International Review of Industrial Property and Copyright Law, 14*, 1-35.

Swire, P., & Litan, R. (1998). *None of your business: World data flows, electronic commerce, and the European privacy directive.* Washington, DC: Brookings Institution Press.

ENDNOTES

[1] Although the topic lies beyond the scope of this chapter, it is worth noting that the EU has adopted with some success a similar strategy in the case of proprietary database protection; the benefit of EU database protection statutes is available only to businesses from jurisdictions with equivalent protection.

Chapter VIII

Analysis and Justification of Privacy from a Buddhist Perspective

Soraj Hongladarom
Chulalongkorn University, Thailand

ABSTRACT

The perspective of various Buddhist traditions offers an illuminating insight into the nature and justification of the concept of privacy in information ethics. This chapter begins by outlining the major literature in the West that deals with the issue. What has emerged in the literature is a common assumption of a separately existing individual whose privacy needs to be protected. Then I present the thoughts of two Buddhist thinkers, Nagasena (1894) and Nagarjuna (1995), who are representatives of the two major traditions: Theravada and Mahayana, respectively. The two Buddhist saints agree that the concept of privacy is a construct, since it presupposes the inherently existing individual, which runs contrary to the basic Buddhist tenet of no-self. However, this does not mean that there can be no analysis and justification of privacy in Buddhism, because there is the distinction between two views regarding reality—the conventional and the ultimate views. Both are indispensable.

INTRODUCTION

Privacy has become a key issue in today's information society. It is well-known that the power of information technology is such that information about an individual or, indeed, the entire population now can be easily obtained and manipulated. This can bring about tremendous convenience and benefit, such as when one puts an ATM card into a machine and gets out money, or when one does business with public authorities and can avoid the hassles involved in a seemingly endless amount of paper and filings. However, it is also well-known that the potential for misuse of the information is a real one. In Thailand, there has been much discussion about the government's plan to issue a digital national identification card to each citizen. This idea is not new in Thailand, as each citizen has been accustomed to having a national ID card for a long time. What is new is the digital nature of the new type of card, called a *smart card*, which will be implanted with a microchip and supposedly will contain much more information about the cardholder than before. There were talks about putting such information as health records (so the holder does not have to bring along all of his or her health information and medical history when seeing a doctor anywhere in the country), tax ID number (for convenience when contacting the Revenue Department), and other forms of information in one card so that Thai citizens do not have to carry too many cards in their wallets. While clearly offering conveniences of this sort, it is equally clear that there is the tremendous potential for authorities to use this huge database in ways that may not be in accordance with the rights and privacy of the population.

This situation is exacerbated by the fact that Thailand still does not have a specific law protecting personal information. Thus, in principle, the government can decide to do whatever it wants with the information contained in the smart cards. Examples of such misuse are discrimination against certain population groups, such as minority ethnic groups, or perhaps those who are more liable to get certain diseases that would put a heavy burden on the public health service system. It is conceivable that the health records, should they be contained in the smart cards, might lead to a situation in which citizens are denied their rights or are discriminated against. This can happen when the health records in their cards show that they are more likely to contract certain diseases than the general population and, thus, may have to pay more for their insurance, and so forth.

Another serious potential misuse is to use the information and communication technologies for surveillance purposes. The political unrest in southern Thailand has led some politicians to voice their opinions that closed circuit cameras should be installed in key places so that, in the event of violence, the culprits could be identified. In cyberspace itself, there have been talks

of recruiting a number of volunteers who would prowl cyberspace searching for Web sites or e-mail messages containing unlawful content. It is only a short distance from these good intentions to turn into actions that could destroy civil liberties and individual rights of the people. All this was not even conceivable a few decades ago, but with the proliferation of information and communication technologies, these actions are not only possible but are being performed in certain places.

The threat of these misuses of information underscores the need for a sustained reflection on the nature of privacy and its justification. What, in fact, is privacy? What is being guarded when one wants the government to curb its power of gaining information? Another related set of questions is: What justifies the need that privacy of individuals be protected? What kind of principle lies behind the justification attempt? It is the purpose of this chapter to begin to investigate these questions through the Buddhist perspective, especially that of Mahayana Buddhism. The reason I believe the Buddhist perspective is important in this area is that Buddhism has a very interesting claim to make about the self and the individual on whose concept the whole idea of privacy depends. Furthermore, Buddhist ethics also have quite a lot to say in the area of information ethics, especially regarding privacy. As Buddhism finds itself in the early 21st century, where there are widespread potentials to violate an individual's privacy, Buddhism has to find a way to accommodate itself in the new environment and to provide answers to the normative questions that naturally emerge. Hence, at least in Buddhist cultures, one stands in need of answers from the Buddhist tradition that could provide effective guidelines on these matters.

Here is what I would like to accomplish in this chapter: Nagasena and Nagarjuna, two Buddhist saints whose writings form the very basis of both Theravada and Mahayana Buddhism, have a very interesting concept of the self (or lack thereof, as we shall see), which can be applied to contemporary discussions of privacy in information ethics. According to Nagarjuna, the self as an inherently existing entity does not exist, strictly speaking, but as an empirical entity, it certainly does. The concept of privacy prevailing in Western information ethics is predicated upon the concept of the self, and a critique or privacy has to begin with the concept of the self. The idea for this chapter is that if one considers Nagarjuna's concept of the self, then privacy is a contested concept. It does not exist per se. On the contrary, the concept of privacy exists only in accordance with its value. This seems to point toward a more pragmatic concept of privacy. Privacy talks are useful ones, but that does not mean, nor is the talk presupposed by, the putative fact that privacy is already there in some strongly objective sense. While this Buddhist alternative thus will dramatically alter our understanding of the nature of the self underlying privacy, I will argue further that there are, in fact, a number of advantages to this concept in contrast to the prevailing realistic ones (i.e., that take the self to be an essential reality).

Here is the outline of the chapter. I will begin in the next section with a brief survey of the existing literature on the analysis of the concept of privacy and its justification, both from the West and the East. Then I will discuss the Buddhist concept in more detail. The next section will present the key role of compassion in Buddhist ethics and its particular relevance to the discussion on privacy. The basic question is what kind of analysis of the meaning of privacy and what kind of justification can be offered when the premise is that of the Buddhist idea on the self. This leads to some very interesting conclusions. The idea of justifying privacy on the grounds of the ontology of the individual—that there actually exists such a thing as an individual whose rights and privacy are to be respected—is not tenable in Buddhism. There is, however, a way to justify privacy that does not rely on such an ontology. I hope to make this point clearer in the course of this chapter.

PRIVACY INFORMATION ETHICS: EAST AND WEST

In the philosophical literature on privacy, much emphasis has been put on the definition of the concept and its justification. That is to be expected, because it is, of course, the task of philosophy to analyze concepts and to provide justification. In any case, what is interesting is that the majority of the works on the topic has been from the perspective of the West, and it is only recently that there is interest in what the East has to say on definition and justification of privacy. The volume of *Ethics and Information Technology* edited by Charles Ess (2005) is a pioneering attempt to fill this lacuna. In what follows, I will lay the background for my own argument by first detailing what the major published works in the West have to say on privacy, and then we will have a look at some of the articles in the Ess volume. The discussion in this section then will lead to my own argument in the next section.

In "Toward a Theory of Privacy in the Information Age," Jim Moor (2000) has established what is perhaps a now classic concept of privacy. According to Moor, privacy consists in an expression of a core value that is held by all human groups; hence, it is a universal value, because being a part of the core value means that privacy is shared by all human groups. These core values are "life, happiness, freedom, knowledge, ability, resources, and security" (Moor, 2000, p. 204). Thus, for Moor, privacy is a universal value, and he disagrees with attempts to ground privacy as something that has only instrumental value. Privacy, for Moor, is not part of the core values, but it stands alongside them since it is presupposed at least in the value of security. Moor claims that it is an expression of one of the core values; namely, security. Privacy is an expression of the value of security because it protects us from unwanted intrusion that would rob us of the information that we hold dear to ourselves.

For example, somebody wiretapping a person's phone conversations would be a blatant violation of his or her privacy, because we regard phone conversations as a private matter, and a society that allows widespread wiretapping would not protect the security of its members at all. Moreover, the authority that does the wiretapping would violate the democratic ideal, because protection of private information is crucial in ensuring that the authority does not gain an unfair advantage over access of information, which well could lead to abuse of power. For Moor, privacy is justified through its being an expression of the core values that all human groups and communities share. Its justification is based more on empirical grounds, that privacy is presupposed in the core values that empirically all cultures seem to share, than on purely a priori grounds.

In addition, Moor calls for a control/restrict access concept of privacy in which the individual has control over his or her own information through the principle of informed consent, and only those who are authorized to gain access to personal information can do so. His example is a tax investigator who looks at tax records of certain individuals. Insofar as the investigator acts in his or her capacity as an investigator, he or she is authorized to do so, but only to the extent allowed by his or her work as an investigator. As soon as the investigator is snooping around and looks at the records just for curiosity, then he or she violates the principle of informed consent, even though no new information is obtained. For Moor, privacy is more complicated than the simple "either I know or nobody knows" scheme. The level of access that a person is allowed to gain access to another's information is defined through a complex of situations. Moor states, "Ideally, those who need to know do, those who don't, don't" (Moor, 2000, p. 209).

Another concept is that of Adam D. Moore (2003). He agrees with Jim Moor that privacy is an empirically grounded concept and is universal in all human cultures. In support of this claim,

Moore cites a number of empirical studies in anthropology and cultural studies that claim that privacy is empirically grounded in all cultures and, thus, is part of cultural universals (Moore, 2003). He adds that although privacy is universal, its specific form does vary across cultures. This topic of universality and empirical grounding of privacy will be the subject of the next sections. He differs from Moor in that he advocates the control-based definition of privacy in which privacy is "our ability to control patterns of association and disassociation with our fellows" (Moore, 2003, p. 215). Moor would disagree with this, for he believes that it is not possible to control all of the "greased" information about ourselves that is available through all of the electronic means. Hence, Moor's is a weaker concept that allows for some space in which personal information can be obtained, but only through authorized personnel.

In another well-known article, W. A. Parent (1983) defines privacy as "a condition of not having undocumented personal knowledge about one possessed by others" (p. 269). The idea is that if the personal knowledge in question is documented, then presumably, it is in a public domain in the sense that anybody can look it up and learn about the information without thereby violating the privacy of the person whom the information is about. Parent disagrees with those such as Fried (1970) and Wasserstom (1979), who argue more toward a control concept of privacy in which privacy is defined more as the control an individual has over the information related to himself or herself. According to Parent, an individual should be entitled to reveal as much or as little information concerning himself or herself to those he or she trusts. The individual has control over the information about himself or herself, but it does not seem that his or her privacy is either threatened or protected, because he or she voluntarily reveals his or her private information to others. The individual has control, but not necessarily privacy. Another important point in

Parent's view is his justification of privacy. The reasons why privacy should be valued are three-fold, according to Parent. First, if others have information about us, they have power over us. Second, people generally are intolerant of others' lifestyles and so forth, so privacy protects this. Finally, privacy is among the values that, taken together, constitute the liberal ethics. In Parent's (1983) words, "individuals are not to be treated as mere property of the state but instead are to be respected as autonomous, independent beings with unique aims to fulfill" (p. 276).

Hence, it seems that Parent subscribes to the instrumental view of privacy as a value, since he believes that privacy is valuable because it brings about desired values, such as individual autonomy and protection against abuse of power by others, protection of diversity in lifestyles, and so forth, and the need for individuals to be treated as ends, not mere means, as Kant would say. This instrumental view accords with Fried (1984), who argues for privacy as a necessary ingredient of intimacy among persons. Their views thus contrast with those of Moor and Moore, both of whom look at privacy as a more or less universal concept. We will discuss this point later on when we look at how the Buddhists look at the problem of privacy.

What is common in these concepts of privacy, even though there are many differences among them, is their presupposition of the existence of the individual or the self whose privacy is the object of analysis here. For people like Moor, Moore, Fried, and Parent, privacy is that of the individual. The question is what it means for an individual to have privacy as well as why privacy is valuable or important to him or her. I would like to call this the *individual-centered view* of privacy, because it seems to take for granted the existence of the individual self. Parent's definition, for example, presupposes that there is personal knowledge that should be protected from others. Moor's idea that information about oneself needs to be controlled and that only restricted personnel

are authorized to gain it in relevant contexts also shares the presupposition that it is information about oneself; that is, about the individual self who subjectively purviews the information about himself or herself and decides which information could be divulged to others and which cannot.

This does not mean that privacy does not exist at broader levels. According to Westin (2003), there are three levels of privacy: political privacy, sociocultural privacy, and individual privacy. The first is the kind of privacy that citizens in a political entity enjoy and that can be violated only when the interests of the whole polity is at stake (Westin, 2003). The second level concerns privacy in lifestyles, beliefs, and behaviors—privacy that should be protected from undue intrusion by authorities. In other words, cultures also can have their privacy as do individuals. The third level is that of the individual, whose private life should be accorded some space, which would allow him or her to make decisions and to express his or her ideas, which are necessary for democracy (Westin, 2003). Thus, Westin (2003) sees privacy as a "social good" that requires "continuous support from the enlightened public" (p. 434).

To turn to the right to privacy, Judith Jarvis Thomson (1975) famously argues that there is no such right; instead, there is a group of rights related to the person, which are more basic. Her argument is that the right that usually is considered a right to privacy is, in fact, a right to some more basic conditions, such as property or person. A quarreling couple, for example, might not enjoy having their quarrels listened to through a bugging device, but Thomson sees this more as the right not to be listened to, which is a part of the right over the person, not the right to privacy. Cutting someone's hair while he or she is asleep does not harm him or her, but his or her right is violated nonetheless, and that is the right over the person according to Thomson. The basic idea, then, is that any putative instances of violation of the right to privacy turn out to be, on closer analysis, a violation of the right to the person or the property

(Thomson, 1975). Against this, Thomas Scanlon (1975) argues that there is, indeed, a common ground to the right of privacy, and that is the condition of "being able to be free from certain kinds of intrusions" (p. 315). The intrusions of our bodies, behaviors, and interactions with others are some of the clear examples of intrusions that violate the norms of privacy.

From this brief review of the numerous literature on privacy in the West, it should be clear that the common thread that runs though all these differing concepts is the presupposition that the individual exists objectively and distinctly from other individuals. The control theory of privacy assumes that it is the individual that should be in control of his or her information. The restricted-access view also is based on the belief that the individual exists, access to whose information should be restricted. Parent views privacy as a protection given to personal knowledge, which is the kind of knowledge about an individual who, from his or her own first-person perspective, does not want others to share. The key issue here is the individual and the first-person perspective, which is its defining characteristic.

This has not always been case, even in the West. Tamás (2002) details the development of the concept of privacy in the West and found that before the advent of modernity, privacy consisted mostly in the private life in one's own house or among one's own family. It is only with the modern emphasis on the pure subjectivity of the individual (evidenced in René Descartes' famous "*cogito, ergo sum*" statement) that the concept of privacy changed toward something based on the point of view of a single individual who is defined solely through his or her personal viewpoint, his or her idiosyncratic perspective, which can be shared by no one.

In a critique of the modern concept of privacy, which clearly contrasts it with the ancient concept, Tamás (2002) has the following to say:

Privacy as subjectivity hurts itself at the unchanging public sphere and at its political might, which makes the subject feels inessential, politically irrelevant; the subject still remains free to be herself, indeed the more herself she is within her private moral homestead, the freer she is; but in the public realm she is increasingly unprotected as long as rebellion is redefined as dissent and, of course, she has a "right" to dissent. (p. 220)

So the ancient concept concerns having authority in one's homestead, and according to modernity, such a homestead has receded to lie solely within the limit of pure subjective consciousness, which, as Tamás (2002) points out here, runs the risk of being eroded by the kind of politics that destroys the public sphere in which citizens exercise their right to take part in governance. What is interesting in our case is that all the key figures in contemporary debates and analyses on privacy in the West seem to subscribe to this modernist idea of privacy as subjectivity. It is thus highly interesting to see how works on privacy from the Asian perspective compare with this Western concept.

As previously mentioned, Charles Ess (2005) has made an important contribution to this comparative perspective on privacy in his special issue of *Ethics and Information Technology*. The papers in the volume point to an emergence of a new perspective on privacy that does not rely solely on the metaphysics of pure subjectivity that we have seen to be presupposed by the Western concept. For Ess, the most salient difference between the Asian and Western concepts is this basing of privacy on the individual subject, and he points out that this runs counter to the teaching of Buddhism:

In particular, in those countries such as Japan and Thailand where Buddhism plays a central role in shaping cultural values and identity, the Buddhist emphasis on "no-self" (Musi in Japanese) directly undermines Western emphases on the autonomous individual as the most important reality (at least since Descartes), the source of morality (in Kant), the foundation of democratic polity, and in all these ways the anchor of Western emphases on individual privacy. As Buddhism stresses instead the importance of overcoming the ego as the primary illusion at the root of our discontent—it thus provides a philosophical and religious justification for doing away with "privacy" altogether, as in the example of Japanese Pure Land Buddhism (Jodo-shinsyu), which inspires some authors to move towards salvation by voluntarily betraying private, even shameful personal thoughts. (Ess, 2005, p. 5)

Moreover, when the awareness of the need for privacy enters the life world of the cultures of the East, Ess sees that what happened is a kind of hybridization in which the elements of the West (i.e., individualism, emphasis on pure subjectivity) and of the East (i.e., emphasis on community and dissolution of the individual self) are mixed up. It is a purpose of this chapter to elucidate the nature of this mixture, and it will be seen in the next section how a theory of privacy according to the Buddhist perspective could be started.

For more specific perspectives of privacy in the East, Lü (2005) provides a detailed analysis of Chinese culture in terms of privacy. What is notable is that Lü (2005) states that, for the Chinese, privacy is regarded as having an instrumental rather than an intrinsic value (Ess, 2005). This also will be an important topic in the discussion of the Buddhist view, which I will develop in the next section. Furthermore, Kitiyadisai (2005) presents a powerful critique of the Thai government's recent attempt to issue smart cards to all its citizens, cards that have strong potential to violate the right to privacy of all Thai citizens. As much more personal information can be contained in the microchip that is implanted in the smart card, the potential for abuse is much greater than before. More alarming is perhaps the

tremendous power over the citizens that the Thai government could have, once the cards are issued to all citizens. (By law, each Thai citizen more than 15 years old is required to have a national identity card.) This power includes population profiling, criminal records, genetic categorization, and so forth. Kitiyadisai (2005) correctly points out that the lack of legal mechanisms against such abuse remains a thorny issue, and it appears that the government is not much interested in sponsoring a law that would restrict its own power. Hence, this is one of the many issues of which Thai citizens need to be constantly aware so the democratic ideal of checking and balancing the political power can be realized.

Another perspective comes from Japan. Nakada and Tamura (2005) say that privacy as practiced nowadays in Japan has its roots in traditional Japanese culture. What is emphasized here is the contrast between the Western notion of the individual as somehow atomic, in which one is more or less separated from another, and the Eastern notion of the individual as defined in terms of the relations the individual has with other individuals and of roles he or she has within the society (Ess, 2005; Nakada & Tamura, 2005). This is a standard Confucian teaching on the individual in society (for more detail, see Ames & Rosemont, 1998). The idea, broadly construed, is not unlike Buddhism. Even though there is no explicit rejection of the individual self in Confucianism (the self is constituted through networks of relation, but that, by no means, implies that such a self does not, in fact, exist), the thrust of both traditions seems to be that social relations among individuals define both the identities of the individuals themselves (only conventionally in Buddhism) and their expected roles. Hence, it would be instructive to see how Buddhism and Confucianism would view the notion of privacy and to compare this with the modern concept as put forth in Western literature (e.g., those by Moor, Parent, Moore, etc.).

In any case, a broad picture emerges from this comparative review of the literature on privacy. On the one hand, the West tends to view privacy in terms of a property of an atomic individual. Being atomic seems to imply that the individual is accorded some degree of privacy. This also can be compared with the ancient concept in which one's private domain is the estate that one possesses, and no outside influences are to intervene (within certain limits). Breach of privacy is tantamount to trespassing one's property. The difference is that for the modern concept, the domain in question has receded to the individual consciousness, or pure subjectivity. This is not to say that the estate or the individual possession such as land and other property has no role to play. Obviously, these have a large role to play in modern societies, but it points to the fact that in modern consciousness, the justification of privacy ultimately relies on pure subjectivity or private reasoning. Here, one is reminded of the ethical principles of Kant, in which the ultimate linchpin of ethical judgment is the individual reasoning mind itself (Capurro, 2005).

On the other hand, the situation in the East, at least as emerged from the previous discussion, tends to be one in which the line separating one individual from another is fuzzier. One might want to compare this situation with the general social condition in Asia in which individuals tend to live together in large family groups, sharing many things together, and in which the need for private space is not emphasized. One also might imagine a large family house in which the boundaries among individual members are close to nonexistent (Kitiyadisai, 2005; Ramasoota, 2000). As for the private subjectivity, there is not much emphasis on it in the philosophical traditions of the East. Buddhism treats it as parts of the five constituent elements (*skandhas*) of the self, consisting of bodily form (*rupa*), feeling (*vedana*), perception (*samjña*), disposition (*samskara*), and consciousness (*vijñana*). The private self thus is composed of four basic elements in the Buddhist

thought, and the idea of personal subjectivity is that it consists of these more basic elements. Hence, one can see from the beginning that in Buddhism, the personal self is broken down into these elements, and there is no assertion that such a self exists as a self-subsisting entity. In more mundane terms, this could be taken to mean that in the East, the emphasis is on the interrelation of oneself with others, as seen in the Japanese examples mentioned in Nakada and Tamura (2005), rather than on the atomic or substantival characteristic as in the West.

Nonetheless, one should not be persuaded to have an idea that things are entirely black and white. The West has its understanding of the interrelatedness of individuals as well as an emphasis on the role of communities, and the East also has its way of emphasizing the separateness of individuals. For example, the communitarian tradition, based largely on the works and thoughts of Hegel, is a clear indication that the idea that individuals are interrelated is not lost in the West. In the East, today's globalized world has dictated that the idea of privacy is to take root and find ways of concrete realization (Lü, 2005). The task for the theorist, then, is to search for a system of justification of privacy that respects these diverse cultural traditions but at the same time is powerful enough to command rational assent of all involved. In order to start to do this, I discuss in the next section the Buddhist view on the self and its implication for privacy.

THE BUDDHIST VIEW OF THE SELF AND PRIVACY

Ess' (2005) attempt to bring the perspectives of the East into the contemporary discussion and debate in information ethics is highly commendable. However, as is the case with pioneering attempts, more details need to be added so the account is more complete. It is the argument of this chapter that Buddhism itself does not reject privacy; on the contrary, one could rely on its teachings to justify its continued use and its enforcement, even in Asian and especially in Buddhist polities. One should not be persuaded by a hypothetical and simple argument that since Buddhism rejects the individual self (more on this difficult topic later) and since the individual self is the linchpin of privacy, then Buddhism rejects privacy. This is so because one needs to distinguish between the absolute and conventional levels of assertion. Conventionally speaking, there is privacy. That the individual does not exist in the absolute sense does not imply that he or she does not exist in empirical reality, and if this is so, then his or her privacy is there also as a consequence of the individual's social roles. From the absolute point of view, there is no distinction that can be made between subject and object, for such a distinction presupposes that there is an inherently existing self whose very existence is denied in Buddhism. Thus, the proposal is that privacy is grounded on the conventional idea of the self and individual, and the justification of privacy cannot be conceived separately from the democratic ideal. Privacy is necessary for democracy. Loss of privacy typically leads to abuse of power; privacy, hence, appears more as an instrumental value than as an intrinsic one (and here I find myself in broad agreement with at least the contributors to the Ess special issue mentioned earlier). However, the distinction between intrinsic and instrumental values rests on a presupposition that there exists some kind of core in the values such that when the core possesses a property inherently in a value, then the value is said to be intrinsic, but if not, then it is regarded as instrumental. The idea here is that talk of values being intrinsic or instrumental are just a way to argue that some values are those from which we do not want to part and some are more adventitious. But if we realize that the reason we do not much want to part from those values we call intrinsic is no more than our attachment to them, then we can begin to see how the whole distinction is constructed. The upshot is that one

should not be worried about values being intrinsic or instrumental, because the distinction appears to rest on a rather insecure foundation, or so I would argue.

The argument in the previous paragraph naturally needs quite a lot of explication. So let us flesh this out step-by-step. First of all, let us look at the Buddhist analysis of the self and then at the different levels of perception and analysis as conventional and ultimate. In *The Questions of Milinda*, one of the most well-known texts in all of Buddhism, the Venerable Nagasena, in reply to questioning by the Greek King Milinda, has the following to say:

The king said: "Is there, Nagasena, such a thing as the soul?"
"What is this, O king, the soul?"
"The living principle within which sees forms through the eye, hears sounds through the ear, experiences tastes through the tongue, smells odours through the nose, feels touch through the body, and discerns things (conditions, 'dhamma') through the mind—just as we, sitting here in the palace, can look out of any window out of which we wish to look, the east window or the west, or the north or the south."
The Elder replied: "I will tell you about the five doors, great king. Listen, and give heed attentively. If the living principle within sees forms through the eye in the manner that you mention, choosing its window as it likes, can it not then see forms not only through the eye, but also through each of the other five organs of sense? And in like manner can it not then as well hear sounds, and experience taste, and smell odours, and feel touch, and discern conditions through each of the other five organs of sense, besides the one you have in each case specified?"
"No, Sir."
"Then these powers are not united one to another indiscriminately, the latter sense to the former organ, and so on. Now we, as we are seated here in the palace, with these windows all thrown open,

and in full daylight, if we only stretch forth our heads, see all kinds of objects plainly. Can the living principle do the same when the doors of the eyes are thrown open? When the doors of the ear are thrown open, can it do so? Can it then not only hear sounds, but see sights, experience tastes, smell odours, feel touch, and discern conditions? And so with each of its windows?"

"No, Sir."

...

"Then, great king, these powers are not united one to another indiscriminately."

"I am not capable of discussing with such a reasoner. Be pleased, Sir, to explain to me how the matter stands."

Then the Elder convinced Milinda the king with discourse drawn from the Abhidhamma, saying: "It is by reason, O king, of the eye and of forms that sight arises, and those other conditions—contact, sensation, idea, thought, abstraction, sense of vitality, and attention—arise each simultaneously with its predecessor. And a similar succession of cause and effect arises when each of the other five organs of sense is brought into play. And so herein there is no such thing as soul." (Nagasena, [1894], Book II. Chapter 6)

Nagasena is refuting the King's belief that there exists the "living principle" that is supposed to be responsible for our understanding of the sense data coming to us and for our self-consciousness as a separate entity as opposed to other individuals. It is this principle, so the King appears to believe, that is one who sees, hears, tastes, remembers, feels, and so forth. This is perhaps comparable to the Western individual self that we discussed earlier. At least the notion that the living principle here is one who does the seeing, hearing, tasting, thinking, and feeling makes it a very strong contender for the Western individual, private self. Nagasena, however, argues that such a living principle does not, in fact, exist, because all it does is see, hear, think, and so forth, and these actions always are performed in relation to the relevant faculties.

If there were the living principle, then, on analogy with the king and Nagasena as capable of looking through any window in the palace, this living principle presumably would be able to see through the ear or think through the nose, since the eyes, the nose, and so forth are the doors through which the living principle (or the soul) comes in contact with the outside world. But since the seeing function of the soul always is connected to the eye, an essential part of the living principle has to rely on this bodily part. Seeing is part of a chain of causes and effects that arises from light reflecting from a surface, travels to the eye, falls on the retina, gets changed to electrochemical signals and transmitted to the brain, and so forth. Nowhere is this living principle found. This is also the case for the other faculties. As for the thinking faculty, one might think, "This is me," and get a notion that the individual self actually exists. (This is the basis of Descartes' famous argument that the *I* that does the thinking actually exists because it always is found in any act of thinking or being conscious, and Kant's argument that the "I think" always accompanies any act of thought such that the thoughts are able to be related to the same individual [Descartes, 1986; Kant, 2003]). But when analyzed by Nagasena, "thinking" here is just one episode in the series of "thinkings" and feelings that occur in rapid succession one after another. Nowhere in these episodes is the living principle or the soul found either. Hence, it is concluded that there is no soul and, thus, no inherently existing self. This argument against the inherent existence of the self is accepted by all schools and traditions of Buddhism.

One should bear in mind, nonetheless, that this analysis of the self does not imply that what is commonly understood as the self does not exist at all. To do so would be a blatant denial of empirical reality. The self in conventional reality does exist, and it is only after analysis that the conventional self is shown to be a mere illusion in ultimate terms. Let us look at the following text from the *Mulamadhyamakakarika* (The

Fundamental Verses of the Middle Way—MMK) by Nagarjuna:

The Buddha's teaching of the Dharma
Is based on two truths:
A truth of worldly convention
And an ultimate truth

Those who do not understand
The distinction drawn between these two truths
Do not understand
The Buddha's profound truth.

Without a foundation in the conventional truth,
The significance of the ultimate cannot be taught.
Without understanding the significance of the ultimate,
Liberation is not achieved. (*MMK* XXIV, pp. 8-10)

Understanding the difference and distinction between the two truths is crucial in the whole of Buddhism. What Nagarjuna is saying is that the Buddha's teaching is based on two levels. First, there is the level of conventional truth. It is the basic teaching that language as it is being used in everyday life, together with its system of meaning and its way of dividing up the world to correspond to the meaning, is conventional in the sense that one cannot grasp reality as it really is through language alone. In this, Nagarjuna is roughly on the same wavelength as Immanuel Kant (2003), who famously argues that ultimate reality consists in things in themselves, which cannot be known save through the system of categories that are essential to the understanding. It is only when conventional reality—in Kant's terms, phenomenal reality—which is necessarily based on language and concept, is understood in its very nature to be nothing more than an illusion, something that is projected by the mind out of the more basic, ultimate reality, that the distinction between the conventional and the ultimate level of understand-

ing is grasped. Just as for Kant, the phenomena as the appearance of things in themselves represent to us two sides of a unitary reality, so Nagarjuna is clear in pointing out that the two levels of truth here do not imply that there are two separate realities. On the contrary, there is only one reality, the one with which we are all accustomed. But when this familiar empirical reality is analyzed and found to be not as it appears, it is understood to be merely conventional.

The case of the self, or the individual *I* is no exception. The referent of the word *I* in a statements such as:

(1)   I weigh 76 kilograms.

is nothing but my own body. I may weigh 76 kgs. at the time of writing this chapter, but just a few years ago I weighed less, and there is no guarantee that I'll weigh the same in the future. But the *I* also may refer to mental states, such as in the statement:

(2)   I am trying to understand what Nagarjuna means by the two truths.

In this case, the *I* refers to my thinking at the moment, which naturally changes quite rapidly. In both cases, the *I* in (1) and (2) refer to the empirical or conventional *I*, whose existence Buddhism has no qualm in recognizing and accepting. It is only when there is an inference from a collection of empirical statements such as (1) and (2) to an affirmation that there exists an overarching *I* that somehow binds all these empirical episodes together that Buddhism disagrees, since it is this overarching *I* that is the object of analysis and is found to be nonexistent. At the conventional level, then, there are many episodes of empirical *I*s such as in (1) and (2), but at the ultimate level, one cannot find the overarching *I* or the living principle that has been refuted by Nagasena in the passage that we have already seen. Hence, Nagasena's analysis contrasts with that of Kant, who argued for a transcendental unity of apperception, which accompanies all episodes of thoughts of an individual that provide a fulcrum point for the individual being *one* individual (Kant, 2003).

The implication for the analysis and justification of privacy is that on the one hand, privacy, being a concept that is used in everyday life and is part and parcel of normal understanding of the (social, cultural, legal) world, is not denied in Buddhism at all. Conventional reality is as true and as real as the ultimate one. In fact they are one and the same. As the conventional, individually based self does exist, so, too, is his or her privacy, which is a normative notion established to safeguard his or her personal information from the prying eyes of other individuals or political authorities.

On the other hand, privacy is justified in Buddhism through its being a necessary element in the realization of democratic ideals that require individuals to be respected and accorded a certain number of rights that would allow them to function effectively in the task assigned to citizens in a democratic polity, such as deliberation and participation in public policy process. In such a scenario, violation of individual privacy would mean that the violator gains an unfair power over the individual; thus, the basic underlying principle of democracy would be undermined, the principle that individuals are equal in power in need of some space within which they can live, think, and communicate freely. For example, a society that routinely checks its citizens' e-mail communications would not be democratic in this sense, because e-mail communication is private, and the information gained from such snooping might be used against the senders and receivers in an unjust manner. At the practical level, as Buddhist cultures find themselves in the 21st century in which such uses of technologies have tended to become commonplace, they would need to find out how their religious tradition could serve as a foundation for democracy. This can be done, for example, on the premise that Buddhism ac-

cords a lot of importance to the capacity of each individual to gain liberation by himself or herself. Since achieving the ultimate goal relies on individual effort and since even Buddha himself can do no more than show the way, there is the idea of equality that is pervasive. Each individual (of course, this is taken in the conventional way) has to rely on herself or himself for liberation; no one is better or worse than another in this regard. One then can extrapolate from this and argue that, for Buddhism, democracy is ingrained, since democracy relies on the notion that individuals possess an equal degree of rational capabilities that would enable him or her to function effectively in deliberation. Surely this line of argument would need to be developed further.

I think this is a strong enough justification, and one does not seem to need arguments to the effect that privacy is ingrained in the individual self such that it is inalienable for the individual in the same way some philosophers argue that rights are inalienable. If one subscribes to the Doctrine of Two Truths and realizes that the individual self exists firmly on the conventional side, then one realizes that the self as well as the rights that are but corollary to the self are merely conventional; that is, they do not exist *tout court* on their own right. When the self does not exist in the ultimate sense, neither do the rights that belong to the self. In this light, talk of rights being inalienable seems to be merely a way of speaking so that the justification looks strong (MacIntyre, 1984), but, in fact, there is really no need, and if the Doctrine of Two Truths and the Doctrine of No-Self are accepted, such a justification would be incoherent. This is so because, as the self may exist at the conventional level, it does not at the ultimate level. At this ultimate level, the walls separating an individual self from other selves break down, and it makes no sense to talk about this or that self anymore. At the ultimate level, when the usual empirical self is analyzed and found to be nothing but juxtaposing episodes of mental states, there is not much sense in saying that these states do belong to one individual (what is there that remains the same such that it could justify there being one individual?), and when that is the case, there is not much sense in saying that there is a difference between one individual and others, either. The upshot is that from the ultimate perspective of a Buddha, privacy just makes no sense whatsoever. Since a Buddha is omniscient, he (or she!) actually can read the thoughts and minds of anybody, but that is, of course, no cause for concern, for a Buddha is full of love and compassion, and there is no possibility that any harm would arise from that.

So how about the attempts by Moor and Moore, both of whom would like to base privacy on empirical facts of the matter, which allegedly are shared by all cultures? Both Moor and Moore want to find a firm foundation for privacy in such a way that it does not vary too much from one culture to another. For Moor, privacy is an expression of the universal value of security, which is shared by all cultures. The Buddhist, I believe, would have nothing against this. She might point out, though, that the inference of privacy as a value from these core values should not be taken to mean that the individual self actually does exist inherently. So long as one bases one's argument on the conventional side of reality, keeping in mind that the individual self that underpins the notion of privacy is nothing but a construct for the purpose of living harmoniously or in accordance with the democratic ideals, things will be fine (Kitiyadisai, 2005). It is only when there is a reification of the self that problems seem to arise, including those that gave rise to the whole problem of privacy in the first place. When one wants to gain an unfair advantage on others, then one would want to encroach upon others' private, personal information. But that is only because those who want to gain the information mistakenly believe that these advantages will bring what they believe to be useful to themselves, such as when the unfair advantages gained from violating the privacy of others translate into material benefits

(as is always the case). Here is the root of all the problems. Violating privacy is motivated by what Buddhists call mental defilements (*kleshas*), of which there are three—greed, anger, and delusion. Since violating privacy normally brings about unfair material benefits, it is in the category of greed. In any case, the antidote is to cultivate love and compassion. Problems in the social domain, according to Buddhists, arise because of these mental defilements, and the ultimate antidote to social problems lies within the individuals themselves and their states of mind.

THE IMPORTANCE OF COMPASSION

But one might then ask: What is the benefit of trying to eliminate suffering by getting rid of the defilements? And why should one strive to attain liberation when the subject matter at this moment is justification of privacy, which seems a very long way from nirvana? The answer is that realizing the importance of liberation and the way toward it is an important Buddhist contribution to the current debates on the nature of privacy in information ethics. The key here is compassion. Realizing that there are, in fact, no walls that separate one individual from all others is a crucial step toward realizing the universal interdependence of all individuals and, indeed, all things. Compassion naturally arises from this realization when one realizes that other beings are no different from oneself. All want to get rid of suffering, and all do want happiness. The benefit of this realization for information ethics is that compassion is the key that determines the value of an action. In an earlier paper (Hongladarom, 2005) on electronic surveillance in the workplace, I emphasized the role of compassion in using surveillance technologies in the workplace. The idea is that if employers and employees are compassionate toward each other, there is really no need for surveillance devices. The implication for information ethics is that ethical issues, such as surveillance in public places or violation of privacy in general, arise because those involved lack compassion. On the one hand, employers who believe that their employees might spend time idly or nonproductively install surveillance devices; this shows a lack of compassion and trust toward the employees. On the other hand, some employees may not use their work time in a fairly productive manner, which gives rise to the need for installing surveillance devices in the first place. All of these show that both parties lack compassion toward the other. The key is to develop a set of virtues that would prevent one from doing bad things rather than subscribe to universal rules. In that paper and in this chapter, I would venture to say that virtue ethics is more in accord with Buddhism than the more mainstream liberal ethics of Kant or Mill.

The upshot is that instead of relying on the Enlightenment project of founding ethical judgments on rational capability of human beings or on maximizing utilities, whatever that means, I believe that ethical deliberation is better served by recognizing that value judgments are more like tools that purport to get us what we need or what we believe to be desirable. Purists may say that this line of thinking robs ethics of its supposedly universal and objective foundation, but if we, perhaps following pragmatists like Richard Rorty (1979), realize that these talks about ethical objectivity are but devices to give ethical judgments a firm foundation so that they have some force, then we are, I believe, on the right track. Purists also might add that basing ethical judgments on what we actually desire would render ethical values merely instrumental, hinting that the values may not be objective and that judgments may be relativistic. If privacy is considered to be an instrumental value only, then there might be circumstances in which strict observance of personal privacy is not justified, and hence, information ethics would be relativistic. But we do not need to follow this line of thought. The Buddhist views on the two

truths and the no-self teach us that this distinction between values being instrumental and intrinsic is only a construction, something imputed by the mind on raw, unconceptualized reality. Once it is realized that the distinction between values being instrumental and intrinsic relies on the values being mistakenly considered to exist in and of themselves, then things should be all right. This is so because when values are seen to be mere tools that can change more or less to the circumstances, then they can be considered instrumental, and when they are fixed (e.g., when people view them as something that should be applied across a broad range of situations and cultures), then they are considered intrinsic. In any case, values are only tools, and ethical deliberation based on Buddhist teachings should reflect this.

REFERENCES

Ames, R., & Rosemont, H. (1998). *The analects of Confucius: A philosophical translation*. New York: Ballantine.

Capurro, R. (2005). Privacy: An intercultural perspective. *Ethics and Information Technology*, 7(1), 37-47.

Descartes, R. (1986). *Meditations on first philosophy: With selections from the objections and replies* (J. Cottingham, trans.). Cambridge: Cambridge University Press.

Ess, C. (2005). Lost in translation? Intercultural dialogues on privacy and information ethics. *Ethics and Information Technology*, 7(1), 1-6.

Fried, C. (1968). Privacy. *The Yale Law Journal*, 77(3), 475-493.

Fried, C. (1970). *The anatomy of values*. Cambridge, MA: Harvard University Press.

Fried, C. (1984). Privacy. In F. D. Schoeman (Ed.), *Philosophical dimensions of privacy*. New York: Cambridge University Press.

Hongladarom, S. (2005). Electronic surveillance in the workplace: A Buddhist perspective. In J. Weckert (Ed.), *Electronic monitoring in the workplace: Controversies and solutions* (pp. 208-226). Hershey, PA: Idea Group Publishing.

Kant, I. (2003). *Critique of pure reason* (N. Kemp Smith, trans.). Basinstoke: Palgrave Macmillan.

Kitiyadisai, K. (2005). Privacy rights and protection: Foreign values in modern Thai context. *Ethics and Information Technology, 7*(1), 17-26.

Lü, Y.H. (2005). Privacy and data privacy issues in contemporary China. *Ethics and Information Technology, 7*(1), 7-15.

MacIntyre, A. (1984). *After virtue.* Notre Dame, IN: University of Notre Dame Press.

Moor, J. (2002). Toward a theory of privacy in the information age. In R. M. Baird, R. Ramsower, & S. E. Rosenbaum (Eds.), *Cyberethics: Social & moral issues in the computer age* (pp. 200-212). Amherst, NY: Prometheus Books.

Moore, A. D. (2003). Privacy: Its meaning and value. *American Philosophical Quarterly, 40*(3), 215-227.

Nagarjuna. (1995). *The fundamental verses of the middle way: Nagarjuna's Mulamadhyamaka-karika* (J. Garfield, trans.). New York: Oxford University Press.

Nagasena. (1894). *The questions of King Milinda* (R. Davis, trans.). Oxford: Clarendon Press.

Retrieved February 20, 2006, from http://www.sacred-texts.com/bud/sbe35/sbe3506.htm#page_86

Nakada, M., & Tamura, T. (2005). Japanese conceptions of privacy: An intercultural perspective. *Ethics and Information Technology, 7*(1), 27-36.

Parent, W. A. (1983). Privacy, morality and the law. *Philosophy & Public Affairs, 12*(4), 269-288.

Ramasoota, P. (2000). *State surveillance, privacy and social control in Thailand (1350-1998)* [unpublished doctoral dissertation]. Canada: Simon Fraser University.

Rorty, R. (1979). *Philosophy and the mirror of nature.* Princeton, NJ: Princeton University Press.

Scanlon, T. (1975). Thomson on privacy. *Philosophy & Public Affairs, 4*(4), 315-322.

Tamás, G. M. (2002). From subjectivity to privacy and back again. *Social Research, 69*(1), 201-221.

Thomson, J. J. (1975). The right to privacy. *Philosophy & Public Affairs, 4*(4), 295-314.

Wasserstom, R. (1979). Privacy: Some assumptions and arguments. In R. Bronaugh (Ed.), *Philosophical law* (pp. 148-167). Greenwood, CT: Greenwood Press.

Westin, A. F. (2003). Social and political dimensions of privacy. *Journal of Social Issues, 59*(2), 431-453.

Section II

Specific Viewpoints

Chapter IX
Information Privacy
in a Surveillance State:
A Perspective from Thailand

Pirongrong Ramasoota Rananand
Chulalongkorn University, Thailand

ABSTRACT

This chapter examines information privacy as manifested and understood in Thai society. Multidisciplinary perspectives—philosophical, anthropological, historical, legal, policy-oriented, and communicative—are used to explore information privacy, which arguably is emerging as an ethic in Thailand. While the diffusion of ICTs along with the country's aspiration toward an information society may have given rise to this conceptual emergence, the longstanding surveillance that characterizes the Thai state is reckoned to be a major hindrance to a meaningful realization of this ethic in Thai society.

BUDDHISM AND PRIVACY: AN INCONGRUENCE (?)

In studying normative concepts in Thai society, many scholars, foreign as well as local, have turned to one preeminently potent philosophical force that has shaped Thai culture for centuries: Buddhism. Thailand is a predominantly Buddhist culture with more than 95% of the population professing the religion. As far as the ethic of privacy is concerned, Buddhism may shed some light on the existence or lack of it in Thai society, as will be discussed.

By some philosophical accounts, Buddhism is said to bear resemblance to liberalism, upon which the theory of privacy originally was founded. This is with particular regard to both philosophies' emphases on the individual capacity to seek and attain emancipation. However, the two philosophical traditions diverge in their goals and concepts of human emancipation in accordance with the different social contexts in which they evolve. While liberalism emphasizes emancipation as the creation of individuals who struggle to achieve rights and freedom in secular and material terms, Buddhism teaches the transience of matter and being and encourages individuals to discard material belongings and worldly comforts in order to achieve spiritual freedom, as embodied in the ultimate condition of nirvana.

Likewise, on a philosophical plane, privacy appears to be incongruent with Buddhism in at least two important ways. First, the philosophical environment of Buddhism is anchored in the idea of interrelatedness rather than in a model of the individual vs. the society or the state. In this regard, the problem is the relationship between the inner and the outer rather than the private vs. the public. The fact that Buddha himself left the household life behind to seek enlightenment may indicate that Buddhism leaves the liberal problematique behind or is fundamentally indifferent to it.

Second, unlike liberalism, which focuses on individualism, natural rights, and human dignity, Buddhist thinking sees the obsession with one's individual self and one's possessions, material or not, as the root cause of suffering. Emancipation, according to Buddhist teaching, means disillusionment with and relinquishing of preoccupation with the self and worldly desires. Therefore, individuality can be seen as both the beginning and the end to human emancipation in Buddhism.

To put it another way, Buddhist philosophy operates on a different level from that of liberalism. Aside from its relatively modest contribution to promoting rights-oriented political culture, Buddhism also pays little attention to physical freedom, which is a crucial basis for privacy.

In any case, it ought to be noted that these philosophical interpretations are filtered mainly from classical Buddhist teaching, which may not necessarily reflect the behavior of relatively secularized Buddhists in contemporary Thai society.

ANTHROPOLOGICAL EVIDENCE OF PRIVACY IN THAI SOCIETY

The Thai language does not have a word for privacy but refers to it by descriptively translating it from English as *khwam pen suan tua* or *khwam pen yu suan tua*, meaning "the state of being private."

According to a prominent Thai anthropologist,[1] the Thai public-private divide is inherently distinct from that of the West. Citing the example of an interior design of traditional Thai houses in the Northeast, this anthropologist points out how the room that is considered most private—the spirit room—can be shared by all members of the family. This spirit room, he explains, usually is located at the center or in the least accessible corner (from outsiders) in the house and is considered a sacred space that needs to be protected from outside intervention. Meanwhile, this room also is designated as a space where all family members perform religious rituals and functions together, since it is where the ancestral shrines and the ashes of ancestors are kept. What this signifies, he says, is that the traditional Thai concept of privacy is fundamentally collectivistic. It is the kind of privacy that is shared by intimate members of the household. By this token, individualistic privacy is said to have no place in traditional Thai culture.

Similar to this interpretation is an anthropological study at a local university, which finds privacy implications in the evolution of house forms and habitation patterns of Thai peasants in the Central Region over the past 100 years. When peasants first settled in this region, their habitation units featured a large common space, which was used for several purposes (social rituals, workspace, and playground) and relatively small living space (kitchen and sleeping areas). Most of these traditional houses do not have separate bedrooms, since family members usually sleep together in one big central room. Most of the common space, regarded as social space, was located outdoors so that neighbors could join in the activities.

But as the capitalist economy grew and took over the peasant community, traditional farming was no longer adequate to cope with the modern way of life. Many farmers became migrant laborers in the city, and new farming technologies were adopted by those who still farmed to increase production. With more time freed up and with the penetration of television, many farmers found themselves spending more time indoors. This directly affected the house forms. Most evident was the way private space increased at the expense of common space. Separate rooms with doors are now common in peasants' houses, and so are rooms with new functions. For instance, the emergence of the TV/living room has become a norm for architectural patterns across the peasant community in the Central Plains.

Clearly, privacy in the physiological sense has increased in the peasant community. However, this did not have bearing on the ethic of privacy in the sense of private rights against the intrusion of others and an aspect of human dignity. This claim will be substantiated in the ensuing accounts on the history of state surveillance in Thailand and the perception of privacy by Thais, particularly in the context related to information and communication technologies (ICTs).

HISTORY OF STATE SURVEILLANCE IN THAILAND: FROM WRIST TATTOOING TO SMART CARDS

Thailand, formerly Siam, has had a long heritage of the state controlling people through different means of surveillance. In the ancient period (13th to mid-19th centuries) when human power was scarce, a majority of the male population (the commoners) had to have their wrists tattooed with codes that would signify their subordination to a certain noble.[2] The nobles, on the king's behalf, would control these men and extract from them forced levies of produce or taxes, *corvée* labor and soldiering forces. This system of manpower control and wealth mobilization also was complemented with periodic population surveys and detailed recordkeeping of each male commoner and his family. However, such traditional methods of surveillance were not very successful in coping with the commoners' various subterfuges to avoid *corvée* recruitment and to avoid being tattooed.[3]

When the first wave of Western modernization reached Siam in the mid-19th century, the country underwent a major reform known as the Chakkri Reformation.[4] Then, more rational and bureaucratic means of surveillance replaced the brutal wrist tattooing. Registration documents and surveys became new practices of "civil registration," which later was established as a major institutional component of the newly constructed Ministry of Interior.

Since the early 20th century, all Thais have been required to report the births, deaths, and moves in their families to local offices of the Ministry of Interior. From the 1950s to the early 1970s, two identification cards were launched in response to wartime crisis and dictatorial rule that insisted on identifying Thai citizens from those immigrants who fled from neighboring war-torn countries in Indochina. In addition to the identification card, the household registration paper was another crucial identification item for Thai citizens. Gradually, the two documents became indispensable documents in the lives of Thais. They are mandatory for almost all transactions from education, banking, employment, and conscription to getting a home and a cellular phone. Over the years, Thai people have become accustomed to the use of both documents, hence contributing much to the social control that the state desires. Nevertheless, the actual surveillance capacity of the state still was marred by several factors, including red-tape bureaucracy, traditional clientele relationship, inherent inefficiency, and rampant corruption.[5]

In 1983, some of these difficulties were overcome partly by the application of ICTs to the management of civil registration information. The Population Information Network (PIN), as the much-prided project of the Ministry of Interior was called, consisted of two major phases of operation. The first phase (1983-1988) primarily involved the issuing of personal identification numbers and the creation of a central population database (CPD) that hosts basic personal information on all citizens within one centralized computer storage. The second phase (1996-2001), partly inspired by the inefficiency of PIN I,[6] featured the establishment of online linkage between the CPD and all civil registration offices nationwide and the issuance of new personal identification cards with a magnetic stripe capable of storing more information than before. This card, which is the third generation of ID cards in Thailand, contains basic registration data, a photo, and a digital scan of both thumbprints of the cardholder.[7]

In the closing year of PIN II, a new government led by telecommunications tycoon Thaksin Shinawatra took office. In 2002, the Thaksin government staged a bureaucratic reform and introduced a new ministry called the Ministry of Information and Communication Technology (MICT). One of the tasks assigned to the newly founded ministry was to be in charge of a new multipurpose ID card, or smart card. In 2003, the cabinet asked the MICT to oversee the procurement and management of the new smart card, including the cooperation among other government bodies concerning smart cards. The main collaboration for the smart card, however, was between the MICT and the Ministry of Interior, or, more specifically, the Department of Local Administration, which has been in charge of the PIN project and the CPD.

The new smart card will contain a microchip capable of storing numerous fields of information that are relevant to all the participating record-keeping organizations. These organizations, which will be data sources for the new card, include the Ministry of Interior's civil registration bureau, the social security department, the health and welfare ministries, the land transport department (for driver's licenses), the civil servant bureau, and the agriculture ministry, among others. The information on the card will include the cardholder's name, addresses, date of birth,

religion, nationality, blood type, allergies, medical conditions, biometric images (fingerprints, face, and iris), parents' names, marital status, social security details, health insurance, driving license details, taxation data, the Bt 30 healthcare scheme, and details of those officially registered as poor.[8]

The smart card project, as approved by the cabinet in 2004, is divided into three phases. The first phase aims to produce 12 million smart cards with the budget of Bt 1.67 billion for the fiscal year 2004. The second phase, with the budget of Bt 3.12 billion for the 2005 fiscal year, will distribute 26 million cards. The third phase has the budget of Bt 3.12 billion for the remaining 26 million smart cards in 2006. By the end of the project, it is expected that all of Thailand's 64 million people will have a smart card.[9]

The smart card plan has sparked some, although not widespread, criticisms mainly from the civil society. Much of the criticism centers on the lack of legislation on privacy or personal data protection in Thailand and the plausible misuses of personal information stored in the card.[10] Some critics voiced concerns about the inclusion of sensitive information, such as blood group and genetic information in the healthcare segment of the card, while others expressed worries about the transparency of government agencies in handling and managing databases of information contained in the card. Due partly to these criticisms and technical problem, the smart card project was delayed in its implementation.

Prompted by recent insurgency movements and rampant violence that intensified in the Muslim-majority provinces bordering Malaysia,[11] PM Thaksin in October 2005 pushed the long-delayed smart ID card to be issued first to 1.2 million residents of three provinces: Yala, Pattani, and Narathiwat.[12] According to the premier, this is a way to curb the violence in these provinces, since it is believed that militants are abusing dual citizenship to escape across Thailand's border with Malaysia after committing attacks. Once the cards are issued, Thaksin hopes Malaysia will share information about its citizens so that Bangkok can determine which people are claiming dual citizenship and force Thai Muslims to choose one nationality. In effect, the smart card is foreseen to end the long-existing dual citizenship problem with Malaysia.

Interestingly, since the smart card was reintroduced and urgently launched in association with the security crisis in the South, there has been no criticism against it whatsoever. The media's seeming indifference to the issue may be attributed partly to their reluctance to clash with the outspoken prime minister, who often likened media criticisms on the handling of the Southern issue to lack of patriotism.[13]

Prior to the urgent issuance of the smart card, the prime minister in July 2005 pushed for the passing and immediate implementation of the executive decree on administrative rule in emergency situations, which gives him absolute power while restricting people's freedoms. The law, as widely criticized and opposed by academics and the press, echoes edicts issued in earlier times, such as Revolutionary Order No. 17, the National Administrative Reform Council's Order No. 42, and the Press Act of 1941.[14] These critics are concerned that the government is exploiting the Southern violence as a reason to issue the law to curb press freedom and the rights of the public. Aside from severely restricting freedom of expression, the law also infringes on the right to privacy. For instance, Article 11(5) of the decree allows government officials to investigate, intercept, or terminate any letter, print, telegraph, telephone, or other means of communication, as deemed necessary. This newly granted authority must be viewed in the context absent any legal measures that would provide a check on excessive or unjustified use of government power.

In addition to new aggregate surveillance mechanisms like the smart card, the present government is also notorious for other, more targeted, big-brother practices. According to the 2003 annual report of the Office of Official Information Committee, for instance, the disclosure of telephone use and phone tapping practices by government agencies was listed as issues that urgently need to be considered. As stated in the report, such practices have clear privacy implications, and they frequently were publicized in the news. Telecommunications operators were cited as saying that they were constantly approached by security organizations and law enforcement agencies to tap or intercept telephone communication of individuals.[15]

Similarly, Internet service providers and network providers routinely revealed caller ID of their subscribers when they were contacted by the police who wanted to investigate individuals and organizations on the Internet.[16] In the legal vacuum of cybercrime, the Internet has been exploited for many unlawful ends, hence giving law enforcement officials legitimacy to probe into any Internet user's personal information. Such practices were done entirely without a warrant and went unchecked by any regulatory authority, even though they clearly violated information privacy of the investigated parties.

PRIVACY AND DATA PROTECTION IN THAI LAWS

Until now, Thailand has had no coherent legislation that directly and exclusively regulates privacy, or *khwam pen (yu) suan tua* in Thai. Although there are a number of articles on different legislation and the constitution that address matters related to privacy in its multifarious dimensions, these provisions mainly deal with privacy in conjunction with other rights and legal protections. There are no direct stipulations about violation of privacy, per se, since abuses typically have been framed in terms of trespass, defamation, or breach of trust or confidence instead.

Insofar as data protection is concerned, there has been evidence of legal protection of government information since the ancient period of Ayutthaya.[17] However, the protection of personal data belonging to individual citizens was not legally recognized until sometime in the early 20th century after the Chakkri Reformation. With the introduction of new information and communication technologies (e.g., radio and telegraph), a legislation to govern their use, the Radio and Telegraph Act, was passed in 1914. This law contains a section that prohibits and sets forth penalties for unauthorized opening of documents or telegraphs that belong to others. In 1934, the Telegraph and Telephone Act was passed, which regulated against unauthorized opening, eavesdropping, and disclosure of information transmitted by telegraph or telephone. Notably, the legal trend then had been toward a concept of privacy focusing on ownership and property rights rather than on personal freedom. A slight shift occurred in 1949 with the amendment of the constitution to incorporate the new section on rights and liberties, which followed the Thai government's adoption of the UN Universal Declaration of Human Rights. Article 47 in this section lays down the first constitutional protection of a set of rights that are akin to the rights of privacy in the West. It reads:

The rights of individuals in their families, dignity, honors, reputation and privacy are recognized and shall be protected. Public communication and dissemination of personal information, using whatever means, which may affect the rights of individuals in their families, dignity, honors, reputation, and privacy are prohibited unless they are done in the public interest.[18]

This provision remained unchanged for the next 60 years and was adopted again in the section on rights and liberties of Thai citizens in the latest constitution promulgated in 1997 as part of political reform. From it, one can deduce that privacy is understood not as a separate category of right but as one that is recognized in conjunction with other types of rights.

Following the 1949 constitutional amendment, a number of laws were passed with contents addressing matters relating to privacy and data protection. These are mostly civil and criminal laws that regulate information between private parties. Very few deal with the protection of people's information privacy from government interference.[19] Despite the existence of these legal provisions, information privacy is hardly given adequate recognition and protection in practice. While it may be unfair to blame this deficiency solely on the lack of implementation, given the general apathy toward the issue in Thai society, there undeniably are shortcomings in existing privacy-related laws that need to be rectified.

First, the penalties for violation are usually minimal. For instance, in the Juvenile Justice System Act, the penalty prescribed in cases of abuses involves a maximum fine of 500 Baht (about US$ 15) or a maximum six-month jail term. In the past, it was quite commonplace to see the identity of juvenile suspects revealed in newspaper coverage. It was only with the strong and consistent campaigning of child rights NGOs and activists that newspapers discontinued this practice in recent years.

Second, civil and criminal law causes of action as well as appeals to constitutional law are not adequate to protect privacy, especially when it comes to the regulation of computerized files. As mentioned, the protection of privacy under civil and criminal law depends upon litigation brought under torts of trespass, defamation, or breach of confidence. To establish a civil or criminal wrong against a person or his or her property, it is essential to prove that the wrong was either intentional or that an injury arose from negligence. In the case of defamation, for instance, the truth of a statement is the basis for litigation. In the context of computerized recordkeeping, use, and transfer, a file could be true but nevertheless could cause injury when used in a different context or when combined with other data. With the now common practice of computer matching across different databases and interagency record linkage, an individual's privacy can be invaded without causing harm, as recognized by law. Furthermore, within the routine environment of automated data practices, it would be very difficult to demonstrate the intention to cause harm.[20]

In addition, like most legal statutes on rights and freedoms in Thailand, these privacy-related laws are subject to limitations usually on the basis of collective public interests—national security, public safety, and so forth. In fact, such exceptions even gravitate toward a norm in Thailand, given the country's extensive history of dictatorial rule, its security situation during the Cold War, and the constant threat of a *coup d'etat* under civilian governments. During the problematic period of the late 1960s and early 1970s, national security became a shorthand for the government's suppression of suspected insurgents and dissidents. Many repressive laws were passed in the name of protecting national security, in effect undermining the constitutional protection of people's rights and liberties.

Insofar as laws that regulate the collection and use of personal information by government agencies are concerned, a similar trend of making exceptions in the interest of national security is also evident. The 1991 Civil Registration Law, which was enacted in response to the introduction of computerized recordkeeping and data processing, is a case in point. Apart from making such exceptions, this law also allows other government departments to share in the use of civil registration information through requests for copies of information as well as through computer linkage. Such a provision surely helps to facilitate computerized manipulation of personal data, which are growing by leaps and bounds in the Thai bureaucracy.

In 1997, when the historic Freedom of Official (Government) Information Act B.E. 2540 was passed, information privacy emerged under the section Personal Information and Data.[21] This section contains five articles that clearly imitate the eight basic fair information practice principles of the OECD's Guidelines for the Protection of Privacy and Transborder Flow of Personal Data.[22] While these regulations follow internationally recognized principles of data collection, they still contain some loopholes, which, again, appear in the form of exceptions. For instance, Article 24 of the law articulates the principles of use limitation and disclosure limitation. This article forbids government agencies to disclose personal information in their recordkeeping systems to other government agencies or to third parties without first obtaining the informed consent of the data subject, albeit with the following exemptions: internal use, planning, statistics, census, research, national archives, criminal investigation and litigation, and matters of life and death. Furthermore, the court, government officials, and/or government agencies and departments that are identified as the appropriate authority by other laws are allowed to obtain information about data subjects from any government database. This lengthy list of exemptions closes with an open-ended provision to allow as exceptions any other cases that may be stipulated in subsequently enacted royal decrees.

Nevertheless, the section on data protection in this relatively new bill is not without merit. First, the technique used in information storage—manual vs. computerized—is not an issue. Personal information is defined broadly to cover both manual and computerized personal records. That both types of records are subject to regulation is a good thing, since tampering with manual records can be just as dangerous. Also, the contained data protection principles definitely represent an improvement over the previous status quo, since they recognize, in principle, that the individual citizen has a legitimate legal interest in the information pertaining to him or her contained in government files.

It deserves mentioning that the introduction of data protection within the freedom of official information law was, indeed, strategic. According to a well-respected lawmaker who had been involved in the enactment of this law, the inclusion of personal data protection was an initial step toward further legislative action in the future. Since public awareness about data protection was still minimal, it made sense to introduce the issue to the legislature under the umbrella of access to government information, which was a more timely topic and one that had significant public support. For the same reason, defensive governments would be more likely to let their guards down due to the pressure from representatives of the public who had been vying for a greater access to government information.[23]

In another development, as Thailand was joining the rest of the world in the information society/economy bandwagon in the early to mid-1990s, a new direction of policy and planning that emphasized widespread diffusion of ICTs emerged. To accommodate this, it was deemed necessary by the responsible policy unit—the National Information Technology Committee (NITC)[24]—that information laws be created, particularly those that address automatic information processing and electronic commerce. As a result, six ICT laws were drafted, including a data protection law, starting in 1998.[25] It deserves mentioning that these legislative concerns were taken mostly at face value. They are void of any political or philosophical grounding and are meant to be instruments to meet the requirements of the envisioned information society only.

In the case of the data protection law, one of the NITC's rationales in drafting the new law was to accommodate the European Union's Direction on Transborder Data Flow and on the Protection of Individuals in relation to the Processing of Personal Data. Article 25 of the Directive notably prohibits the transfer of data to a third country that does not provide an adequate level of protection. Since Thailand has had quite close trade relationship with the EU, it was obliged to adopt this legal requirement into its policy agenda. The emergence of a data protection legislation in Thailand thus may follow the model described by Colin Bennett (1998), who writes extensively on information privacy policy, as a penetrative process of policy convergence.

After the bureaucratic reform in 2005, which gave birth to the Ministry of Information and Communication Technology (MICT), the drafting of ICT laws was transferred to the new Ministry, while NECTEC was relegated to be only a center for ICT research. The draft law, which was drawn up twice, followed the guidelines used by the EU Directive on data protection and data protection laws in Australia, Hong Kong, and New Zealand. The completed draft law underwent a review by related agencies, including the Office of Official Information Commission (OOIC)[26], who disagreed with many of its provisions. From then on, the OOIC has assigned a legal research center at Thammasart University to research data protection laws overseas in order to develop another version of the data protection law.

According to recent research (Serirak, 2004), the two draft laws on data protection have many similarities. For instance, both of them serve as general provisions on data protection and recommend that a special regulatory body be set up and assigned the task of implementing the new law in the same fashion as the OOIC for the preceding Freedom of Official Information Law. Also, the stipulations contained in both drafts are meant to protect individuals as well as legal entities. Both draft laws also recommend that all organizations, public and private, develop a clear data protection policy that is in line with the provisions in the new law.

Meanwhile, the two drafts differ on a few points. First, the OOIC's draft rules that all data controllers and processors be registered with a regulatory committee to be set up, while the ICT's draft does not make this compulsory but places it under the consideration of the committee. Second, the OOIC's draft also proposes that there be only one regulatory body, which will be known as the Office of National Information Committee, to oversee all information-related issues, including freedom of information and data protection. This new office, as the OOIC envisioned, will function as another department within the government's bureaucracy under the care of the Ministry of Prime Minister's Office. The ICT's draft, however, recommends that the Office of the Data Protection Committee be set up as a separate regulatory agency that specializes only in regulating data protection. The new office will be under the MICT and will be outside the government's bureaucracy in order to allow for greater work efficiency and flexibility.

Despite the development in both draft laws, the data protection act is yet to be passed. With the insurgency crisis looming in the South, it is likely that more state surveillance measures will be introduced, hence undermining the importance of privacy and the need to pass a data protection law in the near future.

THAI PERCEPTION OF INFORMATION PRIVACY

While data protection law has emerged in the context of globalizing policy convergence and international diffusion of the Internet, it is quite questionable whether the general Thai public indeed considers information privacy important. Here, information privacy is defined as "control over the circulation of one's personal information, including access to, transfer, exchange, and communication of that information."[27]

As far as information privacy on the Internet is concerned, local research found that 92% of Internet users surveyed were aware of and gave importance to their right to information privacy in that context. Age and income were found to positively influence their level of awareness; that is, the older and more economically established

a person is, the more will he or she realize the importance of information privacy on the Internet. When it comes to violation of information privacy in cyberspace, the studied Internet users interestingly placed the least importance on looking up an IP address by law enforcement officers while giving the most emphasis to making personal data that may have moral implications publicly available. Meanwhile, they ranked private information collectors higher in their potential big-brother list than government recordkeeping organizations. Data from the same research also show that information privacy was not understood as an intrinsic value, desired for its own sake. The surveyed Internet users were found to regard privacy more as an instrumental value that was necessary to achieve other important ends, such as security, employment, and legal protection (Khananithinand, 2002).

Correspondingly, focus group interviews of subsets of the Thai public on the issue of information privacy and state surveillance found that participants in the higher socioeconomic strata were more apprehensive about the application of new ICTs in organizational recordkeeping and were more definite in maintaining a boundary between public and private realms. They also exhibited less trust in the handling of personal information in government files than those from lower socioeconomic backgrounds. The latter group was apt to see government's documentary activities as a benign force that benefits the collective interests of the public. As would be expected, participants who were Internet users, mostly from higher socioeconomic groups, expressed a greater awareness and understanding of information privacy than those who were nonusers, mostly from lower socioeconomic groups.

Meanwhile, there was a clear reflection of indifference and economic utilitarianism in evaluating information privacy and government surveillance from the participants in lower socioeconomic groups. So long as surveillance practices benefited them economically, they would tend to accept it as part of the status quo. These participants did not value privacy much, because they saw it not as a part of their basic need. They could get by with less of it in their daily lives. To them, the greater priority was to make ends meet. Their tendency to not question government information practices was reinforced by their feelings of powerlessness vis-à-vis the state and its ignorance of the ramifications of new surveillance technologies that were in widespread use.

In addition, the study found that personal experiences and vulnerability played a crucial role in helping to crystallize the participant's orientation to aspects of privacy. Participants who were HIV-positive and those who had worked with HIV-positive persons were more critical of the government's approaches toward health surveillance and were more cognizant of the importance of a reliable body of laws that could restrict serious invasions of information privacy. Interestingly, unlike the participants in the lower socioeconomic groups, the HIV-positive participants, who came from relatively similar backgrounds, felt that they were in a position to politically mobilize against unfair government information practices or in support of legal measures that would restrict a serious invasion of privacy (Ramasoota, 2000).

EMERGENCE OF PRIVACY ETHIC ON THE INTERNET

As far as regulation of Internet content in Thailand is concerned, the ICT Ministry, since its inception in 2002, has been the central authority in legal enforcement with strong support from the Office of National Police. Meanwhile, self-regulatory efforts are emerging in the industry as well as in civil society circles. At the forefront of self-regulation is the so-called Thai Webmaster Association (TWA) (formerly the Thai Webmaster Club), which was established in 2002 by a group of Thai Webmasters with social concerns. In 2002, the TWA defined a set of ethical rules and guide-

lines to ensure safe access to the Internet and to serve as measures in dealing with different types of content provision. This code of ethics is to be enforced by the newly constructed self-regulatory body called the Webmaster Council of Thailand (WCT), which comprises selected members from the TWA and a number of appointees from the public and private sectors.

Interestingly, the TWA's code of ethics holds striking resemblance to that of the more established Press Council of Thailand (PCT). Eighteen out of 24 articles in the TWA's code echo those in the PCT's code. This includes the following ethical principles:

- Accuracy and completeness of information
- Information authenticity and copyright
- Right of reply
- Prompt correction of information
- Language decency
- Specification of information source and protection of source anonymity
- Respect of human dignity, especially the rights of juveniles, women, and the underprivileged
- Clear measure against obscene materials
- Fairness in criticism and commentary remarks
- Clarity in presenting advertising information (not advertorial in disguise)
- Avoidance of misleading information
- Avoidance of privacy violation except for public interest
- Professionalism and integrity
- Public order and morale
- Avoidance of dispute and conflict with others in the same profession.

The ethics that are not borrowed from the PCT's code include the following:

- No spreading of viruses
- No spreading of information that causes personal damage

- Clear privacy policy
- Clear identification on the Web site of a Webmaster's contact address
- Good judgment in balancing public interest with employers' demands, professionalism, and the Webmaster

There are three major explanations for this cross-media transfer of ethical standards. First, the Webmaster of a few online newspapers holds a prominent role in the TWA and was a leading force in the drafting of the TWA's code of ethics. Second, and related to the first, it is a known fact that the newspaper industry now represents the most established form of self-regulation in all information-related industries. So, their code of ethics readily may serve as a blueprint for other forms of mass media. In addition, most Webmasters in Thailand, particularly the more technocratic IT professionals in the TWA, had little knowledge about such a loaded concept like ethics. So, they most likely rendered the responsibility in the drafting of the code to those with journalistic backgrounds.

Notably, this cross-media transfer of ethics is done within a philosophical vacuum and with little recognition of the technical differences between print media and the Internet and, thereby, associated implications for privacy. Also, the code contains a similar tendency toward exception, as would be the case of other information-related laws, as discussed earlier.

CONCLUSION

Information Privacy Ethic and the Surveillance State: Strange Bedfellows in the Age of Globalization

While globalization and the internationalization of information society ideology may have given rise to the emergence of information privacy on the legislative agenda and as a professional code of ethics, these two forces (i.e., referring to globalization and internationalization of information society) to implant it in the Thai value system. If ethics is to be construed as "beliefs regarding right and wrong behavior in accordance with generally accepted social norms" (Reynolds, 2003, p. 4), then information privacy may only be a pseudo-ethic in a surveillance society like Thailand. It is not so much the lack of realization by the general public about the critical importance of privacy ethic applied to ICTs as it is their insensitivity and ignorance toward social-scale surveillance practices that made this implantation of value very difficult. What lies deeper than this habituation and conformity to surveillance are the philosophical underpinnings of Thai culture that may be incongruent with the concept of privacy. In the absence of critical scholarship and public learning that could create avenues for resistance to the growing technological surveillance, what is certain is that information privacy in Thai society always will have uneasy bedfellows.

REFERENCES

Bennett, C. J. (1998). Convergence revisited: Toward a global policy for the protection of personal data. In P. E. Agre & M. Rotenberg (Ed.), *Technology and privacy: The new landscape.* Cambridge, MA: MIT Press.

Fried, C. (1968). Privacy. *Yale Law Journal, 77*(3), 475-493.

Khananithinand, N. (2002). *Awareness of information privacy by Thai Internet users.* Unpublished master's thesis, Chulalongkorn University, Bangkok, Thailand.

Miller, A. (1971). *The assault on privacy: Computers, data banks and dossiers.* Ann Arbor, MI: University of Michigan Press.

Phongphaichit, P., & Baker, C. (1995). *Thailand, economy and politics.* Oxford: Oxford University Press.

Ramasoota, P. (1997). Information technology and bureaucratic surveillance: A case study of the population information network (PIN) in Thailand. *Information Technology for Development, 8.*

Ramasoota, P. (2000). *State surveillance, privacy and social control in Thailand* (1350-1998). Unpublished doctoral thesis, Simon Fraser University, Canada.

Ramasoota, P. (2003). *Internet content regulation.* A research report submitted to the Thailand Research Fund (TRF) under the Media Reform Project.

Ramasoota, P. (2004). Communication rights in Thailand: Towards whose information society. In *Proceedings of the Regional Symposium on Communication Rights in Asia,* Manila, The Philippines.

Reynolds, G. (2003). *Ethics and information technology.* Boston: Thompson.

Serirak, N. (2004). *Data protection law and implications towards good governance.* Unpublished doctoral thesis, Thammasart University, Thailand.

Westin, A. (1967). *Privacy and freedom.* New York: Atheneum.

Wilson, K.G. (1988). *Technologies of control: New interactive media for the home.* Madison, WI: University of Wisconsin Press.

ENDNOTES

[1] Dr. Nithi Aeusriwongse, former professor of Anthropology and Sociology, Chiang Mai University, interview by author, October 13, 1996, Chiang Mai University, Chiang Mai.

[2] This is a different system from slavery. All free commoners were supposed to report to a certain noble or to the king in order to be entitled to basic legal protection. The commoners usually had the right to choose the noble with whom they wanted to be, while the slaves would always be tied to one noble because of debt bondage.

[3] Some commoners co-opted with the nobles through a patron-client relationship to avoid arduous *corvée,* while others bribed officials who carried out the tattooing to exempt them or to make an invisibly minuscule tattoo.

[4] The reform, named after the ruling Chakkri dynasty, began formally in 1892 and took more than two decades to complete. Aside from a major bureaucratic reform, king Chulalongkorn, who initiated it, also launched a series of other reforms, including the emancipation of slaves, the abolition of the *corvée* system and outdated customs, the establishment of a modern military force, legal reform, educational reform, and the creation of new and modern means of transportation and communication such as highways and the telegraph. See more in Pasuk Phongphaichit and Chris Baker's (1995) *Thailand, Economy and Politics.* Oxford: Oxford University Press.

[5] Pirongrong Ramasoota (1998). Information Technology and Bureaucratic Surveillance: A Case Study of the Population Network (PIN) in Thailand. *Information Technology for Development, 8,* 53.

[6] After PIN I was completed, a proposal for PIN II was raised in 1992. Due to discontinuity in governments, limited budget, and the need to pass a new civil registration law, however, PIN II was significantly delayed and did not take off until 1996.

[7] Ibid., 54.

[8] http://www.boingboing.net/2002/11/25/Thailand

9   http://www.thaipro.com/news_00/201_Thai-smart-cards.html

10 Personal data protection draft law has been in the process for a number of years but has never passed. According to a newspaper analysis dated November 2003, it would take at least one more year for the drafting of the law to be ready. The article also commented that the draft legislation focuses only on data possessors and ignores the issues of data controllers and processors, who might be capable of misusing personal data stored in the databases.

11 As a result of insurgency attacks in the three provinces, more than 960 people have been killed since January 2004.

12 This number only accounts for residents aged 15 to 70 out of a total of 2.2 million people that reside in the three provinces.

13 Prime Minister Thaksin Shinawatra was quite (in)famous for his outspokenness, particularly with regard to his critics and the media. In September 2003, there were news reports about 130 Muslims in the problematic Southern provinces who fled to Malaysia in political exile. The PM was furious and openly asked the local media to stop reporting this news. His exact words were, "Aren't you media people Thai? If so, stop reporting this news immediately."

14 These laws imposed dictatorial control on freedom of the press and the people's rights and liberties. As a result of strong campaigning by the press and its civic alliance in the early 1990s, the former two were abolished. As for the Press Act of 1941, many of its provisions were made obsolete by articles that addressed freedom of expression and freedom of the press in the new Constitution promulgated in 1997. See more details about the protest by the press against the new executive decree in "Press Up in Arms Against Decree," *The Bangkok Post*, July 21, 2005.

15 See more in Pirongrong Ramasoota (2004), "Communication Rights in Thailand: Towards Whose Information Society," Proceedings of the Regional Symposium on Communication Rights, Manila, August 7-9, 2004.

16 Pirongrong Ramasoota (2003), "Internet Content Regulation," a research report submitted to the Thailand Research Fund (TRF) under the Media Reform Project.

17 The Ayutthaya period—named after Ayutthaya, kingdom's capital—spanned more than 417 years from 1350 to 1767.

18 Article 47 of the Thai Constitution 2534 B.E. (1991), amended version (No. 5), section 3: Rights and Liberties of Thai citizens.

19 See an inclusive review of these laws in Pirongrong Ramasoota, State Surveillance, Privacy, and Social Control in Thailand (doctoral thesis, Simon Fraser University, 2000), 258-259.

20 See more detailed discussion on the issue of computer-related litigation in Wilson (1988, p. 54).

21 The movements that gave rise to the passing of this new law came from the civil society. A group of academics, NGOs, and activists argued on grounds that existing laws did not provide adequate public access to official information while politicizing instances of social injustice and negative consequences in the cases of denied access. The movements coincided with the rising democratic sentiments in the aftermath of the crackdown on pro-democracy demonstrators by a military-led government in 1992.

22 The OECD Guidelines were a result of collaborative work by experts at the Washington, D.C.-based World Peace through Law Center and its affiliated organizations of lawyers, judges, and jurists. The eight fair basic information principles could be summarized in the following terms: collection limitation, data quality, purpose specifica-

tion, use limitation, security safeguards, openness or transparency, individual participation, and accountability.

23 Dr. Borvornsak Uwanno, former dean of Faculty of Law, Chulalongkorn University, interview by author, October 11, 1998, Vancouver, Plazcek Residence.

24 The NITC was hosted by the technocratic National Electronics and Computer Technology Center (NECTEC) of the Science and Technology Ministry.

25 The areas addressed by the six draft laws include computer crime, electronic data interchange (EDI), digital signature, electronic fund transfer, information infrastructure, and data protection.

26 The OOIC was created in 1997 to oversee and help enforce the newly enacted Freedom of Official Information Act. Housing a 30-member staff, the office is headed by a full-time director and a part-time committee that convenes periodically to decide on various information-related topics. Apart from receiving complaints from the public on access to government information, it also acts as ombudsmen and coordinator between members of the public and government agencies on issues related to government information.

27 This definition derives from a review of prominent definitions given to privacy by Westin (1967, p. 7), Fried (1968, pp. 475-493), and Miller (1971, pp. 211-216).

Chapter X
Interactions among
Thai Culture, ICT, and IT Ethics

Pattarasinee Bhattarakosol
Chulalongkorn University, Thailand

ABSTRACT

Information is important to humans because without information, no task can be performed. Therefore, information and communication technology (ICT) was invented and implemented to serve the needs of people. This facility has both positive and negative impacts on Thai society. However, it is generally the information technology ethics of the user that determines the direction of use of the technology. This chapter presents the relations among Thai culture, ICT, and IT ethics, in which all impacts are considered and described. The discussion in this chapter indicates that there are various factors related to development of IT ethics, but the one main factor is family background. Thus, in order to increase the IT ethics of users in an ICT world, the proposed solution in this chapter is to create a strong family and instruct children in their religion. Although this method is long-term, the outcome is worth the wait.

INTRODUCTION

Information and communication technology (ICT) is a technology whose main activity to make information accessible to communities using computer networks. ICT has experienced rapid growth and has become part of the human lifestyle all over the world, including Thailand. Since information is very important to people in many ways, computer scientists are trying to invent techniques to improve information transfer methodology to the point where people around the world can obtain information easily and quickly without boundaries. Consequently,

most daily activities rely on ICT-based machines that perform quickly and perfectly.

Although computer scientists constantly are developing new technologies for ICT use, the results of using these technologies are still in the hands of people who use them. It is true that everything has two sides, as does ICT. If ICT is applied to rights, or legal activities, the outcome can be expected to be positive to society; otherwise, its results may be negative.

Considering the fact that people are components of society and every society has a unique culture, one finds that culture in each society is what binds its members together. One significant part of the human culture is ethics. Although people in different communities have different cultures, what remains rather constant in each culture is that there is an ethical system that protects human rights.

As mentioned previously, human activities rely on information, but how the information is used depends on the IT ethics of the user. Since people have many chances to receive various kinds of information, some information may motivate users to violate their IT ethics in order to gain the highest benefits for themselves without being concerned with the negative outcome of these activities.

Thai culture and ethics have influenced Thai living styles for centuries, long before ICT was implemented. People carry on with their lives in accordance with what they have been taught by their ancestors. After ICT was implemented, Thai people had access to knowledge and information that were different from what they had been taught; this information is useful for their businesses and/or their lives. Moreover, ICT allows people to work anywhere, anytime, and whenever they want. Thus, the lifestyle of some Thais has started to change according to the information and convenience they have obtained through ICT.

The consequence of the changing life style of the Thai people may alter the ethics that they inherited from the past. Since Thai culture typically shows a significant connection with nature and since most activities belonging to Thai culture are related to religion, there is a possibility that the IT ethics of Thai people at the present time are influenced both by Thai culture and ICT. One might show this in a mathematical formula. If *LE* represents the level of IT ethics of a person, *ETC* is the effects of Thai culture, *EICT* is the effects of using ICT, and *e* is a small effect from environment, then the model of Thai IT Ethics can be formulated as $E = R(ETC, EICT, e)$, where $R()$ represents relation, which can be either function or nonfunction among parameters.

This chapter will focus on the impact of ICT on the IT ethics of the Thai people and their culture. Additionally, a solution to improve Thai IT Ethics in the cyberworld is suggested.

BACKGROUND

According to the Webster's dictionary, the word *culture* means the act of developing intellectual and moral facilities, especially through education, and it also can mean the integrated pattern of human knowledge, belief, and behavior that depends upon a person's capacity to learn and transmit knowledge to succeeding generations. Therefore, if the behavior of people in a society changes, it definitely will change the culture of that society.

Moor (1985) defines the meaning of computer ethics as follows: "Computer ethics identifies and analyzes the impacts of information technology upon human values like health, wealth, opportunity, freedom, democracy, knowledge, privacy, security, self-fulfillment, and so on." Considering the current roles of ICT, one finds that it has been implemented in every corner of human life. Although the original aim of developing ICT was for information transfer among organizations, this technology has been developed to support mankind in every activity everywhere. For example, people can communicate anywhere because of the development of mobile technology; people can exchange information because of the existing Internet. The ability to transfer and exchange information has enabled business units to improve their strength and increase their competitiveness.

Although ICT has been implemented all over the world, most people on the Internet expect that other users will use the Internet under the same rules of ethics. Unfortunately, the consequences of using ICT are in the hands of the user. Thus, ICT usage can be classified both legal and illegal, depending on the objectives of the user. However, Mowshowitz (1978) said that the ethical judgment in using computers was based on the impacts through the organization. Additionally, searching for appropriate methods for ethical judgment and control in an organization must deal with the reality of the power of professionals.

In order to create a clear understanding of computer ethics, professional codes of ethics have been defined by various organizations. For example, a well-known code of ethics is the standard Ten Commandments based on Barquin (1992), which was announced by the Computer Ethics Institute. In 1998, the Association for Computing Machinery (ACM) also announced the ACM Code of Ethics and Professional Conduct, whose content is quite similar to the Ten Commandments by Barquin (1992). Moreover, another worldwide organization, the Institute of Electrical and Electronics Engineering (IEEE), announced the IEEE Code of Ethics for all engineers to follow, establishing a standard for ethical judgment.

Since information easily flows to all users, some users use it to commit crimes, while others use it for creating a good society. However, some users may use ICT without knowing that their actions are against the IT ethics rules, such as sending a tracking agent into other persons' computers or posting fake data on the Internet to cause confusion for others, and so forth. Therefore, in order to prevent unintentional crime, Solomon (1993) and Cappel and Windsor (1998) suggested that people should be provided knowledge about ethics in their professional training. However, the study of Cappel and Windsor (1998) has shown that ethical decision making is still dependent on professional experiences.

Since immoral uses of ICT have increased, the attitudes of people toward others have been altered. In the old days, people could live together without guards or fences. Currently, we are living in an environment surrounded by high security systems, even though we are using the Internet at home. This indicates that people do not trust each other as in the old days.

Considering Thai culture in which people live with caring, sharing, and trust, we can see that the strength of community is bound up intimately with culture. Some influences upon Thai culture are from religion. According to their religion, people were taught to believe that causing harm to others is a sin, and consequently, they will go to hell after they die. However, has this culture been maintained, or has it been changed by the ICT world?

Since a part of Thai culture was established through the community's religion, and since the purpose of each religion is to teach people to be a good person for the society, rules in Thai culture are then consistent with the codes of ethics in IT. Thus, "What can Thai culture do for IT ethics?" is the next question that will be answered in this chapter. Nevertheless, if people use IT without ethics, serious damage will arise and will be hard to fix. Therefore, the next question to be answered is, "What would happen to ICT if there were no IT ethics?"

This chapter begins with a short description of Thai culture. The following sections then will discuss the relationship between Thai culture and IT ethics as well as how Thai culture can influence the actions of Thai users, or vise versa. Problems of using ICT without IT ethics will be stated, ending with a conclusion on the impact of ICT upon Thai culture. The last section will show the entire picture of interactions among Thai culture, ICT usage, and IT ethics.

THAI SOCIETY AND CULTURE

Thai culture has been around for more than 1,000 years. Hongladarom (1992) and Mahidol University (2002) referred that Thai culture can be regarded as a combination of two great cultural systems: Chinese and Indian. Since religion is a

Figure 1. Relationship among Thai culture, society and religion

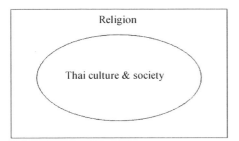

significant part of Thai life, there is a high impact of religion upon Thai culture. In other words, religion in Thailand is the best representative of the culture of the Thai people. Figure 1 presents the relationship among Thai culture, society, and religion.

As mentioned by Phillips (1965), the Thai community is usually composed of a group of individualities bonded by their religion with small emotional commitment. Furthermore, Komin, (1990) stated, "The Thai social system is first and foremost a hierarchically structured society where individualism and interpersonal relationship are of utmost importance."

Although Thai culture is based on religion, the Thai character is not the same as other countries that believe in the same doctrine. Komin (1990) concludes that Thai character is reflected in the nine value clusters as follows:

1. **Ego Orientation:** Thai people usually have the highest ego value of being independent and of self-esteem. The ego for the Thai is very important and is always a main factor in any decision making. Maintaining "face" in society is an automatic action of a Thai in any situation.

2. **Grateful Relationship Orientation:** Thailand has been called the Land of Smiles. In general, Thai people are friendly, sincere, and helpful, with deep reciprocal relation-

ships. This grateful relationship value also is based on gratitude toward others. Thus, reciprocity of kindness, particularly the value of being grateful, is a highly valued characteristic trait in Thai society.

3. **Smooth Interpersonal Relationship Orientation:** The values of Thai society are different from Europeans, whose focus is usually on personal achievement. In Thailand, society is based on many different values, such as care and consideration, responsiveness to situations and opportunity, and politeness and humbleness. Currently, these characteristics help bind the economic gap of society in Thailand.

4. **Flexibility and Adjustment Orientation:** For a Thai, there is nothing to be serious about. Thai people hardly hold on to anything. This might be the influence of the Buddha's statement that everything on Earth is impermanent, or empty. Additionally, the feeling of care and consideration also may be a reason to adjust oneself to the situation in order not to hurt others.

5. **Religio-Psychical Orientation:** Owing to the fact that more than 90% of the population in Thailand believes in Theravada Buddhism, it is obvious that Buddhism has a significant role in the Thai lifestyle.

6. **Education and Competence Orientation:** Thai society puts a high value on education. People who achieve a high level of education always obtain high respect from others. Education can be compared to a social ladder on which people climb to success and a firm social position.

7. **Interdependence Orientation:** In the rural area of Thailand, people in villages always help each other in any task, such as rice harvesting, wedding ceremonies, or the ordination day of anyone's son in the village. Apart from Thai ego and smooth interpersonal relationship, this characteristic

helps Thai society to facilitate coexistence of various ethnic groups in Thailand.

8. **Fun-Pleasure Orientation:** This value relates to many other values already mentioned. The value of grateful relationship is the creation of pleasure for others. Additionally, the value of religio-psychical is the belief of emptiness and impermanence. Therefore, Thai people never take anything seriously like the Japanese. Thus, Thai people always smile, whether facing troubles or participating in parties. Smiling is a method to relieve negative pressure in one's mind. Moreover, this action can comfort the actor for another positive side of life.

9. **Achievement-Task Orientation:** A part of the Thai educational system is to push children for hard work. Teachers always eulogize students who are smart and highly responsible for their assignments. Moreover, teachers usually set up these students to be class leaders. Thus, this attitude is embedded in children's minds and reflected when these children grow up to be adults. Unfortunately, the fact is that the winner in society is the person who has good relationships with others, not a person who performs good work.

Besides these characteristics, there are some characteristics of Thai that have not been stated by Komin (1990), but they are stated by Soopatra Soupap (1975) in the article, "Thai Society and Culture." For example, Thais love gambling and risk taking, Thais never show disagreement and easily believe in things, they don't like others to be as good as themselves, and so forth. These characteristics lead to changes in Thai society when information and communication technology moves into their lives. Unfortunately, these changes also affect the level of IT ethics.

Soupap (1975) mentions that Thais like to do things easily. This appreciation stimulates some Thai people to create tools to support their tasks. Thus, the need for making things easily can be

counted as an internal factor for the change in Thai society. However, this change is a slow movement and, generally, does not turn over the normal lifestyle.

It is a fact that human life always changes, and external factors from different environments and different cultures can accelerate changes in society. Since Western people arrived in great numbers into Thailand, the rate of change has accelerated. Moreover, the direction of change also has been different from the past. At present, modern Thai society has been influenced by Western lifestyle in many areas, such as the education system, the economic system, commercialism, consumerism, arts, and entertainment.

Considering the model of Thai society, we find that the doctrine of every religion exerts a powerful influence on the behavior of the society. One worldwide acceptable behavior is ethics. This qualification of a human being usually is obtained from a strong belief in religious teachers. However, the ethics of a people also can be changed by both internal and external factors. Moreover, standards of ethics of the citizens can direct changes in society. A high standard of ethics leads to positive change; otherwise, the society will fall into trouble.

Referring to the details already mentioned, Thai society (TS) can be written as a model of relations between ethics (E), religion (R), culture (C), internal factors ($IntF$), and external factors ($ExtF$); that is, $TS = R(E, R, C, IntF, ExtF)$. Since IT ethics is similar to general ethics in society, the model of Thai society in modern technology also is related to IT ethics and can be written as $=$, where E represents IT ethics.

Figure 2 represents the relationship among Thai society, ethics, religion, culture, internal factors, and external factors.

RELATIONSHIPS AMONG FACTORS

We learned from the previous section that there are links between IT ethics, Thai society, religion,

Figure 2. Relationships among Thai society, ethics (IT ethics), religion, culture, internal factors, and external factors

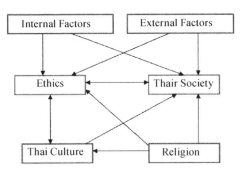

culture, internal factors, and external factors. Since Thai society is a model of religion, Thai culture, internal factors, and external factors, the lines link between these parameters (boxes) have only one direction. Furthermore, there is a two-directional link between IT ethics and Thai society. This link means that when IT ethics of people change, the situation in the society, or the society, will change, or vise versa.

Due to the fact that IT ethics is highly related to religious belief and religious precepts that will never change, there is only one direction line link between IT ethics and religion. On the other hand, the edge between IT ethics and Thai culture is bidirectional, because when the culture changes, the level of ethics changes, and vise versa. The model of IT ethics is the reverse relation of Thai society, which can be represented as $E = R(TS, R, C, IntF, ExtF)$, where E is the level of IT ethics; TS represents Thai society; R and C represent religion and Thai culture, respectively; $IntF$ and $ExtF$ refer to internal and external factors. This relation is similar to the reverse relation of Thai society.

THE CHANGES

As society grows due to the increased activities of modern capitalism, every business also grows, and human life becomes busier than normal. For example, shops have more customers to serve, schools have more students, and so forth. The daily lifestyle is not as easy as it used to be. Owing to the situation where a large amount of data must be computed in every organization in which manual calculation was the only method at the time, human error naturally occurred. Loss of benefits in the commercial world became a critical issue for business organizations. Frustrations in the working staff increased. Too much paper needed to be kept for reference, and so forth. Therefore, the computer system was invented to serve the fundamental needs of computation and data storing.

Some of the results of using a computer system in an organization are reduction in human error, increase in organization performance, and reduced space for paper storage. Additionally, the working staff is relieved of stress. Thus, the working environment is better. However, the data are still transferred manually.

Once the organization is well-organized by a computerized system, its service and productivity increase. Thus, an automatic data transferring system was another user requirement. Why is this so? Consider a system that has hundreds of documents to be distributed. If there is only one postal worker for this job, it would take many days to finish. A manual transferring system is not only slow, but it also may lose some documents along the way, or some receivers in the list may not receive the documents. These errors cause interruption in business processes and are not positive for the business organization.

As a means to reduce the errors mentioned, computer network technology was developed in order to link all computers together and to allow people on the network to transfer data freely. This system has a common name—information and communication technology (ICT). Thus, a revolution in data communication in society began.

At present, the modern Thai lifestyle relies on ICT to a large extent. Most of a Thai's daily life at work or at home depends on computers and network facilities for information exchange and data communication. ICT provides facilities to its users until it seems like there is no boundary to its usage. Thus, ICT provides tools that were created by humans to support their tasks in the same way as other invented tools, except that the power of ICT is enormous and, hence, rather difficult to control.

Are all these changes the only changes in society? The answer is no. Another area of change that may not be obviously perceptible concerns human thought. In the early age, talks about works referred to functions to be performed but not to the question of who performed the functions. Now, talks about works do not consider functions to be processed, but people think first of the question, "Who will do the job? Then, functions to be performed will be assigned based on qualifications of the object that was assigned to perform those functions. This thought is the thought of objects.

This situation can be explained rather easily when we look at the development of computer language. Early programming languages, such as FORTRAN, COBOL, and PASCAL, are functional-oriented programming languages. The functional programming language supports the functional programming design; this means the design that concerns the functions to be performed by programs. Currently, functionally oriented technology is out-of-date, and organizations turn to use the object-oriented technology (OOT) instead.

The concept of OOT was based on things, which also can be called objects. The development process using OOT starts by defining objects in the developed system. These objects can be people, documents, equipments, and so forth. The second step is to define relationships among the objects, following the characteristics of each object, grouping objects under some constraints, and so forth. In the design process of OOT, the designers will start with the same process as the

analysis process; that is, to define all necessary objects for the new system.

What does this change mean? The change from functionally oriented to object-oriented computer programming languages reflects the change of the human mind. But how? Usually, programming is a technique in which people pass on their thoughts into codes that force a computer to run jobs. The functionally oriented approach is not concerned with who will perform the tasks, while object-oriented programming does care about who must perform the tasks. Using a functionally oriented language, anyone can perform the tasks. This reflects a helping and sharing system. On the other hand, object-oriented languages reflect the different idea of independent and individual systems.

Thai society is an open one, and it has received ideas and influences from everyone with whom it comes into contact. Thai people love to follow others, especially now Europeans and Americans. Since one of the Thai characteristics is that they are people who love to do things easily (Soupap, 1975), using computers and ICT are, thus, favorite tools in modern Thai life. Many activities are performed by computers and ICT, such as e-banking, e-commerce, and e-learning.

According to the policy of the current Thai government, every task should be able to be transformed in the digital world, so all services will be fast and accurate with the right and completed documents in digital format (Bhattarakosol, 2003). Therefore, most government processes are transformed into the digital process under ICT facilities. This change makes Thai life more convenient; nonetheless, it is also a mirror reflecting that Thai society is also a busy society fully immersed in the cyberworld.

Once the digital system is applied in the Thai working environment, the concept of independent and individual system has been integrated into Thai society without awareness. Thai society is the same as other societies in the world. So, all businesses in Thailand, including government businesses, are expanding and changing their scales. Some Thais are struggling for survival in their work, having no time for their families. A defect of working with computer applications is that every process must be in "right—authority," "order," and "rules." Once a process is called without order or breaking a rule or without authority, then an error occurs. Thus, Thai staffs try to avoid these errors by not helping friends process their jobs.

Implementing ICT in Thai society, Thai citizens have chances to obtain knowledge from everywhere, anytime by themselves. Additionally, the chance to engage in discussions across countries is increasing. Thus, the Thai population has the opportunity to gain knowledge and experience different cultures via the Internet without having to attend classes.

In conclusion, Thai society has changed into a convenience society with a busy lifestyle. People are more independent, and, most importantly, family life has become looser.

IMPACT OF CHANGES—PROBLEMS

It is well known that human needs are unlimited; the desire of people is not limited only to necessary things, but they always want everything. These needs have pushed the development of ICT further and further with no end to serve these unending needs. Thus, ICT increases the power of mankind.

From the previous section, one can see that there have been many changes in society with ICT. These changes are as follows:

1. People are independent.
2. People are concerned with "object."
3. People are smarter.
4. People have much freedom to exchange their thoughts through technology.

5. People's lives depend on digital documents and equipments.
6. Human life is full of tools to support one's work.
7. Family life is less important than work.

Consider the society model, $TS = R(E, R, C, IntF, ExtF)$, in which TS represents Thai society; E is the level of ethics; R and C represent religion and Thai culture, respectively; $IntF$ and $ExtF$ refer to internal and external factors. After ICT was implemented in Thai society, ICT become a new external factor in Thai society. Thus, the model of Thai society has been changed to be a convenience society with a busy lifestyle, independent, and most important, a looser family life.

Refer to the ethic model, $E = R(TS, R, C, IntF, ExtF)$, and Figure 2, in which E is the level of ethics, the relationships among parameters E, TS, and C are two-way relationships. Thus, when Thai society (TS) changes, the level of ethics (E) changes, and the culture (C) also is changed. Once these parameters are changed, problems may occur in the society. The impacts of changes are described next.

Impacts of Change in "Independence"

When society becomes a busy society, full of work and responsibilities, people have to concentrate on their lives more than others in order to survive. Although computers and ICT are fascinating tools for their work, there are some constraints of which users have to be aware.

Working with computers and ICT is not as simple as one might think. It requires "right," "order," and "rules." "Right" means "authentication" and "authority." A user cannot run applications without having the right to do so. Any computer applications usually authenticate their users before granting authority to run or use the program and data. Thus, each user must have the correct user name and password to log on to the system. These user names and passwords must be kept secret from other users, because whenever an error or any harm occurs in the system, the user name and password are used to identify the responsible person. For example, a student cannot use his or her login name and password to change grades of the enrolled subjects, because students have no right to perform such a task. Therefore, the application will authenticate users before allowing them to enter any transactions.

"Order" means processes of applications that must be inputted in correct sequence; otherwise, the applications will not run properly or correctly. For example, users must enter the user name and password before pressing "Enter" to enter the system.

"Rules" are the constraints that are usually implemented under the requests of organizational managers. In order to perform some processes, some conditions must be validated and be true. For example, students cannot enroll in subjects without having taken prerequisites.

Looking back on Thai society, we find Thai people are always helpful to others. The normal situation in the past was that when a staff member (A) was sick, another staff member (B) would take care of A's jobs. Unfortunately, according to "right," "order," and "rules," people cannot help each other to perform the tasks because of fear of unexpected responsibility when errors occur. Therefore, when A gets sick, his or her job will be left for him or her until he or she returns. So, caring and sharing is wiped out from Thai society. This is an indicator that Thai culture has been changed in a negative way.

When computers are implemented and when most tasks are preformed by machines, quality management is applied to organizations in order to measure performance of working staff. Therefore, whenever evaluation indicates that the performance is lower than the expected investment cost, a reengineering and layoff process usually begins. Thus, people will do everything

to maintain their positions; this includes corruption or being unfaithful to their responsibilities and their partners. Since ICT is an effective tool, performing fraud is easy, fast, and difficult to trace. Thus, using ICT to perform illegal tasks means that the ethics of IT users is decreasing.

Finally, the impacts of a change from dependence to independence can be concluded as negative in the change of culture and decreasing of ethics of IT users.

Impacts of Change in "Object Concerns"

According to the evaluation in the workplace, every task must be quantifiable in some way. This can be done, for example, by counting the number of papers to be printed or delivered, the number of hours to spend for a service, and so forth. These traditions create feelings of object concern more than mental concern.

The object concern strategy is the situation in which people focus only on the things or objects they need. The word *things* or *objects* refers to any tangible and intangible things, such as money, which is tangible; or sexual desire, which is intangible. The object concern is hardly aware of being right and wrong, but it focuses only on whether the demands were met properly or not.

The mental concern strategy is a situation in which people focus on the feelings of others, similar to Thai character in the past. The mental concern does not focus on objects or demands of a certain person, but it determines the right and wrong for the entire society. The defect of this strategy is that some requirements may not be served as needed, and the performance of the organization is lower than the expectation.

In the past, people usually worked with their hearts. Efficiency was measured by considering effort put on work, not the number of products. Therefore, forgiveness and understanding were the main mechanisms for organizational management. Unlike in the past, however, organizational management today is based on the number of benefits returned, which must be countable in some format, such as number of increased customers per year or number of girlfriends a man can have. Therefore, people are striving for objects to be counted.

Just like the previous issue, whenever people are concerned with objects or their needs more than with feelings of right and wrong, caring and sharing also decrease, because they are afraid of losing their objects to others, or they are afraid that their demands will not be met. Therefore, people may perform illegal actions in order to increase their objects or to serve their desires. An example of this is when the system of Orange prepaid mobile phones was hacked by a Thai teenager, who gained more than 100 million Baht (Thai Rath, 2005). Another case is that of a teenage girl who was raped by a man whom she had known only on the Internet (Kaosod, 2005). All of these actions indicate that IT ethics of people is missing, because they use ICT to serve their requirements without considering others or the law.

Impacts of Change in "Being Smart"

Every country wants its population to be smart, so an education system must be implemented in every corner of society. The Thai government also supports the implementation of an e-learning system to the entire country (Bhattarakosol, 2003). Information is distributed over the Internet, and people can access it via a modem at home or at the workplace. These channels support learning skills so that people can have much knowledge to perform their work without paying a fee.

One good thing about being smart is that people know how to serve their needs easily. However, this good point can be a big problem for society, because people might use their knowledge in the wrong way, to serve their desires. Thus, having good knowledge in technology is a double-edged sword that either can harm or support the society in which objectives are main factors for

the outcome. The objective of using knowledge relies on the morality and ethics of a person. If a person is strong in ethics, the objective to apply the knowledge to society will be positive; on the other hand, it can cause negative results.

Impacts of Change in "Freedom to Exchange Their Thoughts"

The ability of ICT to expand the rate of distribution of information to the world means that various pieces of information are floating across societies. In the past, people usually stayed in their own communities and were taught the same model of life. Accepting different lifestyles is interesting and motivates change in society. These changes are both positive and negative. The positive changes are that people are able to find their roles or have an alternative lifestyle that supports their future and society. An example is the revolution in the Philippines in January 2001 caused by short message service (SMS), or text messaging. Citizens of the Philippines distributed SMS via mobile phones, allowing them to assemble and force President Joseph Marcelo Ejercito Estrada to resign and be arrested afterward (Ellis, 2001).

The facilities of ICT never have been limited. Thus, powerful ICT definitely increases human expectations. Therefore, the impact from ICT usage is very serious, as it could destroy an entire social or community system. Considering Thai culture, we find that Thai children usually are obedient to their parents. Thai society is a seniority society or hierarchical society in which older persons are given higher priority than the younger ones. Ethics and morality are taught to kids without question, and they usually believe what they have been taught. Once the new culture of freedom of mind spread into Thai society, children began bargaining with their parents. They acted against the normal culture and believed in equality without considering their responsibilities; they loved challenging their lives in abnormal ways. Therefore, teaching ethics to children is much more difficult because they will compare them to the actual world they see, and the question, "Why do we need ethics?" will always arise.

It is undeniable that the world is full of crime and that most of these crimes are uncontrollable, especially digital crimes that are hardly detected and captured. These criminals can get away with their crimes, get rich, and be happy. This negative but true information is distributed throughout the Internet. Examples are used as models to be copied, because users on the Internet will feel that using ICT without ethics may bring about negative results to society, except to the person who used it. Once a person emulates the illegal process and gets away with it, others will follow the same path after knowing the technique.

In conclusion, if there is freedom for receiving information from the ICT world, a news filtering systems also should be used. Otherwise, the receivers can develop their behaviors in the opposite direction of the law. This indicates that the overload of information can cause a decrease in ethics.

Impacts of Change in "Digital and Equipments Dependencies"

According to the architecture of the ICT system, digital equipment is the most important part. Without this equipment, no communication can occur through the Internet. Since most information and functions of every organization are stored in digital systems called computers, the entire business functions rely on the completeness of the computers and their applications. Additionally, connections over the network also must be perfect; otherwise, the information transfer cannot be completed.

Considering the fact that a computer application is written by programmers and maintained by programmers and system administrators, the entire company actually is dependent on these groups. Since computers cannot work without coding, whether the program's running codes are

correct or incorrect depends on the correctness of codes. If programmers or system administrators are not faithful to their jobs, incorrect coding may exist and may cause critical loss for the company. Thus, the dependency of people on the machine should be considered under the loyalty of persons.

Although there is no illegal function in the application, some fraudulent documents do exist. For example, a British man was captured by the Thai police because he created fake tickets for Scandinavian Airlines and sold them to tourists at half price (Matichon, 2005). These fake tickets were similar to the real tickets of Scandinavian Airlines, because he used the same technology to print them. Moreover, he used ICT to connect to the Scandinavian Airlines database and update the customer's booking information.

So, the impacts of relying on digital documents and equipment may cause trouble in daily life when its functions are not performed correctly or when someone hacks into the system for his or her benefit. However, people remain in the digital world, while technicians are creating tools to protect all illegal processes. People cannot maintain trust or an easy mind, because they never know what will happen to their lives or their property.

What are the real effects of spending life in the digital world? As mentioned previously, people will be scared by the society around them because they will not be able to distinguish real or unreal documents, or they will not be able to trust the results from computer applications. Therefore, society is changed to an untrustworthy society.

Impacts of Change in "Tools"

In the modern world, organizations are computerized. Computers run applications to perform tasks for working staff. Since there are various kinds of demands, there are various applications invented for computers. The applications that people use to create their outputs and benefits are called *tools*.

Since computer technology is changing rapidly, various applications must be updated to suit the new invention and environment, such as the Microsoft operating system and its applications. These changes affect users because they need to keep updating their knowledge in order to be able to run with the technological world. What will happen if the user's knowledge is obsolete? If the user's knowledge is out-of-date, it is possible that the user can be cheated by unfaithful technicians. Therefore, people must learn about tools and their technologies in order to protect themselves.

Consider the problems of computer viruses, which make it necessary to install virus detection systems on each machine. If the detection software is out-of-date, new viruses can attach themselves to the computer without protection, and serious damage can occur.

Generally, tools are good for users; they help users to perform tasks easily, accurately, and quickly with reliable results. Therefore, users count on these tools without worrying that someday the system may break down. Since applications perform all complicated tasks for the users such that they need not know how to solve it manually, when the system is down, officers may have problems. They cannot perform their jobs even with their knowledge.

Therefore, from the previous paragraphs, conclusions on the effects of using tools are: (1) people must update their IT system frequently; otherwise, they may not be able to perform some tasks; (2) without the knowledge of new technologies, people can be cheated easily; and (3) people do not know how to think or solve problems without tools.

How do these results affect society? It is quite obvious that a society of people with tools is lazy, as everything is dependent on tools; machine-dependent more than self-dependent or encouraging teamwork; and somehow extravagant in its spending money for new tools.

Impacts of Change in "Loose Family Life"

The last issue for impacts of change is about the situation of the family in modern society. The family structure in Thailand or other Asian countries is that of close families; that is, family members (1) are close to each other, (2) respect elderly members, (3) are dependent, and (4) are considerate of others' feelings.

However, when ICT was implemented as a necessary tool, people became independent, self-centered, object-oriented, and careless. Therefore, most of the time, people spend time to serve their own needs more than sharing time with family members. Thus, relationships among family members are not as strong as the time without ICT.

In a new society in which technology leads the living styles, children in the big city usually are excessively self-confident; they receive too much information from the Internet, and their relationships with their parents are rather loose. Thus, these children have chances to make wrong choices for their lives. Additionally, these kids may not know what is right or wrong because (1) there is no one who teaches them at home, or (2) they believe in what they received from the real society or the Internet.

According to the previous paragraph, the level of ethics of children is decreasing because (1) children do not know the meaning of ethics, and (2) children do not see the importance of having ethics. When these children grow up to be adults, society will be full of adults with a low-level of ethics.

SOLUTIONS

When ICT is integrated into human life, many changes arise in society. These changes also affect the level of IT ethics of society members. It is hard to find the solution to solve problems of lack of IT ethics, because there are many causes of losing IT ethics.

Consider the model of the level of IT ethics, $E = R(TS, R, C, IntF, ExtF)$ in which E is the level of IT ethics; TS represents Thai society; R and C represent religion and Thai culture, respectively; and $IntF$ and $ExtF$ refer to internal and external factors. To increase the level of IT ethics (E), parameters in the model must be changed in a positive direction. However, it is impossible to enforce every parameter to have a positive direction as needed. The obvious uncontrolled parameters are $IntF$ and $ExtF$, which refer to internal and external factors. $IntF$ is not able to be controlled because humans' needs usually are unbounded, while $ExtF$ is obviously uncontrollable.

The remaining parameters are TS and R and C. Since TS is also dependent on R and C, the important factors are religion and Thai culture. According to the definition of Thai culture from Section 3, Thai culture is obtained or is a part of the religion of the people. Therefore, the only significant factor that can maintain a good level of IT ethics is to maintain the religion of the Thai citizen.

The belief of a child is a transferring process from the child's family. Thus, if society wants to maintain IT ethics in the ICT environment, the family in that society must be strong. The strength in the family maintains realizations of right and wrong of people. Children will trust and obey their parents or elderly members in the family. They will open their minds and learn about good and bad results from their guardians. Therefore, $IntF$ and $ExtF$ factors cannot lead these kids down on illegal path in the ICT environment.

Unfortunately, some children may not have parents and are brought up as orphans. Thus, they do not have a chance to learn from their parents about ethics or religion. Nevertheless, every child must go to school. Therefore, establishing a subject teaching about rules in religions is necessary in order to establish what is legal and illegal to kids. Once these kids grow up to be adults,

society will consist of responsible adults, and society in the world of technology will develop in positive way.

WHAT WILL HAPPEN NEXT?

It is quite scary that the societies of the world are becoming societies of problems. Some examples from the statistical records of Fraud and Technology Crimes by 2002/03 British Crime Survey and 2003 Home Office Online Reports have classified technological crimes in various points, such as computer viruses, computer hacking, offensive messages and Web sites, and copyright theft. These crimes occur all over the world, and many techniques are invented to protect against those crimes.

The prevention methods can be classified in two categories: prevention by laws and prevention by technology. Prevention by laws is the announcement of codes of ethics from various institutes as well as statutes for property rights, e-commerce, and so forth. Applying codes of ethics and codified laws is one fundamental way to guide users in their actions. However, there is no social punishment. Unlike codes of ethics, laws are enacted by the government, and any breakers will be punished for their illegal actions. Unfortunately, in Thailand, these laws and codes still are not widely known, and many important laws concerning information technology ethics have yet to be drafted. In any case, the number of victims continues to increase.

The technological prevention method can be separated into two solutions. The first solution is to implement hardware to protect the system, such as implementing routers to filter the arriving packets before these packets enter the network of the organization. The second solution is to install software to protect the system from intruders, such as installing a firewall to protect the system from unauthorized users or installing virus protection software to protect and kill viruses on the system.

Consequently, the results of the changes and impacts of changes can be seen in the development of new laws and technologies. These developments are performed to balance all changes and their effects. Thus, the society can be maintained on the object side.

Since society appears now to be full of crime, various patterns, and various approaches, people in the society usually do not maintain a peaceful life, because they have to be aware of things (visible and invisible) around them. Therefore, the mentality of mankind in the future may not be as happy as people in this age; this is a comment in the mental side.

In conclusion, there are possibilities that various developments in laws and technologies will arise to protect against technological crimes. Moreover, people in the future will live without trust and will be worried about being cheated. Therefore, satisfaction in life will be low. Furthermore, this trend is not suitable for living, because it is the same as the situation in business organizations in which the period of competition is 24 hours a day, seven days a week.

If the family system is altered, as recommended in the previous section, society slowly will turn back to be a pleasurable environment in which people can depend on others. However, adjustment in the family is not that simple, as there are many factors involved, and these factors mostly are uncontrollable. Therefore, the solution should be applied to a small community as a prototype and then should expand slowly to other communities. Additionally, the cooperation between families and schools must be well-maintained in order to support one another in creating good ethics. This process will take years to succeed, but starting now is better than not.

CONCLUSION

In this chapter, Thai culture is described, and factors related to it are also elaborated upon. Since Thai culture represents the religion of the people, and since ethics is related to Thai culture, ethics is also related to the religion. IT ethics is a part of human ethics according to the use of ICT. Thus, there are interactions among IT ethics, ICT, and Thai culture. However, the belief in commandments of each religion relies on the family.

The consequences of implementing ICT into Thai society are both positive and negative. Unfortunately, the negative effects have caused problems for the entire world. These effects are caused by persons who ignore IT ethics. Even though new technologies, new methods, or codes of ethics are invented or installed to protect technological crime, it will not reduce crime. This indicates that the existing methods are not the right solutions to stop technological crime. Moreover, these methods are temptations for hackers and crackers to intrude upon the system.

In order to completely solve the problem of lack of IT ethics, the main reason for these effects must be solved. In this chapter, the main factor is family, and lack of IT ethics is the result of loose family life. Thus, IT ethics can be built up only when these family problems are solved.

Even though the proposed solution is not easy, it is not impossible. Starting in small communities is the first step to create a good society and ethics. As a result, people will have ethics, including IT ethics, no matter how much they are involved with ICT.

REFERENCES

Barquin, R. C. (1992). *In pursuit of a "ten commandments" for computer ethics.* Retrieved September 30, 2005, from www.brook.edu/its/cei/papers/barquin_pyrsuit_1992.htm

Bhattarakosol, P. (2003). IT direction in Thailand: Cultivating and e-society. *IT Professional. IEEE, 5*(5), 16-20.

Cappel, J. J., & Windsor, J. C. (1998). Comparative investigation of ethical decision making: Information systems professionals versus students. *ACM SIGMIS Database, 29*(2), 20-32.

Ellis, E. (2001). How text messaging toppled Joseph Estrada. *Asia Buzz: Revolution.* Retrieved October 15, 2005, from http://www.time.com/time/asia/asiabuzz/2001/01/23

Hongladarom, S. (1992). *Science, civil society, and Thai culture.* Retrieved October 9, 2005, from http://www.stc.arts.chula.ac.th/STC/papers/Science_Civil_Society.html

Kaosod. (2005). Retrieved October 17, 2005, from http://www.thaiitjobs.com/itnews_listitnews.asp?newsid=11919&ibcid=22

Komin, S. (1990). *Psychology of the Thai people: Values and behavioral patterns.* Bangkok: National Institute of Development Administration, Research Center.

Mahidol University. (2002). Retrieved October 9, 2005, from http://www.mahidol.ac.th/thailand/culture.html

Matichon. (2005). Retrieved October 17, 2005, from http://www.thaiitjobs.com/itnews_listitnews.asp?newsid=11465&ibcid=10

Moor, J. H. (1985). What is computer ethics? In T. W. Bynum (Ed.), *Computers and ethics* (pp. 266-275). London: Blackwell.

Mowshowitz, A. (1978). Computers and ethical judgment in organizations. In *Proceedings of the 1978 Annual Conference of ACM/CSC-ER,* New York (Vol. 2, pp. 675-683). New York: ACM Press.

Phillips, H. P. (1965). *Thai peasant personality: The patterning of interpersonal behavior in the village of Bang Chan.* Berkeley: University of California Press.

Solomon, R. (1993). *Ethics and excellence.* New York: Oxford University Press.

Soupap, S. (1975). *Thai society and culture.* Retrieved October 17, 2005, from http://www.thaicov.org/resources/documents/thai_values.html

Thai Rath. (2005). Retrieved October 17, 2005, from http://www.thaiitjobs.com/itnews_listitnews.asp?newsid=11404&ibcid=18

Chapter XI
We Cannot Eat Data:
The Need for Computer Ethics to Address the Cultural and Ecological Impacts of Computing

Barbara Paterson
Marine Biology Research Institute, Zoology Department, University of Cape Town, South Africa

ABSTRACT

Computer ethicists foresee that as information and communication technology (ICT) increasingly pervades more and more aspects of life, ethical issues increasingly will be computer-related. This view is underpinned by the assumption that progress is linear and inevitable. In accordance with this assumption, ICT is promoted as an essential component of development. This notion ignores the cultural origin of computing. Computer technology is a product of the Western worldview, and consequently, the computer revolution is experienced differently by people in different parts of the world. The computer revolution not only threatens to marginalize non-Western cultural traditions, but the Western way of life also has caused large-scale environmental damage. This chapter argues that computer ethics has to critically analyze the links between computing and its effects on cultural diversity and the natural environment and proposes that the Earth Charter can function as a framework for such holistic research.

INTRODUCTION

Computer ethics is a fast-growing and increasingly important field of practical philosophy. Deborah Johnson (1999) predicts that because the majority of moral problems will be computer ethics issues, computer ethics will cease to be a special field of ethics (Bynum, 2000). Kristina Gòrniak-Kocikowska (1996) predicts that the computer revolution will give rise to a revolution of ethics

and that computer ethics will become a global ethics relevant to all areas of human life. Bynum and Rogerson (1996) and Moor (1998) suggest that the second generation of computer ethics should be an era of global information ethics. These views seem to ignore the reality that the effects of the computer revolution are experienced differently by people in different parts of the world. While for some the challenge is to keep up with the continuous new developments, others are still struggling to put in place the infrastructure that may allow them to ride the waves of the information tide and participate in its benefits.

Nelson Mandela has stated that the gap between the information rich and the information poor is linked to quality of life and that, therefore, the capacity to communicate is likely to be the key human right in the 21st century (Ng'etich, 2001). However, at the beginning of the new century, the digital divide between industrialized nations and the developing world is immense. Eighty percent of worldwide Internet activity is in North America and Europe (Gandalf, 2005), although these areas represent 19% of the worldwide population. The ratio of Internet users to nonusers in developing countries is 1:750, compared to 1:35 in developed countries (Ng'etich, 2001). Although Internet usage in Africa grew by 429.8 % between 2000 and 2005, it only represents 2.5 % of worldwide usage, and only 2.7% of Africans are Internet users (World Internet Usage Statistics, 2005). In Africa, poverty and illiteracy prevent many people from accessing computer technology.

Many believe that these hurdles are simply a question of income per capita and infrastructure (Anyian-Osigwe, 2002; Grant, Lewis, & Samoff, 1992). In the first world, computing is experienced as a crucial element in the competitive market and, therefore, also is promoted in the third world as a vital part of development. The notion that computers are the solution to bridge the gap between the rich and the poor overlooks the fact that computers are the product of a particular worldview promoting values such as efficiency, speed, and economic growth (Berman, 1992; Bowers, 2000).

Computer use requires people to act and think in a prescribed unified way (Heim, 1993, as cited in Gorniak-Kocikowska, 2001, 2004; Kocikowski, 1999, as cited in Gorniak-Kocikowska, 2001, 2004). Not only is there the danger that the computer revolution will marginalize cultural traditions other than the Western one, but the Western

way of life also has precipitated environmental degradation to the extent that we are now facing an environmental crisis of global warming, natural resource depletion, and accelerated species extinction.

The term *West* can have different meanings, depending on its context. *Western* is no longer simply a geographical distinction but also a cultural and economic attribute. Here, *West* is used to refer to societies of Europe and their genealogical, colonial, and philosophical descendants, such as the United States, Australia, or Argentina. The term *Western culture* will be used to refer to the common system of values, norms, and artefacts of these societies, which has been shaped by the historic influence of Greco-Roman culture, Christianity, the Renaissance, and the Enlightenment.

Different cultures have unique ways of storing, representing, and transmitting knowledge, such as mythologies, storytelling, proverbs, art, and dance. These modes cannot all be equally well-represented through computerization, but all are equally valid and deserve to be preserved (Hoesle, 1992). We cannot assume that computer technology will solve the complex social and environmental problems at hand. In order to adequately address these complex issues, a diverse body of knowledge is required, and we simply cannot afford to lose any sources of knowledge.

Although there is an increasing gap between the first and third worlds, and the environmental crisis presents some of the most pressing and difficult moral issues (Hoesle, 1992), there is only a small body of research in computer ethics that addresses the problem of the digital divide between the first and third worlds and the relationship between computing and the environmental crisis (Capurro, 1990; Floridi, 2001; Gòrniak-Kocikowska, 2004). Just as computerization is a product of the West, most computer ethics is explored and defined by Western scholars. Although writers such as Johnson (1997) and Gòrniak-Kocikowska (2004) acknowledge that computer technology was created from within a particular way of life, most current computer ethics research ignores the cultural origins of the technological determinist stance. This stance is prevalent in writing on computing and also affects computer ethics (Adam, 2001; Winner, 1997). The evolutionary view of progress and its impact on the human world leaves other cultures no choice but to adopt computerization and to assimilate the values that are embedded in computerization (Bowers, 2000). Moreover, current computer technology adopts a logico-rational paradigm that often relies on convergences by eliminations and aggregations. It is not clear that computers will develop in such a way so as to mimic or represent values or value choices that invoke those elements at the core of any human being. This consequence might not only lead to information colonialism but also may arguably reinforce a worldview that is ecologically unsound.

In this chapter, it is argued that computer ethics has to critically address the links between computing and its effect on cultural diversity and the natural environment. A framework for global ethics is being provided in the form of the Earth Charter, which has been developed in a decade-long global process in order to realize a shared vision of a sustainable global society. It is suggested that computer ethics make use of this framework in order to carry out the holistic research that is required to see how information and computer technology can be used responsibly to create a future that is ecologically and economically sustainable and socially and culturally just.

BACKGROUND

The field of computer ethics is underpinned largely by the assumption that technological progress is linear and inevitable. This observation has been made by Adam (2001) for the more popular writings and those dealing with professionalism, but it is equally true for the more academic computer ethics research. For example, James Moor (1998) states that the "computer revolution has a life on its own. … The digital genie is out of the bottle on a world-wide scale." Kristina Gòrniak-Kocikowska (1996) predicts that the computer revolution will affect all aspects of human life and that, consequently, computer ethics will become the global ethics of the future not only in a geographic sense but also "in the sense that it will address the totality of human actions and relations."

The notion of a computer revolution carries the theme of a technology out of control, continuously developing while humans are limping along, hardly able to keep up with the innovations but always looking forward to the inevitable next step in computing power (Curry, 1995). In this view, technological progress is unavoidable and determines society rather than being determined by human need. Innovation becomes a goal in its own right (Veregin, 1995). This technological determinism takes the objectivity of the world for granted and ignores the complex relationships between society and technology, thus obstructing analysis and critique of technological development (Adam, 2001).

Technological determinism is supported by the tool-based model of technology, which carries the implication that technology develops independently of social and scientific contexts, thus ignoring that technological innovation takes place against a background of social context and profit motives and that every technology imposes limits on thought and action (Pickles, 1995; Veregin, 1995; Winograd & Flores, 1986). The more technology becomes an integral and indispensable part of life, the greater is its influence (Veregin, 1995). The determinist stance is further reinforced by the increasing complexity of information systems and the increasing dependency on the technical knowledge of experts who understand them. For the average person, a computer system resembles a black box whose inner workings remain a mystery.

Furthermore, technological determinism informs an evolutionary view of progress that places different cultures in a competitive struggle. Seeing computerization as inevitable means that nontechnological cultures must adopt computerization or become extinct (Bowers, 2000). The Declaration of Principles formulated at the World Summit on the Information Society affirms that "the Information Society should be founded on and stimulate respect for cultural identity, cultural and linguistic diversity, traditions and religions, and foster dialogue among cultures and civilizations" (WSIS, 2004). Nonetheless, Gòrniak-Kocikowska (2004, p. 3) predicts that the computer revolution will lead to "a takeover and ruthless destruction of traditional values of local cultures by the new digital civilisation." The computer is a product of Western civilization, and the field of computer ethics is dominated by Western scholars who tend to overlook problems outside their cultural experience. This ethnocentrism marginalizes the need to consider the long-term implications of displacing diverse cultural narratives.

THE COMPUTER AS A PRODUCT OF WESTERN CULTURE

The computer has its roots in 16th- and 17th-century Europe, an era of increased mechanization and increased focus on mathematics. The mechanic philosophy, which emerged during the Renaissance and the scientific revolution, was based on the assumption that sense data are discrete and that problems can be analyzed into parts that can be manipulated by mathematics. For Hobbes, the human mind was a machine, and to reason was to add and subtract (Merchant, 1980). The binary system and its significance for machines were advocated by Leibniz in the latter half of the 17th century (Freiberger & Swaine, 2003). As more and more processes of daily life were being mechanized, the desire also to automate cognitive processes such as calculation came naturally. The computer is the result of the effort to achieve both high-speed and high-precision automatic calculation and a machine capable of automatic reasoning (Mahoney, 1988).

The classical view of reality is still influential in Western common sense thought and in the notion that Western science produces objective, value-free, and context-free knowledge (Merchant, 1980). Although "it is an inherent characteristic of common-sense thought ... to affirm that its tenets are immediate deliverances of experience," common sense is an organized cultural system composed of conclusions based on presuppositions" (Geertz, 1983, p. 75). The mechanistic metaphor has shaped Western culture's view of nature, history, society, and the human being (Merchant, 1980). This metaphor has influenced the birth of economics with Smith's (1976) "The Wealth of Nations," which analyzed market economies as self-governing mechanisms regulated by laws and giving rise to an orderly society. The scientific revolution has brought about a strong focus on quantification and computation. The industrial revolution and its emphasis on increasing production through mechanization has given rise to a strong focus on economics attested by the development of both capitalism and Marxism.

Twentieth-century information theory, the mathematical representation of transmission and processing of information, and computerization manifest the view that problem solving is essentially the manipulation of information according to a set of rules (Merchant, 1989, p. 231). The method of computer science is formalization (i.e., symbolization of real-world phenomena so they can be subjected to algorithmic treatment. The computer is thus a result and a symptom of Western culture's high regard for abstraction and formalization; it is a product of the mathematician's worldview, a physical device capable of operation in the realm of abstract thought.

Epistemological Issues of Computerization

One cornerstone of the rationalistic tradition is the correspondence theory of language (Winograd & Flores, 1986). This theory has influenced thinking about computers and their impact on society. Quantification and computer representations are taken as models of an objective reality. Whereas humans have developed a complex system of languages to interpret, store, copy, or transmit information that they receive in analog format through their senses, computers facilitate the external processing of information in digital format by representing it in binary form. Thus, computers reduce experience to numerical abstraction. As a consequence, the natural and social worlds are treated as being made up of discrete and observable elements that can be counted and measured. Reality is reduced to what can be expressed in numbers (Berman, 1992).

Using a computer is an isolated activity of the individual. Although computers have revolutionized communication in terms of scope and speed, computers are not conducive to cooperation and teamwork. Human-computer interaction generally is characterized by a one-user-per-computer ratio. Collaboration with other computer users generally means division of a task into a linear sequence of subtasks, which can be addressed by single individuals. Furthermore, computer-based experience is a partial experience predominantly limited to the visual. The manipulation of objects displayed on the screen emphasizes the interaction between the active subject and the passive object, which is characteristic of a scientific mind that has been exposed as being male and disembodied (Keller, 1985). This interaction is underpinned further by a domination logic that objectifies both the natural world and people as other (e.g., women or indigenous people) to justify their exploitation (Merchant, 1980).

The disengagement between subject and object reinforces a psychological distance between the individual and the social and natural environment (Veregin, 1995; Weizenbaum, 1976). Computer-based experience is individualistic and anthropocentric and no longer influenced by geographic space. Computerization creates an alternative, unnatural environment, or infosphere (Floridi, 2001). The computer has created a different world in which most activities involve information technology; in addition, the concepts regarding these activities are shifting and becoming informationally enriched (Moor, 1998). Digitization has become a worldview in itself (Capurro, 1990). Such views may adequately describe the experiences of people whose lives are permeated by computerization but emphasize how different these experiences are from the realities of the majority of people on the planet. The value dualism of hard vs. soft information ignores the reality that the computerized abstraction of the world is not absolute but rather dependent on cultural context, scientific paradigm, and technological feasibility. The digital world excludes and obscures important aspects of the realms of society and natural environment.

Contrary to the individualism of computerized experience, African thought emphasizes the close links among knowledge of space, of self, and one's position in the community. Although African traditions and cultural practices are diverse, there are underlying affinities that justify certain generalizations (Wiredu, 1980). In African philosophy, a person is defined through his or her relationships with other persons, not through an isolated quality such as rationality (Menkiti, 1979; Shutte, 1993). African thought does not know the sharp distinction between the self and a world that is controlled and changed. The world is a place in which people participate in community affairs. In fact, participation is the keystone of traditional African society. Participation integrates individuals within the social and natural networks of the world. The members of a community are linked by participation, which becomes the meaning of personal and collective unity and connects people both horizontally and vertically, the living and the dead as well as the physical environment that surrounds them (Mulago, 1969). Setiloane (1986) calls participation "the essence of being"; "I think, therefore I am" is replaced by "I participate, therefore I am" (Taylor, 1963, p. 41). The individual's personhood is dependent on the community, but the continuation of the community depends on the individual. The life of the ancestors is continued through the individual; the individual life is continued through the dependents (Mulago, 1969). Unlike the Western concept of community, the African meaning of community does not refer to an aggregation of individuals (Menkiti, 1979) but prioritizes the group over the individual while still safeguarding the dignity and value of the individual (Senghor, 1966). Shutte (1993) explains that the notions of a person as a free being and that of being dependent for one's personhood on others are not contradictory. Through being affirmed by others and through the desire to help and support others, the individual grows, personhood is developed, and personal freedom comes into being. African thought sees a person as a being under construction whose character changes as the relations to other persons change. To grow older means to become more of a person and more worthy of respect. In contrast to Western individualism and its emphasis on the rights of the individual Menkiti (1979) stresses that growth is a normative notion: "personhood is something at which individuals could fail" (p. 159). The individual belongs to the group and is linked to members of the group through interaction; conversation and dialogue are both purpose and activity of the community. Consequently, African socialism aims to realize not the will of the majority but the will of the community (Apostel, 1981) and, therefore, rejects both European socialism and Western capitalism because both are underpinned by subject-object dualism, which produces relationships between a person and a thing rather than a meeting of forces. Subject-object dualism, as is reinforced through

computerization, alienates the individual from others. While Western rational thought values individuality, African tradition is afraid of solitude and closed individuality, and values solidarity, consensus, and reconciliation.

Users who share the cultural assumptions embedded in computer technology are not aware of the inherent bias, but members of other cultures are aware that they have to adapt to different patterns of thought and culturally bound ways of knowing (Bowers, 2000; Duncker, 2002; Walton & Vukovic, 2003; Winschiers & Paterson, 2004). The uncritical acceptance of the computer obscures its influence on the user's thought patterns. The digital divide is seen as a problem of providing access to technology. However, it may be that the digital divide is an expression of the dualisms inherent in the cultural concepts underpinning computerization. Hoesle (1992) stresses that the main issue of contrast between industrialized countries and the third world is cultural. Capurro (1990) warns that a critical awareness of how information technology is used to manipulate both ourselves and the natural environment is necessary. Such awareness must include the linkages between progress in developing countries, which goes hand-in-hand with more widespread use of computers and the emergence of Western individualism and subjectivism (Bowers, 2000) and impacts on the environment.

THE LINGKAGES BETWEEN INFORMATION TECHNOLOGY, DEVELOPMENT, AND THE ENVIRONMENT

Information technology generally is seen as an essential component of development and strongly promoted by international development agencies. It is assumed that information technology enhances both economic development and democratic practices. This promotion implies that unless developing countries apply information technology and join the fast train of the computer revolution, they will be left behind (Berman, 1992). Publications on ICT development in Africa describe African societies as "lagging behind" (Schaefer, 2002), while ICT structures in Africa are compared to "the North American picture ... in the first half of the twentieth century" (Kawooya, 2002). This line of argument not only supports technological determinism but also subscribes to a development ideology that is based on a particular concept of history. This concept is as linear as the concept of technological progress, assuming that every society has to go through the same stages until they reach the same economic levels as countries considered developed.

Information Technology and Democracy

The notion that information technology contributes to a more democratic society is based on the assumption that information technology is nondiscriminatory in that it potentially provides equal opportunities to everyone. However, equal access does not ensure equal benefit (Neelameghan, 1981). In addition, this assumption ignores the existing imbalances and asymmetric societal structures that do not allow everyone to participate equally (Adam, 2001; Grant Lewis & Samoff, 1992; Veregrin, 1995). Information technology is not inherently neutral but is linked to power from which moral implications arise: "Those who filter and package information for us in the [global information infrastructure] will hold enormous power over us" (Johnson, 1997). As a study by Introna and Nissenbaum (2000) suggests, the criteria by which search engines filter information are not transparent, and particular sites systematically are excluded. This conclusion runs counter to the democratic value associated with the Internet.

As long as the public sphere continues to prioritize information from the North over information generated in the South (Lor & Britz,

2002), it is questionable whether people in Africa and other developing nations actually do have access to appropriate and useful information. Simply providing the infrastructure to tune in to the North-to-South information flow cannot bridge the gap between the information-rich and the information-poor. The information-poor have to generate information for themselves and about themselves. Thus, the issue raised by Johnson (1997) of power being exercised by those who filter and package information over those who receive this information is a pertinent one for Africa and other non-Western countries whose voices are marginalized in the global information scenario.

Although the scope of online communication allows people to engage with a vast number of other people all over the world, Bowers (2000) argues that the learning of moral norms is of higher importance to democratic decision making than is access to information. Global communication, although spanning a much broader geographic scope, tends to join like-minded people who share a common interest. Online communities provide little opportunity for participants to understand the needs of others and one's responsibility to them (Adam, 2001; Bowers, 2000; Johnson, 1997). The more time people spend communicating online with like-minded people, the less time is spent communicating with those whose geographic space they share. As a result, people engage less in debate and tend toward already formed biases. The paradox of growing insularity through increasing connectivity prompts Johnson (1997) to raise an old question: Is democracy possible without shared geographic space? In the African context in which multi-ethnicity is the norm rather than the exception, and tribalism and ethnic discrimination are a major obstacle for democracy, the question is extremely pertinent. In the light of Johnson's and Bowers' analyses, there seems to be the danger that computer-mediated communication may exacerbate the existing ethnic divide in many African countries by harboring insularity.

Information Technology and Economic Development

Ogundipe-Leslie (1993) argues that development itself is characterized by cultural imperialism and ethnocentrism and interferes with the natural internal processes in the society to which it is introduced. Development is based on the assumption that every society shares the same values that characterize developed societies, such as efficiency, speed, and competitiveness. These values are evoked through references to the super information highway that will lead African countries into a future of material security and possession of particular goods and services that are typical of industrial societies. This eurocentric point of view is used as a standard of measurement so that societies who do not conform are not perceived as different but as primitive, traditional, or underdeveloped (Ogundipe-Leslie, 1993). The notion of development as an economic upliftment ignores a nation's values, aspirations, beliefs, and patterns of behavior. As a consequence, measures to develop according to the Western economic model interfere with the natural internal processes in society and uproot the individual and collective lives of the people. Ogundipe-Leslie (1993) criticizes development not only for its cultural imperialism and ethnocentrism but also for ignoring the social costs that people have to pay for the interruption of their social dynamics.

Computerization and particularly the global information infrastructure increasingly enforce Western ideology onto other cultures. Computerization is shaping consciousness and bodily experience to accept computer mediation as normal; consequently, computer illiteracy is considered socially abnormal and deficient, and those who do not use computers are less-developed and less-intelligent. Capurro (1990) confirms that the influence of modern information technology is shaping all aspects of social life. For example in the industrialized world in which computerization is permeating society, it is becoming apparent that computerization rationalizes humans out of work processes (Bowers, 2000). Increasingly fewer people do more complex tasks in a shorter time, thus excluding more people from this process. One of Africa's hidden and untapped assets is its human resources (Britz, 2002). Computerization is seen as a means to provide information, education, and economic opportunity to all people to overcome the problem of unemployment. There is, however, the danger that computer technology in Africa might further enforce and enlarge the gap between the advantaged and the disadvantaged.

Berman highlights the origins of computer technology by stressing that during and after World War II and the subsequent period of expansion of the welfare state, economic planning data were used by the state to gain control over people. African countries inherited the concept of authoritarian state control in colonial rule. The computer's logical structure, which emphasizes hierarchy, sequence control, and iteration, reflects the structure of bureaucratic organizations. This focus on control is obscured by the assumption of scientific objectivity. Hence, the power, which is exercised through computer application, is hidden behind the appearance of expert decision. The computer is a technology of command and control (Berman, 1992). Not only do computers reinforce authoritarianism, but they also become a symbol of advanced development and efficiency. But because computers narrow the scope to quantifiable information, indigenous knowledge is further marginalized, which makes it difficult for the state to take the qualitative aspects of social structure and culture into account.

While some level of ICT may be important for development in the sense of improved well being and decreased suffering of African people, no level of ICT will be a sufficient condition for these hopes. The perception that ICTs are necessary for economic development ignores that technology invents its own need. The multitude of new consumer products and the rate at which they are introduced indicate that producers create needs where none existed (Veregin, 1995). The global ICT market is characterized by ever-decreasing intervals of software releases that force African countries continuously to invest in new software in order to avoid a further widening of the digital gap (Winschiers & Paterson, 2004).

The Environment

Bowers (2000) warns that the globalization of computer-based culture is not only a form of colonialism but that the cultural assumptions and lifestyles reinforced by the digital culture are ecologically problematic. Merchant (1980) stresses that the mechanistic view of nature sanctions exploitative environmental conduct. The mechanistic philosophy renders nature dead instead of a living, nurturing organism. As a consequence, cultural constraints, which previously restricted destructive environmental conduct, lost impact and were replaced with the machine metaphor (i.e., images of mastery and domination that sanctioned the exploitation of nature). While rural communities are aware that environmental conditions are unpredictable and that scarcity is a possibility, the modern Western way of life is based on the false assumption that progress does not depend on the contingencies of natural systems. Thus, the predominant challenge of the 21st century will be the environment.

The notion of knowledge and information as strategic resources points toward the link between computerization and the industrial revolution and its main characteristic: the transformation of utility value into exchange value (Capurro, 1990). Computerization commodifies information and anything else that falls under its domain. In this sense, the computer revolution "represents the digital phase of the Industrial revolution … it perpetuates the primary goal of transferring more aspects of everyday life into commodities that can be manufactured and sold, now on a global basis" (Bowers, 2000). There are "connections between computers, cultural diversity and the

ecological crisis" (Bowers, 2000). The market has become a universal principle encompassing all forms of human activity and commodifying the relationships among people and between human beings and the environment. The mapping and subdivision of lived space based on national or global grids nullify places of local meaning while playing an important part in the functioning of capitalist economy by creating space as an exploitable resource (McHaffie, 1995). Geographic information systems (GIS) have further depersonalized this process. The parallel between information and nature is not accidental; both are considered resources. Nature is a shared resource that is vital for human survival, and information is a resource that is shared among people. Critics of Western-style development, such as Vandana Shiva (1989), have pointed out how the commodification of natural resources, which is typical of the Western paradigm, excludes natural systems from the economic model. In this paradigm, a river in its natural state is not considered productive unless it is dammed. The natural system has to be modified in order to produce value; the use value of the river has to be transformed into exchange value. The preoccupation with quantification contributes not only to the commodification of nature but also to the widespread acceptance of data as the basis of thought. Unless information can be computerized, it is not considered valuable and, hence, undermines the importance of indigenous knowledge.

The global computer revolution perpetuates the assumption underlying development ideology that it is merely a question of time until developing countries will reach the level of industrialized nations. Hoesle (1992) asserts that this assumption cannot possibly be fulfilled. The ecological footprint of the so-called developed nations is not only far heavier than that of the third world but also is unsustainable. It therefore would become an ecological impossibility for the whole world to adopt the same lifestyle. Hoesle (1992) infers that because "the [Western] way of life is not universalizable [it is] therefore immoral." He questions the legitimacy of a world society built according to Western values that have brought humankind to the verge of ecological disaster.

Computerization is instrumental in shaping the ecological problems we are facing, because computerization decontextualizes knowledge and isolates it from the ambiguities and complexities of reality.

The rationalistic tendency to fraction complex holistic processes into a series of discrete problems leads to the inability to address ecological and social issues adequately. Popular cyberlibertarian ideology wrongly assumes that information technology provides free and equal interactions and equal opportunities that neutralize asymmetric social structures (Adam, 2001; Winner, 1997). ICT can only be truly beneficial to Africans if they support the African concept of community and counteract insularity. Besides focusing on the advantages of ICTs, the negative consequences of computerization, such as the rationalization of labor, which are observable in industrialized nations, must be avoided. The current patterns of production (i.e., the high frequencies of hardware and software releases) are ecologically and socially unsustainable and need to change (Winschiers & Paterson, 2004).

Hoesle (1992) therefore stresses the need to bring values back into focus and to recognize humans as part of the cosmos. Modern subjectivism and the sectorial and analytic character of scientific thinking have almost forgotten the advantages of a holistic approach to reality (Hoesle, 1992). The value and legitimacy of Africa's rich tacit knowledge has been undermined because this knowledge is largely informal and does not fit the computer-imposed data formats (Adeya & Cogburn, 2001; Harris, Weiner, Warner, & Levin, 1995). Cultures are reservoirs of expression and symbolic representations with a truth claim of their own and, thus, need to be preserved (Hoesle, 1992). However, Lor and Britz (2002) call attention to the limited contribution that information generated in the South is making to the global knowledge society and point to the bias of the public sphere toward information generated in the North. Only a minute proportion of Internet hosts is located in Africa, although most countries on the continent have achieved connectivity to the Internet (Maloka & le Roux, 2001). The pressing issue is not providing access to technology in order to turn more people into receivers of information that was created elsewhere and may not be useful to them, but, as suggested by Capurro (1990), it is to find ways that African countries can promote their identities in information production, distribution, and use. In terms of a global information ecology, he stresses the importance "of finding the right balance ... between the blessings of universality and the need for preserving plurality" (Capurro, 1990, p. 130). In order to find this balance, a great conversation is necessary that transcends limitations of discourse among members of particular social groups (Berman, 1992; Moor, 1998). Such a global dialogue must be cross-sectoral, cross-cultural, and transdisciplinary. Capurro (1990) reminds us that the electronic revolution is only a possibility that has to be inserted responsibly into existing cultural and social contexts in order to produce the necessary knowledge pluralism to address the complex social and ecological issues we are facing.

In order to fill the need for such global dialogue that addresses the ethical requirements for development that is truly sustainable, a global ethical framework has been developed in the form of the Earth Charter.

THE EARTH CHARTER

The Earth Charter (www.earthcharter.org) development began in 1987 with the Brundtland Report, "Our Common Future," calling for a Charter for Nature (WCED, 1987) that would set forth fundamental principles for sustainable development. The Earth Charter was addressed again during the 1992 Rio Earth Summit and taken forward when Maurice Strong and Mikhail Gorbachev launched the Earth Charter Initiative in 1994. In a decade-long participatory and consultative process involving all major religions and people from different cultures and all sectors of society, the present list of principles of the Earth Charter was developed and finalized in 2000. The Earth Charter consists of a preamble, 18 principles, numerous subprinciples, and a conclusion suggesting "the way forward." The preamble expresses that the future depends on the choices we will make and that "we must join together to bring forth a sustainable global society founded on respect for nature, universal human rights, economic justice, and a culture of peace." The Earth Charter locates humanity as part of the cosmos and stresses the interdependencies among people and between people and nature. The preamble emphasizes that the foundations of global security are threatened by patterns of consumption and production, which undermine communities and cause environmental degradation. The Earth Charter emphasizes that every individual shares the "universal responsibility" of facing the challenges of using knowledge and technologies to build a just, democratic, and ecologically sound future. The Earth Charter principles address four themes: respect and care for the community of life; ecological integrity; social and economic justice; and democracy, non-violence, and peace. As the "way forward," the Earth Charter calls for the development of a sustainable way of life based on a "collaborative search for truth and wisdom" in which cultural diversity is valued.

The Earth Charter and Computer Ethics

Because computing is the product as well as the extension of a way of life and worldview that largely has caused the environmental crisis, and because computers are directly linked to the concept of third-world development, computer ethics has to locate itself more explicitly within the broader context of the environmental issues on the one hand and development ethics on the other.

The Earth Charter framework not only helps to address particular issues in light of their compliance with ecological integrity and respect for nature, but also stresses the gap between rich and poor and global responsibility to address poverty. By stating that "when basic needs have been met, human development is primarily about being more, not having more," the Earth Charter prioritizes qualitative criteria to measure development over quantitative criteria.

The Earth Charter and the WISIS declaration subscribe to the same values: peace, freedom, equality, solidarity, tolerance, shared responsibility, and respect for nature. The two documents do not replace each other but are compatible. While WISIS focuses on ICT development, the Earth Charter is much broader in scope, thus complementing and strengthening the WISIS declaration. Being global both in terms of content and scope (Dower, 2005), the Earth Charter is a proposal for a system of global ethics. It encompasses both human rights as well as less formalized principles for ecological, social, and political development. If ICTs are to be an integral part of this future, it is vital that computer ethics takes cognizance of the existence of this global ethical framework and examines how computing can be inserted into this vision of a sustainable and just future. The Earth Charter asserts the interconnectedness of people and the environment and affirms the wisdom of different cultural traditions, while at the same time confirming the contribution of humanistic science and sustainable technology. The preamble to the Earth Charter highlights the current environmental and social crisis but sees "these trends are perilous—but not inevitable." In other words, the Earth Charter does not subscribe to technological determinism but rather declares that "the choice is ours." The choices we are making as individuals as well as communities determine the future. To change the course of current patterns of thought and behaviors is a matter of human will power and creative energy. It involves a change of attitudes, worldviews, values, and ways of living, such as consumption and production habits.

Unlike the WISIS declaration, the Earth Charter addresses not only states but also the broader public. The global ethic formulated in the Earth Charter provides guidelines for behavior and action. But it is important to realize that the Earth Charter is not to be understood as final. It provides a framework and catalyst for reflection and discussion. As such, this framework is of value to computer ethics. It is the role of computer ethics to guide ICT development toward a sustainable future. By addressing whether the Earth Charter can be endorsed by computer professionals, computer ethics can examine the Earth Charter's justification. The results of such an examination will be fruitful for both the Earth Charter and Computer Ethics. The vision for a sustainable future that is set forth in the preamble to the Earth Charter can guide the development of a vision for the role of computing and ICT in the future. The Earth Charter can be an ethical values framework for improving progress toward sustainability, designing codes of conduct for both professionals and education, and designing accountability systems. The Earth Charter principles set out under the heading Ecological Integrity can help to guide computing and ICT development in terms of environmental performance, which, for example, would refer to issues concerning energy and emissions, both in the production and the use of computer technology; the materials used; the use of resources in production cycles; and the disposal of computing technology, hazardous substances, and so forth. The social impacts of computing (e.g., the danger of increased insularity of users or the rationalization of labor) can be addressed by the principles under the heading Social & Economic

Justice and Democracy. The Earth Charter principles grouped under "Democracy, Non violence and Peace" provide guidance to address issues such as the impact of computing for community participation, the impact of computing on the well being of the community, the impact on community environment, and quality of life.

Today's globalized world is a multicultural world. However, the field of computer ethics is dominated by Western perspectives. It is necessary to overcome this eurocentric tendency by examining the implications of computer technology from different cultural paradigms. The Earth Charter, on the other hand, has been developed by people from various cultural contexts. Computer ethicists may examine how computing either can support or violate the principles and values stated in the Earth Charter. Using the Earth Charter as a framework for addressing ethical issues arising in computing will enable computer ethicists to examine these issues from the perspectives of different cultural backgrounds as well as the implications for the environment and the development of a sustainable global society. Using the Earth Charter to address particular computer ethics issues will help to put them in a larger global context, supporting a more critical and inclusive examination without giving in to technological determinism or information colonialism.

Rather than accepting the current destructive tendencies of industrial civilization and imposing them on developing nations, the Earth Charter encourages the reinvention of industrial civilization through changes of cultural orientation and extensive revision of systems, practices, and procedures. As such, the Earth Charter is closely linked to development ethics (Dower, 2005). Computer ethics needs to acknowledge the linkages between computing, development, and environmental conduct. The Earth Charter provides a tool for the development of a computer ethics that is global in both content and scope and contributes toward a sustainable future for all.

CONCLUSION

There are several positions in computer ethics that purport the global character of computer ethics. These views, however, ignore the observation that the digital divide is a divide between a minority of people whose lives are permeated by computerization and a majority of people whose lives largely are unaffected by the computer. These views also seem to ignore that computerization itself is a product of a particular culture and worldview. In spite of the advantages that computerization and information technology have to offer, there is the danger of traditional worldviews and cultural practices being transformed and replaced with Western values embedded in the technology. This replacement is a form of information colonialism and a threat to the environment endangering human survival. Gòrniak-Kocikowska (2004) predicts that although it would be desirable that the emergence of a new global ethic is a participatory process of dialogue and exchange, it is more likely that Western cultural values and worldviews will be imposed through computerization. It is the responsibility of computer ethics to prevent such ethnocentrism.

To avoid that computerization enforces the adoption of a Western worldview, a broad cross-cultural dialogue is necessary. Such dialogical ethical research requires a balanced framework that takes cultural diversity and the need for ecological sustainability into account. A suitable framework for global ethical dialogue is already in place in the form of the Earth Charter, a set of principles that lays down an inclusive ethical vision that recognizes the interdependencies of environmental protection, human rights, equitable human development, and peace.

ACKNOWLEDGMENTS

Les Underhill, Britta Schinzel, Tim Dunne, and John Paterson read earlier drafts of this chapter.

REFERENCES

Adam, A. (2001). Computer ethics in a different voice. *Information and Organization, 11,* 235-261.

Adeya, C. N., & Cogburn, D. L. (2001). Globalisation and the information economy: Challenges and opportunities for Africa. In G. Nulerns, N. Hafkin, L. Van Audenhoven, & B. Cammaerts (Eds.), *The digital divide in developing countries: Towards an information society in Africa* (pp. 77-112). Brussels: Brussel University Press.

Anyiam-Osigwe, M. C. (2002). Africa's new awakening and ICT. Toward attaining sustainable democracy in Africa. In T. Mendina & J. J. Britz (Eds.), *Information ethics in the electronic age. Current issues in Africa and the world* (pp. 36-46). Jefferson, NC: McFarland.

Apostel, L. (1981). *African philosophy: Myth or reality.* Gent, Belgium: Story-Scientia.

Berman, B. J. (1992). The state, computers, and African development: The information non-revolution. In S. Grant Lewis & J. Samoff (Eds.), *Microcomputers in African development: Critical perspectives* (pp. 213-229). Boulder, CO: Westview Press.

Bowers, C. A. (2000). *Let them eat data: How computers affect education, cultural diversity, and the prospects of ecological sustainability.* Athens: The University of Georgia Press.

Britz, J. J. (2002). Africa and its place in the twenty-first century. A moral reflection. In T. Mendina & J. J. Britz (Eds.), *Information ethics in the electronic age: Current issues in Africa and the world* (pp. 5-6). Jefferson, NC: McFarland.

Bynum, T. W. (2000, Summer). A very short history of computer ethics. *Newsletter of the American Philosophical Association on Philosophy and Computing.* Retrieved July 2005, from http://www.

southernct.edu/organizations/rccs/resources/research/introduction/bynum_shrt_hist.html

Bynum, T. W., & Rogerson, S. (1996). Introduction and overview: Global information ethics. *Science and Engineering Ethics, 2*, 131-136.

Capurro, R. (1989). Towards an information ecology. In I. Wormell (Ed.), *Information quality. Definitions and dimensions. Proceedings of the NORDINFO International Seminar "Information and Quality,"* (pp. 122-139) Copenhagen.

Curry, M. R. (1995). Geographic information systems and the inevitability of ethical inconsistencies. In J. Pickles (Ed.), *Ground truth* (pp. 68-87). London: The Guilford Press.

Dower, N. (2005). The earth charter and global ethics. *Worldviews: Environment, Culture, Religion, 8*, 15-28.

Duncker, E. (2002). Cross-cultural usability of the library metaphor. In *Proceedings of the Second Joint Conference on Digital Libraries (JCDL) of the Association of Computing Machinery (ACM) and the Institute of Electrical and Electronics Engineers Computer Society (IEEE-CS) 2002,* Portland, Oregon (pp. 223-230).

Floridi, L. (2001). Information ethics: An environmental approach to the digital divide. *Philosophy in the Contemporary World, 9*(1). Retrieved June 2005, from www.wolfson.ox.ac.uk/~floridi/pdf/ieeadd.pdf

Freiberger, P. A., & Swaine, M. R. (2003). Computers. In *Encyclopædia Britannica 2003*. [CD-ROM]. London: Encyclopedia Britannica.

Gandalf. (2005). *Data on Internet activity worldwide (hostcount)*. Retrieved July 2005, from http://www.gandalf.it/data/data1.htm

Geertz, C. (1983). *Local knowledge. Further essays in interpretive anthropology.* New York: Basic Books.

Gòrniak-Kocikowska, K. (1996). The computer revolution and the problem of global ethics. *Science and Engineering Ethics, 2*, 177-190.

Gòrniak-Kocikowska, K. (2004). The global culture of digital technology and its ethics. *The ETHICOMP E-Journal, 1*(3). Retrieved May 2005, from http://www.ccsr.cse.dmu.ac.uk/journal

Grant Lewis, S., & Samoff, J. (1992). Introduction. In S. Grant Lewis & J. Samoff (Eds.), *Microcomputers in African development: Critical perspectives* (pp. 1-24). Boulder, CO: Westview Press.

Harris, T. M., Weiner, D., Warner, T. A., & Levin, R. (1995). Pursuing social goals through participatory geographic information systems. Redressing South Africa's historical political ecology. In J. Pickles (Ed.), *Ground truth* (pp. 196-222). London: The Guilford Press.

Heim, M. (1993). *The metaphysics of virtual reality.* New York: Oxford University Press.

Hoesle, V. (1992). The third world as a philosophical problem. *Social Research, 59*, 227-263.

Introna, L., & Nissenbaum, H. (2000). Shaping the Web. Why the politics of search engines matter. *The Information Society, 16*, 169-185.

Johnson, D. G. (1997). Is the global information infrastructure a democratic technology? *Computers and Society, 27*, 20-26.

Johnson, D. G. (1999). Computer ethics in the 21st century. In *Proceedings of ETHICOMP99*, Rome, Italy.

Kawooya, D. (2002). The digital divide. An ethical dilemma for information professionals in Uganda? In T. Mendina, & J. J. Britz (Eds.), *Information ethics in the electronic age: Current issues in Africa and the world* (pp. 28-35). Jefferson, NC: McFarland.

Keller, E. F. (1985). *Reflections on gender and science.* New Haven, CT: Yale University Press.

Kocikowski, A. (1999). Technologia informatyczna a stary problem totalitaryzmu. *Nauka, 1*, 120-126.

Lor, P. J., & Britz, J. J. (2002). Information imperialism. Moral problems in information flows from south to north. In T. Mendina & J. J. Britz (Eds.), *Information ethics in the electronic age: Current issues in Africa and the world* (pp. 15-21). Jefferson, NC: McFarland.

Mahoney, M. S. (1988). The history of computing in the history of technology. *Annals of the History of Computing, 10*, 113-125.

Maloka, E., & le Roux, E. (2001). *Africa in the new millennium: Challenges and prospects*. Pretoria: Africa Institute of South Africa.

McHaffie, P. (1995). Manufacturing metaphors. Public cartography, the market, and democracy. In J. Pickles (Ed.), *Ground truth* (pp. 113-129). New York: The Guilford Press.

Menkiti, I. A. (1979). Person and community in African traditional thought. In R. A. Wright (Ed.), *African philosophy* (pp. 157-168). New York: University Press.

Merchant, C. (1980). *The death of nature: Women, ecology, and the scientific revolution*. San Francisco: Harper and Row.

Moor, J. (1998). Reason, relativity, and responsibility in computer ethics. *Computers and Society, 28*, 14-21.

Mulago, V. (1969). Vital participation: The cohesive principle of the Bantu community. In K. Kickson & P. Ellinworth (Eds.), *Biblical revelation and African beliefs* (pp. 137-158). London: Butterworth.

Neelameghan, A. (1981). Some issues in information transfer. *A third world perspective. International Federation of Library Associates (IFLA) Journal, 7*, 8-18.

Ng'etich, K. A. (2001). Harnessing computer-mediated communication technologies in the unification of Africa: Constraints and potentials. In E. Maloka & E. le Roux (Eds.), *Africa in the new millennium: Challenges and prospects* (pp. 77-85). Pretoria: Africa Institute of South Africa.

Ogundipe-Leslie, M. (1993). African women, culture and another development. In S. M. James (Ed.), *Theorising black feminism: The visionary pragmatism of black women, A.P.A. Busia* (pp. 102-117). London: Routledge.

Pickles, J. (1995). Representations in an electronic age. Geography, GIS, and democracy. In J. Pickles (Ed.), *Ground truth* (pp. 1-30). New York: The Guilford Press.

Schaefer III, S. J. (2002). Telecommunications infrastructure in the African continent. 1960-2010. In T. Mendina & J. J. Britz (Eds.), *Information ethics in the electronic age: Current issues in Africa and the world* (pp. 22-27). Jefferson, NC: McFarland.

Senghor, L. (1966). Negritude—A humanism of the 20th century. *Optima, 16*, 1-8.

Setiloane, G. M. (1986). *African theology: An introduction*. Johannesburg: Skotaville Publishers.

Shiva, V. (1989). *Staying alive: Women, ecology, and development*. London: Zed Books.

Shutte, A. (1993). *Philosophy for Africa*. Cape Town: University of Cape Town Press.

Smith, A. (1976). *An inquiry into the nature and causes of the wealth of nations* (R. H. Cambell & A. S. Skinner, Eds.). Oxford, UK: Clarendon Press.

Taylor, J. V. (1963). *The primal vision: Christian presence amid African religion*. London: S.C.M. Press.

Veregin, H. (1995). Computer innovation and adoption in geography: A critique of conventional technological models. In J. Pickles (Ed.), *Ground truth* (pp. 88-112). London: The Guilford Press.

Walton, M., & Vukovic, V. (2003). Cultures, literacy, and the Web: Dimensions of information "scent." *Interactions, 10,* 64-71.

WCED (1987). *Our common future. Report of the World Commission on Environment and Development (WCED)* (pp. 323-333). New York: Oxford University Press.

Weizenbaum, J. (1976). *Computer power and human reason: From judgement to calculation.* New York: W.H. Freeman.

Winner, L. (1997). Cyberlibertarian myths and the prospect for community. *ACM Computers and Society, 27,* 14-19.

Winograd, T., & Flores, F. (1986). *Understanding computers and cognition.* Norwood, NJ: Arlex Publishing Corporation.

Winschiers, H., & Paterson, B. (2004). Sustainable software development. *Proceedings of the 2004 Annual Research Conference of the South African Institute of Computer Scientists and Information Technologists on IT Research In Developing Countries (SAICSIT 2004)—Fulfilling the promise of ICT,* Stellenbosch, South Africa (pp. 111-115).

Wiredu, K. (1980). *Philosophy and an African culture.* London: Cambridge.

World Internet Usage Statistics. (2005). *Data on Internet usage and population.* Retrieved November 2005, from http://www.internetworldstats.com/stats1.htm

WSIS. (2004). *The world summit on the information society: Declaration of principles.* Retrieved November 2005, from http://www.itu.int/wsis

Chapter XII

Current and Future State of ICT Deployment and Utilization in Healthcare:
An Analysis of Cross-Cultural Ethical Issues

Bernd Carsten Stahl
De Montfort University, UK

Simon Rogerson
De Montfort University, UK

Amin Kashmeery
University of Durham, UK

ABSTRACT

The ever-changing face of ICT can render its deployment rather problematic in sensitive areas of applications, such as healthcare. The ethical implications are multifaceted and have diverse degrees of sensitivity from culture to culture. Our essay attempts to shed light on these interplaying factors in a cross-cultural analysis that takes into account prospective ICT development.

PREAMBLE

Satisfactory provision of healthcare is central to our quality of life. At the same time, healthcare is a central cost factor in our personal as well as public expenditure. Healthcare systems in different countries face different challenges and provide different levels of services. It is probably fair to say that there is no one model that can address or overcome all issues. It is probably also fair to say that most healthcare systems are trying to use technology in order to address some of the problems they are facing. Among these problems, one can find issues of cost minimization, consistency of care provision, quality control, labor saving, and a variety of others. This chapter will explore the relationship of culture, ethics, and the use of information and communication technology (ICT) in healthcare. As this suggests, we will not be able to do justice to the intersection of these four topics. Instead, the chapter will attempt to identify some dominant issues that are of relevance today.

The main purpose of this chapter is to develop a framework that will allow us to understand how culture can shape the perception of the ethicality of the use of ICT in healthcare. It is meant to provide the foundation upon which we can build valuable empirical research. We are interested specifically in the question whether there are cultural differences with regard to the perception of ICT in healthcare between individuals from cultures in a non-Western setting and those from European, specifically British, culture.

Given the size and complexity of the topic, we will use this chapter to outline some of the relationships among the main concepts and to identify areas worthy of research. Following basic definitions of pertinent concepts, the chapter will start by discussing the relationship between culture and health informatics and then proceed to describe some of the ethical issues of health informatics. These two strands of thought then will be combined to develop the concept of cultural influence on the perception of the ethics and morality of health information systems. We then will describe several scenarios that will render it clear what kind of issues we believe to be likely encountered. Establishing the descriptive and theoretical part of our topic will pave the way for developing methodological considerations that are pertinent to empirical research and to the cultural impact and ethics of ICT use in healthcare.

Ethics and Morality

It long has been established that, for the sake of practicality and application, a distinction should be made between ethics and morality. Morality can be defined as the set of acceptable social rules that are adhered to in a given community. Following this, one can define ethics as the workable scheme for the theory of morality. Ethics

then can be used to describe, define, and justify morality. This distinction is not required by the etymology of the concepts, and it is not always used in English language writings on ethics. It is more widely adhered to in continental European philosophy (Stahl, 2004). We nevertheless believe it to be useful because it can help us distinguish between fundamentally different issues. Morality is a social fact and can be observed through the use of established social science methods. For example, we can observe patients in hospitals and find out whether they believe that a certain action is good or bad, whether they believe that a certain use of technology is acceptable or not. This question is fundamentally different from the ethical question of why the use of a technology is good or bad. While most individuals follow a morality of which they are aware, many of us rarely engage in explicit ethical reflection. That means that patients' ethical convictions, while important for their moral attitudes, often are implicit and much harder to determine. This has methodological consequences that will be discussed later.

Another reason the distinction between ethics and morality is important for our project is that it roughly corresponds to the difference between descriptive and normative research. One can undertake purely descriptive research on the social fact of morality, but when it comes to ethical justifications and normative suggestions, one changes the level of analysis. This is important for researchers to reflect on, and the conceptual distinction will make it easier for us to do so.

CULTURE AND INFORMATICS

This section will briefly review the relationship between culture and health informatics. For this purpose, it is useful to state why we are speaking of health informatics rather than information systems, software engineering, or computer science. The reason is that the term *informat-*

ics is more inclusive and aims at use and social context rather than at the technical artefact itself. This is particularly pertinent, given that technology applications in healthcare are never ends in themselves or pure gadgets, but are always there to facilitate the aims of providing care. Such care also is always embedded in situations, cultures, and communities, which must be reflected by the technology. The very term *informatics*, therefore, indicates that we are looking at a wider picture. Interestingly, a large part of academic and practitioner publications dealing with ICT in healthcare use the term. Having thus explained the use of the term *healthcare informatics*, this section now will discuss the concept of culture and its relationship to health informatics.

Culture

Culture is a multifaceted concept that is hard, if not impossible, to define. For our purposes, we can start with an understanding of culture as the totality of shared meanings and interpretations of a given group. This repository of shared understandings and interpretations of the word is represented by emblems whose meanings and interpretations members of the same culture share (Castells, 2000; Galtung, 1998; Ward & Peppard, 1996). The exchange of meanings and the agreement on appropriate interpretations of emblems breed skills of communication, which begin with primitive means but evolve the more the communities develop. Eventually, communities become communication aficionados to the extent that the very existence of the culture depends on it. The nature of the culture will be reflected in the nature of communication with information or meaning being implicit or explicit. This often is referred to as low context communication and high context communication (Nance & Strohmaier, 1994). This, in turn, underlines the social nature of cultures.

This is a rather wide understanding of culture that requires further specification. It is useful, however, because it allows an understanding of culture as a multiple phenomenon with areas of overlap and frequent change. For example, it facilitates cultures of different reach, such as organizational culture and national culture. Most organizations will have some particularities that are meaningful to their members and that outsiders cannot access easily. This is particularly so within a culture of collectivism (Nance & Strohmaier, 1994). They thus fulfill the definition of culture, and they arguably require a culture in order to facilitate their long-term survival (Robey & Azevedo, 1994). A similar description can be found for national cultures; namely, that they are the collection of things, ideas, and techniques, including institutions, which a society needs to persist (Gehlen, 1997). It should be clear that such a definition of culture will not allow easy delimitations and distinctions. Most individuals will be members of a variety of cultures (e.g., work, sports clubs, ethnic groups, families, nations, and regions). These memberships may be mutually reinforcing, but they also may be contradictory.

An important aspect of culture is that it has a normative function. This means that cultures contain an idea of how things should be and how its members are expected to behave. This means that they are inherently utopian and imply a good state of the world (Bourdil, 1996). There are different ways in which the normative character of cultures is transmitted. One of these ways is what we usually call ethics or morality. These refer to the norms that are accepted in a given culture and the justification of such norms. This also can be translated in terms of values that are implicit in all cultures. Therefore, one can say that culture is a "value-concept" (Weber, 1994, p. 71). A related and very important aspect is that of tenet. Tenets and creeds constitute what we call meta-ethics. Their essence, usually imposing values and principles on communities that share belief in them, is normative guidance. Some religions are so comprehensive that their creeds and tenets can collectively govern all aspects of life of individuals, including their interactions with other members of the community. To these communities, ethical rules that they would abide by are only those ordained by their religion.

All of this should render it clear that cultures are linked deeply to questions of identity. On an individual level, identity as the answer to the question "Who am I?" is answered by a collection of narratives. These narratives draw on the cultures of which the individual is a member. Despite wide debate of a classification nature between relativists, utilitarianists, teleologists, and deontologists, it remains a fact of life that basic morality in the human species that commands decent conduct (i.e., do not lie; do not steal; do not deceive; etc.) are connate and *natura insitu*s and, therefore, for that part universal. Culture, one thus can claim, is a universal ingredient of human existence. Clashes of cultures can evolve when interests conflict and desires intersect. In ramifications of the perplexity of today's modern life, including those of technological applications, paradigm shifts might redefine postulates. When that happens, some cultures might tend to impose their compromised values on others, thereby leading to contradictory influences on identity and to cognitive dissonance, which can lead to pathological developments.

This point will be addressed in this chapter, since description of distorted cultural values and their influence on the perception of ethics health informatics constitute part of an ongoing debate.

Culture and ICT

The last section indicates that there is a close link between culture and technology. If culture imposes necessary conditions for reproduction, for instance, then it would become clear that reproduction technology and culture will be mutually dependent. By analogy, understanding technology as a rational approach to the environment, which typically uses artifacts for the subordination of nature, we are safe to say that culture is one of the human constants.

The close link of technology and culture extends to different types of technology but, most notably, to the most important and prominent technologies of a given culture. Early agricultural cultures can be characterized by their use of ploughs or other technologies that allowed them to develop agricultural production. Similarly, the cultures we live in today are characterized by their relationship to ICT. Talk of the "information society," the "global village," or similar constructs indicates that we are aware of the importance of ICT for our culture. ICT also is linked to the other defining technologies of our age, such as biotechnology and nanotechnology, but also to modern developments of more traditional technologies such as mechanical production technologies.

ICT thus allows the functioning of social institutions in Western societies such as the UK. Public administration and economic activities would look different without it. On the other hand, the social institutions we find in our cultures allow the use and development of ICT. Apart from this high level of interdependency between culture and ICT, there are also links that are less visible but as important. If we go back to the definition of culture as a set of shared meanings, norms, and interpretations, then we will see that culture strongly influences our perception of ICT and of the uses we believe to be acceptable. Again, this is a two-way relationship in which technology also affects the repository of available signs and their interpretations. For example, we find it normal to speak of humans as information processing machines and to compare our cognitive functions with those of a computer. This indicates that technology has found its way into the set of symbols and metaphors that we believe to be meaningful. The issue becomes more complicated when culture and, consequently, ethics plays on several notes or acts on a multitude of fronts. Ethics of ICT in healthcare demands macro- and micro-analyses of not only the impact of ICT application on societal values but also the product of associated impacts of the combined forces interplaying in the overlapping parts of ICT and healthcare domains.

ETHICS AND HEALTHCARE

Healthcare procedures touch most of us on many different occasions. They are there during the most existential moments of our lives, from birth right across to death. They can affect our well being directly by providing remedies and alleviating pain and indirectly by offering us the certainty that we will be taken care of when needed. In light of the importance of healthcare for our physical and mental well being, it is easy to say that healthcare and ethics are closely related. But, nevertheless, it will be helpful to clarify the concepts used and to indicate some of the areas that we believe to be of relevance to our research.

Value-Based Practice (VBP) vs. Evidence-Based Practice (EBP) in Healthcare

Contemporary applications of ICT expand across the spectrum of healthcare fields. New developments in areas such as ICT are still unfolding and will continue to do so for some time to come. This situation usually creates what could be described as a policy vacuum (Moor, 1985). Applications of ICT in healthcare systems lead to yet a further step of ambiguity and uncertainty. This is because a policy vacuum breeds an ethics vacuum. In order for action policies to be formulated, a conceptual framework needs to be created through appropri-

ate analysis of the situation in question. This is very much the case in healthcare. In healthcare settings, current and future extensive use of ICT undoubtedly would result in a new state of affairs, which needs to be conceptualized in order for it to be given the legal, moral, and ethical codes that would keep its deployment in an acceptable manner—legally, morally, and ethically.

Over the past five decades, the world has been going through the initial, introductory phase of communication technologies, followed immediately by a boom in information technology applications and then a convergence of computing, communication, and media technologies. We currently are witnessing the new phase, which is still pervading diverse aspects of our lives in an unprecedented interfusion. Thus, this phase merits the title *permeation stage*. The ethical dimensions of healthcare ICT deployment under such circumstances can best be elucidated, if investigations covered areas, where vulnerable groups constitute the matrix. These mainly include neonates and infants, the elderly, palliative care, and mental illness patients. ICT could transform our concepts to the extent that the question is not anymore "Would it enhance healthcare?" but rather "What is healthcare?" When that happens, we then will realize how intangible healthcare has become. It is in such areas that ambiguity is evident as to whether health decision making should be the product of values or facts.

In terms of systematic categorization, recent researchers divide this domain into two distinct major subsections; namely, values-based practice (VBP) and evidence-based practice (EBP). Bill Fulford, one of its prominent advocates, defines VBP as the theory and skills base for effective healthcare decision making, where different (and, hence, potentially conflicting) values are in play (Fulford, 2004). On the other side of the debate, Ronald Levant, an advocate of EBP, describes their initiative as a movement that strives to achieve accountability in medicine, psychology, education, public policy, and even architecture. He maintains that professionals are required to base their practices to whatever extent possible on evidence (Levant, 2005).

How Relevant is the VBP/EBP Debate to Health Informatics?

Values in a broader sense are "standards of behaviour" (Waite, Hawker, & Soanes, 2001). But this definition falls short of giving even a framework, if values were to be used for applied purposes, such as healthcare practice. In that sense, Sackett, Straus, Scott-Richardson, Rosenberg, and Haynes (2000) maintain that specifically patients' values mean their unique individual preferences, concerns, and expectations. In practical terms, what these bring to clinical encounters should be integrated for the purpose of making sound, clinical decisions that would serve these patients' interests. Combining the two definitions, it would appear that standards of behavior can become a function of preferences, concerns, and expectations; in short, the interests of all parties involved. Other definitions go as follows, singling out people's interests: Value-based practices (VBPs) are practices that are grounded in people-first values, such as choice, growth, personhood, and so forth (Anthony, 2004).

Seedhouse (2005) in his recent work sets out his vision for a democratic future for healthcare decision making in which values of all stakeholders in the healthcare system will be taken into consideration. Values, being a subjective domain, require practice skills and methods of delivery when applied as a tool for healthcare decision making. Interaction between patients and providers is an essential part of the healthcare process. Value-based practice takes such activity into account and considers its proper application a responsibility that the provider should strive to achieve. Among subheadings relevant to informatics and ICT, *knowledge* and *communication* stand out in this context. These are two terms used for information retrieval, acquisition, and accumu-

lation. Information usually is acquired through first-hand narratives, polls, surveys, and media reports. In order for communication to be effective in terms of value-based practice in healthcare, the human factor is indispensable. Elements, such as attentive listening, empathy, sympathy, and reasoning, are attributes only of human beings. Methods such as Internet polls, postal surveys, and camera surveillance are potential recipes for communication failure, which, by the same token, will impact the value-based assessment and decision making. The knowledge thus acquired might have a wider impact of a negative nature not only on the users (patients) but also on other groups involved in the process, such as managers, social workers, insurers, and so forth (Colombo, Bendelow, Fulford, & William, 2003).

As interests vary from person to person and from group to group, the question as to how conflict is handled becomes inevitable. In fact, this is the paradox of value-based practice in healthcare. Therefore, the term *value* ought to be analyzed further into its micro-dimensions, which constitute a spectrum ranging from the abstract sense of ethics and over self-fulfilment criteria (wishes, desires, needs, etc.) right up to principles and beliefs. Another feature that renders the value concept problematic is the fact that values are not static; they change with time and can be modified under certain circumstances. This situation is exacerbated by the fact that some cultures allow such changes to take place, and others allow that to happen only within a very narrow margin. Also, the attitudes toward such changes can bear different connotations. They can be defined as developments in the positive sense of the word, but they also can be defined as degradation.

Evidence-based practice, on the other hand, can be executed with the least reliance on the human factor. Artificial intelligence, expert systems, and diagnostic software are vivid examples. When sufficient material for decision-making precursors is at hand, opinions based on facts and evidence come into play. As mentioned above, EBP advocates concentrate their concern on accountability and pursuit of fact and evidence to verify it (Levant, 2005). Others have their own agenda for EBP implementation, which, in their view, should be guided by the recovery-oriented process and its values (Stultz, 2004), a matter that would transform EBP into VBP as well.

It is worthwhil to briefly considering the status of these considerations in terms of ethics and morality as outlined previously. If morality consists of the accepted norms and if ethics are the justifications, then values would seem to be part of both areas. Values are those things that we value and, thus, can be immediate generators of moral norms. On the other hand, values also can be part of the justificatory context of morality. The introduction of the term *value* to the debate also raises another issue: What are we to do if values contradict? As already stated, basing medicine on evidence is an immensely value-laden starting point. It implies assumptions on the nature of reality and of our abilities to access this reality. Evidence-based practice is thus value-based, even if this is not often recognized. Another problem of the concept of values refers to competing and contradictory values. When we speak of value-based medicine, we should realize that there is no single value and no coherent set of values that could guide this. The question thus appears—which values to choose among competing ones? An answer to this question would lead us beyond the current chapter and would have to go back to ethical theory. Very briefly, one solution could be the introduction of a hierarchy of values that would help us to identify which values we should prefer in case of a value conflict (Stahl, 2003).

Is Ethical Impact Proportional to Technology Sophistication?

In order to answer this question, it would be sensible first to define sophisticated ICT applications in healthcare and what degrees of sophistication are meant. Two broad areas frequently are being identified by prominent bodies such as UNESCO: telehealth and telemedicine. "The former ... [includes] health services, education and research supported by ICT, while the latter refers more specifically to medical care and procedures offered across a geographical distance and involving two or more actors in collaboration, often in interdisciplinary teams" (UNESCO, 2005) As such, both are seen as related to healthcare informatics.

Equity, as a basic concept in all aspects of life, is a value that should be observed by all parties involved in any given setting in which spheres of interests overlap and lines of rights intersect. It is particularly so in healthcare systems. If we consider the situation of healthcare in a third world setting, inhabitants of remote rural areas who hardly have any care at their disposal would find equity a luxury that they cannot afford. ICT can benefit people who inhabit these isolated areas. In terms of observing, for example, the value of equity in healthcare under such circumstances, telemedicine applications are of particular benefit in that they do the following:

- Enhance access to better diagnosis to all people through computerized techniques.
- Enable online consultation with specialists, thereby reducing cost to the benefit of care providers.
- Enable follow-up through easy feedback on the efficiency of the prescribed treatment.
- Allow a chance for local medical professionals to receive training without having to move to more urbanized areas.
- Allow the establishment of databases for easy access to medical records.

Operations such as this could expand to an international level reaching as far as the technology can geographically go, thereby surpassing limits beyond which control becomes increasingly difficult. It is this degree of sophistication that could cause concern. Amidst these vast operations, it would become obvious that values such as confidentiality would be liable to breach with less and less control possibilities. Confidentiality as a personal requirement, however, is being dwarfed in comparison to security at a national or communal level.

An explanation might be that wide-scale research, such as clinical trials, can yield an enormous amount of information. If such information compiled by research conducted on whole communities is of a sensitive nature, such as DNA and genes, the breach of information confidentiality can become alarming. Genes can carry information that reveals traits common in the genetic pool of the whole community to the extent that their very existence could be at risk. Future bio-weapons fall into this category. This is supported by the fact that pharmacogenetics is a reality, which means that certain individuals, groups, or communities are more ready to respond to certain drugs than others, depending on their genetic makeup. This is being vigorously researched under the pharmaceutical domain for enhancing therapeutic and medical treatment. By the same token, however, individuals, groups, or whole communities can be inflicted specifically by disease through certain drugs or chemicals, depending on their genetic makeup. This is very much the case in societies whose building blocks are tribes or clans. We will explore this aspect further later on.

CULTURAL INFLUENCE ON THE ETHICS OF ICT USE IN HEALTHCARE: PARADOXES FROM WESTERN AND NON-WESTERN SETTINGS

In this section, we will have to choose some pertinent characteristics of the cultures that we hold to be representative and contrast them with certain uses of technology. It will end up with a collection of scenarios that will elucidate some issues of concern and shed more focused light on their complexity.

Issues in British Culture

British culture, as a vivid Western example of dynamic liberalism and utilitarianism, can serve the purpose of contrasting Western vs. non-Western settings. The liberal tradition translates into a high regard for the individual and the belief that social phenomena can be reduced to the sum of individual ones. This is important for healthcare, because the individual's rights are considered of primary importance, whereas collective considerations tend to be viewed as secondary. At the same time (and closely related to liberalism), British culture is influenced strongly by utilitarianism. This means that it is a generally accepted ethical principle to sum up all utilities and disutilities of a given act and to make decisions according to the comparison of the aggregate utility of an act. Utilitarianism often is vulgarized into a cost-benefit analysis in which the methodological problem of measuring utilities is replaced by measuring financial costs and benefits. This means that cost-benefits considerations are deemed appropriate in ethically charged situations. It also means that there is an intrinsic contradiction between the two main pillars. While utilitarianism is based on a methodological individualism and, thus, compatible with liberalism, it is also deeply collectivist, because the rights of the individual can be (morally) overwritten by the overall collective utility.

Another aspect of mainstream British culture is that it is modernist, meaning that it relies on and trusts reason and science. While there is some resistance to this modernist view, it probably is safe to say that in mainstream British discourses, scientists are regarded as reliable and trustworthy, and the results of scientific research are seen as valid. This links to utilitarianism, which can be seen as the attempt to render ethics scientific. Science is justified, because it will help bring about a greater sum of happiness. It also means that there is an intrinsic bias toward evidence-based medicine and by association healthcare, because this is based on the scientific approach. Considerations of value are not seen as equally valid.

Examples of Issues in British Culture

On the basis of liberalism, utilitarianism, and modernism, British culture is fundamentally appreciative of new technologies. This is true for technology in healthcare as well. New healthcare technologies generally are described as positive and benevolent. There is, however, a stream of literature and research that looks at the intrinsic contradictions that grow out of the traditional view of technology in healthcare. Berg, whose work was done in the Netherlands and is transferable to the UK, describes some of these issues. The modernist view of ICT assumes that there is one governing rationale and that technology can be used accordingly to further the well being of patients. Doctors use technology to help and heal patients. This overlooks that modern societies are much more complex. One explicit reason for the use of ICT is thus to support organizational issues (Berg, 1999). Such an approach overlooks that healthcare is a complex system with a multitude of conflicting actors and interests. But even if it works, ICT then can be used to change the way in which healthcare workers and patients interact. Technology can lead to disliking doctors and nurses. On the other hand, it also can widen the access to health services. Technology, which formally structures processes, also will lead to bureaucracy, which produces costs and, thus, is not always desirable from the utilitarian point of view.

Another interesting problem can be found in the intersection between healthcare, technology,

and rationality. The modernist view of linear and individual rationality that objectively can determine desirable solutions (which is also the basis of evidence-based medicine) is not just problematic, because it underestimates the complexity of organizations. It is, to some degree, self-contradictory because it requires the very ad hoc and pragmatic activities to survive that it sets out to replace (Berg, 1997). More importantly, it also can be seen as an ideology that promotes particular interests. Using the case of a new online service, NHS Direct, Hanlon, et al. (2005) argue that "the supposed dominance of this technocratic consciousness hides class, gender and jurisdictional struggles" (p. 156). The Electronic Patient Record is a good example of these issues. Fairweather and Rogerson (2001) argue for a morally appropriate balance between the various moral standards that are in tension in the field of electronic patient records (EPRs). EPRs can facilitate doctor-patient relationships. However, at the same time, they can undermine trust and so harm the doctor-patient relationship. Patients are becoming increasingly reluctant to tell their own doctor everything that is relevant. A number of moral principles and the question of consent to release records need to be considered.

Issues in Non-Western Culture

Social norms differ from one community to another in different parts of the world. What is acceptable and permissible somewhere might not be so somewhere else. Therefore, healthcare planners and strategists must have a clear vision of what would and what would not trigger sensitivities in the process of healthcare delivery and decision making. For instance, the vital communication element previously mentioned for good value-based practice can become totally defective if carried out, for instance, in a male-to-female setting in which social norms do not accept it. A similar attitude is expected in situations such as vaginal swabbing or artificial insemination, the meta-ethics being tenet-rooted. It is against the social norms and religious codes of many world populations. Muslims, for example, who constitute just over a quarter of the world's population (http://www.islamicweb.com/begin/results.htm) have attitudes that are overwhelmingly governed by Shari'a codes of conduct. These ordain many aspects of life, including those that fall within the sphere of healthcare. Questions concerning issues such as permissibility of a male healthcare provider to examine a female patient (or vice versa) are hot debate topics. This will be investigated further in the scenarios given next.

The influence of culture on the perception of health information and communication technologies are issues in a Middle Eastern setting (women, tribal structures, etc.). Further, to points mentioned previously, issues of ethical dimensions can be exacerbated by cultural influences. In the following section, we will try to take the reader through selected scenarios, some hypothetical and others compiled from real life in parts of the world that have entirely different attitudes toward practices seen in Western settings as acceptable—the effect being cultural.

Some Scenarios

Scenario 1: Outcry to the King

Ali takes his wife, who is in labor, to a university teaching hospital. Shocked to learn from the receptionist of the obstetrics and gynecology department that the attending physician is male, not female, he reluctantly leaves the hospital to send a bitter letter of complaint through the media to the highest authority in the country: the king.

Let us imagine how the situation would be if this scenario were repeated, and the wife had complications and would require consultation and on-air monitoring via telemedicine.

Scenario 2: 30 Years in Pursuit of a Female Orthopedist

Yassir writes on May 18, 2005, to a medical forum asking for help. His mother has been suffering from debilitating orthopedic problems for 30 years and is reluctant to be seen by a male orthopedist; there is no female specialist in the area where they live.

Yassir's mother could not be helped, even by telemedicine intervention, so long as the hands that would touch her were those of a man, as she put it. The patient received numerous messages of support and sympathy.

Scenarios 1 and 2 are in total compliance with the Islamic code of conduct. The Islamic Jurisprudence Council of the Mecca-Based Muslim World League issued in its 14th session, convened in January 1995 in Mecca, its Fatwa (dictum) emphasizing the impermissibility of healthcare professional attending patients of the opposite gender. The Fatwa allowed for a margin of permissibility only under circumstances of absolute necessity. As is the case in all other similar situations, the degree of necessity is left to the individual to evaluate. In our two scenarios, the persons in question did not categorize their situation as absolute necessity and, therefore, abided strictly by the given Fatwa.

Scenario 3: Miss L. and the Monitoring System

Miss L. is admitted to the hospital in the summer of 2003. During her stay in a single room on the surgery ward, a young male in a professional outfit made frequent visits to her, paving the way for a relationship to develop between the two. Eventually, kissing and hugging took place. Without realizing that the monitoring system was active, she enjoyed it. Soon, another man appeared and showed her photographs of her intimate encounters, threatening to make them public on the World Wide Web, unless she gave in to his demands, which turned out to be sheer sexual blackmail.

Scenario 3 is a typical example of the abuse that technology could undergo as a powerful tool with which opportunistic people might fulfill their desires. The perpetrator knows that Miss L. faces a very difficult situation, as cultural and social values of her society would not approve of her behavior.

Scenario 4: Mr. A.F. and the Monitoring System Again

Mr. A.F. was admitted to the hospital as a private patient and stayed in a private, luxury room for two weeks for pulmonary infection treatment. On one occasion during the convalescence days, his wife, who was visiting him at the time, happened to be with him alone in the room. He locked the door and had a very steamy, intimate encounter with her, without realizing that the monitoring system was active. The hospital management, while reiterating the fact that they were doing their job, soon acknowledged the unfortunate incident, offered an apology, and promised to destroy the film that carried the embarrassment, reminding Mr. A.F. that the essential function of hospital rooms is healthcare and receiving visitors for the purpose of the patient's welfare, but nothing beyond that. Mr. A.F. was adamant in not accepting the apology and insisted on suing the hospital. His argument was based on the conviction that his welfare extended to the activity he performed and that the hospital should have warned him beforehand of the monitoring system and what activities they had in mind for monitoring. He also maintained that had the monitoring system been run by a human being, he or she would have stopped filming the action immediately. Leaving it up to a machine led to the embarrassment, for which the hospital should be held responsible.

Scenario 5: Genetic Screening and the XL Clan of the LL Tribe

Tribes in Middle Eastern regions and in some other parts of the world constitute the main building blocks of many societies extending across geographical boundaries and trespassing political borders. They share common ancestry and, therefore, a gene pool. The chronicle of this ancestry extends deep in history. Qahtani tribes, for instance, are named after Noah's descendant Qahtan, and Adnani tribes after Adnan, one of the descendants of Ishmael son of Ibrahim. Their branches and subsections are numerous and extend throughout the Arabian peninsula and beyond. For instance, about 70 tribes can now be identified in the UAE alone. Through the tribe and its hierarchy, the individual has the right of protection of the tribe and is obliged to abide by its rules. Disputes among members of the same tribe are dealt with by heads of clans, leaders of the subtribes, or the chief (sheikh) of the tribe. Verdicts and rulings thus formulated are binding to all parties. These stem from traditional tribal conventions and practices (urf), known to everybody. The traditional tribal system even makes a young man's own choice of his bride largely immaterial, as it strongly advocates first and second cousin marriages. The first option is usually the daughter of his paternal uncle. It is, therefore, not surprising that some of these clans who have been living in isolated, remote areas for millennia have an exceedingly high rate of consanguinity and, hence, are expected to have a reasonably distinct genetic makeup (http://www.al-bab.com/yemen/soc/manea1.htm).

This is dependent on population frequencies of specific alleles, though not to be taken as race-specific, as no extensive studies have been made available thus far to define race based on genetics. It also should be made clear that the tribes in question at the writing of this chapter have not been subject to studies within the population genetics domain that clearly point out 1% frequencies of certain alleles, which is by definition a polymorphism.

Under such conditions, culture can put into action factors that are not reckoned with in the West. The sensitivity of information in a healthcare setting, such as patients' records and stigmatization, can form a combination of devastating effects in that culture. Saudi Arabia, for example, recently has introduced nationwide mandatory premarital screening tests, the impact of which on the social level is yet to unfold with a possibility of an unpleasant outcome if the tribal structure of the society is taken into consideration. The positive side of these tests is self-explanatory. In recognition of the high incidence rates of genetic diseases such as sickle cell anemia and thalassaemia in some regions of the country, such measures no doubt would reduce these rates. However, in the long run, with the accumulation of more and more genetically related information, whole clans and tribes could be stigmatized and girls with certain genetic traits victimized (in terms of spinsterhood), if procedures are not properly executed and/or information systems are not efficiently run and managed (Kashmeery, 2004). Our scenario is hypothesized for future projection.

The XL clan extends across the borders of three neighboring countries. Their branch on the western side of the borders had in abidance by genetic screening rules set by their government to consider allowing such tests to be performed on its members. Within a few months, a trend was established from the compiled data that the clan members have a NOTCH4 gene triplet repeat polymorphism. Without realizing the significance of the finding, the medical record facility did not impose tight security measures on the results. An abstract leaked in a bona fide manner to the local media, which published a layman report on the procedure and praised its underlying policy. In academic circles, the impact was different. This polymorphism was known to have some association with a serious psychological defect: schizophrenia (Wei & Hemmings, 2000). Rumors spread swiftly, blowing the issue out of proportion. The chief on the top hierarchy of the tribe on the eastern side of the border got upset by the news that reached him anecdotally and ordered the XL clan chief not to cooperate with the genetic screening scheme. XL clan, chief, and individuals have their loyalty to the tribe more than to the state. They all decided overwhelmingly to boycott the screening schemes, current and future ones, and thereby came into conflict with local authorities, who stood by their agenda and work plans. The issue assumed national proportions, following confrontations and arrests. Social unrest began to reach police records wherever members of the XL clan were engaged, at work or social activities. XL clan becomes more and more isolated and alienated, with intermarriage rates with other groups of society falling rapidly, leaving stigmatized women haunted by the state of spinsterhood, which is a woman's nightmare in that society. The impact of these developments spilled over the borders to the east and south where other subsections of the same tribe live, and the scenario repeated itself, forcing members of the LL tribe to go through the same ordeal.

Scenario 6: The Bed-Ridden Elderly in the Care of Extended Family

At the age of 82, Mr. S.K. had been bed-ridden for three years due to leg muscular dystrophy. He also was diabetic and hypertensive and, therefore, needed close health and nursing care. Values, culture, and tradition would not allow his family even to discuss the principle of admitting him to a nursing home. The social norms where Mr. S.K. lived demanded that he be looked after by his nearest of kin. To facilitate such a stipulation, members of the extended family usually live together in large premises. Mr. S.K.'s three sons were living with him in such a setting and managed to share the responsibility of his care. They were grown up professionals engaged in diverse occupations ranging from diplomacy and university professorship to high-ranking civil service. None of them was ever heard complaining or expressing the least bit of discontent, except for their admitted lack of expertise in some aspects of the care they were practicing.

Despite their continuous pursuit for knowledge from physician friends of theirs, they have always felt that the scheme would have worked more efficiently had there been a handy, simple software that gave guidelines for executing their tasks in a more professional way.

Their worries always peaked during the night when they were in their rooms and while they all were away at work, for fear of not being there for help, if needed. They used to hypothesize an emergency situation and have always felt that an adequate monitoring system, connecting them simultaneously to the patient's healthcare professionals who could intervene in the right moment, would have perfected the scheme.

These shortcomings were dwarfed in relation to the great advantage of having their father looked after in the comfort of his own home surrounded by members of his own family, who would do anything to please him, reiterating to him time and again that they do that with pleasure and passion.

Of course, he did not know that there are millions of parents in other parts of the world who go through the ordeal of leaving their homes and their loved ones when they desperately need them, and of losing their property in order to cover the expenses of nursing homes, where they might face a fate they frequently read about in the media. He didn't know that. But what he knew very well was that looking after him and preserving his dignity, no matter how demanding that might be, are ordained by tenet and are a debt carried with pride from generation to generation.

EPILOGUE

Given the review of the literature and the scenarios just elaborated, the reader should have an idea of what sort of issues we expect to find. The reader also will realize that the research we are suggesting is at the crossroads of a number of disciplines and theories. So far, this chapter contains a collection of thoughts that is meant to support the contention that research in the cultural aspects of the ethical properties of ICT in healthcare is desirable. We have refrained from developing a specific theory that will explain the relationship between culture, ethics, and ICT in healthcare. Instead, we intend to investigate these matters from the starting point outlined previously, but we will keep an open mind to issues that have not yet been raised. To some degree, we thus propose to follow a grounded theory approach that aims to develop theory inductively from observation (Glaser & Strauss, 1967).

The purpose of this chapter was to outline an area of research between culture, ethics, and ICT. We hope that the chapter succeeded in persuading the reader that such a project is worthwhile. Given the early stage of the research, we expect the chapter to provoke vigorous debate and hot discussion about this topic—something that will help us to develop these considerations further. It is also a call for other researchers with similar interests to contact us in order to develop collaborative ties.

REFERENCES

Anthony, W. A. (2004). The principle of personhood: The field's transcendent principle. *Psychiatric Rehabilitation Journal, 27,* 205.

Berg, M. (1997). Problems and promises of the protocol. *Social Science & Medicine, 44*(8), 1081-1088.

Berg, M. (1999). Patient care information systems and health care work: A sociotechnical approach. *International Journal of Medical Informatics, 55,* 87-101.

Bourdil, P. (1996). *Le temps.* Paris: Ellipses/Édition Marketing.

Castells, M. (2000). *The information age: Economy, society, and culture, volume I: The rise of the network society* (2nd ed.). Oxford: Blackwell.

Colombo, A., Bendelow, G., Fulford, K. W. M., & William, S. (2003). Evaluating the influence of implicit models of mental disorder on processes of shared decision making with community-based multidisciplinary teams. *Social Science & Medicine, 56,* 1557-1570.

Fairweather, N. B., & Rogerson, S. (2001). A moral approach to electronic patient records. *Medical Informatics and the Internet in Medicine, 26*(3), 219-234.

Fulford, K. W. M. (2004). Ten principles of values-based medicine. In J. Radden (Ed.), *The philosophy of psychiatry: A companion* (pp. 205-234). New York: Oxford University Press.

Galtung, J. (1998). *Frieden mit friedlichen Mitteln—Friede und Konflikt, Entwicklung und Kultur.* Opladen: Leske + Budrich.

Gehlen, A. (1997). *Der Mensch: Seine Natur und seine Stellung in der Welt* (13th ed.). Wiesbaden: UTB.

Glaser, B. G., & Strauss, A. L. (1967). *The discovery of grounded theory: Strategies for qualitative research.* New York: de Gruyter.

Habermas, J. (1981). *Theorie des kommunikativen Handelns* (Band I/II). Frankfurt a. M.: Suhrkamp Verlag.

Hanlon, G., et al. (2005). Knowledge, technology and nursing: The case of NHS direct. *Human Relations, 58*(2), 147-171.

Kashmeery, A. (2004). Who owns the human genes? An East-West cross-cultural analysis. *Oxford Research Forum Journal, 2*(1), 81-85.

Levant, R. F. (2005). Evidence-based practice in psychology. *Monitor on Psychology, 36*(2). Retrieved April 19, 2005, from http://www.apa.org/monitor/feb05/pc.html

Moor, J. H. (1985). What is computer ethics? *Metaphilosophy, 16*(4), 266-275.

Nance, K. L., & Strohmaier, M. (1994). Ethical accountability in the cyberspace. *Ethics in the Computer Age* (pp 115-118). Gatlinburg, TN: ACM.

Waite, M., Hawker, S., & Soanes, C. (2001). *Oxford Dictionary, thesaurus and wordpower guide.* Oxford, UK: Oxford University Press.

Robey, D., & Azevedo, A. (1994). Cultural analysis of the organizational consequences of information technology. *Accounting, Management and Information Technologies, 4*(1), 23-37.

Sackett, D. L., Straus, S. E., Scott-Richardson, W., Rosenberg, W., & Haynes, R. B. (2000). *Evidence-based medicine: How to practice and teach EBM* (2nd ed.). Edinburgh: Churchill Livingstone.

Seedhouse, D. (2005). *Values based health care: The fundamentals of ethical decision-making.* Chichester, UK: Wiley & Sons.

Stahl, B. C. (2003). The moral and business value of information technology: What to do in case of a conflict? In N. Shin (Ed.), *Creating business value with information technology: Challenges and solutions* (pp. 187-202). Hershey, PA: Idea-Group Publishing.

Stahl, B. C. (2004). *Responsible management of information systems.* Hershey, PA: Idea Group Publishing.

Stultz, T. (2004). Model transformation: From illness management to illness management and recovery. *ACT Center of Indiana, 3*(4), 2.

UNESCO. (2005). Retrieved May 5, 2005 from http://www.unesco.org/webworld/observatory/in_focus/010702_telemedicine.shtml

Ward, J., & Peppard, J. (1996). Reconciling the IT/business relationship: A troubled marriage in need of guidance. *Journal of Strategic Information Systems, 5*, 37-65.

Weber, M. (1994). Objectivity and understanding in economics. In D. M. Hausman (Ed.), *The philosophy of economics: An anthology* (2nd ed.) (pp. 69-82). Cambridge: Cambridge University Press.

Wei, J., & Hemmings, G. P. (2000). The NOTCH4 locus is associated with susceptibility to schizophrenia. *Nature Genetics, 25*, 376-377.

Chapter XIII
Business Ethics and Technology in Turkey:
An Emerging Country at the Crossroad of Civilizations

Gonca Telli Yamamoto
Okan University, Turkey

Faruk Karaman
Okan University, Turkey

ABSTRACT

IT ethics cannot be analyzed without assessing business ethics in general and the cultural environment. This study is based on the Turkish case. Turkey lies at the crossroads of civilizations, making it hard to define a generally accepted set of ethical principles. Western, Islamic, and Turkish cultures are in competition with each of them, and a synthesis has not yet been achieved. Therefore, a common identity and common ethical standards cannot be acquired. In fact, such a synthesis could be categorized as a new civilization. This disagreement causes proliferation of unethical behaviors such as the illegal copying of software. The majority of highly educated technical people in Turkey approves of the illegal copying of software, if it is necessitated by the interests of the country. This shows that we have a long way to go to reach global ethical standards, and country-specific differences cannot be eliminated in the short term.

INTRODUCTION

While the IT sector is growing exponentially and converging with every aspect of our lives and work, it also has effects on business ethics, and various moral or ethical problems can arise. The Internet also presents us with utterly new ethical challenges for which we have no precedents in our efforts to struggle (Bynum, 2005; Ess, 2002).

There are several definitions made through IT ethics. Some defined computer ethics; others defined information ethics. According to Bynum (2001), Deborah Johnson (1985) defined computer ethics as one that studies the way in which

Figure 1. The conceptual map of IT ethics

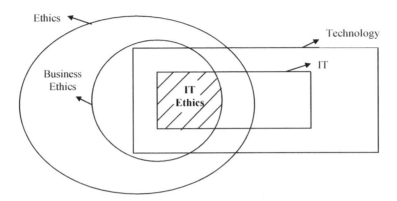

computers "pose new versions of standard moral problems and moral dilemmas, exacerbating the old problems, and forcing us to apply ordinary moral norms in uncharted realms" (Johnson, 1985, p. 1). Moor (1985) also defined computer ethics as a field concerned with policy vacuums and conceptual muddles regarding the social and ethical use of information technology.

On the other hand, information ethics is characterized as a biologically unbiased extension of environmental ethics based on the concepts of information object/infosphere/entropy rather than life/ecosystem/pain (Floridi & Sanders, 2002).

In Figure 1, we present a conceptual map of IT ethics. Business ethics is a subset of ethics, and IT is a subset of technology. The intersection of IT and business ethics is IT ethics. Business or IT ethics develops within the context of culture; geography; history; legal, economic, and political environments; and so forth. Unethical behavior in one country or civilization may be seen as ethical in another. For example some highly educated technical people in Turkey approve of the illegal copying of software, if it is necessitated by the interests of the country. A common example is cracking the Hotmail e-mail account in order to use a 250 MB quota. In fact, such high quotas are available only to American citizens.

For IT ethics, this presents an important obstacle, since IT products are used worldwide and cultural disparities hinder the establishment of globally accepted, standard IT ethics. The solution may be that each major culture and civilization should be analyzed from the perspective of individual businesses and IT ethics, and then, common denominators should be found.

The ideal solution would be the global acceptance of a particular country's environment and reducing the cultural differences to a minimum. In fact, at the start of the 19th century, Eastern civilization came close to that point; however, it could not succeed. In the 19th century, a great majority of the world was ruled by Western countries. Exceptions were China and the Ottoman Empire (Huntington, 1997; Lewis, 2002). Today, globalization again has become a major trend. However, Eastern cultures' contributions are much more significant. This is due to the relative economic and cultural strength of the East compared to the situation in the 19th century.

That does not mean that a clash among civilizations will take place, as proposed by Huntington (1997). Rather, it simply means that Eastern cultures also should contribute to the formation of a global culture. A globally accepted set of cultural values should not be determined solely by the West. This would diminish the attractiveness of the global culture for Eastern citizens. Global culture and ethics should embrace the best practices of the East. Huntington (1997) argues that differences among civilizations would not diminish but, rather, would widen. He thinks that this eventually would cause global-scale wars. It should be noted here that, although a thought-provoking theory, Huntington's views cannot be seen as Newton rules of global politics, and they are severely criticized. We think that "the clash of civilizations" was an important theory to explain global events, but we also recognize other forces and factors, such as globalization, nation-states, ethnic groups, and so forth. Regional economic pacts such as the EU and NAFTA also should be included. However, we do not see the clash of civilizations theory as totally useless.

Globalization can be seen as an antithesis of the clash of civilizations. However, we do not embrace globalization, too. The ideal mix is in between. Increasingly, the value of cultural diversity is becoming stressed. Cultural differences may pose problems for establishing global standards, but a strictly standardized world may hinder innovativeness, and the diversity of ideas and perspectives can be lost.

In Figure 2, we place the clash of civilizations at one extreme and pure globalization at the other. By *pure globalization*, we mean an ultimate level of globalization in which no nation-state or civilization exists other than the global state and civilization.

In this chapter, after analyzing the improvements and effects of IT all over the world, we will try to introduce the Turkish case for IT ethics and, thus, contribute to the global understanding of the cultural differences affecting the approaches toward business and IT ethics.

IMPROVEMENTS AND THE EFFECTS OF IT

There are several discussions about technology and business improvements and their effects on IT. According to Martin and Freeman (2004), the traditional way of technology posits two alternatives at either end of a spectrum. These alternatives are technological and social determinism. Technological determinism incorporates "the idea that technology develops as the sole result of an internal dynamic and then, unmediated by any other influence, molds society to fit its patterns" (Winner, 1986, p.21)

Such control requires technology to exist outside the construction of society and relies on an artefact's essence, as described by Heidegger (1977). A prevalent metaphor for technological determinism is a railroad line in which "technology is recognized as a separate entity that follows a linear path. Social determinism refers to 'what matters is not technology itself, but the social or economic system in which it is embedded'" (Winner, 1986, p. 20). Technology can be viewed as value-laden with inherent abilities to influence

Figure 2. The clash of civilizations vs. pure globalization

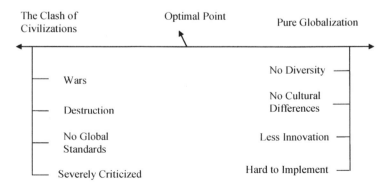

Figure 3. Technological determinism, social determinism

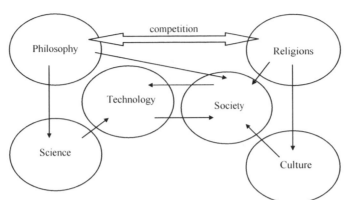

or direct its uses and users all around the world (Martin & Freeman, 2004).

Our view of social determinism and technological determinism is a little bit more sophisticated than that of Heidegger's. We described our view in Figure 3. We think that Heidegger, as a philosopher, presented an oversimplified model for technology and society. We present a more sophisticated model in the figure. Even so, this is also a very simplified view.

Considering an interview with Brenan and Johnson (2004) in an article titled "Social Ethical and Policy Implications of Information Technology," information has been a key driver of globalization. Individuals as human beings and groups as a society gradually are relying on information and information technologies that make technology more prominent in their social and business lives. Intellectual property rights and security issues in information ethics also are concerns (Peace & Freeman, 2005).

Information and ethics should be studied in detail. Convergence of the technologies is an important concept that should be taken into account for predicting the future of IT ethics. The widening generation gap is particularly important.

Unethical and often illegal behaviors in the use of IT seem to be commonplace all around the world. At the same time, however, another study—software piracy and unauthorized access

to computing facilities—are illegal acts in most countries, even in developing and developed countries (Phukan, 2002). Issues such as software privacy, virus development, and illegal system access, which once were viewed as an annoyance, now are considered major problems for organizations (Gattiker & Kelley, 1999). Crime and moral systems adoption should be asserted comprehensively, and emerging new ethical issues should be given more public attention.

Ethical questions arise when issues involve moral standards (Fritzsche, 1990). Therefore, unemployment, changing work life, and marketing styles should be emphasized in an emerging country context. The validity of ethics is based upon the acceptability of the reasons that support and justify them. In other words, emerging ethical issues should be explained to the ordinary citizen.

IT Converges with Everything

Technological revolutions are becoming more frequent, and technological changes are accelerating. Computers, telecommunications, consumer electronics, and entertainment all are converging. Mechanical parts are replaced by electronic parts, and electronic parts are replaced with software. With the manufacturing of cheaper and cheaper computer chips, computing power is now available for a wide range of consumer goods, ranging from refrigerators to automobiles to MP3 players. As Moore's Law is expected to hold for two more decades, the future likely is to be characterized by more intelligent consumer products. According to Moore's Law, the number of transistors on a computer chip doubled every 18 to 24 months, and the corollary is that the speed of microprocessors, at a constant cost, also doubles every 18 to 24 months (Hulbert, Capon, & Piercy, 2003).

Digitally converging technologies already have been revolutionary technologies. Examples are the personal computer, the Internet, the television, video games, and mobile technologies. The term *new economy* frequently was used to emphasize the importance of these new products. It is a frequently criticized idea that that these products were revolutionary. Especially the dot.com crash in U.S. markets supported the views of the critics.

Even so, we reckon that these products were revolutionary. In our view, they have very deep impacts that can be visualized only after a long period of time. This is not to say that we adopt Heidegger's technological determinism as our point of view, but rather, we think that second- or third-order effects also should be considered before declaring these products as not revolutionary. Society may control these secondary or tertiary effects, provided that these effects can be discovered.

Therefore, it will have effects and side effects while it has a hold on everything without borders. Their convergence will have a synergistic effect, augmenting their revolutionary nature. This also makes their impact more complex, and second- and third-order issues should be considered.

Of course, it may seem rather strange to talk about the problems of such exciting new technologies. However, technology changes people's lives, and they will find themselves in a much different world in only a few years.

IT and the Generation Gap

As technological revolutions accelerate, the generation gaps widen. While parents can use the gadgets used by their children, usually parents are less tech-savvy than their children.

The term *digital divide* commonly is used to describe the generation gap in the use of new technology. Older people have difficulty adapting to new technologies. In fact, they need to be retrained in the use of new technologies. Their resistance to the idea of change needs to be decreased if they are to adapt successfully to new technologies. Therefore, special adult education programs are needed.

Information Technologies make new products more complex and harder to handle. In fact, most people cannot use the full capabilities of the products they use, but they pay for the unnecessary features, nonetheless. Companies benefit from this behavior in that R&D investments for the new and unneeded features are financed by such customers. Some of these features become mainstream as society learns how to use them. Younger generations are more accustomed to these kinds of new technologies and implementations.

IT and Crime

New technologies also bring new ways to conduct new types of crimes, since new technologies bring previously unknown, new capabilities. Existing measures against crime assume that criminal people have access only to old technology and can conduct crimes by traditional ways. Legal and regulatory systems are slow to adapt to new technologies, and such adaptation can be made only after a significant number of people are hurt by technology-driven crime.

The challenge of advanced IT products is that such products augment the capabilities of individual technologies, making them hard to regulate. The easiest solution apparently is banning the new technology; however, it is hard to persuade people not to use such attractive technologies. Given the slowness of the regulatory process, predicting the effects of technology on society will help the adaptation of society and its legal system.

IT and the Distribution of Income

In the past, technological changes were not so fast. Societies had more time to adapt to changes. Even then (e.g., in the period of the Industrial Revolution), the social fabric was severely harmed, crime exploded, and the world saw the rise of socialism and communism as a response to these problems. New technologies are eroding the value of some traditional professions and are giving birth to new professions. Thus, some specializations gain value, while others lose value. Those having rising professions will enjoy rising earnings, and those with falling professions will witness declining earnings.

Advanced IT products are much more capable than products of the previous technologies, and they offer a more suitable substitute for human capital. Also, IT products offer more functionality per dollar (i.e., technological capabilities can be purchased at a lesser cost). These factors have caused structural unemployment and a widening income gap. According to the State Institute of Statistics (SIS) data, unemployment rate remained as high as about 10% in spite of the high economic growth in the last three years. The most widely accepted explanation for this contradiction is the view that productivity investments prevented the translation of high economic growth into lower unemployment.

Myopia of the Marketing Function

Changing trends and technology have altered the traditional way of doing business. These trends have caused modifications in the marketing world. We are all concerned with the effects of successful marketing applications associated with the wireless world and new technologies (Yamamoto & Telli, 2005). Technological advances come with a cost. Human society faces increasing difficulty in amassing new waves of technology. In the face of fierce competition, high technology companies continually offer new and more capable products. These products address new and sometimes unknown needs of customers. These products should be transformed based on needs and/or should increase their usage for markets. When customers are not aware of these needs, high technology companies with excellent marketing efforts will stimulate their buying activities. Communication will gain more importance due to the application of these efforts, since interaction with company stakeholders will increase. Therefore, digital and/or mobile communication environments increase the speed and effectiveness of the marketing strategy.

Actually, marketing became the main function for companies with management in developed countries. In fact, the marketing function is more important than R&D functions for many companies. However, in practice, the marketing function by itself can be considered shortsighted, because usually the only important thing for companies is the sale of the product. The shortsightedness of the marketing function is emphasized by the introduction of complex IT products. These products have complex side effects, and in fact, the time of the market stage should include the analysis of such effects. For many companies, however, societal effects of the products they develop and market are not the primary concern.

Strategic thinking is the starting point of change. Changes also depend on the size and age of the company and other environmental factors. Focusing on the future is analyzing the risks and threats in the existing market and trying to forecast probable opportunities in the future. These risks are not only financial or market risks but also political, and technological risks. Even a change in the lifestyle/demographic characteristics of customers will influence customer purchases and the customer decision-making process. The

R&D function should associate much more with marketing in order to create and fill the needs and wants of the consumer. The importance of R&D function should be understood by marketers, and a new synergy should result from that kind of implementation.

IT and New Ethical Issues

In brief, as these various elements show, projected complex IT products make problems stemming from technology more severe. Thus, the previous ways of technology production must be revised, and societal effects and possible problems should be predicted beforehand. This absolutely will lengthen the time-to-market period and add to the cost of the new product development, but this is exactly what society needs; namely, a slower and more responsive process of new technological development.

Complex use of several technologies makes the resulting technology highly complex and powerful. The problems caused by a complex technology are also complex. Such problems are different from the problems caused by separate problems caused by individual problems of the initial technologies that are converging. For example, the digital camera and mobile phone are two distinct products. Consumers can buy them separately. However, advanced mobile phones include a built-in digital camera. Since mobile phones have become indispensable, they are allowed in many places, such as classrooms. However, students may record some parts of the lecture and may distribute the recording via the Internet. Instructors are not protected effectively against such an incident by law or by generally accepted ethical standards. This example is taken from a real experience we faced in our lectures. Apparently, the ethical use of mobile phones with cameras in the classroom setting is unclear, and students have leeway to use their expensive gadgets to harm their instructors.

It is nearly impossible to predict all such second- or third-order impacts. Some of these only will be visible many years after the first introduction of the new technology. One recent example is the mobile phone with built-in digital cameras. Such cameras have unpredicted uses and may be used for spying, for example. This was not apparently the intended usage when these products first were introduced.

A person who is armed with several such new hybrid products enhances his or her capabilities. He or she may use them for terrorist or life-threatening activities. Even worse, most people are not educated in using such tools properly, and society-wide education is ignored due to its cost.

To conclude, the advancement of more complex IT products is not solely a technological issue. It has implications in a wide array of areas ranging from legal and ethical to social. Besides the new horizons brought by the convergence of the technologies, problems also are likely to arise. If we can identify such problems at an early stage, we can get ready for them.

THE TURKISH CASE

With its Westernization efforts, Turkey presents a very special case for analyzing IT ethics. In spite of the great efforts to become part of the Western civilization, Turkey is still struggling to decide to which civilization it wants to belong—Western civilization or Islamic or Eastern Civilizations. Some even argue the importance of establishing a unique Turkish civilization together with the Central Asian Turkish countries.

Business ethics, in general, are not established in emerging countries like Turkey. Although Turkish culture has its own traditional way of dealing with business ethics, the complex issues of the modern world are covered better by Western practices. The reason behind this is that traditional Turkish business ethics of the Lonca-Ahi system of the 15th and 16th centuries could not cope with the social, technological, and demographic changes throughout the world. The Lonca-Ahi system was a voluntary civil organization monitoring its members' ethical behaviors. Members with unethical conduct lost their membership, and nonmembers could by no means practice their occupations.

In other words, at the climax of the Ottoman Empire, Turkish people had developed good practices in many areas of business. Even today's Western civilization is affected partly by these good practices. This is inevitable, since all great empires in history have made their contributions. One example of the Ottoman influence is the Lonca-Ahi system. In this system, a craftsman should become a member of the relevant Lonca. Today, in the U.S., engineers and accountants are required to become members of regulating bodies in order to provide professional services. These were self-regulatory bodies in the Ottoman Empire, similar to today's U.S. practice.

However, as the Ottoman Empire declined, the Ottoman civilization gradually lost some of its qualities, including a high level of business ethics as well as economic power and military strength. On the other hand, Europe and North America both prospered economically and established higher business ethics practices.

In Turkey, in the traditional sectors, there is still some inheritance of good old business practices that are supported by the Central Asian Turkish practices and the Islamic view of business ethics. In the sectors using advanced technology, however, Turkish people can not accumulate comparable good practices yet.

When a civilization or culture does not develop technology, it cannot shape the technology in accordance with its values and cannot adapt itself to new and complex ethical problems forced by technology. In other words, business and IT ethics are high-level achievements for a society. To establish an advanced ethical framework and practice, a country first should solve its economic and security problems. Thus, Maslow's Hierarchy of Needs also can be applied to countries, cultures, and civilizations. When a country or civilization faces economic decline, high-level social qualities such as high ethical behavior also deteriorate, since low-level needs stimulate urgent action without considering far-reaching consequences.

For example, in a country in which software development is minimal, it is hard to persuade people to pay for software, since that society does not even know the meanings of software or similar technological concepts. There is also difficulty in the development process, and society does not give value to those efforts. In fact, software is not seen as property similar to a building or land. It is intangible, and people experience hardship visualizing why it should have a value and why copying it should be illegal and unethical.

This is exactly the situation in Turkey. Even the highly educated, Western-oriented segment of the Turkish population cannot see the impact or ethical problem of copying intellectual property. Society as a whole could not develop an understanding of the software industry, since the only interaction with software is at the user level. In contrast, there is little problem in the case of medical doctors and lawyers, because these are traditional occupations. Society has experience in these fields and respects the value of medical doctors' or lawyers' knowledge. People pay for these traditional services without hesitation but do not want to pay for software. Probably in the future, software also will gain the status of these types of services. People also will recognize software to be as valuable of a service as a doctor or lawyer.

Naturally, in the course of time, Turkish people also will get used to the concept of the value of an intangible asset such as software and will be more willing to pay for it. Intellectual property laws will speed up the process. However, another key issue is that the Turkish regulatory system is caught off-guard by rapid technological changes. A very severe problem is the lack of human capital having expertise both in laws and technology.

Only such multidisciplinary-oriented people can solve the complex ethical and legal problems bought by IT technology. Fortunately, regulatory bodies do recognize the problem and take action accordingly.

The development of a high level of IT ethics in Turkey will take time and should be viewed as a process rather than a one-time, big step. This technology alters all societies, developed or under-developed. However, in emerging countries like Turkey, the results are much more catastrophic. Old institutions became obsolete in a short time and there is little idea about how to establish new ones or reform the existing ones. Obviously, such a transformation cannot be performed overnight.

To understand Turkey, one should understand the roots of the Turkish culture. Modern Turkey's culture can be examined looking closely at the following dimensions:

1. Central Asian Turkish Culture
2. Arab-Islam Culture
3. Western-European Culture
4. Migration to Big Cities and Modernization
5. The European Union (EU) Accession Process
6. A Synthesis or Dissolution

Central Asian Turkish Culture

Ethical behavior in Central Asia was the norm. However, since it was a nomadic civilization, the range of ethical behavior did not include respect for others' land or buildings. Even today in Turkey's central regions, some nomadic families have difficulty understanding why a certain land belongs to a particular person. Today, such families are rare; however, a substantial number of families live in suburban houses built on lands they do not own and, thus, create slum areas. They apparently see the land as public good and think that those who use it also own it. The ownership of real estate is apparently much more systematic in Western countries, given their people's settlement in the same cities for several centuries.

The weak understanding of the rights and privileges of a settled civilization becomes a more severe problem in understanding intangible assets such as company shares, bonds, and so forth. When it comes to intellectual and property rights, it becomes very hard to understand why one should pay for a software CD, especially in the amount of US$1,000 instead of copying and using it. Since it is a conceptual value with little physical attribute other than being a software CD, it is seen as having little value, if not zero. Needless to say, patents and copyrights are not recognized and, thus, cannot be protected.

Of course, that behavior harms the country, because intellectual production is not rewarded. Thus, the country cannot use its full potential and produce scholars, writers, computer programmers, inventors, artists, and so forth. In fact, this is a common problem for most developing countries. In Turkey, however, the problem partly can be attributed to the nomadic roots of the country's people. Although nomadic cultures are strong on building new states and even empires, they are not powerful in science and technology, as settled civilizations are.

Arab-Islam Culture

Turkey's second root is Islam, although lessened in importance after the modernization efforts of the past two centuries. Turkish Islam has differences from its original Arabic versions. Turks are generally strong practitioners of the religion. However, according to the ethical framework in Turkey, the effects of Islam are very deep.

The afterlife concept is stressed very much in Islam. Muslims think that they will be punished for their nonreligious and unethical behavior and be rewarded for their correct behavior. The problem is that the right or wrong behaviors do not match those of the Judeo-Christian Western civilization. Thus, some unethical behaviors in a Western country may be proper in an Islamic country. For example, a divorced woman is rejected by society in some parts of Turkey. In the Western sense, such a behavior does not violate any law, but it is unethical. The Muslim society uses this behavior to discourage a woman from divorcing. In this way, families and children are protected. However, Western civilization gives more value to the woman's freedom than to protecting families and children.

The interesting point is that even well-practicing Muslims may see nothing wrong with copying a book or software and would be reluctant to pay for it unless he or she has no other choice. Those who would consider intellectual property theft to be forbidden are rare. The argument can be that "Western countries sell us expensive goods and enjoy unfair advantage. Those countries are rich, and we are poor. We do not have disposable income to pay for those original books and software. Also, in the past, Westerners have stolen our wealth, so we now steal their wealth in response, and we will not be responsible for that behavior after death." We should note that Turkey is not an Islamic country according to the Arab-Islam culture, but its people have Islamic roots, and some of them are well-practicing Muslims.

Thus, with this kind of reasoning, the strong prohibition in Islam against stealing becomes ineffective in practice when it comes to the theft of intellectual property. This behavior also is attributed to the first factor; namely, nomadic roots. Intellectual property is not real tangible property and has no value—so it cannot be stolen, and its copying cannot be forbidden.

The argument that Westerners have stolen our wealth in the past has a pitfall in that the producers of current intellectual property are not the same Western thieves and most probably are not their grandchildren. Even so, such arguments are seen as strong enough to see the copying activity as an ethical activity, hence pointing to the huge gap between the ethical understanding of a Western country and a non-Western country like Turkey. So, recently, copying has been seen as an opportunity to put the copiers in a retaliation mode.

Western-European Culture

Turkey's interaction with Western civilization started in the Ottoman Empire (ca. 1300-1922), especially in the 19th century. However, the greatest advancements toward Westernization were made by Turkey's founder, Mustafa Kemal Ataturk (1881-1938). In Turkey, Ataturk has a legendary position, and his views have affected Turkish people deeply. His reforms effected change directly in society, largely without any turbulence and disturbance of the community.

Ataturk aimed to modernize and westernize Turkey and succeeded to a great extent. After his death, however, the reforms lost their pace, and Turkey became a country of an eclectic culture. Today's modern Turkey cannot be understood fully by understanding only its cultures based on its major roots. In other words, Turkey has acquired many traits of Western culture, including Western ethics.

Individuality can be described as the quality of being an individual. A human being regarded as a unique personality is one of the strongest Western values (Wel & Royakkers, 2004). This probably empowers some of the highly pro-Western and modern segments of the population; it is common practice to copy books, music, and software. Thus, even the Western culture and ethical environment did not stop Turkish people's copying attitudes from taking root.

Migration to Big Cities and Modernization

In addition to the effects on the identities of the people living in Turkey, a very significant force affecting all the country—namely, migration to big cities—should be examined.

Although Turkey has a presence in industries worldwide, such as textiles, iron, steel, construction, white goods, and so forth, its economy is still dependent on agriculture, with 40% of its people working in agricultural jobs. Even so, that rate is steadily declining, and the recent economic crisis sped up that process.

In other words, Turkey only recently has experienced a transformation comparable to the Industrial Revolution of 19th-century England. The newcomers to big cities experience a culture shock, and their values and beliefs are under attack. The first generation keeps its culture and values taken from the rural areas of Turkey, and they identify themselves with the Turkish and Islamic identities, with the West being unknown or little known. By contrast, it is certain that city inhabitants have adopted Western culture and values as part of their behavior as they lived through the transformation that took place much earlier.

The second- and third-generation newcomers were born in the big cities or have lived for a large portion of their lives in those cities. Thus, they are more open to the effects of the cosmopolitan cultural atmosphere of the big cities. They also are affected by their families, and they live with the conflict of two different worlds. Identity crises are common among these people, and most of them are unsure about the set of values to which they belong. Naturally, ethical problems are not their primary concerns, as they are struggling with their basic needs.

The European Union (EU) Accession Process

In the case of Turkey, the European Union (EU) accession process is likely to fill the gap between Turkey and Europe. So Turkey will become part of a Western culture. There is an interpenetration argument concerning the concordance among Turkish, Islam, and European concepts. Göle highlights the need for a change in the minds of the members of these societies, because there is a horizontal relation taking place between the EU and Turkey (Tepeli, 2005). However, Europe as well as Turkey will be different than the Europe of today and will be less Westernized. This even may increase the differences between the two

major powers of the world: the United States and the EU.

Turkish citizens living in foreign countries are known for their obedience to rules and regulations, although cultural and ethical adaptation takes time. The hesitation of the EU regarding Turkey is understandable, since Turkey also will affect the EU. If the accession is not finalized, the cultural problems in Turkey will deepen. If another set of countries is selected to form an alternative alliance, Turkey's dominant set of ethical values will be reshaped accordingly.

In fact, Turkey can be seen as an important case for setting global ethical standards. Success of such standards in Turkey will be a strong sign for global success, too, since Turkey is at the crossroads of civilizations and is still trying to establish the practice of the right set of ethical standards. The issue is which set of standards will be accepted as right by virtually all citizens. Such a set apparently will depend on the common denominators among people with diverse backgrounds.

Synthesis or Dissolution

Anatolia, which contains most of rural Turkey, is a very fertile land as well as a passage in all directions and, thus, affected by a lot of cultures. These kinds of natural environmental conditions and cross-cultural relations have a lot of influence on the ethical values. On the other hand, looking at Islamic culture, Central Asian Turkish culture, and Western culture in isolation does not define Turkish people. It also should be noted that as a successor of the Ottoman Empire, Turkey also accepts many subcultures. But the cultural, religious, and environmental factors are important and are analyzed in this study.

Lewis (2002) examined the position of the Ottoman Empire as ahead of Western Europe. Up to a certain point, the Ottoman Empire totally ignored the West and saw Western culture as inferior. After increasing military losses, however, Western culture is recognized gradually as superior, and the East is rejected. However, Lewis states that even today, Turkey is not a member of the West. Neither does it belong to the East. In his classic book, Huntington (1997) also defines Turkey as a thorn country together with Russia and Mexico. Such countries are at the borderline of civilization and are defined by distinctive identity crises. Those countries find themselves as fully encapsulated in neither of their distinct neighbors, while such countries nonetheless incorporate much of the cultural elements of their neighbors in their own identities. These cultural mixtures make them less clear and certain as to their national identity, at least compared to their neighbors.

As already seen, each component of the modern culture of Turkey has aspects that support ethical behavior; however, these are disregarded, and ethical issues are paramount. This can be attributed mainly to the remaining differences between Western culture and Turkish culture. Although Ataturk stressed Western civilization, he also emphasized the importance of the local culture and aimed to reach a synthesis of Western culture and local culture.

The problem may be the incompleteness of that synthesis. Turkish society today cannot be deemed homogeneous. There are several subcultures remaining, and naturally, each has different ethical values and different views about right and wrong. A good example is the obedience to traffic laws. In some developed western provinces such as Eskişehir, people do not cross the road when the traffic light is red, even if there is no vehicle passing. However, in Istanbul, pedestrians cross the road whenever they see that traffic slows a little bit.

Even if the ultimate synthesis is achieved one day in the future in the way Ataturk dreamed, it still will be a different culture than Western culture. So, the problem remains. The issue is again the problem of constituting one global set of ethical standards. However, the local differences will hinder such efforts.

In the pessimistic scenario that no such synthesis can be achieved or no one single identity and one single set of ethical standards can be adopted and applied by the great majority of Turkish people, the country may even eventually dissolve and not keep its unity.

THE INTERNET AND ETHICS IN THE WORKPLACE

The Internet is cited as a powerful technological revolution that affects all aspects of business. Early research on the Internet was interested mostly in finance and marketing functions, and the scope was the company as a whole. After extensive research in such tangible and measurable aspects of the firm, attention now turns to intangible assets such as human capital.

In Turkey, the Internet revolution is felt in a delayed fashion as compared to other countries, such as the U.S, Scandinavian countries, and certain Far Eastern countries in which Internet penetration reached high levels earlier. This delay can be attributed to the lack of telecommunication infrastructure, low per-capita income, and low PC ownership and literacy rates in Turkey.

Whatever the reason, Turkey also felt the changing forces of the Internet in a delayed fashion. This is not true for all segments of society, however. High-income segments are highly educated, they follow the global trends more closely, and the Internet penetration in these segments followed a more similar trend to those in the developed countries. Thus, the digital divide became a much more severe problem in Turkey.

Some segments of society, especially those living in the more developed Aegean and Marmara regions, left the agricultural sector early enough to build factories. Thus, people living in these regions became aware of the industrial-age concepts of company shares, capital markets, marketing, production, finance, and so forth, due to this development.

It is then not surprising to see that these segments of society had no difficulty learning to use and adapt to the Internet. Their Internet experience is very similar to that in developed countries and presents little research interest, given the extensive research coverage of the behavior of people in developed countries. Few studies have examined technology adoption and usage behavior in developing countries (Anandarajan, Igbaria, & Anekwe, 2002), few have examined the technology acceptance model across cultures (Straub, Keil, & Brenner, 1997), and few have examined the differences in Internet adoption and usage in developing countries (Brown & Licker, 2003). However, there is not enough documentation about the behavioral experiences in developing countries.

Apparently, the major adaptation problems are felt by low-income segments of society. These people are characterized by the crowded, low-educated families whose members either are still struggling with the traditional way of agricultural life or recently have left their villages and migrated to big cities. They are in transition from the Agricultural Age to the Industrial Age. In a way, they face the problems witnessed by the mid-19th-century England peasants or craftsmen.

In other words, while a segment of Turkish society faces the challenges of the transition from the Industrial Age, the great majority still tries to adapt to the Industrial Age. Even so, information age scientists who presented technologies such as the Internet, mobile communication, and ICT in general are not aware of this situation. There is no restriction for people to buy and use these post-industrial products. But can they use the full potential of them or use them properly? The answer is certainly not affirmative.

In particular, the Internet gives too much freedom and too much enthusiasm for individual space where these are otherwise largely unknown in a society such as Turkey's. In Turkey, the Islamic tradition still has powerful effects, and interpersonal relationships are subject to tight rules. That is changing fast, however. For example,

partners increasingly are found on the Internet, and marriages based on love between individuals rather than as arranged by families become more frequent. The impact is profound among younger generations. Wheeler (2003, 2005) has some studies about Internet and age and gender relationships in Arab countries. It should be noted, however, that Turkey was the only country in the region with a secular system. Therefore, the experience in Arab countries is different than the Turkish case. Women have much more freedom in Turkey, especially in the developed western parts of the country.

In the early stages of the Internet, the primary access in Turkey was the workplace, and Internet connection was used for purposes other than the performance of tasks assigned by employers. In a way, efficiency was brought by the Internet and captured by workers, and they started to finish their tasks in a shorter period of time and use the rest for leisure purposes.

The issue was not of concern until the deep 2001 economic crisis in Turkey, and inefficient working practices prevailed. Until 2001, productivity became a top concern among companies, and they examined the daily lives of their workers more closely. The result was a wave of layoffs and restrictions over the use of the Internet in the workplace.

Nevertheless, home connections grew rapidly, thanks to DSL promotions supported by the local telecom monopoly, Turkish Telecom (TT). Naturally, unlimited DSL connections from home were not limited by supervisors or employers, and the use of P2P applications, chat rooms, MP3 sites, and dating sites exploded.

After the initial prohibition, even the employers were at the stage of accepting the power of the P2P application that they once prohibited and cautiously allowed their use for professional work. Even e-mail was not an acceptable formal way of communication until very recently. However, things are changing fast, especially among the young generations who are friendly to the Internet and joining the workforce.

The current stage in the transformation of the workforce after the Internet is the explosion of distance work. Traditional-style, office-based jobs are highly appreciated in Turkey, and temporary or flexible jobs are not respected at all. This can be attributed again to the late industrialization of the country. Apparently, industrial-age professions were very prestigious among the majority of peasants, and offices were considered as holy places compared to the fields they work.

Apparently, even the highly educated segments of society are affected by the old-fashioned ideas and beliefs of the majority about what an ideal job is. It is easier to follow the crowd, and it is difficult to challenge it. But transformation is inevitable. This may sound like technological determinism. Although we do not strictly follow Heidegger's view, in countries such as Turkey, society has less control over technology. This is related directly to educational levels and low income per capita.

This is a fast, difficult, and bitter experience for Turkish society as a whole. It is one matter to stay alive and another to be swept away by the waves of change. Who will survive and who will not is yet to be seen.

In brief, the Internet does transform Turkish society and the workplace. It is the driving force that is changing the culture and values of its users. The use of P2P programs and decreasing productivity are problems brought with the widespread use of the Internet by employees.

CONCLUSION

From the view of Western IT companies, emerging countries are problematic in terms of intellectual property laws and IT ethics. In these countries, such laws are nonexistent or are not applied strictly. Unethical behavior is also more common.

However, in order to discover the real reasons for intellectual property infringements and un-ethical business practices, the historic, cultural, geographic, economic, and political environments are analyzed. This can be done best by the scholars of that particular emerging country. In this study, we tried to analyze the root causes of the low standards of IT ethics in countries like Turkey. Turkey especially is a very complex case and cannot be understood without considering its history, culture, and neighbors.

In most of the developing countries, per capita GDP is only a small fraction of that of a developed country. However, software and hardware companies set flat prices globally, irrespective of the economic situation of a particular country. Especially for software and content, these disparities among the incomes of people become a motive for using very cheap illegal copies. Such people do not accept the view that they have not acted ethically, and they defend themselves by arguing that their lower disposable income justifies their copying. Thus, for IT companies, new and flexible pricing schemes in accordance with the individual characteristics of the companies might help to alleviate the problem. Illegal copying is also a problem in the developed world. However, these countries are better equipped to fight against it than are the developing countries.

Establishment of global standards in business and IT ethics is an ideal goal. However, there is much to do to reach that point. For many years to come, emerging countries will be headaches for developed countries in terms of IT ethics. However, the solution should start first from understanding and recognizing the situation of these countries. Once root causes are discovered, the rest will be much easier.

REFERENCES

ABI/INFORM Global. (2004). Social, ethical, and policy implications of information technology. *Information Management*, *17*(1/2), 30.

Anandarajan, M., Igbaria, M., & Anekwe, U. (2002). IT acceptance in a less-developed country: A motivational factor perspective. *International Journal of Information Management, 22*, 47-65.

Brown, I., & Licker, P. (2003). Exploring differences in Internet adoption and usage between historically advantaged and disadvantaged groups in South Africa. *Journal of Global Information Technology Management, 6*(4), 6-26.

Bynum T. W. (2001). Computer ethics: Its birth and its future. *Ethics and Information Technology, 3*(2), 109-112. Retrieved September 21, 2005, from en.wikipedia.org/wiki/Business_ethics

Bynum, T. W. (2005). *Computer ethics: Basic concepts and historical overview.* Retrieved November 18, 2005, from http://plato.stanford.edu/entries/ethics-computer

Ess, C. (2002). Computer-mediated colonization, the Renaissance, and educational imperatives for an intercultural global village. *Ethics and Information Technology, 4*(1), 11-22.

Floridi, L., & Sanders, J. W. (2002). Mapping the foundationalist debate in computer ethics. *Ethics and Information Technology, 4*(1), p. 1-9.

Fritzche, D. J. (1990). Emerging ethical issues in international business. *S.A.M Advanced Management Journal, 55*(4), 42-46.

Gattiker, U. E., & Kelley, H. (1999). Morality and computers: Attitudes and differences in moral judgements. *Information Systems Research, 10*, 233-254.

Heidegger, M. (1977). The question concerning technology. *The question concerning technology and other essays.* New York: Harper & Row.

Hulbert, J. M., Capon, N., & Piercy, N. F. (2003). *Total integrated marketing.* New York: Free Press.

Huntington, S. P. (1997). *The clash of civilizations and the remaking of the world order.* New York: Touchstone.

Johnson, D. G. (1985). *Computers and ethics.* Prentice Hall.

Lewis, B. (2002). *What went wrong? Western impact and Middle East response.* New York: Oxford University Press.

Martin, K. E, & Freeman, R. E. (2004). The separation of technology and ethics in business ethics. *Journal of Business Ethics, 53*, 353-364.

Moor, J. H. (1985). What is computer ethics? *Metaphilosophy, 16*(4), 266-275. Blackwell.

Peace, A. G., & Freeman, L. (2005). *Information ethics: Privacy and intellectual property.* Hershey, PA: Information Science Publishing.

Phukan, S. (2002). *IT ethics in the Internet age: New dimensions.* Retrieved from http://proceedings.informingscience.org/IS2002Proceedings/papers/phuka037iteth.pdf

Straub, D., Keil, M., & Brenner, W. (1997). Testing the technology acceptance model across cultures: A three country study. *Information and Management, 33*, 1-11.

Tepeli, S. (2005). Interview with Nilüfer Göle, author of interpenetration l'Islam et l'Europe. *Yeni Aktüel, 11*, 48-50.

Wel, L., van, & Royakkers, L. (2004). Ethical issues in Web data mining. *Ethics and Information Technology, 6*(2), 129-140.

Wheeler, D. (2003). The Internet and youth subculture in Kuwait. In C. Ess & F. Sudweeks (Eds.), Technologies of despair and hope: Liberatory potentials and practices of CMC in the Middle East. *Journal of Computer-Mediated Communication, 8*(2). Retrieved August 20, 2006, from http://jcmc.indiana.edu/vol8/issue2/wheeler.html

Wheeler, D. (2005). Gender matters in the Internet age: Voices from the Middle East. In M. Thorseth & C. Ess (Eds.), *Technology in a multicultural and global society: Programme for applied ethics, publication series no. 6.* (pp. 27-42). Trondheim: Norwegian University of Science and Technology.

Winner, L. (1986). *The whale and the reactor: A search for limits in an age of high technology.* Chicago, IL: University of Chicago Press.

Yamamoto, G. T., & Karaman, F. (2005). A road-map for the development of the content protecting technologies (CPT) for the content based e-business models. *E-Business Review, 5,* 226-232.

Yamamoto, G. T., & Telli, A. (2005). High technology for marketing: New applications & integrated circuits. In *Proceedings of the 4th International Conference on Science Marketing,* Pretoria, South Africa.

Chapter XIV

The Existential Significance of the Digital Divide for America's Historically Underserved Populations

Lynette Kvasny
The Pennsylvania State University, USA

ABSTRACT

During the 1990s, the digital divide figured prominently in the discourses of academics, corporate leaders, educators, and policymakers worldwide. In the U.S., we witnessed a massive infusion of computers and Internet access in homes, schools, libraries, and other neighborhood institutions. This has significantly increased citizens' physical access to information and communication technology (ICT) artifacts and has enhanced citizens' opportunities for acquiring and strengthening technical skills. However, does increased physical access and technical skills signal closure of the digital divide? In this chapter, I address this question by describing the preconstructed ways in which the digital divide is conceptualized by academics and policymakers, and inferring what these conceptualizations suggest about the existential significance of the digital divide as experienced by historically underserved groups in the U.S.

INTRODUCTION

Information and communication technologies (ICT), such as the World Wide Web, e-mail, and computers, have become an integral part of America's entertainment, information, and communication culture. Corporations and government agencies increasingly are offering products, services, and information online. Educational institutions are integrating ICT in their curriculum and are offering courses from a distance. Indeed,

over the past decade, ICT has become indispensable for many middle- and upper-class American households (Hoffman, Novak, & Venkatesh, 2004). However, government analysts warn that historically underserved populations such as low-income households, racial and ethnic minorities, and older and disabled Americans may continue to be distinctly disadvantaged if this divide is not closed, because American economic and social life increasingly is becoming networked through the Internet (U.S. Department of Commerce, 1995).

The *digital divide* is the term used to describe disparities in ICT access. These gaps in access generally formed along the longstanding and systemic fault lines of race, gender, age, income, physical and mental ability, and spatial location. Since the National Telecommunications and Information Administration released its first digital divide report in 1995, access to ICT has increased for most American citizens, but does this mean that the digital divide has been bridged? Is further research in this area warranted, or has the digital divide become passé?

The answer to questions such as these is determined largely by the manner in which the digital divide is conceptualized by academics and policymakers. If we conceptualize the digital divide as a gap in access and skills, then the common technology-centric solutions of increasing public access facilities and training are perhaps sufficient. However, common technology-centric solutions seem limited as we shift the discussion of the digital divide from gaps to be overcome by providing equipment and skills to social development challenges to be addressed through the effective integration of technology into communities, institutions, and societies. Effective integration of ICT requires consideration of the ability of historically underserved groups to access, adapt, and create knowledge using ICT (Warschauer, 2002).

In this chapter, I delve more closely into the question of the existential significance of the digital divide as experienced by historically underserved groups in the U.S. Existentialists embrace the human emotional experience of life and believe that experiences significantly influence human decision making. From an existential perspective, while broader physical access to computing artifacts is important and necessary for bridging the digital divide, the decision to adopt and use ICT is largely a matter of the meanings, values, and experiences of the individual. In what follows, I begin first by reviewing major issues and controversies in digital divide research and conclude with recommendations.

BACKGROUND

The digital divide is an ambiguous term, which contributes to the difficulty in developing effective policy responses. McSorley (2003) argues that the concept of the digital divide has gained some ascendancy precisely because of its central ambiguity; that it can mean all things to all people at once and, hence, mobilize a diverse community of interests. Without conceptual clarity, it is difficult to develop effective policy interventions because there is no solid understanding of the problem at hand, how it can be measured, how it can be tackled, or how it can be prevented.

Contemporary interest in the digital divide is due largely to coverage in government and foundation reports, newspapers, broadcast news, and popular magazines. Our understanding of the digital divide is based largely on survey data. For instance, U.S. households have experienced a rapid gain in computer and Internet access with two million new Internet users per month. In September 2001, 143 million Americans (54%) were using the Internet, and 174 million Americans (66%) used computers (U.S. Department of Commerce, 2002). The gains are largest for low-income families (those earning less than $15,000 per year, which increased at a 25% percent annual growth rate vs. 11% for households earning $75,000 and above) and underrepresented ethnic and racial minorities (33% for blacks; 30% for Hispanics; 20% for whites, Asian Americans, and Pacific Islanders). American Internet users also are engaged in a wide variety of activities—45% use e-mail, 36% use the Internet to search for products and services, 39% make online purchases, and 35% search for health information (U.S. Department of Commerce, 2002). Thus, the U.S. is experiencing a persistent but closing gap in computer and Internet access along the lines of ethnicity and race, geographic location, household composition, age, education, and income level (Hoffman & Novak, 1998; Lenhart, Rainie, Fox, Horrigan, & Spooner, 2000; Lenhart, et al., 2003; Mossberger,

Tolbert, & Stansbury, 2003; Norris, 2001; U.S. Department of Commerce, 2002).

Similarly, national diffusion rates are used for examining global digital divides, particularly the noticeable gaps in ICT infrastructure between developed and developing countries of the world. In the latter, many aspects of the technology may even be seen to constitute an inevitable luxury—they simply cannot afford to do without them, yet can they afford them financially? According to the 2003 Nielsen Net ratings, 580.78 million (9.57%) people worldwide have Internet access. North America accounts for 29% of the global Internet access followed by Europe with 23%, Asia-Pacific with 13%, and Latin America with 2% (Nielsen Netratings, 2003). By 2005, 15.2% of the world's population (approximately 973 million people) is estimated to have Internet access (Internet World Stats, 2005). Internet usage in North America declined to 23% of world Internet usage due to relatively faster uptake in Europe (29.3%), Asia-Pacific (34.2%), and Latin America (7.5%). The highest Internet usage growth is taking place in Africa (429.8% usage growth from 2000 to 2005 compared to 107.3% in North America, the slowest Internet growth region of the world). Yet Africa only accounts for 2.5% of the world's Internet users. Castells (1988) uses the concept of *technological apartheid* to refer to this process of disconnecting complete countries and poor neighborhoods from the world's economic and social systems. According to Norris (2001), these disconnections occur not only as a global divide between developed and undeveloped worlds, but also as a social divide between the information-rich and the information-poor, and as a democratic divide between those who do and those who do not use new technologies to further political participation.

Academics and policy think tanks largely have taken up statistical formulations for both formulating and measuring the digital divide. Consequently, under these conditions, the digital divide comes to scholars preconstructed in terms

of research questions, methods, measurements, and assumptions. This encourages us to define technology in certain ways; to ask certain questions and exclude others; to take up problems defined in advance; and perhaps most tellingly, to accept the terms of public debate as the basis for our research.

The emphasis to date has been to describe the digital divide in statistical terms as a means of presenting trends or demographics. These statistics often are used to create and justify categories such as "people on the wrong side of the divide" and "information have-nots." With positivist thoroughness, we define the have-nots as the typical problem populations (unemployed workers, low-income families, racial and ethnic minorities, single-parent families, high school drop outs, senior citizens, inner-city residents). Statistical rigor provides authority that supports hegemonic discourses that are in sync with international think tanks such as OECD, DOT Force, and World Bank (McSorley, 2003).

In digital divide discourses, haves and have-nots are ranked both by natural attributes such as race and age and by structural conditions of poverty and geographic segregation. These online disparities generally parallel those found off-line (Moss, 2002). Hence, the digital divide discourse becomes preconstructed in the use of science (statistical demographics and digital divide surveys). It also becomes racist in the way that it constructs, names, and ascribes values to groups along social and ethnic lines. Then, in the name of equality and social justice, people engage to aid the groups believed to be inferior (Sterne, 2003).

In the 2000 National Telecommunication and Information Association report, for instance, we see comparisons between racial and ethnic groups with language like "white vs. Hispanic households," "minorities are losing ground," and "the digital divide has turned into a racial ravine." Here's the self-fulfilling prophecy: "Because these factors vary along racial and ethnic lines, minorities will continue to face a greater digital divide as we move into the next century. This reality merits a thoughtful response by policy makers consistent with the needs of Americans in the Information Age" (U.S. Department of Commerce, 1999). If demographic differences become the focus of digital divide policy debates and solutions, why be shocked when those who belong to groups long designated inferior still are not engaged? Are we maintaining old and dangerous myths in our simplified constructions of ICT and its value? Will we participate in propagating shortsighted and heavily prejudiced recitations of the demographic characteristics of the divide?

On its own, the digital divide does not create racism, classism, colonialism, or sexism; these phenomena predate computing. Rather, these logics treat historically underserved groups primarily as opportunities for or impediments to the dissemination of ICT. Because the *a priori* premise of ICT is often profit, its logic concerning social issues such as the emancipation of women and minorities or preservation of the environment becomes largely instrumental. In the context of the digital divide, issues of social justice tend to be reduced to matters of bottom-line calculus—tolerated when costless, enthusiastically promoted when profitable, but too often opposed when change demands substantial diversion of social and economic surplus (Dyer-Witheford, 2000). Unfortunately, much of the contemporary digital divide discourse advocates ICT as a mechanism for alleviating economic inequality, rather than the more comprehensive notion of social inclusion (Couldry, 2003). The digital divide is often framed as what should be (universal access and effective use) rather than what it is (a contemporary basis of inequality experienced by structural minorities such as urban poor or small/under-resourced businesses).

The assumption underlying the framing of the digital divide along the lines of universal access and effective use is that computer and Internet use significantly and directly impacts economic and employment benefits as well as other op-

portunities for upward mobility (Hongladarom, 2003). Policy solutions, therefore, tend to focus on technology fixes such as delivering basic computer training courses, wiring public schools and libraries, and providing computing resources with Internet access in poorer communities (Norris, 2001). Over time, market forces are believed to drive the proliferation of ICT. Aggressive public policies or investments targeted to address digital divide problems no longer will be necessary (Compaine, 2002). Indeed, as statistics report growing numbers of American Internet adopters, the use of the term *digital divide* largely has faded from policy debates in the U.S. (Kvasny & Truex, 2001), and federal government support for digital divide programs has declined significantly. For instance, the Technology Opportunities Program (TOP) did not receive appropriations for fiscal year 2005, and funding for the Community Technology Center program was reduced from $32 million in 2002 and 2003 to $10 million in 2004 and $5 million in 2005. The proposed budget for fiscal year 2006 eliminates funding to several educational technology programs, such as Enhancing Education through Technology, Star Schools, and Community Technology Centers (CTCs).

In response to these budget cuts and fading US government interest in the digital divide, there have been calls by organizations such as the Benton Foundation's Digital Divide Network, the National Urban League, CTCNet, and the Civil Rights Forum on Communications Policy to renew wider analytic agendas and to extend analysis beyond statistical snapshots of computer access and genres of use. While we know much about the statistical gains in access, we know comparatively little about the actual impacts of increased accessibility for historically underserved groups. Computers and Internet access do not lead directly to digital opportunities for underrepresented groups, communities, and nations. Rather, there are both beneficial and detrimental, intended and unintended consequences (Kling, 1998). Moreover, both technological and social aspects such as power relations, motivation, autonomy, knowledge, policies, technical skills, and resources determine these consequences. Thus, it is somewhat naïve to assume that technological access and market forces are the sole roadblocks to expanded Internet use.

A more complex framing is one of ICT as a configurable computing web of social and technical factors that exist in localized contexts that are important for understanding disparities in the outcomes resulting from computer and Internet use. Without a contextually nuanced understanding of the social and technical nature of the digital divide, we simply perpetuate stereotyped notions about historically underserved groups and developing countries as being on the wrong side of the divide, and propagate shortsighted and heavily prejudiced recitations of the demographic characteristics. If the demographic element becomes the focus of digital divide scholarship, why be taken aback when those who belong to groups long designated inferior still are not engaged in what is naïvely assumed to be neutral technologies? Digital divide discourses that repeatedly describe underserved groups as "catching up" and "at risk of falling further behind" may, in fact, help to perpetuate a self-fulfilling prophecy (Hacker & Mason, 2003).

ICT skills and the capacity to use them are not equitably distributed, even when access is largely available. For example, as underserved groups adopt ICTs, access barriers, proficiency, skills, and a wider range of technologies and applications also must be studied. In fact, gaps in knowledge, skills, and experience come to the fore as access broadens. For instance, Hargittai (2001) introduces the concept of "second-level divides" to signify the considerable difference in people's ability to find various types of content on the Web and time required to complete online tasks. Age is associated negatively with the level of Internet skill, experience with technology is related positively to online skill, and gender does

little to explain the variance in people's ability to find content online. Van Dijk and Hacker (2003) observe that the adoption and use of ICT is cumulative and recursive, because individuals must migrate to new hardware platforms, learn new software applications, and develop new skills. Access, skill, use and cost constantly are shifting and reemerging as new ICTs are introduced and as existing ICTs are upgraded.

There are also studies that focus closely on single demographic groups in order to gain more nuanced understandings about the ways in which ICT is conceptualized and used. Some studies, for instance, have intensively examined racial and ethnic minorities in the U.S. Schement and Forbes (2000) found that African-Americans are likely to buy computers for their children's future, while Hispanic Americans buy computers for work or for their businesses. African-Americans also tend to have more positive attitudes toward ICT than similarly situated European American respondents when they were asked a range of questions such as the importance of the Internet and computers for keeping up with the times and for economic opportunity (Hoffman & Novak, 1998). African-Americans also are more willing to learn new computer skills in a variety of ways (i.e., formal education, online education, informal education) and are more willing to use public access sites (Mossberger et al., 2003). Even among nonusers of the Internet, African-Americans, Hispanic Americans, and urban residents are among the most likely to say they will use the Internet someday (Lenhart et al., 2003).

Thus, the U.S. government's proposition of a closing digital divide is premised on a limited conceptualization based on access to computers and the Internet (Servon, 2002; Warschauer, 2002). The digital divide cannot be addressed adequately without some understanding of the broader context of social and economic stratification (Norris, 2001). Jung, Qiu, and Kim (2001) propose an Internet connectedness index (ICI), a measure for monitoring long-term inequities in the quality of Internet connections among users, especially in terms of whether Internet connections will enhance the chances of people's upward mobility. This model moves beyond the comparison of computer and Internet access for diverse groups by incorporating usage constructs, such as time spent online, computer dependency, location of access points, scope of activities, and personal effects of ICT on the quality of life, in order to provide insights into how the Internet is being incorporated into a world of structural inequalities. This work moves from measures of use and access to measures of connectedness that better capture broader social structures and can help to determine the social benefits of use and access.

EVIL AND THE DIGITAL DIVIDE

In this section, I put forth the argument that the digital divide poses a highly technical solution to the intrinsically human problem of evil. While the digital divide has receded from public debates, the subject of evil has received significant attention in the post-9/11 U.S. For West (1999), evil is the unnecessary social misery, unjust suffering, and unmerited pain experienced by human beings. "All civilizations have a problem with evil, but some—like the U.S.—are in sustained denial even as they view themselves as the embodiment of good" (West, 1999, p. 510). If the U.S. government is conceptualizing the digital divide narrowly as an issue of access that can be remedied with the influx of computers and Internet access, then the country's leaders can safely believe that they have remedied the divide and improved life for most citizens. However, if we see the digital divide as a complex evil that exists in many forms (existential, institutional, social, political, and economic), then it becomes clear that there is still much more work to be done.

ISSUES, CONTROVERSIES, PROBLEMS

For me, the digital divide is fundamentally about evil—it is a painful discourse softened through statistics and dehumanized by numbers. While people in positions of privilege may empathize with those on the wrong side of the divide, few feel deeply and openly enough to enable them to see beyond the statistics. Instead of understanding the everyday practices of people who historically have been excluded from the eWorld and developing technology services and information sources to serve their unique needs, the more common response is to convert and educate the backward masses. We produce discourses that discount their values and cultures and show them why they need to catch up. In fact, their vulnerability may elevate their desire to adopt and use ICT (Kvasny & Truex, 2001). The elites want to provide access and essentially to define away the digital divide, but the people on intimate terms with evil don't have that luxury.

I conducted an ethnographic study in a low-income, predominantly African-American community in order to examine residents' experiences with ICT as well as the meanings and values they attribute to technology (Kvasny, 2005, 2006, in press; Kvasny & Keil, 2006). One particular area of focus was the perceived benefits and actual outcomes of ICT training at a community technology center. I learned that many people experienced ICT as a type of double-bind oppression (Frye, 1983) that occurred when oppressive forces pushed people into situations for which there are few options, all of which are suboptimal. These informants were faced with double binds—do you continue to work in a menial job or do you throw it all away to go back to school for additional training; do you remain on welfare or do you work in a low-paying job that won't move you out of poverty? Either one they chose, they could not win.

For instance, Sandy was employed as a bookkeeper. She always enjoyed working with computers and was extremely optimistic about the prospects of using her computer training on her job. Early in the training, she came to see how she could apply her database skills in the workplace. Since she didn't have a computer at work, she decided to bring her home PC into the office. She began to load customer information into an Access database and soon was printing mailing labels and running reports. Sandy was proud of her accomplishments, but her success did not sit well with her boss. He began to derail her efforts by not allowing her to go to computer classes during her lunch hour. Eventually, her boss delivered a final edict—either take the PC out of the office or quit the job. Sandy took a leap of faith and quit her job in hopes of finding another one that would enable her to work with computers and maintain a livable wage. In the two months after she quit her job, she attended job fairs but was unable to find employment. She surmised that an ICT-related job remained beyond the reach of a middle-aged black woman with no practical computer experience and a computer certificate from a free city-sponsored program.

ICT presented a double bind—will you continue to believe in the espoused benefits of ICT or will you be betrayed by hoping too much? Sandy noted that "computers are everybody's dream of what is right with the world," but she did not receive the outcomes and benefits she anticipated. In many ways, these informants are living lives shaped by forces that are not interlocked accidentally but rather systematically in such a way as to catch them in double binds that penalize motion in any direction. Barriers such as single parenthood, low educational attainment, public assistance, and underemployment cannot be looked upon individually or additively. These barriers are interwoven. To feel the effects, we have to look at the full range of oppressions.

Frye (1983) uses the metaphor of a birdcage that is comprised of several individual wires. Each individual wire is thin, and if you only concentrate on one, you will assume that the bird simply could fly around the barrier and be free. However, if you look at all of the wires, it becomes apparent that the sum of the wires effectively constructs a system of barriers that are as effective as a solid wall in confining the bird. ICT becomes another wire on the birdcage. Digital divide interventions that only deliver ICT access and basic computer literacy are less successful than expected, because they fail to redress the systematic barriers that limit ICT access and skills in the first place. The discourse of technology progress is evil, because it creates a belief system that is imposed upon people who then are provided little chance of actually benefiting materially from ICT use. Valdez (2000) contends that it does not matter how well people accept the professed ideology of greater employment opportunities for people with computer skills, because this ideology does not provide solutions for overcoming the structural constraints of race and class bias. Thus, despite our best intentions, we create a double bind by imploring the historically underserved people to engage with ICT, but we do not deliver on the espoused outcomes.

When I began to question the practical meaning of ICT access and training provided by the community technology center, I began to see that the training was largely outside of the informant's lived experience. For instance, one word processing exercise had informants creating flyers for a ski resort. The document has a picture of a blond woman with ski gear speeding down a slope with the caption "Feel the Thrill, Ski the Slopes." Another exercise called for informants to create a PowerPoint presentation about strategies for studying in college. These lessons weren't integrated with working-class experiences of informants with little or no experience with skiing or college. The detachment of this type of training from the concrete realities of the informants suggests that their needs remained underserved.

Residents came to the community technology center because they generally believed that ICT access and training would help them to overcome their material deprivation. For them, learning about ICT was rarely just for the sake of learning or creating content. Instead, learning was aimed purposefully at improving economic status and social inclusion. Contrary to the statistics that report relatively less ICT use by older Americans, seniors were the most active and innovative ICT users. Although most seniors initially came to the center with no immediate purpose other than to combat loneliness, over time they began to realize that ICT also offered more tangible opportunities. Pearl's narrative suggests tangible benefits such as opportunities for employment and learning and taking a "new lease on life."

I want to make sure that you understand how important this [community technology center] is to us. It is giving us a new lease on life. It increases my thoughts, and my ability to learn. The environment is very encouraging. I now have faith and hope. Now I understand that there are things out there for us, as we get old. The [community technology center] fills a great need. We seniors are now becoming qualified homebodies. We can fill these jobs.

For Pearl, ICT was not only a vehicle for economic empowerment but also a cultural space from which seniors can resist and transform prevailing societal views in which older Americans are seen as idle and unproductive. Martin and Nakayama (1997) describe cultural space as both a physical location that has culturally constructed meanings and a metaphorical place from which we communicate. Employing the latter conceptualization of cultural space, ICT becomes a site for social change. Pearl doesn't want merely to survive, fit in, or cope. She wants to change society's perceptions about older Americans. She sees herself and her peers as "qualified homebodies" who can compete with younger people in the job market.

In this narrative of self-determination, she also notes that "there are things out there for us as we get old." On an existential level, she talks about faith, hope, and a new lease on life.

Ron's narrative also speaks metaphorically from this cultural space as he juxtaposes darkness and light. He talks about being out of the communication loop and feeling "so left behind" due to his lack of ICT skills. For him, ICT is about "feeling connected" and "being part of what's going on."

Technology is the thing of the future. My nieces and nephews tell me that I need to step it up some, so this is my first move to get out of the dark and into the light. ... I want to be more a part of what's going on. I want to feel connected ... I was in the dark. Before I learned about the computers, it was hard to communicate with people ... I felt so left behind, out of it. I was not in the loop for communication. I had no e-mail, so I couldn't keep in touch with my family on a regular basis. I had to use the phone. Now with e-mail, I can communicate on a regular basis because it is less expensive.

Another senior, Ms. Ginny, stated that she came to the center for companionship and social stimulation. She is keenly aware of the risks associated with aging and displays an inner resolve to stay well mentally and physically. She viewed the community technology center as a place for socializing and community building.

I come to the center to socialize. I live alone, so my time at the center lets me mingle with others. I need to constantly stimulate my mind or I might go crazy. I do not want to get old and alone with no one to talk to like some of my friends. I am afraid of getting ill mentally. There are women in my building that don't get out much and they just deteriorate in body and mind. Plus, the program is free. This is what really makes me come because I am on a fixed income. Black people do not take advantage of programs like whites do. That's part of the reason why we are being left behind.

Ms. Ginny appreciates the social aspects of the program, but these are generally framed in physical rather than virtual contexts. She does not articulate the Internet as a communication medium for overcoming loneliness and isolation that she and other seniors experience. Instead, she highlights the importance of the physical coming together at the technology center. She also speaks from a racial standpoint in which she sees blacks as falling behind because they don't take advantage of educational programs as rapidly as other racial and ethnic groups.

Ms. Ginny's comments about the program being free (the community technology center offers courses at no economic cost to participants) are also informative, because even a theoretically free good has associated costs. To get access to this free service, residents must overcome situational barriers such as childcare, financial resources, and transportation. Residents also must overcome institutional barriers such as rules and regulations that impose limits on the duration of use and the type of content that can be accessed. These situational and institutional barriers are essentially the costs that one must pay for using the center, and these costs are not evenly distributed. In particular, younger adults with children and participants with jobs tend to face higher costs, because their daily lives are complicated by time constraints imposed by parenting and employment responsibilities.

Once I recognized that time was perhaps the largest barrier, I looked for opportunities to introduce participants to online services that might help them to save time. I quickly learned that using ICT for something as mundane as shopping for books is more than simply a matter of convenience; it fundamentally challenged cultural practices such as reading and sharing books. Two participants, Ron and Bill, both describe how in their youth they spent time with older men in their communities hanging out in barbershops and pool halls. These older men always had small paperback books in their pockets. They would encourage young boys to read by lending them books and paying them money if they came back to report on what they had read. They used this practice on me during my fieldwork. Once a week, they would give me books to read, and they would quiz me when I returned the books.

Since these gentlemen liked to read, I decided to show them how to search for books online at Amazon.com. I noticed, however, that many of the books that they looked up were ones that they already owned. I began to show them how they could search for books similar to the ones that they owned, read recommendations, and compare prices among bookstores to get the best deals. Neither man was interested in making purchases online. They told me that there is nothing like going to the local store, chatting with the regulars, and browsing in person. They also felt that information on the Internet was somehow censored—"They won't have everything there, only what they want you to buy."

Indeed, greater ICT access and training was perceived as creating new risks like censorship and cultural domination. Mr. Hudson provides a narrative that seems to depict an ethos of despair as he constructs ICT as a nightmare for black fathers with low incomes.

What do I think about the Internet? It is a kind of mind destruction. It is kind of like Christmas where the media comes into your house and just takes over. The white man is invading my home through radio and TV ads. He is programming my family to want this stuff. The black man cannot afford to give his family all of this stuff. Therefore, technology becomes a nightmare for us.

Mr. Hudson internalized the limits set by history and his current economic condition and decided that ICT would not improve the life chances of black men. He saw the same closed doors, dead ends, and limited prospects. When faced with these betrayals, he adopted a bleak and hopeless world-view that shaped his appropriation of ICT.

In summary, people in working-class communities largely remain faceless and nameless have-nots to the wealthy and middle-class people who safely imagine that the rest of the world is like them. While some informants embraced these preconstructed ideologies about ICT and economic advancement, others articulated oppositional standpoints informed by their own class, gender, and racial identities and experiences. In both cases, the existential problems of evil helped to shape informants' motivations, expectations, and actual usage of ICT. These are not the faceless.

SOLUTIONS AND RECOMMENDATIONS

West (1999) argues that the U.S. doesn't deal well with evil. Evils like the digital divide surface during hot times but quickly are pushed to the edge during cold moments. Moreover, the voices of those directly experiencing the ill effects of the digital divide often are absent from the discussion. How can a nation engage in serious discussion of suffering when it can solve its problems simply by declaring that an evil like the digital divide has been solved with the installation of computers and a basic computer literacy courses?

According to West (1999), the metaphor for the U.S. is the "hotel civilization"—a nation that doesn't encourage wrestling with evil, misery, or pain. Instead, the U.S. is more concerned with efficiency, comfort, and convenience. Mobility is the American way because it enables us to turn our backs, check out, and walk away from difficult problems. In the same way that we can lose weight and reverse erectile dysfunction with a pill, relieve debt with a phone call, enlarge breasts and remove wrinkles with cosmetic surgical procedures, we seek to find simple solutions to

the digital divide. In the hotel civilization, people are busy and don't have time for investment in self. Instead, they resort to "purveyors of need" (Bourdieu, 1984)—dietitians, nutritionists, fitness trainers, beauty consultants, and financial planners. Americans are also highly individualistic, tend to ignore history, and look toward the future because it signals progress. Technology is generally prominent in our futuristic visions of society. Thus, we criticize, question, organize, mobilize, and convince people on both sides of the divide that ICT is worthwhile. Everyone is to be part of this progressive ICT culture. ICT provides a clean, low-cost solution to inherently social problems. It makes problem people less human in the sense that ICT mediates our interactions with government, health, education, and other important institutional spheres that determine our life chances. We become an individualistic and highly efficient civilization driven by a market mentality and an endless search for happy endings.

As a scholar deeply engaged in matters of ICT and social justice, I refute this instrumental depiction of the digital divide. What members of this catch-all category of have-nots share is the fact that they are perceived as living outside of the American dream of individual success. The digital divide creates new technological barriers between insiders and outsiders (Floridi, 2001). These barriers need to be dismantled through programs that address both the instrumental and social aspects of the divide. As a metaphor for America, the hotel is the fusion of the home and the market. The warmth and security of the home must exist alongside the calculated efficiency and competitiveness of the market.

The stakes surrounding the digital divide and the science that justifies digital divide policy remedies are large and far-reaching. To date, much of the debate has been technology-centric, viewing the divide as one of access to computers and the Internet. However, digital divides cannot be discussed, much less decided, solely on the terrain of technology. The limitations of this technology-centric view have been engaged in the information systems literature since the 1970s. The relevant findings from this literature often are set in specific (large, for-profit) organizational contexts, which masks the more general contributions of the information systems scholarship. For example, information systems scholarship points out the importance of clear and coherent strategic initiatives, the importance of leadership, attention to developing systems with users' needs and input, the careful control and management of projects, attention to the systemic nature of interdependent systems, the potential value of merging commonplace and emerging technologies, and the need to carefully oversee the entire lifecycle of an information systems effort. Simply, information systems research has much to offer those engaged in the scholarship of the digital divide (Kvasny, Sawyer, & Purao, 2004).

Scholars also must ponder critical questions, such as "How am I implicated with the institutional mechanisms that promote unjustified suffering of oppressed people not just here in the US but around the world?" This question has to do with our fundamental understanding of the digital divide as an existential problem in which everyday people's efforts to live a better life are being impeded and obstructed by ICT. What if continued subjugation is a precondition for the healthy conditioning and flourishing of American democracy? What if just enough ICT training is being provided to grease the economic machine and to produce a permanent underclass in America? These are the critical questions asked by the historically underserved groups who serve as collaborators in my research. If we view the digital divide through the eyes of the underserved, we can begin to comprehend the existential significance of this problem.

CONCLUSION

In this chapter, I have provided competing perspectives for framing the digital divide and the existential significance of the digital divide for historically underserved people. On the one hand, the digital divide is framed in a problem of access that can be solved by markets. The digital divide, from this perspective, is about market values, such as price, deregulation, and competition. On the other hand, the digital divide can be framed fundamentally as a social problem that stems largely from longstanding inequities in income, education, workforce participation, healthcare, housing, and other life chances. The digital divide, from this perspective, is about nonmarket values such as justice, social welfare, and freedom. In the U.S., it is becoming extremely difficult for nonmarket values to gain a foothold. West (1999) argues that ultimately there can be no democratic tradition without nonmarket values. Democracy is about the relationship of public interest and common good to the most vulnerable among us as human beings. Democracy is about curtailing the exercise of arbitrary power. We need a more democratic framing of the intractable problem that has come to be known as the digital divide. Tragically, nonmarket values are relatively scarce, which is one of the reasons it is so tough to mobilize and organize people around this important cause. It is hard to convince people that there are alternative options for which they ought to sacrifice if we are truly concerned about meaningful ways to use ICT to further the social inclusion of historically underserved groups.

ACKNOWLEDGMENTS

This material is based upon work supported by the National Science Foundation under Grant No. 0238009. Any opinions, findings, and conclusions or recommendations expressed in this material are those of the author and do not necessarily reflect the views of the National Science Foundation.

REFERENCES

Bourdieu, P. (1984). *Distinction: A social critique of the judgement of taste*. Cambridge, MA: Harvard University Press.

Castells, M. (1998). *The information age: Economy, society and culture, part 3: The end of millennium*. Oxford: Blackwell.

Compaine, B. (2002). *The digital divide: Facing a crisis or creating a myth?* Cambridge, MA: MIT Press.

Couldry, N. (2003). Digital divide or discursive design? On the emerging ethics of information space. *Ethics and Information Technology, 5*, 89-97.

Dyer-Witheford, N. (2000). *Cyber-Marx: Cycles and circuits of struggle in high-technology capitalism*. Chicago: University of Illinois Press.

Floridi, L. (2001). Informational ethics: An environmental approach to the digital divide. *Philosophy in the Contemporary World, 9*(1), 1-7.

Frye, M. (1983). *Oppression in the politics of reality: Essays in feminist theory*. Freedom, CA: Crossing Press.

Hacker, K., & Mason, S. (2003). Ethical gaps in studies of the digital divide. *Ethics and Information Technology, 5*(2), 99-115.

Hargittai, E. (2001). Second-level digital divide: Differences in people's online skills. *First Monday, 7*(4). Retrieved October 3, 2005, from http://www.firstmonday.org/issues/issue7_4/hargittai

Hoffman, D. L., & Novak, T. P. (1998). Bridging the racial divide on the Internet. *Science, 280*(5362), 390-391.

Hoffman, D. L., Novak, T. P., & Venkatesh, A. (2004). Has the Internet become indispensable? *Communications of the ACM, 47*(7), 37-42.

Hongladarom, S. (2003). Exploring the philosophical terrain of the digital divide. *Selected Papers from the Conference on Computers and Philosophy, 37*, 85-89.

Internet World Stats. (2005). Retrieved December 2005, from http://www.internetworldstats.com/stats.htm

Jung, J. Y., Qiu, J. L., & Kim, Y. C. (2001). Internet connectedness and inequality: Beyond the "divide." *Communication Research, 28*(4), 507-535.

Kling, R. (1998). *Technological and social access to computing, information and communication technologies*. White paper for the presidential advisory committee on high performance computing, communications, information technology, and the next generation Internet. Retrieved September 2004, from http://www.slis.indiana.edu/kling/pubs/NGI.htm

Kvasny, L. (2005). The role of the habitus in shaping discourses about the digital divide. *Journal of Computer Mediated Communication, 10*(2). Retrieved October 3, 2005, from http://jcmc.indiana.edu/vol10/issue2/kvasny.html

Kvasny, L. (2006). The cultural (re)production of digital inequality. *Information, Communication and Society, 9*(2), 160-181.

Kvasny, L. (in press). Let the sisters speak: Understanding information technology from the standpoint of the "other." *The DATA BASE for Advances in Information Systems, 37*(4).

Kvasny, L., & Keil, M. (2006). A tale of two US cities: The challenges of redressing the digital divide. *Information Systems Journal, 16*(1), 23-53.

Kvasny, L., Sawyer, S., & Purao, S. (2004). The digital divide and information systems research: Stepping up or stepping away? In *Proceedings of the MISRC/ CRITO Digital Divide Symposium*, Minneapolis, Minnesota. Retrieved October 3, 2005, http://misrc.umn.edu/symposia/dd/papers/MISRC-CRITO-Kvasny1.doc

Kvasny, L., & Truex, D. (2001). Defining away the digital divide: The influence of institutions on popular representations of technology. In B. Fitzgerald, N. Russo, & J. DeGross (Eds.), *Realigning research and practice in information systems development: The social and organizational perspective* (pp. 399-415). New York: Kluwer Academic Publishers.

Lenhart, A., Rainie, L., Fox, S., Horrigan, J., & Spooner, T. (2000). Who's not online. *Pew Internet and American Life Project*. Retrieved October 3, 2005, from http://www.pewinternet.org/pdfs/ Pew_Those_Not_Online_Report.pdf

Lenhart, A., Horrigan, J., Rainey, L., Allen, K., Boyce, A. & Madden, M. (2003). The ever-shifting Internet population: A new look at Internet access and the digital divide. *Pew Internet and American Life Project*. Retrieved October 3, 2005, from http://www.pewinternet.org/pdfs/PIP_Shifting_Net_Pop_Report.pdf.

Martin, J., & Nakayama, T. (1997). *Intercultural communication in contexts.* Mountain View, CA: Mayfield Publishing Company.

McSorley, K. (2003). The secular salvation story of the digital divide. *Ethics and Information Technology, 5*(2), 75-87.

Moss, J. (2002). Power and the digital divide. *Ethics and Information Technology, 4*(2), 159-165.

Mossberger, K., Tolbert, C., & Stansbury, M. (2003). *Virtual inequality: Beyond the digital divide.* Washington, DC: George Washington University Press.

Nielsen Netratings (2003). *Global net population increases.* Retrieved March 2005, from http://www.nua.com/surveys/index.cgi?f=VS&art_id=905358729&rel=true

Norris, P. (2001). *Digital divide? Civic engagement, information poverty and the Internet in democratic societies.* New York: Cambridge University Press.

Schement, J. R., & Forbes, S. C. (2000). Identifying temporary and permanent gaps in universal service. *The Information Society, 16*(2), 117-126.

Servon, L. (2002). *Bridging the digital divide: Technology, community and public policy.* Malden, MA: Blackwell Press.

Sterne, J. (2003). Bourdieu, technique and technology. *Cultural Studies, 17*(3/4), 367-389.

U.S. Department of Commerce (1995). Falling through the net: A survey of the "have nots" in rural and urban America. *The National Telecommunications and Information Administration.* Retrieved October 3, 2005, from http://www.ntia.doc.gov/ntiahome/fallingthru.html

U.S. Department of Commerce. (1999). *Falling through the net: Defining the digital divide.* Retrieved January 29, 2005, from http://www.ntia.doc.gov/ntiahome/fttn99/contents.html

U.S. Department of Commerce. (2002). A nation online: How Americans are expanding their use of the Internet. *The National Telecommunications and Information Administration.* Retrieved October 2, 3005, from http://www.ntia.doc.gov/ntiahome/dn

Valdez, J. (2000). Searching for a path out of poverty: Exploring the achievement ideology of a rural community. *Adult Education Quarterly, 50*(3), 212-230.

Van Dijk, J., & Hacker, L. (2003). Digital divide as a complex and dynamic phenomenon. *The Information Society, 19*(4), 315-326.

Warschauer, M. (2002). Reconceptualizing the digital divide. *First Monday, 7*(7). Retrieved December 2005, from http://firstmonday.org/issues/issue7_7/warschauer/index.html

West, C. (1999). *The cornel west reader.* New York: Basic Civitas Books.

About the Authors

Soraj Hongladarom is an associate professor of philosophy and Director of the Center for Ethics of Science and Technology at Chulalongkorn University in Bangkok, Thailand. He has published books and articles on such diverse issues as bioethics, computer ethics, and the roles that science and technology play in the culture of developing countries. His concern is mainly how science and technology can be integrated into the life-world of the people in so-called third-world countries, and what kind of ethical considerations can be obtained from such relation. Homepage: http://homepage.mac.com/soraj/web/soraj.html

Charles Ess is a professor of philosophy and religion and a distinguished professor of interdisciplinary studies at Drury University in Springfield, Missouri, USA, and Professor II in the Programme for Applied Ethics, Norwegian University of Science and Technology in Trondheim. Ess has received awards for teaching excellence and scholarship and has published in comparative (East-West) philosophy, applied ethics, discourse ethics, history of philosophy, feminist Biblical studies, and computer-mediated communication (CMC). With Fay Sudweeks, Ess co-chairs the biennial conferences Cultural Attitudes towards Technology and Communication (CATaC) and has served as a visiting professor at IT-University, Copenhagen (2003) and was a Fulbright Senior Scholar, University of Trier (2004). Homepage: http://www.drury.edu/ess/ess.html.

*   *   *

Pattarasinee Bhattarakosol teaches computer science at the Department of Mathematics, Faculty of Science, Chulalongkorn University. She obtained a BSc in mathematics from Chulalongkorn University, an MSc in applied statistics from the National Institute of Development Administration, Thailand, and a Ph.D. in computer science from Wollongong University in Australia.

Dan L. Burk is the Oppenheimer, Wolf and Donnelly Professor of Law at the University of Minnesota, USA, where he teaches courses in patent, copyright, and related topics. An internationally prominent authority on issues of high technology, Burk is the author of numerous papers on the legal and societal impact of new technologies, including articles on scientific misconduct, Internet regulation, biotechnology patenting, and competition policy. Burk holds a BS (1985) in Microbiology from Brigham Young University, an MS (1987) in Molecular Biology and Biochemistry from Northwestern University, a JD (1990) from Arizona State University, and a JSM (1994) from Stanford University.

Theptawee Chokvasin is lecturer and researcher in logic and philosophy at the Institute of Social Technology, Suranaree University of Technology, Thailand. His interest is in logic, metaphysics, and philosophy of technology. His previous works include research papers *Martin Heidegger and Phra Dhammapitaka (P.A. Payutto)'s Views on Technology: A Comparative Study* (2002) and *The Interpretations on Categorical Propositions in Aristotle and Modern Logic* (2003) (research grant from Suranaree University of Technology). He currently is working on the theory of tool analysis and instrumental realism in philosophy of instrumentation.

Frances S. Grodzinsky is a professor of computer science and information technology at Sacred Heart University, where she has developed and taught a wide range of courses, including Computer Ethics, Software Engineering, Networking, Systems Analysis and Design, and Theory of Programming Languages. She is co-chair of the Hersher Institute of Ethics at Sacred Heart. She has presented papers on Computer Ethics at SIGSCE, Ethicomp, CEPE, SIGCAS, SAC, APPE, ICIE, and CCSCNE. Her papers have appeared in *The Gender Politics of ICT* (Archibald, Emms, Grundy, Payne, and Turner, eds., Middlesex University Press, 2005); *Journal of Information, Communication and Ethics in Society*; *Readings in Cyberethics* (Spinello and Tavani, *Journal of Computers and Society*); and others. She is a Visiting Scholar, Research Center on Computer Ethics and Social Responsibility, Southern Connecticut State University, New Haven, Connecticut and serves on the board of INSEIT (the *In*ternational *S*ociety for *E*thics and *In*formation *T*echnology).

Thomas Herdin is an assistant professor at the University of Salzburg, Austria, Department of Communication Science. His fields of research include intercultural and trans-cultural communication, communication management, and cultural industry and tourism research. His regional focus is Southeast and East Asia. His latest publications and talks include The Cultural Dimension of Leadership; Digital Culture: A Dialectical Interplay; Cultural Industry in China; Netizen and Information Culture; Intercultural Competence in Tourism-Management; and others. His current research projects include Value Shift in China. Tsunami Research includes Sustainable Development in Thailand in the tourism sector. Contact: tom@herdin.at

Wolfgang Hofkirchner, PhD, studied political science and psychology at the Paris-Lodron-University of Salzburg; since 2001, he has been an associate professor for technology assessment at the Institute for Design and Technology Assessment, Vienna University of Technology; since 2004, he has been professor for Internet and society at the Center for Advanced Studies and Research in Information and Communication Technologies & Society; Paris-Lodron-University of Salzburg. Hofkirchner specialized in science-technology-society, his current focus is on information society theory and foundations of information science. Hofkirchner has published more than 100 contributions in the field, including 15 books.

Faruk Karaman holds a BS in electrical and electronics engineering from the Bosphorus University, Istanbul-Turkey (1993) and an MBA from the Marmara University, Istanbul-Turkey (1997). In 2001, he was awarded a PhD in management at the Marmara University, Istanbul-Turkey. Currently he is giving graduate and undergraduate level lectures on e-commerce and financial management at Okan University and consults SMEs in the Istanbul area. His research interests include e-commerce, Internet security, intellectual property laws, content protection, technological trends, and futurism.

Amin Kashmeery obtained a PhD in physiology from Durham University in the UK. He is a professor of physiology and founding director of the Centre for Islamic Biomedical Ethics, Institute for Middle Eastern & Islamic Studies, Durham University. Before that he was head of the Biomedical Ethics Programme, Oxford Academy for Advanced Studies, Oxford, UK (1997-2001); and professor of physiology, founding director, Centre for Biomedical Ethics, King Faisal Specialist Hospital & Research Centre, Riyadh, Saudi Arabia (2001-2004).

Lynette Kvasny is an assistant professor in the College of Information Sciences and Technology at Pennsylvania State University. She earned a PhD in computer information systems at Georgia State University. Her research explores the ways in which race, gender, and class identities shape and are shaped by the adoption and use of information and communication technologies. More information is available at http://ist.psu.edu/faculty_pages/lkvasny/

Lorenzo Magnani, philosopher and cognitive scientist, is a professor at the University of Pavia, Italy, and the director of its Computational Philosophy Laboratory. He has taught at the Georgia Institute of Technology and at the City University of New York; currently he directs international research programs in the EU, the U.S., and China. His book, *Abduction, Reason, and Science* (New York, 2001) has become a well-respected work in the field of human cognition. In 1998, he started the series of International Conferences on Model-Based Reasoning (MBR).

Ursula Maier-Rabler is an assistant professor and academic director of the Center of Advanced Studies and Research in Information and Communication Technologies & Society (ICT&S Center), University of Salzburg. Maier-Rabler's research areas include Internet and society, Internet assessment, integrated online communication, e-policy, e-democracy, digital networks, and knowledge management. Information and communication technologies include digital networks and the Internet and the digital information highway. Her focus is on sociopolitical and information cultural aspects in the context of the increasing diffusion of digital network technologies in our society. Maier-Rabler is a contributing editor for *New Media & Society* (Sage, 1998-2002); *European Journal of Communication* (Sage); section head of the Communication Technology Policy Section of the International Association for Media and Communication Research (IAMCR) (1998-2002); President of the Austrian Communication Association (1996–2000); and member of the program on Changing Media—Changing Europe that was set up by the European Science Foundation. Contact: ursula.maier-rabler@sbg.ac.at

Barbara Paterson is a computer scientist committed to solving conservation problems. She grew up in Germany and obtained a master's (Magister Artium) degree in linguistics, philosophy, and computer science from The Aachen University of Science and Technology in 1995. She then moved to Namibia, where she has developed extensive volumes of software for the Namibian Nature Foundation and the Ministry of Environment and Tourism of the Namibian government. She obtained her PhD from the University of Cape Town (UCT), South Africa. Her research explores the interdisciplinary gaps between information technology and conservation and ethics, against the cultural background of a post-colonial society in which the deficits of the past constrain the impact of technological interventions. She is now a post-doctoral fellow at the Marine Biology Research Unit at UCT.

Pirongrong Ramasoota Rananand is currently assistant professor in the Department of Journalism and Information, Faculty of Communication Arts at Chulalongkorn University. She is an alumnus of Simon Fraser University's School of Communication in Canada. Her areas of research include policy issues of Information and Communication Technologies (ICTs), children and the new media, content regulation of media, media and democratization, and social implications of ICTs.

Simon Rogerson is the director of the Centre for Computing and Social Responsibility at De Montfort University, UK. He is Europe's first professor in computer ethics. He received the 2000 IFIP Namur Award for outstanding contribution to the creation of awareness of the social implications of IT and in 2005 became the first non-American to receive the prestigious ACM SIGCAS Making a Difference Award. Following a successful industrial career, he now combines research, lecturing, and consulting in the management, organization, and ethics of IT. He is vice president and council member of the Institute for the Management of Information Systems.

Johnny Hartz Søraker (Cand. Philol.) is a researcher with the Programme for Applied Ethics at the Department of Philosophy, Norwegian University of Science and Technology. He has a background in both philosophy and computer programming and primarily teaches and researches computer and information ethics, focusing especially on embedded values in technological architectures, cross-cultural communication, and the (moral) value of information.

Bernd Carsten Stahl is a reader in critical research in technology of the School of Computing and a research associate at the Centre for Computing and Social Responsibility of De Montfort University, Leicester, UK. His interests cover philosophical issues arising from the intersections of business, technology, and information. This includes the ethics of computing and critical approaches to information systems. He is the editor-in-chief of the *International Journal of Technology and Human Interaction*. More information can be found at http://www.cse.dmu.ac.uk/~bstahl/

Herman T. Tavani is a professor of philosophy at Rivier College and co-director of the International Society for Ethics and Information Technology. He also holds appointments at the Harvard School of Public Health, where he is a visiting scholar/ethicist in the Department of Environmental Health, and at Boston College where he teaches ethics courses in the Carroll School of Management. Tavani is the author, co-author, editor, or co-editor of more than 100 publications, including five books on ethical aspects of information technology. Currently, he is book review editor for the journal *Ethics and Infor-*

mation Technology, bibliography editor of *Computers and Society Magazine*, and editor of the *INSEIT Newsletter*.

Maja van der Velden is a research fellow at the Department of Information Science and Media Studies, University of Bergen in Norway, where her research focuses on the impact of information and communication technologies on the diversity of knowledge. Before beginning her academic work, Maja worked for many years supporting organizations that were developing and using information and communication technologies for social justice in a number of countries around the world, building on her broad background as a researcher and activist in The Netherlands, Canada, the Middle East, and Africa.

Gonca Telli Yamamoto is an associate professor in the School of Business Administration at Okan University. She was formerly director of Social Sciences Institute and the coordinator of MBA and PhD programs. She currently teaches, consults, and conducts research on mobile and integrated marketing, university marketing, customer value, customer relations, and new learning technologies in business. She also is interested in the broader business, social, and policy implications associated with the emerging information society. She has some books related to sales and integrated marketing. She also has several articles in national and international journals.

Index